Mark —
I hope you understand
how much I respect your
work and your support.

David

CONFORMITY
COLLEGES

CONFORMITY COLLEGES

THE DESTRUCTION OF INTELLECTUAL CREATIVITY AND DISSENT IN AMERICA'S UNIVERSITIES

DAVID R. BARNHIZER

Skyhorse Publishing

Skyhorse Publishing books may be purchased in bulk at special discounts for sales promotion, corporate gifts, fund-raising, or educational purposes. Special editions can also be created to specifications. For details, contact the Special Sales Department, Skyhorse Publishing, 307 West 36th Street, 11th Floor, New York, NY 10018 or info@skyhorsepublishing.com.

Skyhorse® and Skyhorse Publishing® are registered trademarks of Skyhorse Publishing, Inc.®, a Delaware corporation.

Visit our website at www.skyhorsepublishing.com.

Please follow our publisher Tony Lyons on Instagram @tonylyonsisuncertain

10 9 8 7 6 5 4 3 2 1

Library of Congress Cataloging-in-Publication Data is available on file.

Cover design by Brian Peterson

Print ISBN: 978-1-5107-8028-6
Ebook ISBN: 978-1-5107-8029-3

Printed in the United States of America

This book is dedicated in large part to my longtime friend James "Ridge" Cooper. Throughout our relationship he was my "adopted" brother and even more, a dedicated science teacher in New Jersey schools throughout his life. Ridge was a totally principled person from whom I gained continual insights. But even more important, he was a teacher and guide to thousands of students in his classes whom he taught to think, expand their horizons, and grow as people. As I write this, I am only two days removed from a memorial service celebrating his life, and I miss him even while he will always remain a part of my awareness.

This book is also dedicated to my brother-in-law Marc Moretz, also a teacher. He was an original spirit committed to the ideals of America, and a person who challenged people to be better than we sometimes demonstrate. Marc contributed greatly to my understanding in more ways than I can list here.

I also want to express my deepest respect and admiration for the numerous people who have resisted and challenged what is going on in our universities and K–12 educational systems. Their ranks are growing. They include:

Bari Weiss, Elon Musk, Mark Bauerlein, Alan Dershowitz, Walter Williams, Corey Brooks, Eli Steele, Shelby Steele, Glenn Greenwald, Jay Bhattacharya, Noam Chomsky, Jon Zubieta, Harald Uhlig, Dorian Abbot, Ron DeSantis, Enes Kanter Freedom, Kristi Noem, James O'Keefe, Scott Atlas, Niall Ferguson, John Cochrane, Ayaan Hirsi Ali, Jonathan Turley, Panos Kanelos and the other creators and supporters of the new University of Austin, the leadership of Hillsdale College, Mattias Desmet, Bill Maher, Barbara Kay, Peter Wood, Pete Hegseth, Betsy McCaughey, Roger Kimball, Douglas Murray, Roger Simon, Mark Levin, William Brooks, Nikki Haley, Glen Youngkin, Jeffrey Tucker, James Lindsay, Winsome Sears, Carol Swain, Alveda King, Star Parker, Jennifer Sey, Tom Cotton, Ryan Hawley, Bob Woodson, Larry Elder, Byron Donalds, Tim Scott, Christopher Rufo, Jordan Peterson, Alexei Navalny, Yeonmi Park, and Xi Van Fleet. They all have the courage to "speak truth to power." They are all people who have refused to conform to the dictates of the "Woke," and I have enormous respect for their strength and integrity. The encouraging fact is that their numbers are growing as more people wake up to what is occurring.

I am incredibly grateful for the detailed and high quality editorial professionalism provided by Caroline Russomanno as I worked through this complex and volatile topic.

I also have a special thanks for Barbara Kay, who provided me great comments on an almost-final draft that led me to make significant revisions. As any writer knows, there is a danger in getting too close to your own writing, and a knowledgeable and experienced reader's objective critique is very important.

CONTENTS

Introduction

by Jeffrey Tucker

C OVID feels like a turning point, a time when universities fully embraced the ideology of control, censorship, and compulsion, represented by universal quarantines, masking, and vaccine compliance, all rooted in symbolism rather than scientific realities. And yet this period might be more correctly seen, as it is in this brilliant book by David Barnhizer, as a codification of deep problems that already existed.

The purge of dissident voices away from the progressive/woke religion began many years ago, if not earlier. Even during the 1950s, William F. Buckley Jr. in *God and Man at Yale: The Superstitions of "Academic Freedom* (Regnery, 1951), observed vast problems at Yale University, which he attributed to the excessive deification of intellectual freedom in ways that allowed Yale faculty to abuse that freedom by using it to impose their ideological worldviews and preferences on students. Even he could not anticipate that this freedom was, in that context, a quest for maximum opportunity for full control.

Freedom is the last thing you will find at elite institutions today. The Environmental, Social, and Governance (ESG) and Diversity, Equity, and Inclusion (DEI) bureaucracies are deeply entrenched, and an anti-Western, anti-Enlightenment, anti-American, anti-reason curriculum increasingly pervades the elite academic establishment. It is reinforced at every level, including publishing, promotion, and tenure. For several decades the culture of the university has been one in which anyone who identified as a conservative was in the extreme minority and in some instances university departments were populated by a tiny number of political conservatives, even to the point of that perspective being non-existent.

COVID offered an opportunity to complete the purge. There were three full rounds of it. It began with quarantines and solitary confinement. One must be willing to impose it, celebrate it, and endure it in order to enter the gates of woke heaven. There was yet another test: once having exited quarantine, one must cover one's face at all times. For those who passed those two tests, there remained the biggest challenge of all: accept the government's potion into your arm even though you didn't need it under the best scenario, and it would endanger your life under the worst.

By the end of this ordeal, the final purge of students, faculty, and administrators was complete. Those non-woke voices that remain are too demoralized and afraid to speak up now. The revolution is complete. As a result, the older conception of the university seems almost entirely gone or belonging to only a handful of small liberal arts schools, but seemingly absent at the large institutions that once defined what it meant to have an elite educational qualification.

The university experience is something people think they still understand and value. This is a leftover from the past, a romanticized conception that bears little in common with existing realities.

The medieval conception of the university, institutionally flowing from the monastic experience, was that the final truth did exist in a unified whole but it was elusive of comprehensive understanding due to the fallibility of the human mind. The objective of intellectual work was to discover ever more facets of it, elucidate them to students to develop a tradition of thought, and gradually put together systems of thought that point to that truth.

Whatever the discipline—math, music, logic, theology, biology, astrology, medicine—they were united in a confidence that if some feature of truth was discerned, it could not and would not live in contradiction to that final and universal truth that was God. This confidence, this mission, underscored an ethos of investigation and teaching. It was to be at once humble and fearless, imaginative but governed by methodological rules, creative but also cumulative. And out of this paradigm was born the idea of science. Every sector of specialization benefited from it.

Based on what we know from the history of ideas, the conception in broad terms survived many centuries in the West until the second half of the twentieth, when the whole reason for the existence of the university and even scholarship itself became unmoored from this understanding. With the loss of transcendent concerns, tradition, and even the rules of logic came the evaporation of meaning and then intellectual confidence, eventually replaced by a comprehensive doctrinal ferocity that would have shocked the medieval mind.

These days, it is not even clear why the university exists. Is it vocational training? The rigor of professional certifications seems to cover that in most industries. Is it purely for the sake of gaining knowledge? The internet makes that available for free. Is it to delay adulthood for as long as possible and socialize students into a more ideal circle of friends and contacts? Maybe, but what does that have to do with intellectual life?

We have certainly lived through the decline and fall of the older idea of the university. Now we may yet live to see the end of the university itself and its replacement by something else entirely. Reforms can work, but the reform will not likely come from within the institutions. They must be imposed by alumni and perhaps legislatures. Or perhaps the rule of "Go woke, go broke" will eventually force a change. Regardless, the idea of learning itself will surely return. We are in the transition, and David Barnhizer is our Virgil to give us an outstanding tour of the wreckage left behind and perhaps even a path out of the darkness.

Chapter One

They've Ruined the University

What used to be a vibrant, energetic, rousing habitat of ideas and people in hot debate is now an oppressive, predictable, fatiguing workplace. They've ruined the university.

—Mark Bauerlein[1]

Where We Are Is Not Good

Mark Bauerlein's words bring to mind the William Butler Yeats 1919 poem "The Second Coming," where he wrote in language that everyone should be required to study and discuss:

> Things fall apart; the center cannot hold;
> Mere anarchy is loosed upon the world,
> The blood-dimmed tide is loosed, and everywhere
> The ceremony of innocence is drowned;
> The best lack all conviction, while the worst
> Are full of passionate intensity.[2]

Once obtaining a strong power base in university disciplines, the revolutionaries of race, gender, and other minority interests have metamorphosed from moral beacons fighting and railing against injustice into new dictators. They have created a culture that elevates their interests while repressing those of whom they disapprove. Lord Acton would feel most vindicated.

For Western nations, the ideal of the university and of education generally has been to provide us with analytical skills, knowledge, and the

ability to create and nurture a healthy society that benefits as many people as possible. That ideal, and the university as educational and social
"medium," is under severe attack. The ongoing assault on the integrity
and ideal of the university in America is not a new phenomenon. The
extent to which it has succeeded is, however, stunning. Reversing or even
mitigating what has occurred demands a focused and clear strategy or,
as one critic has stated, America's universities will be nothing more than
propaganda mills for a one-sided political ideology.

The attack is not new. The most serious problems of freedom of expression in our society today exist on our campuses. The new assumption on
the part of what has come to be referred to as the "Woke"—seems to be
that the purpose of education is to induce what that movement considers
to be correct opinion rather than to search for wisdom and to liberate the
mind. This strategy of transforming universities—and education generally—into a one-sided process aimed at producing "true believers" who see
their world only through a single ideological lens has been unfolding for
multiple decades. Walter Williams reminds us, for example, of the 1991
warning voiced by Yale University's then President Benno Schmidt concerning the ideological takeover of the university in America. In his 1991
Baccalaureate address at Yale, Schmidt lamented that "the skepticism and
suspicion with which universities are now greeted and treated even by
friends of learning exceed anything I can recall."[3] Unsurprisingly, having
offended numerous Yale faculty members with his comments, Schmidt
soon resigned from office, effective 1992.

A "War of Attrition"

History has demonstrated repeatedly that highly motivated and strategic groups of fanatical true believers deliberately conceal their true
intentions until the point their movement has gained control. The classic Chinese military strategist Sun Tzu wrote three thousand years ago
in *The Art of War* that the excellent general never allows the enemy to
see his true strategy until after victory has been achieved. Sun Tzu also
emphasized the need for misdirection, deception, and stealth in over-
coming opponents.

A Woke Critical Legal Studies and Critical Race Theory professional friend who taught at Harvard University told me in 1992 that the Left was engaging in a "war of attrition" rather than a frontal assault. This was required, he said, because throughout the 1970s and into the later 1980s, the numbers and power imbalance between traditional university faculty and administrators and the Woke academics and critical political theorists heavily favored the traditionalists.

The "Woke/Crit" strategy involved infiltrating the system, populating the ranks of administrators and faculty with Left-leaning academics who shared the Woke/Crit vision, and gradually seizing power, while progressively eliminating opposition through hiring and intimidation. As that strategy gradually—and then more quickly—took effect, a "critical mass" of like-minded "transformative" people was assembled. Universities then trained a generation of students to share a vision of being "social justice warriors," and the crusade was launched.

That strategy is precisely what we have experienced for more than four decades as the Woke/Crit movement took hold and expanded its control over critical institutional points of power and leverage. Such strategic "stealth" behavior allowed the "revolutionaries" to have effects far beyond their actual numbers. The fact is that an intolerant minority *can* take power in a political system, controlling what is allowed and destroying democracy in the process. It has been done before and is occurring now.

The University of Virginia's Garrett Sheldon offers a strong view on what he considers a disastrous decline in the soul and spirit of the university in America. In his article "The Decline and Fall of the University in America," he writes:

> [T]he "life of the mind" within a rigorous but friendly community is an ideal . . . But the "system" of academic freedom and its attendant experiences of intellectual growth [long] prevailed. . . . I never can remember, even in the midst of terrible fights that led to presidents being fired or programs being altered, or board members resigning, that anyone questioned the right to free speech, academic inquiry, or liberty of conscience. . . . That is the classic statement of academic

freedom: a "free marketplace of ideas" that develops individuals and society. And it is especially important in a democracy, where the people are self-governing. It holds that the solution to bad ideas is not to censor or ignore them, but to *refute* them with good and reasonable ideas. . . . Political correctness (PC) effectively replaces free, diverse debate and a positive collegial community with Nazi-like speech control. In place of a "free-marketplace of ideas" examining all subjects and perspectives is one official ideology that eclipses all the other views.

That PC doctrine, essentially, is that Western Civilization in general, and America in particular, is racist, sexist, imperialist, and unjust. This means that nothing good can be said about certain figures or subjects (Jefferson, the founding, Christianity, etc.) and nothing bad or "offensive" can be said about "protected groups" (women, minorities, gays, Muslims, illegal immigrants, etc.). This ideology has pretty much captured the humanities and social sciences in American universities (as well as the most prominent academic associations and journals, and the most prestigious awards).[4]

America's Educational System Has Become a Means of Indoctrination

Until recently the assault on the university and America's entire educational system has been a largely stealth process where most Americans never even knew what was going on. Similarly, to our general society, members of university faculties were thought of as being among the most intelligent and intellectually balanced members of our society. They were deep "thinkers" after truth, immersed in knowledge creation and learning, and divorced from raw politics, identity agendas, and one-sided activism. We assumed they were imparting their skills, knowledge, methods, and balanced perspectives to university students. We were wrong. We also trusted our K-12 teachers, administrators, and boards to be wise and dedicated professionals rather than Woke ideologues. Once again, we were wrong.

As is detailed in my book, *"Un-Canceling" America* (2021), many teachers and educational administrators are working to "destabilize" and transform their students, educational institutions, and America itself. Numerous examples are set out in *"Un-Canceling" America* of administrators telling teachers to keep on with what they had been doing to advance a Woke agenda and Critical Race Theory themes, but telling teachers and administrators to hide that agenda from parents. As *"Un-Canceling" America* demonstrates through numerous examples, Woke teachers even bragged about their activism and the fact that they were seeking to turn young children into Woke activists who would advance their agenda. After uncovering numerous examples of such deceptive and still ongoing behavior, my impression was that their comments created an impression of little children thrilled at being able to "put one over" on their own parents.

Universities have been "investigating," suppressing, and canceling faculty members who resist their Woke and Critical Race Theory strategically and cleverly legitimated by the seemingly benign mantra of Diversity, Equity, and Inclusion (DEI). Hundreds of university faculty around the nation have been subjected to petitions and complaints that led to investigations for not being sufficiently "correct" in political views, for being culturally "insensitive," or for using linguistic terms the Woke consider inappropriate. FIRE, the Foundation for Individual Rights and Expression, released a 2022 analysis of what was occurring in America's universities. The report, *"FIRE Statement on the Use of Diversity, Equity, and Inclusion Criteria in Faculty Hiring and Evaluation"* included the following observations:

> Since 2015, FIRE has seen over 600 attempts to sanction scholars for protected speech, and most of those have been successful. The frequency of these incidents is accelerating: More than half have occurred since 2020. For some professors, even tenure is no longer a reliable shield against encroachments on academic freedom. In the last several years, nearly three dozen tenured professors have been fired for their protected expression, scholarship, or pedagogy. Meanwhile, hundreds of colleges and *universities* maintain bias reporting systems that encourage students to anonymously report peers or faculty for

offensive-but-protected speech. Many hold training programs that compel speech, attempt to embed ideological bias in research review.

An institution dedicated to advancing the frontiers of human knowledge should recognize the fallibility of the human mind and promote the value of seriously entertaining the possibility of being wrong. Instead, many DEI statement mandates do the opposite, closing the debate on issues of societal importance. They require faculty to endorse or apply specific positions on race, gender, and related issues as if they are beyond question, and as if a professor who disputes them is ipso facto incompetent. . . . Moreover, in FIRE's experience, DEI statement policies generally are not created by faculty—who, according to the principle of academic freedom, are the proper judges of their disciplinary peers' academic qualifications—or tailored to particular positions or disciplines. Rather, DEI statement policies are commonly authored and imposed by administrators, and they often apply globally to an entire college or university.[5]

Like Mark Bauerlein, Garrett Sheldon, Dorian Abbot, Barbara Kay, Carol Swain, Harald Uhlig, Peter Wood, and many others, I believe so deeply in what the university represents as a driving force in advancing human creativity and the health and collective diversity of our political community across generations, that I am totally committed to the belief the institution must be saved from the intellectual and spiritual corruption that is taking place. Although there have been multiple variants of the university institution, and the system has always been subject to various degrees of political and external control, the institution's core essence as an ideal involves honesty of thought, rationality, interactive discourse, and adherence to the best evidence and knowledge we are capable of creating and discerning. At their foundation, universities exist to make us better as individuals than we would otherwise be. A key part of their role is to educate us in ways that assist in the evolution of healthier societies through application of the wisdom and insights the institutions and their open-minded leaders strive to impart to us through research and teaching.

Still, the reality is that we are experiencing what Belgium's Ghent University faculty member Mattias Desmet described as a "mass formation psychosis."[6] Nor is it an accidental event. Many faculty and administrators in America's universities have formed into a single-minded ultra-authoritarian mob whose members are intent on gaining power and dominance while forcing their political agendas on the nation's youth. As with China, the former Soviet Union, and Nazi Germany, the intention of that mob or "mass" of true believers, ideologues, and power-seekers is to turn the university and the nation's total educational system into instruments of propaganda and systemic transformation into what historically has always turned out to be a flawed and ultimately failed political form of government.

It is vital we avoid being seduced by elegant rhetoric. The activist faculty, Woke administrators, and students who have been indoctrinated into becoming "social justice warriors" as part of their "learning" frequently preach tolerance and empathy but brook no dissent. They attack relentlessly, invent high-sounding and often baseless "theories," and seek to silence, and "cancel" anyone with the audacity to expose or even question their narratives, opinions, theories, arguments, acts of intolerance, and abuses. Any counter argument about what they are doing is condemned as a "conspiracy theory," bigotry, racism, sexism, or some form of shameful "phobia."

A Takeover by Militant Faculty, Administrators, and "Woke" Hypersensitive Students

Our universities have become filled with militant faculty and administrators seeking to proselytize others into accepting and advancing their vision of society. As shown in the excerpts set out next describing the culture at Duke University, Woke and hypersensitive students are a core part of a repressive system. Their perspectives are heavily oriented toward what their particular political movement is seeking to achieve. The underlying thesis of this authoritarian strategy is to "get our youth" while they are young and only partially formed in terms of their core worldviews. As with the Maoist Red Guard, Hitler Youth, Komsomol, and the like, creating cadres of true believers through what propaganda and indoctrination masked as education and social justice is a vital part of a movement's quest for transformative power.

This is a condition Albert Camus describes as a distortion that occurs whenever individuals who are engaging in the struggle to achieve what they think to be social justice, simultaneously claim to be clear-thinking scholars or philosophers rather than driven ideologues in pursuit of a political agenda. Camus discussed the subjectivity of this self-deluding phenomenon in the context of the creativity of the artist versus the scholar's need to keep a sufficient distance from the heated conditions of society in order to retain a clear perspective and avoid excessive subjectivity. He writes:

> [I]t is not possible to be a militant in one's spare time. And so the artist of today becomes unreal if he remains in his ivory tower or sterilized if he spends his time galloping around the political arena. Yet between the two lies the arduous way of true art. It seems to me that the writer must be fully aware of the dramas of his time and that he must take sides every time he can or knows how to do so. But he must also maintain or resume from time to time a certain distance in relation to our history.[7]

In challenging us to resist the effects of excessive subjectivity, Camus added that: "Real mastery consists in refuting the prejudices of the time, initially the deepest and most malignant of them, which would reduce man, after his deliverance from excess, to a barren wisdom."[8] He goes on to warn:

> We all carry within us our places of exile, our crimes and our ravages. But our task is not to unleash them on the world; it is to fight them in ourselves and in others. Rebellion, the secular will not to surrender . . . is still today at the basis of the struggle. Origin of form, source of real life, it keeps us always erect in the savage, formless movement of history. In this situation: "it is essential that we must never let

criticism descend to insult; we must grant that our opponent may be right. . . . It is essential . . . that we remake our political mentality."[9]

A 2004 Sampling of Academic Political Affiliation at Duke University Found Zero Faculty Diversity in Multiple Departments

Hunter Lewis, in his article "Political Debate Sweeps Campus," writes that the DCU (Duke Conservative Union) revealed the political affiliation of faculty from several departments (at Duke University) to be in favor of registered Democrats over Republicans. These included history, literature, sociology and English. (Lewis reports) The departments had a (political) ratio of 32-to-0, 11-to-0, 9-to-0 and 18-to-1, respectively.[10] Such a distortion is actually mind-boggling and could never occur solely by accident.

Duke's "diversity" has not improved during the ensuing seventeen years. Ivan Petropoulos, a Chemistry student at Duke and an open-minded thinker in the traditional Liberal sense, demonstrated great courage and integrity in publishing the following remarks in the *Duke Chronicle*. Among his most telling observations is one that unfortunately describes the culture not only at Duke, but at far too many of America's universities. He writes: "If Duke's purpose is to cultivate the future leaders and freethinkers of our generation, then I can't help but think that we've failed in that regard."[11] Unless this ongoing disintegration of our educational systems is reversed, the nation will continue to decline.

He continues:

> "Being a conservative feels like a joke at Duke." I don't often agree with my friend (who made this statement) on political issues, but he's right about this one. In this age of acceptance, you'd be hard-pressed to find a group on campus more unpopular than Duke's conservative population. From the posts we make on social media, up to the professors we expel from the classroom [such as Evan Charney who taught for 20 years at Duke], it seems like students here just aren't comfortable with political disagreement. And how could we ever be? A recent poll of first years found that 74.6% self-identified as "liberal"

or "very liberal." With one ideology dominant on campus, debate ceases to exist; we no longer can have civil discussions, because there is nothing to disagree about. Not only is this a boring way to go about college, but it's also at odds with the fundamental purpose of a liberal education—the pursuit of which is rooted in seeking to understand those with opposing worldviews.[12]

Petropoulos then goes on to explain how the current "Woke" culture contradicts in the most fundamental ways his pre-existing expectations of what a university is supposed to be about:

> Coming into Duke, I imagined it to be a melting pot of ideas, where everyone could be heard without fear of being rebuked, silenced, or ostracized. My friends on the right know more of the opposite to be true. They worry that if they express their political views, they run the risk of losing friends, lower grades and fewer job opportunities. . . . Proving their point, all of those who talked with me preferred to not be publicly outed as Republican to the Chronicle. This is deeply disheartening: considering that politics can be such a huge part of our identity, it can be particularly isolating for the roughly 6% of us who find themselves following a seemingly forbidden ideology at Duke. . . . As a liberal at Duke, political discussions are mind-numbingly-agreeable; unless you're talking to a borderline communist, your politics will be challenged more often when talking to a brick wall than when talking to the average student. . . . Here, you don't learn how to carefully formulate your own ideas, how to present and debate your own beliefs, or how to peacefully negotiate a middle ground with your political adversaries—you only learn how to properly rehearse the truths deemed acceptable by the university and the student population. If Duke's purpose is to cultivate the future leaders and freethinkers of our generation, then I can't help but think that we've failed in that regard.[13]

"Academic Freedom Is Dead!" Dr. Jay Bhattacharya

An example of the intolerance that is taking place in America's universities is provided by the experience of Stanford professor Jay Bhattacharya. No one is safe from the wrath of the Woke. Bhattacharya is a tenured professor at Stanford and a skilled, respected, and extremely professional scientist. His sin? He dared to challenge the "official" controlling narrative of the COVID-19 pandemic's insistence on lockdowns and shuttering schools. The fact that he and his colleagues have been shown to be correct even now doesn't seem to matter. Their problem is that they didn't go along with the dominant, but severely flawed, narrative being pushed by a combination of the federal government, mainstream media, Big Pharma, the National Education Association, the American Federation of Teachers, and politically powerful segments of the "scientific" medical profession. A report describes Dr. Bhattacharya's experience at Stanford:

> A Stanford University professor of medicine says "academic freedom is dead" after his life became a "living hell" for challenging coronavirus lockdown orders and the "scientific clerisy" during the pandemic. "The basic premise is that if you don't have protection and academic freedom in the hard cases, when a faculty member has an idea that's unpopular among some of the other faculty—powerful faculty, or even the administration . . . If they don't protect it in that case, then you don't have academic freedom at all." . . . Bhattacharya is a tenured professor of medicine at Stanford University and also an economist who serves as director of Stanford's Center for Demography and Economics of Health and Aging.
>
> He came under fire during the pandemic after co-authoring the Great Barrington Declaration, which was an open letter signed by thousands of doctors and scientists in 2020 denouncing lockdowns as harmful. Bhattacharya was joined by Harvard professor of medicine Dr. Martin Kulldorff and Oxford professor Dr. Sunetra Gupta in co-authoring the document. The declaration was quickly denounced by other health leaders, including National Institute of Allergy and Infectious Diseases director Dr. Anthony Fauci, who

slammed the call for herd immunity in the document as "nonsense and very dangerous."[14]

University of Alabama Professor Leaves the Institution: "Universities Are No Longer Places that Embrace the Freedom of Exchanging Ideas"

A University of Alabama professor left a teaching position due to the "obsession" over the university's push for equity in science and the "rise of illiberalism." Dr. Matthew M. Wielicki, a Polish immigrant and Earth Science professor . . . [stated] "over the last decade or so, but especially the last few years, the obsession with universities and grant-funding institutions on immutable characteristics of faculty and students and the push for equity in science above all else has dramatically changed the profession of an academic professor," Wielicki said. He added that the "rise of illiberalism in the name of DEI is the antithesis of the principles that universities were founded on."[15]

"Thank Goodness It's Not Me": Fear and Trembling in the University

What is happening in our main educational systems is not a fake "conspiracy theory." It is real. Philip Carl Salzman, no stranger to being a target of the Woke, describes the intolerant Identity culture that has emerged in American and Canadian universities:

Almost every university in North America has committed to what is called "social justice," which is the implementation of identity politics through the mechanisms of "diversity, equity, and inclusion." Identity politics divides everyone into one of two categories: evil oppressor or innocent victim. Through official mandatory policies, universities have transformed academic culture from a quest to discover truth about the world and its beings, to the indoctrination of identity politics and enforcement of "social justice" policies.[16]

In China, Teachers Are Required to Be "Mouthpieces for the Regime"

Hans Yeung was a manager at the Hong Kong Examinations and Assessment Authority. He is also an historian in modern Hong Kong and Chinese history. Yeung describes the ideological takeover of Hong Kong's universities, calling it "educational cleansing." It is a lesson we must heed in America. Yeung writes:

> Educational cleansing became rampant after the Hong Kong National Security Law was passed in 2020. The release of the Education Bureau (EDB)'s Guidelines on Teachers' Professional Conduct (Guidelines) last week means another spell on teachers, who will only be obedient and act as mouthpieces of the regime in the future. This is not an overstated judgment, especially when we compare the Guidelines with the rescinded Code for Educators drafted by the Council on Professional Conduct (Code), which the EDB has abolished. The [replaced] Code represents a much more liberal educational ecology. It has a whole chapter on teachers' rights, which clearly states that "as citizens, professional educators should enjoy all rights conferred by law and fundamental human rights" and that teachers have the right to "exercise professional judgment to present, interpret and criticize all kinds of information and views, including that on controversial issues," . . . As the [rescinded] Code stipulation that teachers "should strive to cultivate in their students a sense of freedom, peace, equality, rationality, and democracy" is also taken away in the Guidelines, teachers who choose to adhere to this belief may cross the red line of "provocations against the social order," a term which is not defined at all. . . . All these rights, which Hong Kong educators have long taken for granted, are found nowhere in the Guidelines. This indicates that teaching now becomes a profession with responsibilities without rights.[17]

Chapter Two

As Marshall McLuhan Explained, the Medium Is the "Message" and the University Is a Very Powerful "Medium"

Marshall McLuhan was a brilliant thinker who is probably best known for his insight that the medium is the message.[1] This stands for the idea that the systems we use to communicate and educate are "mediums" that inexorably lead to specific behaviors, structures, and systems of thought and behavior depending on the scale, focus, and power of the specific medium in question. Universities, and our entire educational "medium," including the K-12 system that feeds its graduates into the university and societal systems, are powerful and overarching mechanisms that shape our understanding.

The heightened connection between social movements and universities has altered the nature of the university as an intellectual and knowledge "medium." The goal has been to transform the "message" being transmitted to students and the society. The civil rights movement of the 1960s and 1970s was a fantastic phenomenon. I am proud to have been a part of it as a civil rights and federal civil rights lawyer in the Reginald Heber Smith Community Lawyer program sponsored by the US Office of Economic Opportunity (OEO) prior to the creation of the Legal Services Corporation.

Throughout my life I have sought to continue such efforts, but realized that there were distinct lines that needed to be drawn between my responsibilities and aims as a university professor and the other undertakings in which I engaged as an advocate, activist, scholar, consultant, litigator and legal strategist on behalf of groups and disadvantaged clients as well as other activities in which I was engaged. A teacher's job is to assist students to develop their skills and awareness to the highest levels they are capable. It is to think with clarity and precision while possessing a great range of information and knowledge that allows an honest and comprehensive understanding of the world with which they are engaged. It is, in fact, our responsibility to educate students in ways where they become their own "teacher" because, ultimately, that ability is the ideal for which we must all strive. Intimidation, indoctrination, propaganda, "shout downs," silencing of alternative viewpoints, one-sided politicized assertions and interpretations all contradict and offend the essential spirit and legitimacy of the educational process.

Liz Peek has offered an analysis of how we arrived at the precipice of societal chaos, explaining the role of universities in the process. She writes:

> Wonder where today's "cancel culture" comes from? It comes from college campuses, fueled by young people and abetted by an older generation that has not had the courage to say no. This is how the slide toward totalitarianism begins. Silencing the opposition is essential to creating "legitimacy" for despots like Vladimir Putin or Kim Jong Un; if political opponents have no voice, people will assume they don't exist.[2]

As Peek notes, universities have been the driving force for the CRT/Woke movement. Our universities are where our current K-12 teachers and administrators are being molded by political zealots who are firmly convinced their perspectives are the only legitimate options. Their K-12 students are then sent to universities with an already formed political mindset that is then further intensified. Anyone who disagrees with the "intellectual" ideologues is condemned as a bigot or racist. They are attacked and "canceled" by bullies "high" on the narcotic of power. In far too many instances, that power is being abused through shaming, bullying, and punishing not only those who dare to disagree, but anyone who fails to affirmatively support the ideologues by condemning and shunning the unfortunate offender.

Woke/CRT Is a "Mass Movement" of Disciplined and "Exclusively Political" Identity Groups That Are Seeking Power and Control: DEI Is at Its Heart

In *The New Realities*, Peter Drucker warned about the "new pluralism" and its intense desire for power and rejection of the individual. He warned it is also an assault on the assimilative ideal of the American political system. Drucker explains:

> The new pluralism . . . focuses on power. It is a pluralism of single-cause, single-interest groups—the "mass movements" of small but highly disciplined minorities. Each of them tries to obtain through power what it could not obtain through numbers or through persuasion. Each is exclusively political.[3]

Consistent with Drucker's warning, America's universities have been captured by a "mass movement" of "small but highly disciplined" Identity Groups. The result has been a serious and dangerous degradation of our educational institutions. Many "new scholars"—particularly those in the "soft" and malleable noncumulative disciplines—possess agendas that cannot be pursued without resort to radical, condemnatory, and dishonest pseudo-intellectualism and demonization. This has produced an academic culture in which intimidation of discourse in teaching and scholarship has become a dominant trait.

From the perspective of universities, one effect of the Civil Rights movement is that it made the walls of academia more porous for those entering with a commitment to social justice and against discrimination and the denial of opportunity to every American. That progressive, social justice orientation was vitally needed in the American society of that time. The problem, however, is that as with many impassioned revolutionary movements, the transformation of the university in America ultimately went too far due to its grounding in aggressive activism. Universities require a degree of distance from the intensity of social disputes and conflicts. This does not mean they don't take those challenges into account in relevant areas of teaching and inquiry, but maintaining a distance from the "madding crowd" is vital.

There is a real distinction between well-considered strategic accommodation and the large scale flooding of a system. Allowing a very rapid inflow of radically different people filled with an intense commitment to activism into teaching and administration has transformed the university institution in both good and bad ways. Even though we can criticize the university of the pre-Civil Rights era for its deficiencies that included too often ignoring issues of social justice, the ideals of "learnedness," the pursuit of truth, balance, reasoned thought, evidential research and investigation, and analytical discipline, are vital elements for the university. They are critical in aiding and strengthening the society the university is supposed to serve. That core focus has largely been lost.

It is now almost impossible for anyone aspiring to become a member of a university faculty in America to achieve that dream unless they demonstrate "undying loyalty" to the Woke/Critical Race Theory agenda. There has been a dramatic and still widening shift toward a heavily politicized faculty and to the administrative and curricular base in our universities. This shift has been replicated in our elementary and secondary systems of K-12 after several decades of indoctrinated university graduates have entered the K-12 teaching and administrative ranks.

This widening split—one found not only in universities but throughout American society—has intensified the already politicized nature of the university and altered the nature of the educational "medium" in profound and questionable ways. The victors of the "cultural revolution" have seized effective control of much of the university's administrative structure, curriculum, and the system of rewards and punishment. This is particularly so in the "soft" disciplines, ones where rhetoric, belief, assumption, and opinion dominate content, interpretation, and method far more than do tested data and methodology.

The concepts and prevailing interpretations dealt with in the "soft knowledge" disciplines make it even more essential that we develop a sense of healthy skepticism about powerful sounding assertions of meaning, and that we educate students in ways that create the ability to question, make critical distinctions between claims and arguments, understand the importance of facts and evidence, and assess the motivations of those who are making overarching assertions of validity that advance their own politicized agendas.

At the heart of the problem is that many Woke faculty are seeking to proselytize rather than develop students' capacities for intelligent and interactive discourse aimed at full understanding as opposed to acquisition of power. Martin Buber captured the distinction as well as any. He wrote:

> In our age, in which the true meaning of every word is encompassed by delusion and falsehood, and the original intention of the human glance is stifled by tenacious mistrust, it is of decisive importance to find again the genuineness of speech and existence as We. . . . Man will not persist in existence if he does not learn anew to persist in it as a genuine We.[4]

Buber highlighted the vital importance of having open and honest discourse rather than preemptive strikes and argumentative deceit. Discourse requires interaction and tolerance, not preemptive strikes. Buber offers a sense of the difference between honest discourse and propaganda.

> Genuine conversation, and therefore every actual fulfilment [sic] of relation between men, means acceptance of otherness. . . . The strictness and depth of human individuation, the elemental otherness of the other, is . . . not merely noted as the necessary starting point, but is affirmed from the one being to the other. The desire to influence the other then does not mean the effort to change the other, to inject one's "rightness" into him; but it means the effort to let that which is recognized as right, as just, as true . . . take seed and grow in the form suited to individuation. Opposed to this effort is the lust to make use of men by which the manipulator of "propaganda" and "suggestion" is possessed.[5]

Critical Race Theory, the 1619 Project, and Wokeism Are Masquerading as Presumptive "Theories of Everything" in Race and Gender

It is no accident that the "soft" disciplines of history, social studies, political science, race and gender studies, anthropology, interdisciplinary studies, and communications are where the "Woke" and Critical Race "Theorists," propagandists and demagogues congregate. This is because belief, opinion, assertion, and assumptions about problems, causation, and "truth" are the coin of the realm. You don't even have to prove what you say in certain "off limits" or taboo areas such as race and gender. Nor can anyone safely question the assignment of accountability to individuals and systems. For many Woke/CRT activists, their assertions and accusations are sufficient standards of "truth" because it is their "lived experience," however subjective their interpretations might be, and because it serves the movement's political agendas. That anti-intellectual process has allowed one-sided and politically-driven attacks by Woke faculty and administrators to be treated as valid for whatever propositions they assert.

The unfortunate reality is that the Woke/Critical Race "Theorists" have concocted a failed "pseudo-theory" akin to what in physics is called the "Theory of Everything" or TOE. In the realm of physics, the hope was that the deep levels of matter research would be able to show the single common force that underlay the fundamental structures and dynamics of the universe. Even though there is a new movement among some physicists to return to that TOE undertaking, the reality is that the Theory of Everything efforts of the 1970s era are acknowledged as having failed in the face of the enormous complexity of what they are attempting to understand, as well as overweening researcher hubris that blocks alternative perspectives.

The disturbing reality that is being denied by the Woke is that just because a bunch of allegedly "smart" people in a discipline invent a movement and call it a "theory" of this-or-that does not mean they are right or that there is total, or even significant, validity in their assertions. An example is provided by what we are encountering in the area of Critical Race Theory and the overstated assertions represented in the 1619 Project, an undertaking that the *New York Times'* Bret Stephens scathingly described as a "theory in search of evidence." Since its release, the 1619 Project in one form or another has been driven into schools and is serving many situations and curricula as a core instrumentality of Critical Race Theory's assertion that race permeates every aspect of American society. It is therefore important to understand the 1619 Project's context. This is brought forward in a compelling op-ed written by the Stephens in 2020, one severely criticizing the 1619 Project. Stephens writes:

> If there's one word admirers and critics alike can agree on when it comes to *The New York Times*'s award-winning 1619 Project, it's *ambition*. Ambition to reframe America's conversation about race. Ambition to reframe our understanding of history. Ambition to move from news pages to classrooms. Ambition to move from scholarly debate to national consciousness. . . . But ambition can be double-edged. . . .
>
> As fresh concerns make clear, on these points—and for all of its virtues, buzz, spinoffs and a Pulitzer Prize—the 1619 Project has failed. . . . Monocausality—whether it's the clash of economic classes, the hidden hand of the market, or white supremacy and its consequences—has always been a seductive way of looking at the world. It has always been a simplistic one, too. The world is complex. So are people and their motives. The job of journalism is to take account of that complexity, not simplify it out of existence through the adoption of some ideological orthodoxy.
>
> This mistake goes far to explain the 1619 Project's subsequent scholarly and journalistic entanglements. It should have been enough to make strong yet nuanced claims about the role of slavery and racism in American history. Instead, it issued categorical and totalizing assertions that are difficult to defend on close examination. . . . An early sign that the project was in trouble came in an interview last November with James McPherson, the Pulitzer Prize-winning author of "Battle Cry of Freedom" and a past president of the American Historical Association. He was withering: "Almost from the outset,"

McPherson told the World Socialist Web Site, "I was disturbed by what seemed like a very unbalanced, one-sided account, which lacked context and perspective."

In particular, McPherson objected to Hannah-Jones's suggestion that the struggle against slavery and racism and for civil rights and democracy was, if not exclusively then mostly, a Black one.

As fresh concerns make clear, on these points—and for all of its virtues, buzz, spinoffs and a Pulitzer Prize—the 1619 Project has failed. . . . None of this should have come as a surprise: The 1619 Project is a thesis in search of evidence, not the other way around. Nor was this fire from the right: Both Wilentz and Harris were at pains to emphasize their sympathy with the project's moral aims.[6]

My point is that the overwhelmingly sweeping assertions being made by the "theorists" of the Critical Race political movement are a thinly veiled effort to recreate a "Theory of Everything" for a specific political movement. That movement is pursuing a pre-determined political agenda in which the activists are seeking power by utilizing "cherry-picked" examples, overly broad allegations of the evils of total "systems" that contain flaws in the same way that any human system does, and the extremely powerful moral force of racial discrimination. The Woke/CRT arrogation of power through the weaponization of racial accusations applied through their newly imagined Theory of Everything, masquerading as "Intersectionality," is dividing—and likely to ultimately collapse—the American nation.

The result is that we are engaged in a hotly conflicted struggle over not only the nature and functions of the university, but our entire educational system. This struggle is an important part of a larger effort by the Woke/CRT movement to seize, "dismantle," and transform all of American society. Capturing the universities, and then the K-12 educational system, has been a key part of the strategy because that is where the thoughts and minds of people are shaped and a core of future loyalists produced.[7]

The challenge goes considerably beyond the university, even though that institution is a driving force for creating the crisis that is besetting our society as an eroding democratic community. The Brownstone Institute's Jeffrey Tucker offers a perspective worth noting. He describes a system-wide movement toward what can only be described as authoritarianism, and if we are honest about Woke/CRT's connection to its admitted Marxist roots and to a political system at risk of becoming a totalitarian political state. Tucker writes in the context of how the "crisis" of the COVID-19 pandemic was manipulated to gain greater control:

> The institutions on which we used to depend to defend our liber-
> ties and rights—nonprofits, courts, intellectuals, academia, tech,
> media—have failed spectacularly. We had no idea just how many
> of them had long ago been already captured. We did not know that
> feds were deeply embedded at Facebook, Instagram, Twitter, and
> LinkedIn. We did not know that they had already captured the news
> pages of the *New York Times* and so on. We thought that these insti-
> tutions were merely ideologically biased. We did not know that they
> had become tools of the regime.[8]

The Takeover Developed "Gradually" and Then "Suddenly" Once a Critical Mass of Faculty and Administrators Was Achieved

I find Victor Davis Hanson to be a fount of insight on numerous criti-cal issues. In a recent essay, he outlined the crisis now being experienced by the American university, a crisis he described as "the Woke university implosion." Hanson writes:

> In a famous exchange in *The Sun Also Rises*, Ernest Hemingway
> wrote: "How did you go bankrupt?" Bill asked. "Two ways," Mike
> said. "Gradually, then suddenly." "Gradually" and "suddenly" applies
> to higher education's implosion. During the 1990s "culture wars,"
> universities were warned that their chronic tuition hikes above the
> rate of inflation were unsustainable. . . . Left-wing indoctrination,
> administrative bloat, obsessions with racial preferences, arcane, jar-
> gon-filled research and campus-wide intolerance of diverse thought

short-changed students, further alienated the public—and often enraged alumni. Over the last [thirty] years, enrollments in the humanities and history crashed. So did tenure-track faculty positions. Some $1.7 trillion in federally backed student loans have only greenlighted inflated tuition—and masked the contagion of political indoctrination and watered-down courses. But *"gradually"* imploding has now become "suddenly."[9]

The very rapid entry into universities of impassioned ideological activists, and the hiring priorities through which those individuals have benefited, has resulted in a situation where there has been a dramatic shift in who serves as academic faculty, as well as an extensive expansion of "Woke" university administrators who impact heavily on what faculty do. As this transformation of administrators and faculty took place and Woke/Critical Race Theory advocates increasingly dominated universities, it has made entry into faculty and administrative positions increasingly difficult. At this point, entry into faculty and administrative positions in universities ranges from difficult to virtually impossible for candidates possessing more traditional or less ideological values. This is particularly true in the "soft" disciplines such as history, social science, and other inherently political disciplines contrasted with more technical-and science-based undertakings represented by STEM subjects.

Universities Are Gripped by a "Soft and Unforgiving Totalitarianism"

The situation we face is akin to that of the fiery Latin American revolutionaries who, after struggling mightily to overthrow an undeniably unjust dictator, become dictators upon gaining power. As we were warned, "power corrupts." The mutation of old revolutionaries and their new allies into controllers and dictators has taken place because it is one thing to attack power, but quite another to possess it. While "all power corrupts," we are entering a phase where we have to understand that "absolute power corrupts absolutely." It is a dangerous moment due to the degree to which the university and K-12 educational systems have been captured by the Woke/CRT movement.

Emory University Professor Emeritus Mark Bauerlein explains how far universities and faculty have sunk, describing faculty and administrators as "total conformists" adhering to a Woke "Party Line." He describes what has developed in universities, institutions that should be centers of discourse and critical thinking, as a "soft totalitarianism."

> We have a Party Line firmly in place, and all the faculty members know it. They're scared; the adversarial temper is gone. The courage of the independent thinker, the fearless critic taking on the Greats, the researchers and scholars who follow the evidence wherever it leads—they are rarely seen or heard, and we've watched too many occasions of reprimand and worse, when some heedless fellow opened his trap in the wrong way and had to apologize or go home . . . The result is a conformity I never would have expected to spread so widely. . . . "Contesting received wisdom is exactly what we're supposed to do." . . . It is, indeed, a soft totalitarianism, and few people have the stomach to describe what now unfolds in plain sight.[10]

Walter Williams offers a powerful counter to the Woke mantra asserting that capabilities and methods of inquiry such as rationality are bad and even racist, that the individual is a danger to the collective, that merit is an exploitative and discriminatory tool, and that free speech done by anyone other than themselves is destructive or "a danger to democracy." He emphasizes how unique and vital has been the Western philosophical and political elevation of the ideal of the individual as a key contributor to the overall community.

> "The indispensable achievement of the West was the concept of individual rights, the idea that individuals have certain inalienable rights that are not granted by government. Governments exist to protect these inalienable rights. It's a tragic state of affairs when free speech and inquiry require protection at institutions of higher learning. Indeed, freedom in the marketplace of ideas has made the United States, as well as other Western nations, a leader in virtually every area of human endeavor. . . . The true test doesn't come when he

permits people to say those things he deems acceptable. The true test comes when he permits people to say those things that he deems offensive. . . . Attacks on free speech to accommodate multiculturalism and diversity are really attacks on Western values.[11]

The Woke Are Absolutists Who Tolerate No Dissent

Bauerlein offers a description of the American university as of 2021. He writes that we now have a stifling and punitive hegemony in control of the university. His compelling analysis bears strong resemblance to that of Hans Yeung who writes that the CCP's new educational rules force China's teachers to "be obedient and act as mouthpieces of the regime."

We now have a hegemony in higher education that's more binding, more stifling and controlling and punitive than anything the faculty, administrators, and students ever exerted and imposed back in those oppressive, conformist years of the 1950s. The Woke outlook is absolute. Professors don't dare cross it. Undergraduates who have other concerns keep their heads down when the protesters pass. Administrators react to the Woke demonstrations with the dispatch of an attendant at the court of Henri IV hearing the king's latest request. Be quick, be wary, stay safe! That's the policy, even for professors with tenure and long achievement. They have a paycheck for life as long as they don't engage in serious misconduct, but they act as if they have no security, no protection should the mob arise. They see a colleague targeted and keep quiet. They don't come to his defense and demand due process (for whatever crime he's supposed to have committed). No, they only think, "Thank goodness it's not me."[12]

Shame on the "Ivies": They Are Aggressive Enablers of What Is Happening

The power of Harvard and Yale's enormous prestige is playing a significant part in the disintegration of vital university norms across the board. Those institutions have produced numerous recent examples of faculty, administrative, and student-led behaviors that contradict many of the ideals we

consider the university to advance. This has been multiplied by other incidents at the University of Pennsylvania, Princeton, and Columbia. All-in-
all, the Ivy League is proving to be a saboteur of the fundamental ideals
we have long considered essential in American education and for the benefit of the society.

The Foundation for Individual Rights and Expression (FIRE) published its *2022–2023 College Free Speech Rankings*, and the results do
not look good for the Ivies.[13] The report on campus free speech ranked
Columbia dead last and described it as "abysmal." The University of
Pennsylvania was close behind. Yale was ranked sixth from the bot-
tom, and Harvard and Princeton came in with a "poor" ranking. The
elite University of Chicago (a non-Ivy) was ranked the most free. Writing
about the report in the *New York Post*, Rikki Schlott states:

> If you like free speech, don't go to Columbia. A leading free speech
> organization ranked the best and worst college campuses for freedom
> of speech and New York's top school, Columbia University, came
> in dead last. . . . Columbia University came last and was the only
> school to be slammed with a Speech Climate rating of "abysmal."
> Scoring just 9.91 out of 100, New York City's Ivy was dragged down
> by its high number of scholars who were sanctioned for expressing
> their views. Between 2019–2020, seven academics faced investigation
> or disciplinary action for tweets or comments deemed unacceptable.
> Columbia did not immediately respond to The Post for comment.
> The University of Pennsylvania was second to last, with a score of
> 14.32 out of 100.[14]

The Harvard/Yale system exudes a powerful presence in America, just as
the Oxbridge system of Oxford and Cambridge universities dominates the
British intellectual and political system. The power and prestige of those
universities' ultra-desirable degrees is not really related to any demonstra-
bly higher quality of the education itself compared to that being provided
to students in "lower" institutions. Many American colleges and universities provide an equal or superior educational culture for their students,

and have faculties who are far more engaged with their students. The reality is that the benefits of Harvard, Yale, and the other prestigious Ivies are, like the United Kingdom's Cambridge and Oxford "Oxbridge" combo, far more the product of the influential connective networks created by access to other graduates, and the snob appeal status bestowed by having the "stamp" of Harvard or Yale on one's record and the preferences of potential employers.

The bad aspect of this incredible level of influence is that the faculties of those universities are almost all of a strongly Left orientation and this has a significant effect on the beliefs and political worldviews of those they teach. This means that in many universities, and particularly those thought elite, the new and progressive graduates have been exposed to a monolithic experience of political and philosophical content and aims, not one that is in fact "diverse" or "inclusive." In a key study, it turned out that only one percent of Harvard's faculty identified as Conservative, with the university's vast majority of faculty being on the Left. These institutions correctly see themselves as institutions that are educating the future leadership of America. As such, Harvard and Yale select students in part for what they perceive to be their political outlook. They then educate them through perspectives that enhance the already existing orientation, and send them out into a world where they have disproportionate access and opportunities to the "best" jobs from which they can shape the future.

In other words, they are pretty much all Woke and, due to the power of the Ivy credential, they have a heightened opportunity to be part of "dismantling" and "transforming" the existing system. Victor Davis Hanson suggests the Ivies might eventually have some difficulties, although by the time anything of negative consequence to their dominance actually occurs, it probably will be too late to save us from some of the increasingly intense developments. Hanson writes:

> Eventually, even elite schools will lose their current veneer of prestige. Their costly cattle brands will be synonymous with equality-of-result, overpriced indoctrination echo chambers, where therapy replaced singular rigor and their tarnished degrees become irrelevant.

How ironic that universities are rushing to erode meritocratic standards—history's answer to the age-old, pre-civilizational bane of tribal, racial, class, elite and insider prejudices and bias that eventually ensure poverty and ruin for all.[15]

Chapter Three

The "Spiral of Silence"

Yeonmi Park's Eyes Are Fully Open to What Is Happening in America

Yeonmi Park is a courageous young North Korean woman who fled that country, traveled across the Gobi Desert during her escape, experienced terrible conditions and extreme abuses while doing so, and worked her way through South Korea and then to America. Park said she sees troubling similarities between the United States and North Korea. In an interview with the *New Zealand Herald*, Park shared thoughts.

> "North Korea was pretty insane. Like the first thing my mum taught me was don't even whisper, the birds and mice could hear me. She told me the most dangerous thing that I had in my body was my tongue. So I knew how dangerous it was to say wrong things in a country." . . . She says there are signs the US education system is doing the same thing to its citizens. "That's what it does when you're brainwashed," she said. "In some ways they (in the US) are brainwashed. Even though there's evidence so clearly in front of their eyes they can't see it."[1]

In addition to writing *In Order to Live* (Penguin, New York, 2015) with Maryanne Vollers—a bestselling book about her journey—Park enrolled in Columbia University in 2016. She found the culture there to be repressive and drew damning comparisons between North Korea and the culture she encountered as a student at Columbia. Here are some excerpts from her description of the Columbia experience published in the *New Zealand Herald*.

Yeonmi Park says she thought she was entering a country that promoted free speech—instead, she found the opposite when she went to university. Park attended Columbia University and she soon realised she was in a system that focused on political correctness and contained anti-Western sentiment. She says she thought the system would encourage free thinking and open dialogue but instead found they were being forced to think a certain way.[2]

At Columbia: "Every problem, they explained to us, is because of white men."

"Going to Columbia, the first thing I learned was 'safe space,'" she said. "Every problem, they explained to us, is because of white men." Some of the discussions of white privilege reminded her of the caste system in her native country, where people were categorised based on their ancestors, she said. She found she would get into arguments with lecturers and students about subjects and eventually learned "how to just shut up" in order to maintain her good grades. "I literally crossed the Gobi Desert to be free and I realised I'm not free, America's not free."[3]

While the Woke and Crits represent only a small portion of the population, they have consolidated into a coordinated, aggressive, and ruthless mass formation of the kind described by Ghent University academic Mattias Desmet in his book, *The Psychology of Totalitarianism* (2022). This has produced a chilling effect for university faculty and administrators who understandably don't want to be the objects of vindictive attacks and fear the potential impact on their careers. A recent report by FIRE describes the chilling of academic discourse. In Rikki Schlott's *New York Post* report on the suppression and fear being experienced by US academics, she explains:

Academic freedom is under siege. A new survey from the Foundation for Individual Rights and Expression (FIRE) reveals professors are shutting their mouths and biting their tongues out of fear of being canceled. In their newly released report, *The Academic Mind in 2022: What Faculty Think About Free Expression and Academic Freedom on Campus*, FIRE surveyed nearly 1,500 professors from colleges and universities across the country. The results show mass self-censorship and a widespread fear that saying the wrong thing could cost them their reputations—or even their jobs. . . . Some 72% of conservative faculty members and 56% of moderates felt this way, while 40% of liberal faculty members did. Roughly one-third (34%) said they often feel they can not [*sic*] express their opinions because of how students, colleagues or school administration might respond. More than half (52%) of professors reported being "afraid of losing their jobs or reputations because someone misunderstands something they said or did, takes it out of context, or posts something from their past online." . . . 11% of faculty members say they've either been disciplined or threatened with discipline by administrators for what they taught in the classroom. An additional 4% were threatened or punished for research, academic talks or work in non-academic publications.[4]

The fear among those who are supposed to be America's guiding intellectuals is legitimate. The consequences they face are real, including careers ruined through innuendo. But it is not only faculty who are silenced. Apprehension has spread to students over whom the Woke faculty and administrators exert control through immediate grading consequences, as well as providing recommendations for jobs or access to graduate education. When your future is at stake, self-censorship and a public appearance of support for the Woke and CRT agendas can be the result for faculty, students, and university administrators who are not part of the radical movement but seek to avoid its wrath.

Brianna McKee explains the consequences of universities being "enablers" of the repressive behavior of the Woke movement:

The failure to protect freedom of speech at universities threatens education's core purpose, which is to impart knowledge and hone the mind through debate and challenge. Worse still, it threatens the future of democratic institutions which rely on the free flow of ideas in the public square. The civil contest of ideas is not only the very essence of university life but the very essence of political life in a flourishing liberal democracy.[5]

Self-Censoring by Students, Faculty, and Administrators and the Abuse and Misuse of Accusations of "Racism" to Intimidate and Silence

In describing the emotional dynamics of what we are experiencing, and why the Progressive left's strategy is so successful, one prospective speaker at the University of New Mexico, who was scheduled to present a talk about the importance of constitutional rights, offered the following comments.

> "[M]ost people cower in fear when they're called a racist, they go into a place of paralysis. We are in the era of weaponized name-calling where people ask for forgiveness immediately, and they apologize for no reason just because they're called this." Today's Democratic Party doesn't believe in individualism or speech, Charles Kirk added, noting how the left prefers to categorize each person by arbitrary subgroups based on immutable characteristics rather than merit.[6]

As former president of Calvin College Anthony Diekema puts it:

> Faculty simply do not always say what they believe, or what they know to be true, because they don't want to deal with what may be the resulting hassle—peer alienation, negative student opinions, or the ire of a constituent community. Self-censorship is often a matter of personal convenience for faculty. They simply assess the potential costs before speaking out.[7]

Noah Carl is a British sociologist and intelligence researcher who writes about self-censorship by students and academics. This includes warning about the threat that our democratic system's divisiveness and growing intolerance of competing ideas and policies produces in undermining free speech and the quality of intellectual development at universities. He explains:

> [S]elf-censorship is indicative of an atmosphere in which costly social sanctions are leveled against those who express controversial beliefs. A single act of self-censorship may give rise to additional acts via the so-called spiral of silence. This is where a minority viewpoint gradually disappears from the public conversation, due to the fact that each individual who might express that viewpoint becomes increasingly less likely to do so as the number of other individuals expressing the viewpoint decreases. Given the level of vitriol to which some campus dissidents have been subjected, it would hardly be surprising if many students and academics chose to keep their opinions to themselves.[8]

Carl then describes the results of several surveys in which significant numbers of university students admitted to being afraid to share their views due to concerns about being found "offensive":

> In a 2017 survey of US college students . . . 49% of respondents said they were reluctant to speak about politics because they feared that other students might find their views offensive, while 34% said they were reluctant to do so because they feared that a professor might find their views offensive. In another 2017 survey . . . 30% of respondents said they had "stopped themselves from sharing an idea or opinion" in class because they feared that other students might find their views offensive, while 39% said that they had stopped themselves from speaking up outside the classroom for the same reason.
>
> In a 2018 survey commissioned by the William F. Buckley Jr. Program at Yale, 53% of respondents said they had often "felt intimidated in sharing [their] ideas, opinions or beliefs in class" because they were different from those of their professors, while 54% said they had often felt intimidated in sharing them because they were different from those of their peers.[9]

David Bernstein, founder of the Jewish Institute for Liberal Values, says "Woke" ideology not only stops open discourse but is creating greater antisemitism. The fear of being attacked for opposing the Woke ideology is causing people to self-censor. This fear has spread throughout the university, K-12 schools, and most of American society.

> "Americans are self-censoring at rates higher than they were during the McCarthy era in the United States," Bernstein said. The Cato Institute found that 62 percent of Americans have political views they are afraid to share. The Foundation for Individual Rights and Expression (FIRE), in partnership with RealClearEducation, commissioned College Pulse to conduct a survey of over 37,000 students at 159 colleges, who were asked about their experiences with free speech on their campuses. Eighty percent of students surveyed answered "I self-censor at least some of the time," and 66 percent said it is acceptable to shout someone down to prevent them from speaking on campus. "The people who deny that it happens like to focus on the 'cancel' part of it, but they don't like to talk about the 'culture' part of it," said Bernstein. "The culture is extremely censorious."[10]

No One Wants to Be "Crushed" by the Mass

Russell Jacoby, professor of History at UCLA, notes that scholars' self-imposed restrictions on their expression of intellectual independence are, in part, a result of prudence. They know that there are consequences to communicating unpopular views and are trying not to offend those who have the power to harm them. Jacoby comments on the disappearance of the independent intellectual. With all the claims by modern group-affiliated activists to be "speaking truth to power," Jacoby cites Voltaire:

> Men of letters, wrote Voltaire, are "isolated writers," who have neither "arguified on the benches of the universities nor said things by halves in the academies; and these have nearly all been persecuted." He added that if you write odes to the monarch, "you will be well received. Enlighten men, and you will be crushed."[11]

Scholars have no more desire to be "crushed" than anyone else. They quickly learn the forms of behavior and expression that will help their careers and those that will hurt or destroy their prospects. "Soft" repression works because the ordinary academic is a cautious being, not a courageous one. Many university faculty "run for cover" when surrounded by intensely aggressive critics. Academics seek comfort, contentment, and compensation, not conflict. As part of their defensive coloration, they either take on a public stance in which they appear to be in support of others' agendas, or they withdraw into what they hope is a safe cocoon so as to not draw attention to themselves.

For new and untenured faculty particularly, there is a need to "keep their heads down." Being seen as out of step with the Woke can end up "canceling" any advancement to tenure status and job security. Even for tenured faculty, as many have discovered, although they have a significant amount of legal job protection, they can find themselves condemned and marginalized by activist faculty and administrators. As Peter Boghossian, Jay Bhattacharya, and numerous others have found, "social justice warrior" students, administrators, and Woke colleagues can attack teachers by condemning their teaching and research to the point that an intensely hostile work environment is created.

Nor are many faculty "colleagues" willing to defend you, because they are part of the critical "mass," or are afraid of potential consequences to themselves. Boghossian relates how he was even spit at on campus, and Bhattacharya described his experience at the University of Chicago as a "living hell." Scott Atlas was condemned by 85 percent of the Stanford Faculty Senate due to his views on COVID-19 pandemic strategies. The Stanford Faculty Senate never apologized for its members' stunning level of ignorance and closed-minded hypocrisy, even though it turned out Atlas was clearly correct.

Universities Are Shifting from a "Tenure Track" Model to Term-Specific Contracts. That Makes Faculty Even More Vulnerable and Tentative

Another significant part of the dilemma is that, over the last several decades, US universities have shifted to an employment model in which intimidation is easier due to increasingly limited job security. The new model that has arisen in many American universities is one where a very significant part of faculty are not on the tenure track and have limited job security and are on fixed term contracts and periodic employment agreements.

The long-term idea underlying the grant of tenure was that the protections afforded by tenure allowed the scholar/teacher's mind to run free, speak and write openly and critically, and to challenge ignorance and bias. The resulting job security was phenomenal, but it is now fraying due to being abused and even ignored by many academics and administrators. This is not only due to fear of controversy and condemnation, but because they have themselves become politicized and are working within the university institution to use all its benefits and prestige in ways that actually undermine its essence and traditional mission of intellectual depth and integrity.

We are at a point where it is legitimate to ask whether university scholars and teachers have become cowardly, or so intellectually and morally committed to a single political agenda to the point that they have abdicated their responsibility to provide independent intellectual critiques of what is wrong in society and how to resolve the concerns. If that is accurate, they no longer deserve the protections of tenure.

Tenure is a shield, not a spear. It is intended to allow a university academic to be able to "speak truth to power" and not as a weapon to launch one-sided ideological or bigoted assaults. The "speech" of the university academic is to be based on the full evidence, implications, causes, and evidential quality of what is being addressed. That speech will sometimes, or even often, have political implications, but it is only legitimate if it is balanced, honest, clear, and comprehensive as opposed to seeking to advance a faculty member's personal or identity group agendas.

The problem with doing away with tenure's guarantees of employment is that a significant proportion of university academics are highly vulnerable in terms of careers. They do not want to offend the activists who have effectively captured the university and who not only include radicalized faculty but also a host of university administrators. The administrators are a particular problem. Many are Woke themselves, are employed as DEI activists or are fully aware that if they do not go along with the Woke/CRT movement, it will harm or destroy their own ability to move upward in the administrative ranks, or even keep their jobs.

Another part of the problem is that the pay, perks, and privileges of being a university professor are largely unmatched in terms of the overall employment markets. As a law professor, I have always thought of my job like being rich, although without the enormous amounts of money the "real" rich possess. I could set my schedule, read, travel, research, write, engage in very interesting projects, work with organizations outside the university, and more.

The freedom to do what you want and like, largely without any real oversight or interference, is something granted few people, and it is wonderful. This creates a situation in which the threat of losing such a great job is actually frightening because the work conditions and freedom are so fantastic. After a few years in the position and culture of being able to do what you want and to focus on matters important to you, it would be difficult to adjust to a work setting similar to what Hermann Hesse described as being "beneath the wheel."[12]

It is also the fact that there may be no equivalent employment opportunities available elsewhere. For example, I have absolutely no idea whether many, or any, of my former colleagues would be able to find productive employment in a situation with anything even close to the salaries, "perks," and status they receive as university faculty. If they were forced out of the university, many would suffer dramatic financial and psychological consequences. That fact has to be frightening and understandably convinces most academics and university administrators to go along with the crowd of Woke/CRT. Otherwise they could find themselves "on the streets."

Chapter Four

Jacques Ellul's *Propaganda* and *Technological Society*

One of my intellectual heroes has long been French natural law philosopher Jacques Ellul. For me, his works on natural law pale in relation to his analyses on technology and propagandist manipulation. The
power, shaping effects, and scale of institutional structures are part of the
phenomenon that Ellul defined as "technique." More than sixty years ago,
in two fantastic books, *The Technological Society* and *Propaganda*, Ellul
warned of the transformation of social structure and behavior through
the rise of technique and propaganda. He argued that we are increasingly trapped within a "technological society" that defines and dictates the
terms of human behavior and causes a progressive loss of our humanity.
In those two brilliant 1960s works, Ellul warned: "The conflict of propaganda takes the place of the debate of ideas."[1]

When we fast forward to the present day, it is clear we are experiencing
an accelerating shift to an authoritarian and propagandized "technological
society." This shift is overwhelming our society as information capabilities
evolve and are seized by educational, economic, and governmental activists
committed to the pursuit of power, profit, and the full implementation of a
Woke vision of society. In ways that anticipate Mattias Desmet's concept of
Mass Formation and a Mechanist society, Ellul provides insight into why
impassioned and fanatical Identity Groups are so dangerous. Such divisive
social organizations often result in rigid and fanatical stereotypes among
their members, and the "dumbing down" of the best of human capability.

We need only to scan our daily media and listen to the statements of our "leaders" to understand the accuracy of Ellul's warning. He explains the consequences of stereotypical "group-think":

> A stereotype is a seeming value judgment, acquired by belonging to a group, without any intellectual labor. . . . The stereotype arises from feelings one has for one's own group, or against the "out-group." Man attaches himself passionately to the values represented by his group and rejects the cliches of the out-groups. . . . The stereotype . . . helps man to avoid thinking, to take a personal position, to form his own opinion.[2]

Whatever designation we use, Ellul is describing a transition to a Mass Formation conformist society driven by the powers of a new technology. In *The Technological Society*, Ellul wrote about the dangers posed by a far less powerful technology than what we now face. He wrote that a technologically-dominated system, in which everything is rigidly compartmentalized and specialized to the point that the individual disappears into the "machinery" of the culture, will inevitably impose a repressive authoritarian conformity. In such a fully orchestrated and monitored culture, intellectuals no longer provide independent insight and essential perspective to the society. The few who might try, find themselves speaking to the intellectually deaf. Others become no more than "true believers" and agents and servants of those in power.

For members of "true believer" groups who believe what they must in order to remain part of the group, the sense of commitment offers a powerful source of stimulation. It provides a sense of belonging, personal significance, and human relationships in a troubling and terrifying world. At the same time it compresses the mind into a tight and impenetrable form that accepts only messages that fit their specific worldview. Open-minded thought and analysis disappear and we effectively become "drones" programmed to serve our "masters."

The problem is that knowledge, experience, and critical thinking are precisely the kinds of skills we have traditionally trusted our universities to provide. But universities are defaulting on that duty, shutting down thought and enhancing divisiveness. Ellul warns what happens when that occurs.

> The intelligentsia will no longer be a model, a conscience, or an animating intellectual spirit for the group. . . . They will be the servants, the most conformist imaginable, of the instruments of technique." In this "mode" of discourse we are unwilling to communicate because it is interest group politics rather than intellectual discourse.[3]

"The Coddling of the American Mind"

Less than a decade ago, Greg Lukianoff and Jonathan Haidt published an analysis in *The Atlantic* that detailed what was occurring in American universities. In "The Coddling of the American Mind," they wrote: "Something strange is happening at America's colleges and universities. A movement is arising, undirected and driven largely by students, to scrub campuses clean of words, ideas, and subjects that might cause discomfort or give offense."[4] The authors went on to warn:

> This new climate is slowly being institutionalized, and is affecting what can be said in the classroom, even as a basis for discussion. . . . [T]he deans and department chairs at the [ten] University of California system schools were presented by administrators at faculty leader-training sessions with examples of microaggressions. The list of offensive statements included: "America is the land of opportunity" and "I believe the most qualified person should get the job."[5]

The "new climate" Lukianoff and Haidt described in 2015 has grown in universities far more rapidly, and been institutionalized much more deeply, than expected. It has spread with astonishing speed throughout American society, including our entire educational system, all levels and forms of our media, government, and corporations. In large part this is due to the power of social media. The internet has facilitated an exponentially larger and more powerful and extensive degree of collaboration among ideological groups than was ever before possible.

Lukianoff and Haidt explained how the emergence of social media has progressively disempowered faculty and provided students with a weapon against authority that can be used to intimidate faculty:

> Social media makes it extraordinarily easy to join crusades, express solidarity and outrage, and shun traitors. . . . These first true "social-media natives" may be different from members of previous generations in how they go about sharing their moral judgments and supporting one another in moral campaigns and conflicts. . . . Social media has fundamentally shifted the balance of power in relationships between students and faculty; the latter increasingly fear what students might do to their reputations and careers by stirring up online mobs against them.[6]

For the university culture, one supposedly dedicated to the pursuit of knowledge and truth, allowing activists to seize and control the vital points of institutional power is the equivalent of the "fox in the henhouse." Yet that is what has occurred. As is detailed in my book, *"Un-Canceling" America* (2021), the ongoing transformation is not only afflicting the university culture, but includes dominant media outlets, governmental agencies and legislatures, businesses, and K-12 education systems.

Taken together, the institutions whose integrity is fundamental to our social order sat by passively while a large-scale political transformation driven by the Woke took place. This transformation constructed a culture of silence through intimidation and political correctness. It introduced a "shame" and "bigotry" culture in which anyone who challenged what they were doing was ostracized. In a total contradiction of the ideals of the university and education generally, lies, false narratives, and "frames" are being used to deflect accountability, confuse, and create uncertainty about what is occurring.

A "Quiet Coup" Is Taking Away Our Rights

Consider the experience of former North Korean refugee Yeonmi Park. Her compelling description of coming to America after enduring a horrific journey through the Gobi Desert and China while escaping from the absolute military dictatorship in North Korea, a country where no one has freedom, should be a wake-up-call. After arriving in America, "the land of the free" with a system that is still a shining beacon for many in the nation and throughout the world, Park enrolled in Columbia University.

At Columbia, Park was astonished by the generalized suppression of independent critical thought she witnessed at an Ivy League university long considered an intellectual leader. Park describes her stunned perception and the fact that many Americans simply do not understand, or are unwilling to recognize, the reality of a "quiet coup" that is taking away their fundamental rights. She explained to the *New Zealand Herald*:

> Americans seem willing to give their rights away not realising they may never come back. "Voluntarily, these people are censoring each other, silencing each other, no force behind it," she said. "Other times (in history) there's a military *coup d'etat*, like a force comes in taking your rights away and silencing you. But this country is choosing to be silenced, choosing to give their rights away."[7]

A vital perspective that echoes Yeonmi Park's warning is provided by cybersecurity expert Rex Lee. Lee indicates just how deeply US government agencies have infiltrated Big Tech and how insidious the relationship is. He offers one example of that infiltration and collaboration. More are described at greater length in subsequent parts of this text.

> The Twitter Files released by Elon Musk, showed that the FBI paid Twitter nearly $3.5 million in taxpayer cash. "It's misuse or misappropriation of taxpayer funds, when the FBI, who should be concentrating on terrorists, are now putting their focus on U.S. citizens through a biased lens based on the citizens' political ideology, not that the citizen is doing anything wrong," he said.[8,]

The Consequence Is Fanaticism and Totalitarianism

As Gabriel Marcel warned, one consequence of the social fragmentation we are experiencing is the extreme difficulty of having honest discourse in a politically polarized environment that Deborah Tannen has described as the "Argument Culture."[9] What is happening borders on fascistic behavior within the critical institutions of our American society, including government, media, and education. As is demonstrated at various points in this analysis, in my judgment the Woke/Crit activist movement has in many ways driven us perilously close to that state. What we are experiencing is poisoning the hearts and minds of a wide range of citizens and commentators, while blinding them to the fanatical and intolerant nature of what they are doing. Marcel explains how the fanatical mind defends its beliefs from being weakened by reality: "[T]he fanatic never sees himself as a fanatic; it is only the non-fanatic who can recognize him as a fanatic; so that when this judgment, or this accusation, is made, the fanatic can always say that he is misunderstood and slandered."[10]

Mattias Desmet also warns about the dangers presented by media systems and communications technologies that produce what he calls the "Mechanist Ideology." Its dangers for democratic societies increase exponentially when a political "mass" has the ability to utilize and control the instruments of communication offered by the internet, by surveillance technology, and by social media. In a recent analysis, Aaron Kheriaty, a psychiatrist and the director of the Program in Bioethics and American Democracy at the Ethics and Public Policy Center in Washington, DC, like Desmet, wrote about what he sees as a rapid shift toward totalitarianism:

> The Italian philosopher Augusto Del Noce, who came of age in the 1930s and observed with horror the emergence of Mussolini's Fascist regime in his native country, warned that "the widespread notion that the age of totalitarianisms ended with Hitlerism and Stalinism is completely mistaken." . . . By technological society, Del Noce did not mean a society characterized by scientific or technological progress, but a society characterized by a view of rationality as purely instrumental. . . . Reason is [considered] merely a pragmatic tool, a useful instrument for accomplishing our purposes, but nothing more. . . . [In such a system] it is impossible to deliberate or debate

civilly in a shared pursuit of truth. Reasoned persuasion has no place. Totalitarian regimes always monopolize what counts as "rational" and therefore what one is permitted to say publicly.[11]

The Ideological Makeover of America's Universities

Many of America's universities are dominated by activists and ideologues rather than true teachers and scholars. These "true believers" not only control the behavior of faculties and administrations, but recruit relatively small but highly vocal, aggressive, and unforgiving students who organize and intimidate other students and more traditional faculty members into silence. They do not generally comprise numerical majorities, although they have achieved that status within many university disciplines and at the administrative levels.

A result is that the "principles" of Wokeness, and Diversity, Equity, and Inclusion (DEI) have become critical guidelines for hiring faculty and administrators, the outcome being that it is almost impossible for a non-Woke faculty member or administrator to be hired by an American university. Chapter 26 of this book offers the DEI Hiring Guidelines for Brown and Columbia universities. Those guidelines are quite clearly "loaded" in ways that guarantee only Woke/CRT faculty candidates have any realistic chance of being hired in the Woke university.

The skewed concentration of Woke faculty and university administrators is proving the accuracy of Mattias Desmet's assertion that a formed "mass" can take control of an entire social system when it numbers only 20–30 percent of an institutional or systemic population. Even that "high" number of what is required to control may be overstated. Nassim Nicholas Taleb offers an even more dire warning, arguing that control may only require a political mass of 3 to 4 percent. This control is possible once collaborating activist groups occupy the most critical positions of power and decision-making in key institutions, and are sufficiently aggressive, loud, ruthless, and strategic.[12]

Aaron Kheriaty aptly describes the fact that we are engaged in a no-holds-barred conflict. It is not an intellectual debate in which people with different points of view are engaged in actual discourse aimed at sharing and evaluating each other's point of view. Like Gabriel Marcel's description of the fanatic's mind, we are dealing with people whose belief systems are so rigid that they are incapable of openness to any other views. In the minds of the Woke totalitarians, there are always reasons why the "others" who dispute their assertions and behaviors are wrong. Kheriaty explains this in the following terms in describing how the Woke/Crits respond to anyone who disagrees with their assertions:

> You [the non-Woke] don't think such-and-such because you reasoned logically to that conclusion; you think such-and-such because you are a white, heterosexual, middle-class American female, and so forth. In this way, totalitarians do not persuade or refute their interlocutors with reasoned arguments. They merely impute bad faith to their opponents and refuse to engage in meaningful debate. They forcibly cut their adversaries off from the sphere of enlightened conversation. One does not bother arguing against such dissidents; one simply steamrolls them after placing them outside the realm of acceptable opinion.[13]

"How can you win a fight if you don't fight?"

This is the point where we must demand that our universities fight back against the fanatical groups and movements seeking to control and corrupt America's society. Unfortunately, as described throughout this analysis, many of our universities are a key part of advancing the authoritarian ideology by becoming, in essence, "propaganda and indoctrination systems." Here I am focusing primarily on how rage, hate, resentment, political agendas, and the thirst for power are reshaping and degrading our universities. An initial response to what is being presented here is likely to be something like: "He must be wrong; it can't really be happening, or it can't be as bad as is being suggested." Unfortunately, it *is* that bad because we aren't paying attention.

The rapper Zuby has spoken up about the need to confront and fight back against the Woke. His views are captured with clarity in the

September 22, 2022 report in the *Epoch Times* , "'Silent Majority' Must Speak Up When Vocal Minority Imposes Views on Society":

> If people do not speak up when faced with a vocal minority trying to impose their radical views on society, the silent majority and their children will face dire consequences, said rapper and social commentator Zuby, encouraging the "silent majority" to stop censoring themselves. "A silent majority may as well not exist," he said. "I think there's a silenced majority." As long as people stay silenced, then that vocal minority—even if it makes up only 1 percent of the population—will not be afraid to state their opinions, he said, because they are very vocal and bold.[14]

Zuby then moves to a question with which I am in complete agreement. He asks: "How can you win a fight if you don't fight? How can you win a debate when you don't speak?"

> In a debate, if one person is "spouting off the goofiest, most ludicrous ideas" and the other person just sits there silently and nods, then the one who talks will win the debate, he said. "Most Americans aren't on board with the most extreme and radical and bizarre notions that are floating around out there," he said, referring to the recent assertions that men can become pregnant or give birth. "Over 90 percent of people don't believe that, but those people need to be willing to say something." A silent majority is weak when faced with a vocal minority, he added. . . . "Most people are not being censored by the government or even censored by big tech or censored by social media," Zuby said. "They're censoring themselves."[15]

Ten Years of Cowardice and Submission by a So-Called "Silent Majority"

Zuby concluded:

> "Over the past 10 years, we have had this pandemic of cowardice, and people are unwilling to say things in many cases that are objectively

true. . . . They are afraid of repercussions," he said, adding that cowardice and courage are both habits and they're also both contagious. When people start acting like cowards, it can affect others around who will start behaving like cowards, Zuby said. "When one person stands up, starts speaking out, and using their platform to either state their opinions or to state objective facts, it encourages other people to do the same."[16]

Former Levi Strauss Executive Jennifer Sey Turns Down $1,000,000 So She Could Tell the Truth

Jennifer Sey, a former Levi Strauss senior director of marketing who was reportedly in line for a possible CEO appointment, was forced out of Levi's after she made public statements opposing public school shutdowns. She turned down a $1,000,000 buyout offer because it required she not discuss publicly what had occurred. Sey described the way employees are being silenced in many companies and used the examples of Theranos, FTX, and Enron to show the truth that even if employees have knowledge about bad things going on, they are afraid to speak. Sey singles out universities for the fact that they are educating students in their Wokeness and then sending them out to jobs throughout the nation. This "filling of the ranks" of large scale companies, K-12 educational systems, and governmental agencies has transformed those institutions through the indoctrination into Wokeness students receive in our universities.

Sey said the illiberalism that has traveled from college campuses into companies and taken hold of corporations across the country is "incredibly dangerous." "If you insist on a culture where free speech is not tolerated, not only is it non-inclusive, which is problematic in and of itself, but I actually think it's fraught and rife with the potential for corruption and fraud, like we've seen with Theranos and FTX and Enron," she said. "This pose of wokeness, it's a cloak they wrap themselves in to signal virtue . . . to hide greed, corruption, keeping all the good stuff for themselves," she said. "It's this costume that the left, liberal elite wraps around themselves to say, 'I care about social justice. I care about all these causes. I am a good person.' If you threaten to expose that, you need to be banished."[17]

Chapter Five

The Infantilization of Mind Through "Democratic Despotism"

Alexis de Tocqueville Described the "Infantilization" of Mind That Can Occur Through "Democratic Despotism"

The unfolding situation of a declining educational system in America is of a kind Roger Kimball traces to Alexis de Tocqueville in his classic and brilliantly insightful nineteenth-century work *Democracy in America*. Tocqueville's analysis, written in the 1830s and yet far superior to the quality of our current "discourse," is remarkably contemporary. The force of democratic despotism, Tocqueville wrote, "would be like the authority of a parent if, like that authority, its object was to prepare men for manhood; but it seeks, on the contrary, to keep them in perpetual childhood." Kimball writes:

> In pre-democratic societies, Tocqueville noted, despotism tyrannized. In modern democracies, it infantilizes. Democratic despotism is both "more extensive and more mild" than its precursors: it "degrades men without tormenting them." In this sense, Tocqueville continued, "the species of oppression by which democratic nations are menaced is unlike anything that ever before existed in the world."[1]

The "infantilization" of the mind is taking place in our universities, particularly in the "soft" disciplinary areas of social science, humanities, interdisciplinary studies, English literature, psychology, sociology, philosophy, and other subject areas into which a teacher's or scholar's personalized opinions, interest group identifications, and politics can play major roles. The inherent subjectivity of such disciplinary subject matter allows a highly politicized reinterpretation of the material being studied.

This is seen in the *New York Times'* badly flawed 1619 Project, described earlier in citing the *New York Times'* Bret Stephens analysis, and in the Critical Race Theory dimension that Stephens described as a "theory in search of evidence." It is found throughout what passes for objective political analysis, and in our "new journalism" filled with activists, hustlers, and ideologues rather than honest journalists. It has become common in the increasingly odd Woke interpretations of human and systemic behavior. None of this is accidental. Each is committed to destroying long-held moral, philosophical, and political ideals to create the "space" needed for their dramatic reinterpretations of human and social reality.

In the "infantilizing" of education throughout America's systems, we are dumbing down those who are supposedly being "educated." Part of the process involves progressively turning many of our academic and other leaders into tantrum-throwing "brats" who must have their way and continually proclaim their victimhood. This includes seemingly continual whining about being "scared" and deeply threatened by the mere possibility of exposure, not to the actions, but to the words of those with whom they don't agree. In a nation devoted in its creation to dialogue, impassioned discourse, disagreement, and an understanding that a complex nation required airing of views and compromises, we are suddenly seized by the conviction that words in and of themselves are forms of unforgivable violence that must be suppressed whenever they differ from our agendas and interpretations.

Even this is nothing more than a one-sided political strategy. I am, for example, more than a bit irked and extremely contemptuous of Woke assertions that "white men are the bad guys" in relation to every problem the Woke/CRT Identity Groups blather about. Married to this are divisive and histrionic statements that "all Whites are inherently racist," that masculinity is automatically "toxic" and should be squashed wherever found, and that "terrible" things such as rationality, individualism, mathematics, logic, evidence, and the traditional family structure are nothing more than "White" strategies of repression.

The use of such terms is extremely offensive to me and many others. But the Woke/CRT polemicists don't care about the impact of their twisted accusations on me or millions of others who are representative of a significant range of diversity in culture and perspective. They don't care because their assertions and accusations serve the goal of angering and energizing their revolutionary base. They also are silencing others who are intimidated by such bad faith pseudo-intellectual garbage, and know that if they respond they will be condemned and punished.

If You "Get Them" While They Are Young, You "Own Them"

No one understood the mind-control potential of education better than Mao Zedong. Mao wrote in a 1937 tract that open-minded, thoughtful, and critical Liberalism was a threat to his "revolution." Mao condemned Liberalism in its true and original form because he understood such orientations empowered people to question authority. Mao knew this would cause them to deviate from the dictates of his leadership. To Mao, school's function was to create people who accepted the principles and strategies of "the revolution." This demanded people who followed orders, and anyone who deviated was condemned as a "counter-revolutionary" who suffered severe consequences, even death.

Authoritarian propagandists in the Woke, Critical Race, and Radical Progressive movements, the "Woke/Crits," understand that the best time to take control of children's minds is when they are young and at their most vulnerable. People who never develop the ability to engage in free and critical thought and lack respect for objectivity and the full range of fact and evidence are highly susceptible to emotionally crafted propaganda. They aren't being taught "how" to think, but "what" to think. This is why the slogans, claims, and narratives with which we are currently being surrounded are designed to bypass our rational minds and penetrate us at the emotional level rather than that of fact, evidence, and reason.

Yeonmi Park said she is worried freedoms are being lost in America amid left-wing indoctrination in K-12 schools.

"This is exactly the dictator's handbook. I mean, it's [Adolf] Hitler's youth, Mao's youth and Kim Il-Sung's youth. They always go for young children because they have [not] lived their life enough to . . . have critical thinking skills. Their brains are very plastic, very malleable, and easy to observe information and believe it and [they're] innocent," she said. "And . . . big killers [who] want to seize power from the people, always mobilize the youth. And that is the truth that [worries me that], as a parent myself, that I cannot protect my child right now in America."[2]

Indoctrinating America's Youth

Compared with the "hard" data and evidentiary and methodologically-based disciplinary sectors of the kind represented by STEM research and learning, repeated surveys of the political orientations of university faculty reveal an extreme distinction between Liberal/Left university faculty in the "soft" knowledge fields versus faculty in science, technology, engineering, and mathematics (STEM). In those "hard" disciplines, scholars and teachers must actually base their positions on data, evidence, and a reproducible methodology. To do otherwise is to professionally delegitimize one's own work.

Studies have also shown that while many American students initially begin their course of study at universities studying for STEM degrees, very significant numbers of those students soon shift to the noncumulative disciplines because the STEM courses are "too hard." This unfortunately fits into the reality that the nation's K-12 systems have "dumbed down" with students' skills declining in mathematics and even reading. If and when they enroll in a university, such unprepared students are incapable of performing adequately in rigorous areas of study requiring mathematical and scientific knowledge and total precision and soon gravitate toward disciplines that are less demanding disciplines in that technical sense.

Even here, however, I want to make clear that I am not seeking to insult or denigrate non-STEM fields of concentration. I am an insatiably curious person and have dealt with many disciplines and methodologies in my writing, teaching, client representation, consulting, and study. Hard, tough, challenging analytical work runs a diverse gamut if the point is to develop the strongest ability to think, recognize valid and invalid alternatives through the combination of wide knowledge, and the ability to apply that to understanding the reality of what we face and are being told in someone's political "narrative."

The criticism I am making here is not aimed at undermining the humanistic Liberal Arts–focused forms of education that sought to provide students with the rich range of knowledge, understanding, and skill that has increasingly disappeared from American education but creates perspectives I consider fundamental to the health and wellbeing of our democratic republic. My very strong critique is aimed at the Woke/Crit system that is deliberately undermining and eliminating comprehensive humanistic education through a strategy of creating politicized "drones" who will do the Woke's bidding. The Woke are not allowing far-ranging understanding or critical thinking because they seek to create a politicized system intent on the acquisition of power for their specific Identity Group. It is doing this through indoctrination and intimidation, not through honest, comprehensive, and deep education.

This Woke strategy of indoctrination, propaganda, and intimidation, along with the widespread use of lower evaluative standards, elimination of testing and grading, and "social passes" given regardless of whether students have demonstrated proficiency in math, science, and reading, means we are producing large numbers of poorly educated K-12 graduates who are incapable of performing at higher levels in university educational systems. When those "higher" educational systems continue the process of "dumbing down" students by providing them with a "free pass" and a college degree, the graduates do not possess any significant level of skills, knowledge, and capabilities of the kind and quality required for the preservation of the American Ideal.

The "dumbing down" of America's students has been occurring for several decades, developing to a significant level before we were exposed to the clear evidence of what was being done in a heavily politicized and non-analytical educational system through our experience with the COVID-19 pandemic. This delay in realizing that the educational system was being taken over by the ideological bigots calling themselves Woke and Critical means that many of those who received degrees from universities during that fifteen- to twenty-five-year period were themselves under-educated or their educational experience was projected through a strong ideological lens.

It also reveals that the education and certification of K-12 teachers during that time was significantly politicized in many institutions. Many teachers perceived their role as being political activists and "social justice warriors." Their primary educational responsibility was to "dismantle" and "transform" what they considered to be an unjust and intrinsically evil system. Achieving this meant that they needed to expand their "revolutionary" ranks through proselytization and intimidating and silencing those who didn't "fall into place."

It Is an Ongoing and Relentless Strategy of the "Long March Through the Institutions" of American Society

Mark Hendrickson is adjunct professor of Economics at Grove City College. He is also a fellow for Economics and Social Policy with the Center for Vision and Values, and is on the Council of Scholars of the Commonwealth Foundation. He provides an historical and strategic context for what is happening:

> The tenth plank in Karl Marx's platform for how to steer a society to socialism was "Free education for all children in government schools." That may sound benign and even generous, but the purpose was to indoctrinate children to unquestioningly accept the economic plans and political commands of the elitists running the government. The goal was control of the masses, not the enlightenment and liberation of individuals.

The Italian Marxist Antonio Gramsci (1891–1937) envisioned a multi-generational strategy of infusing popular culture with Marxist notions. The German Marxist Rudi Dutschke rebranded Gramsci's cultural Marxism as the "long march through the institutions," but the goal remained the same: to propagandize and indoctrinate the masses in Marxist ideas until Marxism became the dominant ideology. Fast forward to today, and we see controversy and conflict in our public schools. Both at the primary and secondary levels, students are being subjected to "lessons" that have little to do with developing intellectual capabilities, but everything to do with promoting various progressive agendas.[3]

Liberty, Individual Freedom, and the Foundations of the American Republic

What is now taking place contradicts and offends the basic and unique ideals of the political experiment that is America. The foundations of the American federalist republic are reflected in a simple paragraph in Justice Brandeis's concurring opinion in *Whitney v. California*.[4] It is a commitment that provides us with one of the most vital underlying purposes of our educational systems. *Whitney v. California* was a 1927 US Supreme Court case in which Justice Brandeis wrote a compelling concurrence in defense of free speech under the First Amendment. Brandeis wrote:

> Those who won our independence believed that the final end of the State was to make men free to develop their faculties; and that in its government the deliberative forces should prevail over the arbitrary. They valued liberty both as an end and as a means. They believed liberty to be the secret of happiness and courage to be the secret of liberty. They believed that freedom to think as you will and to speak as you think are means indispensable to the discovery and spread of political truth; that without free speech and assembly discussion would be futile.[5]

It is important not only for the nation, but the entire world, that America's students are provided the ability to think clearly and deeply, to problem solve and innovate, and to recognize the vital need to function as a true social and political community rather than a collection of angry "tribes" at war with each other. The absence of the critical skills of analysis and problem solving, understanding reality, honoring real diversity, and refusing to engage in honest interactive discourse threatens the health and quality of America's social, economic, and political culture. Lacking such fundamental skills sabotages the nation.

This situation has reached the point where we are engaged in a struggle for the quality and heart of how we are allowed to conduct discourse and interact with each other. Without free, interactive, conflicting, and, even bitter, discourse, democracy cannot survive. Within the university the struggle for control of language means that the institution's long-professed culture of intellectual freedom and independence has been twisted into one of political allegiance, conformity, Orwellian "groupthink," and repression. This contradicts and endangers the fundamental ideals of the core beliefs of Western democratic republics.

Aristotle argued that the ideal of aspiring to achieve the highest human development as an individual and as a contributor to our community defined who we are. Edward Younkins, professor of accountancy and business administration at Wheeling Jesuit University, sums it up as follows:

> Aristotle teaches that each man's life has a purpose and that the function of one's life is to attain that purpose. He explains that the purpose of life is earthly happiness or flourishing that can be achieved via reason and the acquisition of virtue. Articulating an explicit and clear understanding of the end toward which a person's life aims, Aristotle states that each human being should use his abilities to their fullest potential and should obtain happiness and enjoyment through the exercise of his realized capacities. He contends that human achievements are animated by purpose and autonomy and that people should take pride in being excellent at what they do. According to Aristotle, human beings have a natural desire and capacity to know and understand the truth.[6]

Two Generations of "True Believers" and "Fault-Finding Men of Words" Are Seizing Power

If we don't want to endure the pain of thinking, there are always the paths of fanaticism, being a true believer, and submitting to what John Gardner called the "pathology of dedication." Echoing Eric Hoffer's analysis of the malady and danger of True Believers, Gardner summed up what we are currently experiencing in his 1987 warning about the dangers.

> [E]very line of behavior has its pathology, and there is pathology of dedication. . . . [T]here is the "true believer" who surrenders himself to a mass movement or to dogmatic beliefs in order to escape the responsibilities of freedom. [He adds] . . . commitment to worthy goals becomes so fanatical (among the groups and organizations) that they destroy as much as they create. A free society does not invite that kind of allegiance. It wants only one kind of devotion, the devotion of free, rational, responsible individuals.[7]

Eric Hoffer described the role of "faultfinding men of words." In *The True Believer: Thoughts on the Nature of Mass Movements*.[8] As seen with numerous European intellectuals who witnessed the rise of the Soviet Union in the 1930s, the role of true believers as "faultfinders" is to undermine the principles of an existing orthodoxy, deliberately weakening the underpinnings of an existing system through intensive criticism so another can replace it. This is a core part of the strategy employed by Woke and Critical Race Theory educational activists. A Critical Legal Studies scholar and activist, Mark Kelman, described this strategy in 1984 as "trashing" the principles and doctrines of the dominant system in order to undermine and transform. That approach has been surprisingly successful.

Although Hoffer was writing in the 1950s and Kelman and Gardner in the 1980s, this "faultfinding" and "trashing" is precisely what is taking place in America today with the activists of the Woke and Critical Race Theory movements. Our dilemma combines the extreme politicization of academia and other critical systems—including media and government.

It is reinforced by the abandonment in those institutions of belief in ideals and duties such as truth and truth-seeking. It is all about power and using the language of opposition and conflict to gain power and keep it. Activism, ideology, and propaganda replace thoughtful interaction. Hoffer's following analysis summarizes our current situation with compelling insight.

"Whatever the type, there is a deep-seated craving common to almost all men of words which determines their attitude to the prevailing order. It is a craving for recognition; a craving for a clearly marked status above the common run of humanity." " . . . the majority of people cannot endure the barrenness and futility of their lives unless they have some ardent dedication, or some passionate pursuit in which they can lose themselves." Eric Hoffer, *The True Believer*:

The true believer, Hoffer tells us, is a frustrated, self-loathing individual who compensates for a weak identity by finding some crusade to invest himself in. The mass movement is perfect for such persons: it "appeals not to those intent on bolstering and advancing a cherished self, but to those who crave to be rid of an unwanted self. A mass movement attracts and holds a following not because it can satisfy the desire for self-advancement, but because it can satisfy the passion for self-renunciation." . . .

Mass movements can be good or bad, wholesome or destructive, but they all "generate in their adherents a readiness to die and a proclivity for united action; all of them, irrespective of the doctrine they preach and the program they project, breed fanaticism, enthusiasm, fervent hope, hatred and intolerance . . . all of them demand blind faith and singlehearted allegiance."

"Mass movements do not usually rise until the prevailing order has been discredited. The discrediting is not an automatic result of the blunders and abuses of those in power, but the deliberate work of men of words with a grievance."[9]

The Demise of the Public Intellectual

Elizabeth Mitchell, a former senior long-form writer for the *New York Daily News* and the author of three non-fiction books, writes about the death of the public intellectual and replacement by specialized academics who are writing for a narrowly focused group of like-minded university faculty whose rewards come from appealing to the agendas and assumptions of other micro-specialists in their area of concentration.

> Our nation has always depended on these [intellectual] heavyweights to guide us, but are they still with us, and if so, who are they? . . . [T]he consensus seems to be: The egghead is dead. This painful conclusion weighs heavily on public intellectuals, who created the country during the 116 steamy days of the 1787 Constitutional Convention, when Alexander Hamilton, James Madison and crew crafted a new nation entirely out of words. Then they bolstered it with 85 newspaper columns under the pen name Publius, now known as the Federalist Papers, to explain and defend their work.[10]

Mitchell goes on to suggest several potential causes in what she feels has been the drying up of "public intellectuals" who seek to comprehensively challenge the range of society's most fundamental problems, linking that decline to a large scale shift to ultra-specialization and the dramatic narrowing of what university academics research and teach in a systemic shift to sub-disciplines representing a progressive narrowing of subject matter.

> Intellectualism got a boost after the Second World War, when the G.I. Bill enabled universities to massively increase capacity. In this fertile period, before specialization fully took hold, philosophers, historians and sociologists explained the postwar world to the new hordes of college-educated women and men hungering for mental stimulation.[11]

The problem is that as the specialization grew to the point it represented increasingly narrow disciplinary niches disconnected from other relevant contexts, the result was a great increase in specialized knowledge and research data. At the same time, this explosion in hyper-detailed areas of inquiry occurred and expanded, we experienced a rapid decline in the overarching and integrative forms of analysis that characterized broad-based philosophical and systemic exploration. Mitchell explains. "[I]n 1985, the Berkeley sociologist Robert Bellah decried that academic specialization had cut our best minds off from the fray. You can't be a truly public intellectual if you speak only to your "in group."[12] Yet membership and communication to the narrow group is precisely what has occurred.

The "Progressive" Narrowing of the Mind

A significant part of the problem is that comprehensive knowledge is impossible at this point. Generally speaking, we have been overwhelmed by the sheer volume and diversity of available information that floods our world like a "data tsunami." Essentially, even the most learned intellectual or scholar is a specialist at this point. We no longer have intellectuals who seek to understand the full range of what has been called the "human *problematique*."

We are increasingly narrow and superficial entities when it comes to comprehending the range of information to which we are exposed. This makes us vulnerable to manipulation of the kind we are experiencing with Wokeness and Critical Race Theory, two politically-driven systems that have made sweeping claims to knowledge that contain seeds of legitimacy but are asserting so-called "truths" that are so inapt that the fact is that the approach is actually illegitimate propaganda.

To provide an idea of how fragmented our world of knowledge has become, and how difficult it is to understand, consider the implications of what James Martin, in *The Wired Society: A Challenge for Tomorrow* described as the incredible explosion in academic journals. Martin, a former IBM information technology engineer, indicates that in 1660 there was only a single scientific journal. By 1750 there were ten journals, and that exploded to a thousand by 1850.[13] A recent estimate indicates the total of scientific journals in 2021 was thirty thousand with an increase of 5–7 percent annually. It is impossible to know more than a tiny piece of the world of knowledge, although it is also fair to say that not very many of those "knowledge fragments" are needed or are of any practical, or even impractical, use.

The "information deluge" gets progressively worse. Almost ten years ago, *Smithsonian Magazine* cited an estimate that 1.8 million articles were published annually, and that often the only readers of what is produced are the writer and the editors. Given the proliferation of online journals, that number has exploded far beyond human capacity.[14]

The "Renaissance Person" is dead. No human could keep up with the incredibly detailed range of knowledge being produced in greater and greater depth. This results not only in esoteric pieces no one reads and micro-specializations to which only the most deeply immersed can possibly relate, but eliminates the more comprehensive philosophical and systemically oriented comprehensive analyses that offer us a broader grasp of our world and its diverse realities.

As we become more and more knowledgeable on "tiny" matters, we become increasingly ignorant of the totality of the systems in which we live. This helps explain why those who dare to claim they understand the effects and dynamics of social and political systems and their "intersections" are being given such latitude in their unproven philosophical assertions. We simply lack the knowledge, concepts, and data needed to expose the distortions and reveal the truths.

The only apparent exception to the dominance of the sub-disciplinary hyper-specialization structure appears to be among scholars in race, gender, and Woke areas of inquiry. There we continually see overblown interpretations and proclamations of cause and effect that, in many instances, are nothing more than strident political assertions others are required to accept without questioning lest they be attacked for their bigotry, misogyny, racism, or phobia. As the University of Chicago's Dorian Abbot discovered when he asked whether there might be issues that needed to be discussed concerning the University's diversity policies, even mild and legitimate inquiries will get you condemned as a bigot or "phobe" with demands you be "canceled." He became the immediate target of students demanding suspension or worse, and MIT canceled an upcoming visiting lecture.

Russell Jacoby has criticized universities severely, and justifiably so. Jacoby is a professor of history at the University of California, Los Angeles, and a critic of academic culture. His fields of interest include the history of intellectuals and education. Robert Marquand, for more than three decades a reporter for the *Christian Science Monitor*, sums up Jacoby's criticisms:

> Jacoby saves his severest critique for the politics and practices of the academy, and the negative influences they can have on young talent—the need to tie one's career to intellectual fashions, to think and write in an inaccessible, specialized language. Academic freedom now means the freedom to be academic, he says. One Jacoby example is the new computerized "citation indexing" services available— where the number of footnotes to one's work in any of the hundreds of scholarly journals (142 for sociology alone) can be instantly tabulated. The more footnotes, the greater the academic stature, hence the unspoken rule to footnote your friends, and see that they footnote you. Quantity, not quality, becomes the yardstick.[15]

The Explosion in Specialized Micro-Disciplines Has Narrowed Our Minds

Robert Schmuhl, professor emeritus at Notre Dame and the inaugural Walter H. Annenberg-Edmund P. Joyce Chair in American Studies and Journalism at that university, echoed Marquand's analysis a decade later. A significant element is the extremely rapid growth in sub-disciplines. Political Science, for example, expanded from five sub-disciplines in 1960 to 104 by the year 2000. Included with this micro-specialization is the fact that, rather than seeking to share wisdom with a wide range of intelligent readers, "thinkers" now were often academic specialists communicating only with others like themselves and publishing in extremely specialized micro-journals. Schmuhl explains:

> Richard Posner places much of the blame on the mania for specialization that's become *de rigeur* throughout the modern university in

recent decades. Narrowing any academic field deepens its work, as the plumbing of abstruse subjects clarifies their meaning with microscopic specificity. But this process also makes resulting research and scholarship more insular, with the ultra specialized knowledge primarily one of professionals communicating only among others in the same sub-discipline.

As Russell Jacoby perceptively points out in *The Last Intellectuals*: "If the western frontier closed in the 1890s, the cultural frontier closed in the 1950s. After this decade intellectuals joined established institutions or retrained." . . . [T]he security of an academic appointment means an author need not worry about the next book royalty or magazine fee to pay monthly bills. It also means a teacher-writer can publish more experimental, avant-garde work that might not appeal to the public at large. So-called "little magazines" and small presses thrive in this university-dependent climate.[16]

Chapter Six

The University Is Being Consumed from Within

Examples of the affliction that has seized America's universities appear in this chapter. The poison of censorship, fear, intimidation, and submission has spread well beyond universities. Six hundred examples of that destructive dynamic are provided in *"Un-Canceling" America*. More are offered in *"No More Excuses!": Parents Defending K-12 Education*. For the university dedicated to the pursuit of knowledge and truth, allowing such activists to seize and control the points of institutional control is educational and even societal suicide as the consequences of one-sided and heavily politicized education spread throughout the university and the entire society, yet that is what has taken place.

Taken together, our educational establishment dishonored its mission and ideals by sitting back quietly while a total political transformation driven by the Woke infiltrated the key points of the collective network. After gaining control, the Woke introduced a "shame" and "bigotry" culture in which anyone who challenged what they were doing was ostracized, and built a culture of silence through intimidation.

What took place was challenged in its earlier phases by former Boston University President John Silber, who was immediately condemned for being a phobic intellectual bigot. A report in the *Boston Globe* discusses Silber's statements and what he labeled "epistemopathologies." The dispute was created by Silber's remarks that Boston University had remained "highly resistant to political correctness and ideological fads."

The areas resisted, Silber said, included "critical legal studies, revisionist history, Afro-centrism, multiculturalism and radical feminism." Silber had stated that "certain versions of radical feminism, multiculturalism, and other intellectual theories should be resisted because they are 'inhospitable to free intellectual inquiry.'" The report added that Marxism was not included in Silber's earlier remarks as an area that had been "resisted." Those mentioned in the April 15 report to [BU] trustees were critical legal studies, revisionist history, Afro-centrism, radical feminism, multiculturalism, the Frankfurt School of Critical Theory, structuralism and deconstructionism, dance therapy, gay and lesbian liberation and animal liberation."[1]

Instantaneous Internet "Lynch Mobs"

For many, the internet has become their "weapon" of choice to the point of creating almost instantaneous internet "lynch mobs" if anyone offends them. The internet has dramatically intensified our social divisions and gives idiots and morons a voice they should not possess. It does this by facilitating the links between people who would never otherwise be able to "find each other. This allows them to share their worst hates, perversions, and fears. Those who harbor inner darkness, dangerous perversions, hatred, and vindictiveness discover they aren't alone.

UCLA's Gordon Klein, for example, followed university policy in not allowing minority students to reschedule final exams after George Floyd's killing, and within a few days had a petition allegedly signed by twenty thousand students demanding his termination. He also needed police protection due to death threats. Another UCLA faculty member referred to the COVID-19 virus as being from "Wuhan" in origin and 1600 people allegedly signed an internet petition demanding his termination due to cultural insensitivity in relation to China.

The internet is not only a communications and research tool. It is a weapon. It isn't only the perverts, "wackos," pedophiles, drug gangs, scam artists, and hate-mongers who are the problem. The internet has allowed us to create our own "gang" in ways that enhance our ability to voice our agendas, preferences, and outrage in believing we have been victimized. In fact, I have often marveled at how frequently media and Identity activists use the term "outrage" to proclaim their reaction to anything they dislike.

Of course there are people and groups who have been ill-treated. The problem is that the internet not only connects us and provides a means of sharing experiences and aims, but stirs up, multiplies, and intensifies our anger and resentment against others. This is demonstrated graphically in relation to Stanford's encouragement of anonymous complaints by students against anything that might subjectively offend one or more of them, even if the perception might not be valid. Such processes place powerful and suppressive weapons in the hands of individuals operating according to motives and mindsets that span a range of intentions and desires from honest perspective to personal dislike, to service of a political agenda.[2]

We Are Dealing With Nasty, Intolerant, Ignorant, Power-Mad, and Bigoted Ideologues. Here Are Some Examples.

New York Black Lives Matter (BLM) leader Hawk Newsome is known for his warning, voiced in the summer of the 2020 "mostly peaceful" demonstrations and riots, that: "Black Lives Matter leader states if US 'doesn't give us what we want, then we will burn down this system.' "I said," Newsome told the host, "if this country doesn't give us what we want, then we will burn down this system and replace it. All right? And I could be speaking . . . figuratively. I could be speaking literally. It's a matter of interpretation."[3]

A strongly implied threat was made recently by a California activist in the context of a proposed $250,000-plus figure for racial reparations. The speaker mocked that number and threatened chaos if Black Californians weren't provided reparations of at least $800,000 each along with some added reference to grants of fifteen to twenty acres of land as well. This kind of virulent hate and threat of violence is now everywhere, and it has poisoned universities where rage, threats, and intolerance permeate the "revolutionary ranks" of academic activists and "Social Justice Warriors."

It is unclear whether the nation will be able to overcome the sickness and extremism that has arisen. An activist warned California's reparations task force of "a serious backlash" if it does not honor his demands for a six-figure payout for eligible Black residents. Deon Jenkins argued that every Black Californian should receive a payment of around $800,000 to reflect average home prices in the state, KRCR reported. "Either they're going to comply or it's going to be a serious backlash," Jenkins said in an interview following the hearing"[4]

The excerpts offered next provide insight into the mindsets of radical progressives in positions of power or people working closely with and influencing those who are. "Revolutionaries" see themselves as fighting a war. Anyone who opposes them or is simply "in the way" is either an enemy or a barrier that must be overcome. In many universities, institutions where deep inquiry, openness, and analysis are supposed to be a driving force, there is absolutely no respect for "difference," "tolerance," or "reasoned discussion." Those virtuous concepts were of great use in the Woke's struggle to obtain power, but the Woke/Crits are not dummies and are fully aware the same ground rules that facilitated their strategy can harm their movement once they are "on top." That is why free speech and honest discussion and debate are now being suppressed in the successfully politicized institution the university has become.

It would be reassuring to believe that people are just kidding around, and that tolerance for people with different points of view remains a value in our constitutional democracy. After all, to a significant extent we have long emphasized the ideals of freedom of speech, reasoned discourse, and freedom of association. Unfortunately, those values have largely disappeared, and hate and outrage are dominant emotions. What appears next is only the slightest taste of what is going on. One intriguing point reflected in the following examples, however, is that while I did not preselect the list based on the gender of targeted individuals and attackers, there is a pattern in which those attacked tend to be men and those who are attacking are women.

"We got to take these motherf–kers out." Britney Cooper, a Rutgers University "women's and gender and Africana studies" professor stated during a conference that "We got to take these motherf–kers out"—referring to anyone who did not agree with the Critical Race Theory and Woke agenda.[5]

A psychiatrist speaking at Yale describes her "fantasies of executing white people." "At Yale, a psychiatrist was recently invited to give a talk to students, described her fantasies of executing white people."[6]

More threats and intolerance at Yale. More than a hundred students disrupted, pounded on walls and desks, and issued physical threats against speakers at a forum seeking to demonstrate how people who disagree on important issues can nonetheless engage in meaningful and productive debate. This included the use of threats of physical violence as well as noise to drown out what they didn't want anyone to hear.[7]

White Males and Otherwise "Privileged" Students Just Need to Shut Up. A sociology professor at Binghamton University told her students that priority is given to "non-white folks" in picking students to call on for classroom discussions.[8]

"Professors who started a free speech group at the Bakersfield College campus" need to be "roped" and taken to the "slaughterhouse." At the Kern Community College District's Board of Trustees meeting on December 13, several speakers attacked professors who started a free speech group at the Bakersfield College campus called the Renegade Institute for Liberty. Community members, faculty, and students accused the group of spreading "hate speech" on campus, threatening violence against Black students, and attacking racial affinity groups. Vice president of the board John Corkins said he believed this group was an "abusive" and "disrespectful" minority and needed to be "culled," and taken "to the slaughterhouse." He said: "They're in that 5 percent that we have to continue to cull. Got them in my livestock operation and that's why we put a rope on some of them and take them to the slaughterhouse." Some board members laughed or smiled at the trustee's comments in the video.[9]

Many University Students Favor "Shout Downs"—and Even Violence—to Silence Those Speaking About Issues the Students Don't Want to Hear. "Among Ivy League students, 36% said that it was "sometimes" or "always" acceptable to shout down a speaker they don't like. Another problem facing students is self-censorship."[10]

Jenn M. Jackson, Syracuse professor calls 9/11 "an attack on the heteropatriarchal capitalistic systems that America relies upon to wrangle other countries into passivity." "Syracuse University assistant professor Jenn M. Jackson . . . tweeted about 9/11 . . . Jackson [tweeted] that the 9/11 terror attacks were an assault on America's "heteropatriarchal capitalistic systems." . . . It was an attack on the heteropatriarchal capitalistic systems that America relies upon to wrangle other countries into passivity. It was an attack on the systems many white Americans fight to protect."[11]

Kaytlin Reedy-Rogier, a "lecturer for Washington University in St. Louis' medical school was caught on camera warning students that if they try to debate her on critical race theory and 'systemic oppression,' she 'will shut that s—down real fast.'" "I have a really hard time being neutral around issues of systemic oppression," Kaytlin Reedy-Rogier told a class of medical students.[12]

Attacks on University Faculty

University faculties are targets. As in the case of Steven Pinker, if you are able to take down one of "the Biggies," the ripple effect spreads throughout the system, silencing many "lesser" figures. Here are several examples to indicate what the university culture has become. Many others are included in *"Un-Canceling" America,* as well as on the websites of the National Association of Scholars and FIRE.

Scott Atlas, Stanford/Hoover. "The Stanford Faculty Senate condemned the COVID-19-related actions of Scott Atlas, a Hoover Institution senior fellow serving as a special assistant to President Donald Trump for coronavirus issues. A resolution . . . approved by 85 percent of the senate membership, specified six actions that Atlas has taken that 'promote a view of COVID-19 that contradicts medical science.' Among the actions cited are: [1] discouraging the use of masks and other protective measures, [2] misrepresenting knowledge and opinion regarding the management of pandemics, [3] endangering citizens and public officials, [4] showing disdain for established medical knowledge and [5] damaging Stanford's reputation and academic standing."[13] Atlas was proved correct on virtually all accusations, and is still waiting for the apology from the Faculty Senate.

Harald Uhlig, University of Chicago. A petition "crusade" attacked highly respected University of Chicago macroeconomist Harald Uhlig. The petition sought Uhlig's removal as editor for a prestigious economics journal, and accused him of: "trivializing the Black Lives Matter (BLM) movement" and "hurting and marginalizing people of color and their allies in the economics profession." Uhlig's sin?—criticizing the push by Black Lives Matter to defund police departments and suggesting the solution lies in better training.[14]

Jon Zubieta, Syracuse. Jon Zubieta is a Syracuse University distinguished professor with a significant record of accomplishments. "He was placed on administrative leave for referring to the 'novel coronavirus as the 'Wuhan flu' on his course syllabus. [He] also called the virus the 'Chinese Communist Party Virus.' 'Syracuse University unequivocally condemns racism and xenophobia and rejects bigotry, hate and intolerance of any kind,' the university said. The DEI administrator at Syracuse ultimately even sought to have a student "Monitor" attend Zubieta's classes and report on any problematic statements he might possibly make.[15]

Keep in mind that the Chinese Communist Party was operating a global propaganda campaign targeting anyone who dared to suggest that China was the source of the COVID-19 release. Also keep in mind that Interim Vice Chancellor and Provost John Liu had numerous contacts and working relationships with China over the years as part of his career. The reaction of the provost was that Professor Zubieta is not only anti-CCP, but he is guilty, by implication, of "hate speech" against Chinese. Liu stated: "The derogatory language used by a professor on his course syllabus is damaging to the learning environment for our students and offensive to Chinese, international and Asian-Americans *everywhere* who have experienced hate speech, rhetoric and actions since the pandemic began." The language Zubieta used was "Wuhan Flu" and "CCP Flu."

> **Adrian Vermuele, Harvard.** "Eleven Harvard Law School student organizations signed a statement calling for administrators to denounce what they characterize as 'highly offensive, discriminatory, and violent statements in online posts' by Law School professor Adrian C. Vermeule. Addressed to five Law School deans, the statement—signed by organizations including the Harvard Parity Project, the Equal Democracy Project, and the Black Law Students Association, among others—describes Vermeule's rhetoric as 'harmful to democracy' and 'unbelievably divisive,' with a particular emphasis on his recent allegations of election fraud. . . . Nicole M. Rubin, who co-wrote the statement, said she felt motivated to take action after realizing several students felt uncomfortable with what Vermeule posted online."[16]

> **Gordon Klein, UCLA.** "A UCLA accounting professor suspended by the university after he refused a request to modify final exams in the wake of George Floyd's death [has stated] that he was following school policy. 'I got a directive, as did my colleagues, that we should absolutely continue the traditional policy [of] the university, and give the exam as scheduled with only the normal excuses, such as you're in a car accident, you had a death in the family,' Gordon Klein [stated] and the school knows it."[17] Reports are that the anti-Klein petition

students circulated obtained twenty thousand signatures from people who almost certainly knew nothing about the situation. This use of the internet and social media highlights how the Mass operates.

Eliezer Gafni, UCLA. "Students at the University of California Los Angeles are calling for the replacement of a computer science department chair appointed just weeks earlier, claiming he is 'unfit to serve' in the role. An online petition they started accuses Professor Eliezer Gafni of showing 'disregard for the racialized experiences of people of color in the United States' and 'disinterest in open communication between all students and UCLA Computer Science administration.' Although the petition commends him for his 'exceptional professional achievements and excellence in his academic work,' signers claim that he has not exhibited a 'strong sense of ethical and societal responsibilities or the collaborative skills—especially with regard to clear communication and inclusivity—that are essential for this role.' Petition signers said Gafni told a student that [the student's] calling the term 'Wuhan virus' offensive politicized the issue. Wuhan is the city in China where COVID-19 was first discovered late last year."[18]

Jay Bhattacharya says his life at Stanford became a "living hell" when he challenged Dr. Fauci over 2020 COVID lockdowns. "Bhattacharya spoke at the Academic Freedom Conference at Stanford's Graduate School of Business and said that in the current era, 'we have a high clerisy that declares from on high what is true and what is not true.' "When you take a position that is at odds with the scientific clerisy, your life becomes a living hell." "You face a deeply hostile work environment." Bhattacharya said that soon after the Great Barrington Declaration gained widespread attention, he received death threats, hate mail and questions on where he receives funding, which he noted, "most of my money has come from the NIH for most of my life."[19]

Eric Rasmusen, Indiana University. "There were numerous calls in 2019 that he be fired for a forwarded link he posted, 'Are Women Destroying Academia? Probably,' relative to volatile issues discussed in which the author (not Rasmusen) argued that women were 'probably' having a negative qualitative effect on academia, and that males had more 'geniuses' than females. Rasmusen's action led to demands by some participants on a website, @SheRatesDogs, that generated over 400 demands that he be fired. Rasmusen then received scathing public media condemnations from Lauren Robel, the IU Provost and Idalene Kesner, the Dean of the Business School.[20]

Steven Pinker, Harvard. "An open letter to the Linguistic Society of America has called for the removal of Steven Pinker from its list of distinguished fellows. . . . The accusations in the letter have been thoroughly contested and rejected by the likes of Nicholas Christakis, Michael Shermer, John McWhorter and Noam Chomsky. . . . This letter wasn't really about Pinker at all. It has a very specific function—to dissuade lesser-known academics and students from questioning the ideological consensus. The letter says, in not so few words: 'It doesn't matter if you're Steven f***ing Pinker. If you don't agree with our ideological prescriptions, you don't belong here.' The letter is really directed towards you—the unknown academic, the young linguist, the graduate student."[21]

William Jacobson, Cornell. Jacobson writes that: "Living as a conservative on a liberal campus is like being the mouse waiting for the cat to pounce." His offense involves writing a blog post critical of Black Lives Matter and what he perceives as the true motivations of its founders, including destruction of the nuclear family and submersion in a Marxist-style collective."[22]

Michael Rectenwald, NYU. He is a now former NYU professor who posted on Twitter criticizing political correctness and student coddling. He was removed from the classroom after his colleagues complained about his "incivility." His offense was that Rectenwald argued against campus trends like "safe spaces," "trigger warnings," policing of Halloween costumes, and academia's growing culture of Political Correctness. Rectenwald was "canceled" by NYU's "Liberal Studies Diversity, Equity and Inclusion Working Group" which manifested some striking "incivility" of its own—engaging in online attacks and saying Rectenwald should receive counseling help for his unacceptable political views.[23]

The "are you kidding me" moment in Michael Rectenwald's situation is provided by the twelve-person committee calling itself the Liberal Studies Diversity, Equity and Inclusion Working Group, that included two deans, several faculty members, and multiple students. This committee published a letter to the editor in an NYU paper. The participating Deans and "Committee" stated: "We seek to create a dynamic community that values full participation . . . " Great thinking. But in a truly incredible episode of academic impropriety and malicious hypocrisy, the "Committee" suggested publicly that Rectenwald was in need of mental health assistance due to his views. Several of Rectenwald's now former "colleagues" went so far as to distribute emails throughout the Liberal Studies department with even worse personal comments.[24]

Dorian Abbot, University of Chicago. "Dorian Abbot, a tenured faculty member in the Department of Geophysical Sciences at the University of Chicago, has recently come under attack from students and postdocs for a series of videos he posted to YouTube expressing his reservations about the way Diversity, Equity, and Inclusion (DEI) efforts have been discussed and implemented on campus. In these videos Prof. Abbot raised several misgivings about DEI efforts and expressed concern that a climate of fear is 'making it extremely difficult for people with dissenting viewpoints to voice their opinions.' . . . Nowhere in these materials does Prof. Abbot offer any opinion that a reasonable observer would consider to be hateful or otherwise offensive.

Shortly after uploading the videos, Abbot's concerns were confirmed when 58 students and postdocs of the Department of

Geophysical Sciences, and 71 other graduate students and postdocs from other University of Chicago departments, posted a letter containing the claim that Prof. Abbot's opinions 'threaten the safety and belonging of all underrepresented groups within the [Geophysical Sciences] department' and 'represent an aggressive act' towards research and teaching communities. The letter also issued 11 demands, many of which would serve to ostracize and shame Prof. Abbot, while stripping him of departmental titles, courses, and privileges. The signatories further demand that the Department of Geophysical Sciences formally and publicly denounce Prof. Abbot's views, and change hiring and promotion procedures so as to prioritize DEI."[25]

Greg Patton, USC. Patton, a business professor at USC, "is no longer teaching his communications course after Black students complained that a Chinese-language example he used during class 'sounded like' a racial slur and 'harmed their mental health.' BUT 'a group of nearly 100 USC alumni, most of whom are Chinese by ethnicity or nationality, came to his defense and wrote to the school's administration in support of their professor, saying his use of the Mandarin word for 'that' was accurate and 'an entirely appropriate and quite effective illustration of the use of pauses.'"[26]

Robert Dailyda, Stockton University. Dailyda was pursuing a PhD at Stockton University: "Given the COVID-19 Pandemic, most communications and courses in 2020/2021 were being conducted through Zoom. Dailyda was hit by six student code of conduct charges after he used a picture of President Donald Trump as a back drop to a Zoom class. The school maintains that Dailyda can be disciplined for saying that he would 'fight to the death for our country.' Dailyda was originally charged with disruptive behavior; discrimination; harassment; hostile environment; harm; and bullying and cyberbullying. . . . Students objected that the image of Trump made them 'feel offended, disrespected, and taunted.'"[27]

Leslie Neal-Boylan, Massachusetts-Lowell. "Leslie Neal-Boylan, the dean of the nursing school at the University of Massachusetts-Lowell, was fired after she received backlash from a student about an email to the campus community saying BLACK LIVES MATTER, but also, EVERYONE'S LIFE MATTERS." Neal-Boylan wrote an email to the nursing school community addressing the ongoing protests across the country against police brutality and racial inequality following the death of George Floyd in Minneapolis. "I am writing to express my concern and condemnation of the recent (and past) acts of violence against people of color," the email said. "Recent events recall a tragic history of racism and bias that continue to thrive in this country. I despair for our future as a nation if we do not stand up against violence against anyone. BLACK LIVES MATTER, but also, EVERYONE'S LIFE MATTERS." A nursing student took issue with the dean's choice of words and posted the email on Twitter saying, "including the statement 'all lives matter' was uncalled for and shows the narrow minded people in lead positions."[28]

Niall Ferguson, Stanford/Hoover. The controversy in question involved support of a student-proposed diverse speakers program that sought to bring some more conservative speakers to Stanford. Ferguson writes: "I was brought up to think of a university as a haven for free thought and free inquiry; a place where established scholars and students communicate ideas, in both directions; a place where old thoughts and new are subjected to rigorous examination. I was therefore appalled by the accusations made against me at a live-streamed Stanford University Faculty Senate meeting on February 11th and published online by Joshua Landy, David Palumbo-Liu and two other faculty members. *I was included in a group of some half-dozen Hoover fellows who were said to have 'abused' the position of the Institution and 'quite possibly, contributed to significant public harm.'* Landy expressed astonishment that I am 'still on the roster' and that Stanford somehow failed 'to publicly censure' me. . . . The time has come to set the record straight.

"[I]n May 2017 I accepted an invitation to meet a group of students associated with the Stanford Review and the College Republicans. Out of interactions over lunch, in meetings and exchanges of emails, I heard these students express their dissatisfaction with a campus dominated by liberal and progressive thought. *From this came the idea, formulated by the students, of a "Stanford Speaker Series" to address the lack of political diversity and debate on campus.* One student suggested inviting the political scientist Charles Murray as part of a conservative speaker series. *However, I wanted to build bridges between Hoover and Stanford, and so I proposed a bipartisan program to model free speech and civil debate. All participants were of the highest quality; some were controversial figures.* . . . As the president and provost wrote in "Advancing Free Speech and Inclusion," published on the "Notes from the Quad" website on November 7th, 2017." [Emphasis added][29]

Erika Lopez Prater, a liberal arts professor, was fired after showing students images of Muhammad in a class about Islamic art and warning students about the works in the syllabus. "Erika López Prater, an adjunct professor at Hamline University, issued a syllabus warning students that the class would contain images of holy figures, including the prophet Muhammad and the Buddha. . . . Students were told they could contact her with any concerns about the course material, but none did. Prater also reportedly warned students that a painting containing an image of Muhammad was going to be displayed a few minutes ahead of time, giving anyone who might be offended by such imagery an opportunity to leave the classroom. Despite the multiple warnings, a senior student in the class later complained to administrators about the imagery and picked up support from Muslim students who were not in the class, resulting in Prater not being welcomed back to the school and setting off national controversy surrounding academic freedom."[30]

Intolerance by University Faculty and Administrators

Alyssa Johnson, LSU. A powerful tool driving this transition has been the invention of the idea of "hate speech," "hate laws," and the ability to label people as "haters" if they don't agree with the views of an identity group. By infusing American society with an ultra sensitivity to things that are subjectively labeled "hate" by an interest or Identity group seeking to advance a political agenda, we internalize the attitude. An example of the "hate speech" transformation is captured vividly in a policy announced by a Louisiana State University faculty member. Fox News reporter Caleb Parke writes that Alyssa Johnson stated she was:

> "keeping a list of names" and would drop from her classes any student who in her judgment engaged in "hate speech" in class or elsewhere. *Johnson wrote, in a now-deleted tweet:* "If @LSU won't take action, we as professors can. [I am] Keeping a list of names and if I see them enrolled in my course, I will drop them. It's not just free speech, it's hate speech and it's a threat to student safety."[31]

Elyse Crystall, University of North Carolina. She publicly "canceled" a student who dared voice a different viewpoint in class. In a Literature and Cultural Diversity course, a student found himself singled out by the instructor for hate speech, after the student said he opposed homosexuality. Crystall wrote in an email to the class that the student was a perfect example of white privilege. She claimed that the student used "hate speech" and it "created a hostile environment in the classroom." . . . "Ms. Crystall didn't stop there. She referred to the student as "a white, heterosexual, [C]hristian male" who "can feel entitled to make violent, heterosexist comments and not feel marked or threatened or *vulnerable*."[32]

Phoebe A. Cohen, Williams College. In a continuing question of "how did this person ever get hired" it is reported that: "The *New York Times* ran a report on the canceling of University of Chicago geophysicist Dorian Abbot for his dissenting views on affirmative action. The paper then quoted a Williams College geosciences professor, Phoebe A. Cohen, who supports Abbot's shunning. She explained her dim view of academic freedom thusly: "This idea of intellectual debate and rigor as the pinnacle of intellectualism comes from a world in which white men dominated." Assuming accuracy of the *Times* report, and of course we can't count on that, this example represents the poisoned fruit of the patriarchy —i.e., a clear demonstration of the willingness to engage in intellectual debate and rigor.[33]

IUPUI's Affirmative Action Officials and Their Nutty Attack on Keith John Sampson, Janitor, Indiana University–Purdue University. This is one of my absolute favorites in terms of "woke" bias and discrimination based on "knee jerk" reactions. It is also a complete condemnation of university DEI offices. Keith John Sampson, a janitor at Indiana University–Purdue University Indianapolis (IUPUI) where he takes classes, spends his rest breaks reading books. "One of the books he was reading was Todd Tucker's *Notre Dame vs. the Klan: How the Fighting Irish Defeated the Ku Klux Klan*. It is a dramatic account of how in a 1924 street brawl Notre Dame students repulsed efforts of the Ku Klux Klan to bring their filthy racist beliefs to their University. The students stole Klan robes and destroyed their crosses, driving the KKK out of town in a downpour. The book's dust jacket had a picture of hooded Klansmen burning a cross. Two of Sampson's co-workers complained about the picture. When John attempted to explain that the book was a story about defeating the Klan, the co-workers ignored him. He then received a letter from IUPUI's Affirmative Action Office. The co-workers had filed a racial harassment complaint."[34]

"Michigan school board member claims 'Whiteness is evil,' faces backlash for divisive tweets: Michigan school board member Kesha Hamilton claimed White people more dangerous than animals." "A Jackson County School board member, Kesha

Hamilton, faced backlash for tweets blasting White people during a public comment on Tuesday, including one resident who called her 'angry and bitter.' The tweets, shared by Libs of TikTok, show the Michigan school board member stating 'These White women are the stupidest' and calling 'Whiteness' an 'evil.' 'Whiteness is so evil . . . it manipulates then says, I won't apologize for my dishonesty and trauma inducing practices and thinks you should applaud it for being honest about its ability to manipulate and be dishonest. #Deceitful #Perfidous,' she said. She also claimed that White people are more dangerous than animals. 'The last thing you have to worry about is an animal—though that could be a very real threat . . . more danger-ous are any whites you may see on the trail!' she said."[35]

"California Dreaming" Through "Deprogramming" K-12 Students and "crushing all forms of oppression and reaction-ary tendencies." "The advocates [of the Ethnic Studies curriculum] say that many state officials fail to grasp that ethnic studies is not a traditional school subject, but a movement and a philosophy best described as 'narrative medicine,' 'radical healing' and even a 'way of life.' It's distinguished from traditional classroom instruction by its emotional, immersive pedagogy designed to deprogram kids from European cultural assumptions, to make teenagers conscious of sys-temic inequities, and to reconnect them with forgotten ancestral knowledge."[36]

Chapter Seven

The Degradation of Merit and Ability

Universities' "Intersectional Feedback Loop" with K-12 Schools

Universities are simultaneously cause and effect of the degradation of American education. We can even borrow Kim Crenshaw's concept of systemic "intersectionality"—or even the idea of an "ecosystem"—to better understand there is a total social and political system in operation.[1] The fundamental institutions that comprise that social ecosystem intersect, interact, and ultimately function as a complete organism in which the parts all work together for various purposes and multiply the effects— good and bad.

The university as institution is just one part of that interconnected system, but the university is a central force in the system, one that supplies knowledge, talent, and ideology to the total socio-economic and political culture. So, of course, is the university's supply chain precursor, the K-12 educational system, where our youth are supposed to receive the fundamental building blocks of education. When that interconnected "educational ecosystem" is working at a high level of quality, so are the other "intersectional" subsystems that universities feed into. The problem is that, as shown throughout *Conformity Colleges'* analysis, the universities have increasingly themselves played a significant role in creating the lack of quality education at both the K-12 and university levels. In doing so, they are undermining not only themselves, but the entire system.

GIGO, or "Garbage In, Garbage Out"

An acronym applied to the creating of analytical models and computer applications is GIGO. That stands for the input/output proposition of "Garbage In, Garbage Out." If universities are receiving poorly educated and ideologically brainwashed raw material from the K-12 system, they are receiving a form of intellectual and conceptual "garbage." When the basic raw material the educational system supplies to the rest of the complex systemic mechanism is defective, the entire social organism is harmed.

Crudely put, we become progressively "dumber" across the board, damaging the quality, integrity, health, and productivity of the overall society. The level of knowledge, skills, and intellectual quality of the students entering the university who have been admitted from the K-12 system is the single most critical factor in what universities are able to teach. This fact holds true even if the university faculty were themselves functioning on the unbiased and non-ideological levels we have long assumed characterized their educational approach and intellectual responsibility. For several decades, however, universities have become increasingly oriented toward what Woke faculty and administrators consider a social justice curriculum. This approach is one where assumption, assertion, and identity politics rule the institution in ways that increasingly brook no opposition.

The result is that we are now dealing with a closed loop educational system that has been heavily politicized in a single direction. The consequences of such a curricular context are at least twofold. The first factor is that universities and colleges are the source of the teachers in K-12. The focus, agendas, and educational quality of what those teachers do, or fail to do, has been taught to them in university schools of education. The second consequence is that, during the period this Woke curriculum has been implemented and steadily expanded, there has been a sharp decline in the measured performance of K-12 students. The old saying is that "the proof is in the pudding" and the significant and accelerating decline in the measured performance of America's K-12 students leaves a bad taste in terms of what is being "cooked up."

Universities are violating their basic responsibility for existing by playing a significant role in the decline. They are doing this through a one-sided and increasingly politicized focus on teaching, research, and the intensely ideological perspectives in which students are being indoctrinated. Universities are producing less capable and knowledgeable teachers, many of whom then go on to "educate" K-12 students when they take positions as teachers and school administrators.

Examples of the Educational System Rejecting Merit and Ability

The examples presented next offer insight into the fact that, at all levels, our educational system has been corrupted as a result of the pursuit of power and the desire to infuse students with an ideological "transformative" agenda consistent with that being advocated by "Woke" teachers and activists. Part of the corruption involves the lack of quality in the knowledge and skills being taught to students. Another critical element, however, is the effort to remove any standards that can be used to judge the capability of individuals asked to do a job, or by which we can be evaluated according to quantifiable and objective standards.

Being seen as less capable than someone else is argued to be emotionally harmful and avoided at all costs because it could make less talented or less competitive people feel bad or inferior. The suppression of legitimate standards of merit in terms of recognizing that some people are best able in a comparative sense of doing a job or task than others is undermining the perception and the reality of our economic and social system. Our traditional rating systems emphasize the primacy of the individual as a core part of a strong social order. This belief system has been at the heart of the American dream and culture since the democracy formed. According to the Woke, they are now the agencies of bigotry and discrimination.

Of course, it isn't that the individual and individualism are the only relevant factors in our democratic republic. But the strong belief is one involving the assumption that, when we create opportunities for all members of society to grow and achieve the highest levels of quality of which they are capable, then the entire political community benefits from the interactive joining of talents, qualities, opportunities, and abilities. Rather than accepting that rewarding superior achievement, creativity, and productivity is vital to a healthy community capable of sustaining all its members in terms of basic needs and fair opportunities, we are in the process of creating a "lowest common denominator" system.

The problem is that, since the Woke and Critical Race Theory movements are essentially collectivist, their belief that the group or collective should be emphasized rather than individual talent eliminates a critical element in a healthy democracy and offends a fundamental part of being human, the aspirational drive to grow and create. This strategy has reached the point that merit and quality are suppressed in favor of a dull conformity in which no one is seen as more capable than others. This sense of lock-step "equity collectivism" ignores the critical roles of creativity, skill, specialized intelligence, and capability as essential driving forces for the evolution and sustainability of the overall community.

America is, or has been, a productivity and imagination-driven system. The belief underlying that system is that the effort to strive for our highest possible personal development is not simply for our own benefit, but for the richness of the complete social and political community to which we aspire. Selecting and rewarding people on criteria other than the quality of their capability, actual performance, and productivity damages the overall system and community. Here are some of the more important issues in that regard.

The Woke and the Crits Are Threatened by Quality, Excellence, Merit, and Ability—Their "Solution" Is To Do Away with Standards of Comparison

Doing away with honest standards of qualitative measurement means teachers and administrators can't be evaluated in terms of their effectiveness, and the students can't either. "[T]he real goal [of the 'no honor roll' and grade movement] is to help the adults who run the schools hide their failures in not getting kids to learn. That's why the teachers unions and their allies in the system . . . oppose standardized tests. [A] new [NYC] DOE guidance warns that 'recognizing student excellence via honor rolls and class rank can be detrimental to learners who find it more difficult to reach academic success.' Even grades can negatively influence 'future student performance.' . . . Staff should 'eliminate practices that penalize students who have been marginalized based on their race, culture, language and/or ability.'"[2]

Students' Knowledge and Skills are "Slip-Sliding" Away

America's K-12 students are not only being passed by those of other nations, but our students' scores are declining in absolute terms. A report by the National Assessment of Educational Progress (NAEP) involving US data from 2019 and pre-pandemic 2020 indicated that decline. Monique Beals reports:

> Math and reading test scores for the country's [thirteen]-year-olds have dropped sharply in comparison to numbers from 2012, with some of the lowest-scoring test takers falling the furthest behind. U.S. News and World Report reported that this was the first major score drop in the subjects since the NAEP began tracking long-term academic achievement trends in the 1970s. Perhaps even more troubling was the study's finding that some of the most significant drops were from students in the lowest-performing percentiles. In math, for example, scores dropped for [nine]-year-olds in the [tenth] and [twenty-fifth] percentiles, and scores fell for [thirteen]-year-olds in the [tenth], [twenty-fifth] and [fiftieth] percentiles.[3]

There Are Consequences Created When We Corrupt the Quality of Education and Turn Our Institutions into Ideological Centers

One consequence for the universities considered most elite is that if potential employers can't trust the quality of new graduates from those institutions, to remain globally competitive, American employers will begin developing their own screening systems to evaluate potential employees. One report indicates employers: "already suspect that prestigious university degrees are hollow and certify very little. Traditional colleges will seize the moment and expand by sticking to meritocratic criteria as proof of the competency of their prized graduates. Private and online venues will also fill a national need to teach Western civilization and humanities courses—by non-woke faculty who do not institutionalize bias. More students will continue to seek vocational training alternatives. Some will get their degrees online for a fraction of the cost. Alumni will either curb giving, put further restrictions on their gifting or disconnect."[4]

Students at the New School, an expensive New York university, occupied the campus and demanded A-grades for everyone.

"Students at an elite, private university in New York City are occupying a campus building with the demand that all be given A grades. . . . [A] letter of demands calls for A grades for all students. It says in part: 'We demand that every student receives a final course grade of A as well as the removal of I/Z grades for the Fall 2022 semester.' The letter insisted, 'Attendance shall have no bearing on course grade.' (According to the New School's website, an 'I' grade is a 'temporary incomplete' and a 'z' grade is an 'unofficial withdrawal.') According to The New School's 'about' page, the university is committed to 'developing students who will have an impact on the world and address the most pressing social issues of our time.' It adds that 'this effort is bolstered by the university's Office of Equity, Inclusion, and Social Justice, which is committed to fostering an equitable, inclusive, and socially just environment for our community.'" [5]

Have transcripts become Monopoly Money? "Consider these facts: A 50-plus-year nationwide study of the history of college grading finds that, in the early 1960s, an A grade was awarded in colleges nationwide 15 percent of the time. But today, an A is the most common grade given in college; the percentage of A grades has tripled, to 45 percent nationwide. Seventy-five percent of all grades awarded now are either A's and B's [*stet*]. The National Association of Colleges and Employers reported in 2013 that [E]mployers have known about grade inflation for years, which is why their most common complaint to me is that college transcripts have become less and less meaningful. After all, virtually all new college graduates sport nothing but A's and B's on their transcripts. For the same reason, grade inflation also hinders the ability of graduate school admissions boards to differentiate meaningfully among student transcripts."[6]

Doing away with "White language" supremacy and eliminating traditional grading so that less capable students' records can look better. "A professor at Arizona State University is calling for the end to 'White supremacy language,' and to do away with the common way of grading papers in favor of labor-based grading that will redistribute 'power.' 'White language supremacy in writing classrooms is due to the uneven and diverse linguistic legacies that everyone inherits, and the racialized white discourses that are used as standards, which give privilege to those students who embody those habits of white language already,' Asao Inoue, professor of rhetoric and composition at Arizona State University, said."[7]

Fighting Back Against the Progressives; "War on Merit." Asra Nomani has become a key figure in the struggle to preserve the integrity of K–12 education. A founder of the organization Parents Defending Education (PDE), she experienced just how twisted is the logic of those intent on undermining education from behind a mask of "equity." Her experience is described next. "It used to be obvious that merit is part of achieving the American dream. But like it's doing to so many self-evident things, the left is attempting to destroy this idea as it pursues a Sovietesque system of 'equity.' . . . When the left succeeds in ending merit in a school, you can be sure the rest of the woke ideas parents abhor have already taken over the curriculum. Beyond that, our schools' loss of rigor has dumbed down our country, and the retreat from pursuing merit has slowed success for so many kids. Virginia mom Asra Nomani recently discovered that in September 2020, her son received National Merit recognition, a prestigious honor given to a handful of kids across the country—but her son's school, Thomas Jefferson HS for Science and Technology, hid it from the family. The majority-Asian school is neck deep and drowning in leftist ideology, pursuing 'equity,' equal outcomes for children based on the color of their skin. Asians are out, as TJ has simply too many successful ones. Nomani's son was the wrong color, and the school's racists decided he should not be presented with the award. Learning this news two years too late, Nomani's son was denied the ability to note the achievement on his college applications and seek scholarships that stem from this award. The school hurt his chances to succeed, and it did it on purpose."[8]

The NYC Department of Education Has Rejected Merit, Educational Excellence, and Ability as Relevant Standards. "[A] new [NYC] DOE guidance warns that 'recognizing student excellence via honor rolls and class rank can be detrimental to learners who find it more difficult to reach academic success.' Even grades can negatively influence 'future student performance.' . . . Staff should 'eliminate practices that penalize students who have been marginalized based on their race, culture, language and/or ability." **Ability?** Insane. A poor grade doesn't 'penalize' students but alerts them, their parents and school staff that they haven't learned material they need to advance in school and later life. Absent any warning, they're all too likely to fall further behind."[9] [Emphasis added.]

The rejection of merit, educational excellence, and ability to perform well is harming New York students. Nearly half of NYC Department of Education graduates who go on to CUNY need to take remedial classes. "Nearly half of all New York City public school graduates who head to local community colleges are forced into remedial classes to survive their first semester . . . Amid chronic absenteeism, widespread grade inflation, and a failure to prepare students for higher education, city school kids are being shoved through an educational revolving door without truly learning, experts told *The Post*. 'Most of the kids we get from New York City schools are underprepared for college,' said Mohammad Alam, assistant dean of enrollment at Borough of Manhattan Community College. . . . The lack of readiness for college work leaves students, some now parents themselves, frustrated—and angry.

"Sáleenal Butler, [twenty], complained that teachers at her former high school, Millennium Art Academy in the Bronx, 'got annoyed when people asked questions'—which was why she had to start her Bronx Community College career in a remedial math class. Post-pandemic test scores are down in K-8 public schools across the city, while chronic absenteeism last year hit an all-time high of 40 [percent]. That means 352,919 kids missed [eighteen] or more days of instruction, or 10 [percent] of the entire year. Among seniors at Bronx high schools, chronic absenteeism hit a shocking 58.2 [percent], according to the DOE. Yet, magically, graduation rates for high school inched up again last year, to nearly 84 [percent] compared to 73 [percent] four years earlier, with lower standards paving the way. 'Dumb it down until everybody passes,' said Wai Wah Chin, founder of the Chinese American Citizens Alliance of Greater New York and a school-choice booster. Lowering the bar in the name of 'equity'—just to get students through the system—harms grads as well as society, Chin argued. . . . As a result, DOE grade inflation—and even fraud—has surged. In 2015, Brooklyn's Dewey High School put hundreds of failing kids in phantom classes without certified teachers. Principal Kathleen Elvin called the scheme 'Project Graduation.' . . . At Maspeth HS, . . . the school created fake classes, gave credits to failing students, and fixed grades to push kids out the door, outraged teachers [said]. . . . In the DOE, kids can pass or graduate without going to class."[10]

The entire California Public University System ended standardized test requirements for admission. "The University of California agreed to no longer consider SAT or ACT scores when making admissions and scholarship decisions under a settlement in a 2019 lawsuit filed on behalf of low income students of color and students with disabilities. . . . The College Board, which produced the SAT, rejected the notion that their standardized tests were inherently racist. . . . 'The SAT itself is not a racist instrument. Every question is rigorously reviewed for evidence of bias and any question that could favor one group over another is discarded.'"[11]

"California State University, the largest public university system in the United States, on Wednesday said it will no longer use college entrance exams in undergraduate admissions. . . . [A]pplicants may still submit their SAT or ACT scores if they wish to do so, but admissions counselors at Cal State will not look at them. Instead, Cal State universities will utilize a 'multi-factored admission criteria' to determine each applicant's eligibility. . . . 'Abandoning the use of objective assessments like the ACT test introduces greater subjectivity and uncertainty into the admissions process, and this decision is likely to worsen entrenched inequities in California,' the ACT said in a statement."[12]

Canceling the "Racist" Discipline of Mathematics. The approach that "racism is in everything in America" reaches some incredibly strange positions. One is that mathematics is racist. I'm still trying to figure this one out because independent of the specifics of mathematics, the demanding precision of the discipline is not simply a formulaic game. Mathematics teaches you how to think critically and clearly and this ability enhances problem recognition and solving. Here is the argument:

"For all the rhetoric in this framework about equity, social justice, environmental care and culturally appropriate pedagogy, there is no realistic hope for a more fair, just, equal and well-stewarded society if our schools uproot long-proven, reliable and highly effective math methods and instead try to build a mathless Brave New World on a foundation of unsound ideology," the letter reads.[13]

Critical Race Theory advocates in education are claiming objectivity and intellectual neutrality are racist. Their assertions include:

"The concept of mathematics being purely objective is unequivocally false, and teaching it is even much less so," the document for the "'Equitable Math" toolkit reads. "Upholding the idea that there are always right and wrong answers perpetuate objectivity as well as fear of open conflict." An associated "Dismantling Racism" workbook, linked within the toolkit, similarly identifies "objectivity"—described as "the belief that there is such a thing as being objective or 'neutral'"—as a characteristic of White supremacy. . . . One of [the guidelines] instructs educators to "identify and challenge the ways that math is used to uphold capitalist, imperialist, and racist views."[14]

How Can Science, Technology, Engineering, and Mathematics (STEM) Be the Answer for America's Future When Our Children Are So Poorly Educated?

It is delusional to approach our future well-being as if America is the sole important piece of the equation. Merit is one issue. Collectivist thought is another. But the truth is that as China, India, Brazil, and other nations aggressively pursue their own well-being, US leaders had better think in competitive terms rather than acting as if we are in full control of the future. If that future is going to be highly dependent on matters of STEM prowess in employment and wealth creation, then we had better commit to turning out the best possible "products" in those dimensions. Otherwise, as our system declines due to being out-competed, jobs are lost to other nations' better educated graduates, demands on the US government to pay to support an increasingly unproductive and unemployed population grow, and social tension and anger rise, we have turmoil that will tear us apart.

In many instances, students have dropped out of STEM programs due to the declining quality of education in America's Woke public schools, and thus the subject matter is too hard or demanding: "Some 50 percent of American college students who major in a STEM—science, technology, engineering and mathematics—field drop out, and the persistence rates for women and people of color are lower than those of their white male classmates, reported researchers at a Cornell conference March 25–26."[15]

NYU's Embarrassing Maitland Jones Debacle

As to the quality of the graduates we are dealing with, consider the recent episode that took place at New York University, where numerous students complained to the administration that a renowned teacher's class was "too hard" and, in an era when disengaged students still expect an "A" grade for mediocre work, complained the grades he gave them were too low. Adam Sabes reports on the situation:

> Maitland Jones Jr., a former chemistry professor at New York University, was fired from the university in August following a petition from students complaining that his course was too hard.
>
> "We are very concerned about our scores, and find that they are not an accurate reflection of the time and effort put into this class," the petition said, according to the *New York Times*. "We urge you to realize . . . that a class with such a high percentage of withdrawals and low grades has failed to make students' learning and well-being

a priority and reflects poorly on the chemistry department as well as the institution as a whole," the petition states.[16]

Jones responded in a comment to the *New York Times* that he has seen a drop in attention from students nearly a decade ago, which was accelerated by the COVID-19 pandemic. "They weren't coming to class, that's for sure, because I can count the house," Jones said. "They weren't watching the videos, and they weren't able to answer the questions." In an op-ed for the *Boston Globe* on Thursday, Jones said that university deans need to learn how to not "coddle students." "Critically, the growing number of administrators, major and minor, who are often without any expertise in a given subject matter, need to learn to stand back from purely academic matters and to support the faculty," Jones said. "Deans must learn to not coddle students for the sake of tuition and apply a little tough love. They must join the community in times of conflict to generate those teachable moments."[17]

American Students Are Frightened of Hard Courses like Math and Science

As the shameful Maitland Jones situation described above indicates, the "dumbing down" becomes a vital concern when we realize that its primary victim is America. In a globalized economy, the fact is that any new employment of the kind that will be left available to human workers generally is not guaranteed to be available to American workers. As seems almost guaranteed by the steady downward movement of American students, many of the young among the American population will lack the basic work habits, skills, and knowledge needed to compete with their counterparts, particularly in Asia. The nation's performance in STEM education described next offers a compelling example of an accelerating decline in capability and quality.

In a [2015] *Pew Research Center report*, only 29 [percent] of Americans rated their country's K-12 education in science, technology, engineering and mathematics (known as STEM) as above average or the best in the world. Scientists were even more critical: A companion survey of members of the American Association for the Advancement of Science found that just 16 [percent] called U.S. K-12 STEM education the best or above average; 46 [percent], in contrast, said K-12 STEM in the U.S. was below average. This could mean that even if there are new jobs available in a globalized and highly competitive economy, Americans will not to be the ones who fill most of them.[18]

The disturbing fact is that in America we are losing our competitive drive and capability as the "lowest common denominator" and extinction of standards of merit culture spreads while other nations are intensifying and expanding their students' educational capabilities. An example is found in the fact that in the United States we commonly hear that jobs involving STEM-educated workers represent the safest employment future for university study. Yet many students undertaking such university majors have dropped out of STEM programs. Why? Because, given their inadequate pre-university education, they find the subject matter too hard or demanding. John Mac Ghlionn, a researcher, essayist, and frequent Epoch Times analyst, covers psychology and social relations. He writes of the national security implications this STEM dilemma presents in the context of the intensifying conflict between America and China:

> The STEM crisis threatens America's national security. As social sciences [disciplinary] majors like anthropology and sociology increase in popularity, hard sciences fade into oblivion. Considering the future is inextricably linked with STEM, and many Americans are ill-equipped for the challenges that await, the future looks rather uncertain. In China, the most popular college majors include software engineering, electronic information engineering, automation, computational science and technology, and applied mathematics.
>
> Are [American students] interested in pursuing STEM careers? The answer appears to be a rather resounding "no." American students, according to Pew researchers, find STEM daunting. Science, math, and engineering, they contend, are just too difficult. More recently, the author Marco Sanau warned that the country is on the

verge of "a significant technology crisis," as it has "fallen behind both China and India in producing math, science, and engineering graduates." This, writes Sanau, will have "significant implications for the competitiveness of the U.S. economy and the effectiveness of Washington's technology-dependent national defense strategy."[19]

China's Educational Test Results May Rank First in the World, But America's Twenty-Fifth Place Ranking Isn't That Bad

Heather Mac Donald of the Manhattan Institute also offers a powerful warning about what is occurring, including the rapid rise of China's student performances on key international tests that allow comparisons between differing countries. She writes:

> Scientific research is about one thing: advancing knowledge. Scientists are not in the business of closing the academic achievement gap; that task falls to families, cultural leaders and schools. Diverting ever more US STEM resources from the pursuit of knowledge to the pursuit of alleged racial equity all but guarantees that a hard-charging, merit-driven China will win the war for scientific and technological dominance, giving it a formidable military advantage. US schools are eliminating gifted and talented programs in the name of racial equity and deemphasizing—if not eliminating—algebra instruction to conceal racially disparate performance in algebra classes. China is taking the opposite course. It identifies its top math talent early on and gives mathematically gifted students accelerated instruction. Its rigorous university entrance exams reward effort and achievement, not identity. Undergraduate math competitions provide a pipeline to the best graduate programs in STEM.

> As of 2018 China ranked number one in the international tests of K-12 math, science and reading known as PISA; America ranked [twenty-fifth]. Chinese teams dominate Stanford's challenge for machine-reading comprehension and the International Olympiad in Informatics. Highly trained STEM Ph.D.s are pouring out of its graduate schools."[20]

Are You Kidding? The American Medical Association Rejects Merit and Ability as Standards, and Adopts Critical Race Theory! The idea that a scientific system ultimately responsible for human lives can vociferously and proudly reject the concept of merit in exchange for Critical Race Theory indicates how far that political movement has progressed, infiltrated, and corrupted America's institutions:

> The American Medical Association (AMA), the largest national organization representing physicians and medical students in the United States, says it will set aside its long-held concept of meritocracy in favor of "racial justice" and "health equity." . . . [T]he AMA set out a three-year road map detailing how the advocacy group will use its influence to dismantle "structural and institutional racism" and advance "social and racial justice" in America's health care system. According to its plan, the AMA will be following a host of strategies, including implementing "racial and social justice" throughout the AMA enterprise culture, systems, policies, and practices; expanding medical education to include critical race theory; and pushing toward "racial healing, reconciliation, and transformation" regarding the organization's own "racially discriminatory" past.
>
> The AMA also makes clear that it now rejects the concepts of "equality" and "meritocracy," which have been goals in the fields of medical science and medical care.
>
> While the AMA doesn't run America's health care system, it holds tremendous influence over medical schools and teaching hospitals that train physicians and other health professionals. Those institutes, the AMA says, must reject meritocracy, which it describes as a harmful narrative that "ignores the inequitably distributed social, structural and political resources." . . . The AMA suggests medical schools should incorporate into their programs critical race theory, an offshoot of Marxism that views society through the lens of a power struggle between the race of oppressors and that of the oppressed. As a result, according to the theory, all long-established institutions of Western society are considered to be tools of racial oppression.[21]

In October 2021, the AMA released a guide describing how the concepts indicated in its May 2021 announcement should be internalized by physicians and the medical profession generally. The following passages demonstrate rejecting merit is only the beginning.

> The American Medical Association recently released a guide on "Advancing Health Equity" that promotes how to fight for critical race theory, includes a list of words not to say and their "equity-focused alternatives," and criticizes concepts like "meritocracy," "individualism" and the "'free' market." The [fifty-five]-page document released on Oct. 28 cites a guide by the organization Race Forward for how to advocate for critical race theory (CRT), which is called "Guide to Counter-Narrating the Attacks on Critical Race Theory." The health equity guide argues physicians . . . must focus on language and collective political circumstances of certain groups.
>
> The guide says doctors should not say "Low-income people have the highest level of coronary artery disease in the United States." Instead, it says, doctors should phrase the same idea like this: "People underpaid and forced into poverty as a result of banking policies, real estate developers gentrifying neighborhoods, and corporations weakening the power of labor movements, among others, have the highest level of coronary artery disease." Rather than using the word "fairness," the guide suggests doctors say "social justice." This is because, it says, fairness "pays no attention to how power relations in society establish themselves but primarily emphasizes outcomes within a pre-given set of rules."[22]

Mandatory Critical Race Theory Training in America's Medical Schools

The AMA wasn't satisfied with mandating anti-merit and quality standards for practicing physicians. It is intent on total CRT-related "reform" at all levels, including medical schools, in terms of admissions, curricula, and standards of medical practice.

Almost all of the nation's top [twenty-five] medical schools are incorporating ideas related to critical race theory (CRT) into mandatory training programs for students and staff, warned a watchdog website documenting leftist indoctrination in K-12 and higher education. Critical Race Training in Education, a project founded by Cornell University law professor William Jacobson, has recently put online a new database on America's most prestigious medical schools. The database finds that [twenty-three] of those [twenty-five] institutions maintain some form of mandatory student training or coursework related to CRT doctrines. The database also observes that [seventeen] schools have mandatory CRT training for employees. For example, Cornell's Weill Medical College requires all faculty and staff to complete "anti-bias training" on an annual basis while it works to "introduce additional educational content related to racism, social injustice, and social determinants of health into the medical curriculum." . . . [T]he subjects of those trainings and coursework . . . usually use terms including "anti-racism," "cultural competency," "equity," "implicit bias," "DEI (diversity, equity and inclusion)" and "critical race theory."[23]

Promoting Woke Culture in 171 Medical Schools, Four Hundred Teaching Hospitals, and Eighty Academic Medical Societies

A recent report reveals the extent to which Wokeism has become part of American medical education. Dr. Stanley Goldfarb, Do No Harm board chair, offers his concerns about the effects on medical education and services he fears will be caused by that dramatic shift toward Wokeism and Critical Race Theory and DEI dogma.

"They [the study's creators] are making this argument that what's best for the health of the American people is that there be this focus on diversity, equity, and inclusion, which simply cannot be justified," Dr. Stanley Goldfarb said. "If you focus on diversity to the exclusion of merit, then patients are at risk of not having the most qualified individual to provide them care." Goldfarb [is the] board chair of the nonprofit watchdog organization Do No Harm (DNH)—an organization spotlighting woke ideologies that DNH says are cropping up in health care and draining resources from the practice of medicine. . . . A flagship medical association that represents major medical schools nationwide has released a November 2022 report (pdf) promoting woke culture in medical schools. The Association of American Medical Colleges (AAMC) is a Washington-based nonprofit comprising 157 accredited U.S. medical schools; [fourteen] accredited Canadian medical schools; approximately [four hundred] teaching hospitals and health systems; and up to [eighty] academic societies. The goal of the report, according to its executive summary, is to improve medical schools' "climate and culture through collective administration of Diversity, Inclusion, Culture, and Equity (DICE) Inventory."

[T]here are many staff and students who don't agree and will be forced to either quit or compromise their values and go along with it by lying, Goldfarb said. . . . Because evaluating medical schools in accordance with DEI standards has become a part of the accreditation process . . . medical staff and students will have to at least pretend to accept a theoretical premise telling them that they are inherently racist, Goldfarb said. . . . "Faculty should not have to discuss what their political ideas are in order to get promoted," he said. Secondly, implicit bias training to maintain or get one's job must go, he said. Thirdly, using race as a criterion of admission must once again become a custom of the past, Goldfarb said, despite the fact that organizations like AAMC are trying to drag them back into the present.[24]

The attack on identifiable standards of intellectual merit provided by traditional testing processes that allow realistic comparisons among individual candidates for educational admission or hiring has intensified throughout our universities. While such testing performance should not be the sole determinant in decision making regarding selection, it borders on the absurd to eliminate comparative mechanisms that have been painstakingly developed to measure capability on the basis of criteria considered centrally related to the educational and employment goals in question for the particular function.

The following excerpts provide how sweeping are the changes. The undeniable fact is that they eliminate the ability to compare candidates based on performance in identical contexts, and this means that decisions can be made on other "softer" emotional and political criteria that have little or nothing to do with candidate's comparative ability. And, of course, doing this is intentional.

> Today, at least two-thirds of higher education institutions, including Harvard and Stanford, don't require the SAT for admission. The American Bar Association recently announced it will drop the LSAT as an admissions requirement for law school. And now, some are calling for the prestigious MCAT to be scrapped as the gold standard for medical school admissions—all in the name of racial equity. . . .
>
> I myself attended universities (Brandeis, NYU) that were far above my family's affordability level precisely because I knew they were investments in my long-term earning potential as well as a way to keep me on the straight and narrow in high school. Sure, as with many Americans—particularly African-Americans like myself—I took on student debt. But the quest for academic success . . . helped me secure a career with good pay and a strong sense of self-worth and satisfaction.
>
> . . . Telling young people—particularly the young people-of-color this "school-blind hiring" purports to benefit—that academic prestige doesn't matter literally reinforces the worst stereotypes of minority cultures. . . . And yet, these well-intentioned initiatives, led mostly by white liberals, completely erase that meaning. This is why school-blind hiring feels so frustrating—and phony."[25]

An Example of How It Works Out in Practice

An "Unfortunate Truth": Critical Race Theory Doesn't Have Room for Asians

I spoke above of a deliberate strategy to eliminate comparative standards in admissions and hiring. There is no clearer example of how the "new" system that is based on whatever criteria the activist system chooses to use in the selection process than is provided by the treatment of Asian-ethnicity candidates seeking admission to the institutions of higher learning ranked as the most elite. Kenny Xu explains how the new system works. Xu is the president of the nonprofit organization Color Us United, and heavily involved in the *Harvard Students for Fair Admissions vs. Harvard* case. He is also a commentary writer for *The Federalist, The Washington Examiner, The Daily Signal,* and *Quillette.* He writes:

> "Asian Americans prove that critical race theory is not true, cannot be true," author Kenny Xu [said]. "Asian Americans never needed politics to succeed in this country. They just want to be treated based on merit." . . . "If America is still a systemically racist country for minorities, how come they have allowed Asian Americans to over-take Whites in education level and socioeconomic status? Asians get higher test scores," Xu said. . . . Xu [added], "Asian Americans prove that, even in the face of whatever racial narratives that you're in, you still can succeed, that this country is the land of opportunity."
>
> "This denigration of merit . . . leads it not only to repudiate the foundational premise of America but also that has a disproportion-ate impact on one racial minority group in the United States more than any other: Asian Americans," James Lindsay wrote. . . . "I think it's deliberate. The reason why is because Asian Americans are the inconvenient minority," Xu said. "Critical race theory really doesn't have any room for Asians." Xu . . . feels the families of most success-ful Asian Americans came to the country without any privilege but thrive because of meritocracy. "If you're an immigrant parent of a child in America, the only way that you see forward to your child

having a better life is to train them to be to be talented, to have merit, so that they can compete in an American meritocracy and critical race theory, you know, says that meritocracy is racist," he said. "[CRT] undermines the entire concept that formulated the ability for Asians to succeed in America."[26]

At UC Berkeley's "Persons of Color Theme House" Many People of Color members moved here to be able to avoid white violence and white presence.

A University of California housing co-op set up by People of Color activists, the "Person of Color Theme House,"

is bizarre and racist. The co-op's discriminatory residence rules did not even allow whites into the housing complex because the POC residents didn't want to have to deal with what I guess is an "aura" of violence and white existence or "presence" that, by itself, made some residents feel threatened or unsettled because they need to have distance from the emotionally disturbing presence of white people.

There are two points that spring to mind. First, is this a statement in which it is being stated that whites are inherently violent? All whites? All white men? White women? Plus, who are we defining as "white"? Are all "people of color" afraid of whites? So we are projecting violent character to all members of a group we ourselves defined, and we are assuming that all POCs share this fear of "white violence"? It seems more than a bit racist to me.

But there is actually another element in this situation that strikes me as odd. It is the idea that, while someone may not fear "white violence," it is still appropriate to have a "standard" in which it is legitimate to allow the residents of Berkeley's "Person of Color Theme House" to block the "presence" of someone who appears to be "white" so that they don't have to even have to look at such people. This approach, described next, is so bizarre it is incomprehensible.

A private housing co-op just off the University of California, Berkeley campus has banned White visitors in common areas or without consent from other tenants. The "Person of Color Theme House" is a housing co-op located near UC Berkeley that "aims to provide housing to low-income, first generation, immigrant and marginalized students of color," according to its website. In a leaked photo of "house rules" for the co-op, tenants are instructed not to bring white guests to the home without permission and to keep White guests from common areas. *"Many POC members moved here to be able to avoid white violence and presence, so respect their decision of avoidance if you bring white guests."* [Emphasis added] White people are not entirely banned from the house's premises, but those wishing to bring White guests into the building must alert other tenants. "Always announce guests in the Guest Chat if they will be in common spaces with you and if they are white." White people are entirely banned from entering shared spaces within the home to allow people of color to avoid "white presence."[27]

Continuing the "Anti-White" theme, a Michigan school board member stated that in her opinion, "White women are the stupidest" and "Whiteness" is an "evil."

The hate and stupidity demonstrated by what are being called Anti-racism activists is stunning. It is like we are being provided a window into the depths of seriously troubled people's minds and hearts, with the individuals revealing the darkness in their souls projecting their twisted views onto an entire segment of the human race. Michigan school board member Kesha Hamilton offers a disturbing example.

A Jackson County School board member, Kesha Hamilton, faced backlash for tweets blasting White people during a public comment on Tuesday, including one resident who called her "angry and bitter." . . . [Hamilton said] "These White women are the stupidest" . . . "Whiteness" [is] an "evil." "Whiteness is so evil . . . it manipulates then says, I won›t apologize for my dishonesty and trauma inducing practices and thinks you should applaud it for being honest about its ability to manipulate and be dishonest."[28]

Project 21's Horace Cooper: "Assuming certain things about people solely because they're White and solely because they're Black" Is RACISM!

Project 21 co-chair Horace Cooper gives his take on the racism of anti-racism speakers, and on individuals being paid tens of thousands of dollars for their racism lectures. Project 21 represents a leading voice of Black conservatives that has existed for over twenty-five years, and is sponsored by the National Center for Public Policy Research. Cooper explains:

[T]here's no doubt that we're living in a culture where when you highlight issues of race, people think they're going to have to stand up and salute smartly. Here's my problem . . . [T]his isn't anti-racism discussion. This is racist discussion. If you listen to some of the nonsense—and a lot of it is nonsense—that these presenters bring to the table, it includes things like assuming certain things about people solely because they're White and solely because they're Black. We used to call that bigotry when that was done, instead of recognizing that people are individuals. Now it's lucrative for these individuals to do these things, but it would be lucrative too if this were 1920, for [the KKK's] David Duke to do this. The only difference is most people of good sense and good will understand they shouldn't say that and they shouldn't pay him."[29]

Chapter Eight

We Need to Get Back to Having "Dangerous Universities"

Albert Schweitzer warned: "The past has, no doubt, seen the struggle of the free-thinking individual against the fettered spirit of a whole society, but the problem has never presented itself on the scale on which it does to-day, because of the fettering of the collective spirit."[1]

The Infusion of "Dangerous Ideas" Into an Orthodoxy

Universities, our supposed hotbeds of free and critical thinking, have become leading co-conspirators in suppressing intellectual independence and stifling the values they are supposed to be instilling in their students. Some of the thematic contributions of activist faculty, including the Woke and Critical theorists, when allowed to compete in an open intellectual system, can generate dialectical insights through the hypotheses they represent. They can also be revealed as superficial or even false. The key, however, in Paul Goodman's terms, is that they infuse "dangerous ideas" that demand analysis and critique into the system and this challenges dominant orthodoxies.[2]

The Renaissance and the Enlightenment were intended to free us from centuries of darkness and ignorance in ways that allowed the full flourishing of humanity. Unfortunately, it seems that we are considerably less interested in open-minded freedom of thought and expression than we assumed, and are regressing to pre-Enlightenment conditions.

Universities are the institutions responsible for advancing our freedom of thought and discourse through the work of scholars and the teaching of each generation of students. But universities and other educational institutions have increasingly set up rules aimed at protecting newly dominant identity groups from criticism.

This has gotten to the point that those increasingly dominant groups are allowed to subjectively self-define almost anything as being "insensitive," "offensive," "harassing," "intolerant," "disrespectful," critical of their core belief systems, "biased," "racist," or "threatening." That shift to a one-sided, almost completely subjective standard by which individuals and Identity Groups with agendas are able to condemn anyone who disagrees with their supposed interpretations degrades the university. It also intensifies our society's conflicts to the point that the entire system is endangered.

Mark Bauerlein is a superb analyst at describing what is occurring. He offers a profound insight into the deterioration of universities:

> In the past, if you wanted to find a place where radical thoughts were in the air, protest and dissent were in ferment, and innovative ideas traded back and forth, you couldn't do better than the college campus in 1965, 1975—all the way to the 2010s. The free speech and anti-War movements of the Sixties made their home there, and the LGBTQ crusade (though it began off-campus) was consolidated into Gender Theory and Queer Theory by academics who gave the activists an intellectual sheen they never would have developed on their own. Today's Critical Race Theory, too, goes back to the law schools and "studies" programs, while the conversion of public schools into factories of progressivism is standard dogma in schools of education. . . . All of them challenged one orthodoxy or another, questioned tradition, upset convention, and aimed to make you think, and think again.[3]

Mark Mercer's "In Praise of Dangerous Universities"

When we speak of "dangerous" universities in a positive sense, what is meant is that honestly presented knowledge and critical thinking are weapons of power that allow, and require, us to see the world clearly and objectively. "Danger" in that sense is created by the fact that we are provided the ability to "Speak Truth to Power" and to work morally and personally to make our community one that rejects abuse and injustice and seeks opportunity for all. That is a key reason the modern university exists, and a reason that is being increasingly corrupted.

The idea of dangerousness in the way that Mark Mercer and others intend represents a return to quality, deeper knowledge, precision of thought, tolerance, and the building of skills and understanding. As is indicated throughout this analysis, we are already being subjected to a socially divisive form of "dangerous" universities that are undermining educational quality, indoctrinating students with alienating and divisive beliefs, and distorting our history and the ideals of American society. That is not the meaning that Mark Mercer intends. His meaning involves the need to recapture the best that higher learning is supposed to reflect through the university ideal, and dealing with ideological faculty and administrators who are sabotaging the true purposes and mission of the university as a fundamental institution.

"Dangerousness" has another face, however, and that is what we are now experiencing with the expanding pool of brainwashed and intimidated people being recruited into a Woke/CRT political movement that is undermining the deeper essence of America. In that form of dangerousness, we are creating the inability and unwillingness to think clearly and honestly. Students are instead being prepared to be "foot soldiers" in a radical movement intent on recreating the nation into an image that only leads to intolerance and repression.

Canadian scholar William Brooks develops Mark Mercer's ideas as set out in Mercer's *In Praise of Dangerous Universities and Other Essays* (2022):

> "In Praise of Dangerous Universities" calls for a return to the rules of open discourse in which students can seek a fuller understanding of their world through critical inquiry and the free exchange of ideas. Mercer stands firmly against teaching political activism. He was outspokenly critical when Dalhousie University introduced an academic course in which students were to be taught how to protest.

He argued that taking sides in social causes is inconsistent with a university's commitment to educate its students. Mercer contends that: "When a course takes a particular position or side on an issue, it cheats students out of the experience of investigating the matter seriously, dispassionately, and open-mindedly, with a concern to appreciate various perspectives."[4]

Mao Zedong Warned It Is "Dangerous" for "Revolutions" When People Are Taught to Challenge, Evaluate, Create, and Think

Mao summarized his thoughts on liberalism in a 1937 pamphlet, "Combat Liberalism": "Any CCP members given to free-thinking or non-conformity, Mao wrote, were undermining Party unity. These demands for obedience and discipline were an early sign of Mao's authoritarianism, which culminated in the 1941 Rectification Movement,"[5]

The independent scholar's and teacher's task is not Maoist conformity of thought and understanding. It is to prepare students to critically test and question everything, not to accept convenient assumptions—no matter how seemingly attractive or comfortable. But conflict and "truths" that don't conform to the dominant assumptions make people uncomfortable, and scholars tend to be easily discomfited. Traditionally, many who entered the cloisters of academia sought peace and reflection, not conflict. The desire to avoid conflict and to receive the privileges and lifetime benefits flowing from alignment with the in-group have inhibiting and directive effects on scholars' work—both in terms of what they say and what they leave out or don't pursue.

The Woke/Crit attacks on the university and our overall educational system have been successful to a disturbing degree. At this point, the competing lines in our fundamental dispute over the preferable nature and functions of society have solidified. The result is that we are possessed by radically distinct and competing visions of society. We are experiencing a battle over speech, communication, social norms, the dynamics of social and political communities, institutional control, and numerous other critical issues. In that struggle, many in the university and elsewhere, including K-12 education, government, corporations, and our media, have become intolerant activists.

Debating, analyzing, and disagreeing over what is best, just, fair, equitable and desirable are core parts of the university ideal. What is not legitimate, however, is that the Woke/CRT advocates are not simply entering their ideas and submitting them into full debate for testing and analysis. On achieving substantial administrative and faculty power in the university, they are engaged in stifling the very processes that created their opportunity to inject their "dangerous" ideas into the university's intellectual universe and critical process. Rather than being faithful to the university ideal, they used it to gain entrance, and as has happened with virtually all the Socialist/Marxist regimes that ultimately gained power, the authoritarian victors created a repressive "new orthodoxy" worse than the system they worked so hard and strategically to undermine.

"Teaching to think intensively and to think critically" IS "Dangerous"

Contrast Mao Zedong's admission that a revolution cannot afford to have Liberals and others who are capable of thinking critically and seeking answers for what they are being asked to do, with the insights of Martin Luther King, Malcolm X, and Nelson Mandela. Dr. Martin Luther King Jr. described a primary purpose of education as "to teach one to think intensively and to think critically."[6] American civil rights leader Malcolm X described the purpose of education as follows: "Education is our passport to the future, tomorrow belongs to the people who prepare for it today."[7] The incredibly courageous South African civil rights and anti-apartheid leader Nelson Mandela offered another powerful insight into the vital importance of teaching critical thinking, wide-ranging knowledge, personal empowerment, and vital skills. Mandela states: "Education is the most powerful weapon which you can use to change the world. Education is the first step for people to gain the knowledge, critical thinking, empowerment and skills they need to make this world a better place."[8]

The problem is that, for people who actually desire to make the world a better place through the highest and best use of critical thinking, through expansive knowledge, skill, and shared vision, this commitment to education is being sabotaged by those who are seeking power for themselves and their closed Identity Groups or competing "tribes." Mao Zedong understood that fact as well as any.

Woke/CRT Is a Carefully Planned System of "Deadening the Mind"

Now compare the insights of MLK, Malcolm X, and Nelson Mandela with what is taking place in many of America's universities, and in the K-12 schools that feed their graduates into our universities. What is occurring, in so many instances, is not education as we have long understood it to be. It is a carefully planned system of "deadening the mind" through a one-sided and dishonest diet of emotional angst, victimization, guilt, and hate. This is being done by the combination of sloganeering, "whiteness" attacks, intense peer pressure, Social and Emotional Learning (SEL) and CRT curricula, and much more. As any propagandist or "brainwasher" understands, first you must tear down an individual's core values, and then fill the resulting "empty space" with your own beliefs and agendas.

King, Malcolm X, and Nelson Mandela would be aghast at what is going on today in America's universities. Their future belonged to people who could think with precision based on honest knowledge. It belonged to people who could get along, negotiate agreements and mutually beneficial compromises, and saw each other as people, not "bags of meat" trapped within different colors of skin. Their future was based on people who respected each other's qualities and dignity. That is definitely not the path that the Woke/CRT Movement is seeking to force us to travel.

America has an increasingly serious education problem rendering many of its graduates non-competitive as well as ignorant. The almost unforgivable tragedy is that urban minority students, most in cities run by Woke/CRT Democrats, are being hurt the worst. Those cities have abysmal public school systems under the control of the Progressive Left, and these school systems are absolute failures. Yet, the messages being trumpeted by the Woke/CRT activists almost entirely ignore and cover up the tragedy of an urban public education system over which they have almost complete control. This is a profound systemic failure, but the system is one created and operated by the Progressive Left.

Clear and honest thinking, detailed analysis, and the manipulation of numbers and data to uncover the underlying implications of a situation, targeted goal, or condition are essential conceptual skills. They are definitely "systems" and "methods" that help us be more productive and capable, allow us to think more clearly in our decision making, and to better understand the pros and cons of situations. They are not an oppressive form of "white systemic racism." The true "systemic" racism discriminating against and oppressing youthful minorities living in America's major urban areas is preventing America's students from acquiring these essential skills and values.

"Dangerous" Universities are About Knowledge, Insight, and Intellect, Not Propaganda, Ideology, and Division

William Brooks further explains our dilemma by quoting Oscar Wilde.

> "An idea that is not dangerous is unworthy of being called an idea at all." Mark Mercer applies this same standard of value to the idea of a university. Dangerous ideas are not necessarily the ones that will divide us. More often, it is the ideas that educational authorities insist we must agree on that limit our capacity for thought. Bold ideas are seldom conceived in safe spaces. Confronting dangerous ideas involves taking risks. Without taking risks, human advancement and the survival of liberty may be virtually impossible. That's why Mercer argues throughout his book that a democratic society of free and equal citizens needs universities that prize their academic mission above the maintenance of politically correct behaviour. Throughout the history of mankind, dangerous circumstances have produced the most courageous thinkers.[9]

Beginning in the late 1960s and early 1970s, and still developing today, widely diverse and non-traditional faculty flooded into universities. I was one, and I still consider what occurred at that point to be a positive development. Many (I hope myself) were in possession of "dangerous ideas." These were such themes as social justice, gender equality, equality of opportunity, racial discrimination, educational access and quality, and other critical issues. Concepts such as equity versus equality, identity choices, and systemic biases of the kind that have been forced into academia over the past thirty plus years have proven quite "dangerous."

Some of these "dangerous new ideas" have helped develop an emerging body of knowledge that is enabling faculty to transcend, extend, and transform the traditional humanistic and scientific core of knowledge that had long been offered by universities. Some of the new ideas are vital insights, while others are a cult of activists' deliberately skewed and distorted attacks on the nation's traditions aimed at turning its population against each other and destroying traditional foundations.

To understand where we are today, and where we must go in seeking to solve the anti-intellectual and anti-community political conflict that is tearing us apart as a society, we need to start thinking about what universities should be about. To do this, we need to have some realistic concept of what universities have been and are supposed to be. That is not easy because we have often deluded ourselves with high-minded idealistic statements we take as fact. It is important to realize that the university is not only an institution; it is a human institution. That is simultaneously its strength and weakness.

Education Is a Vital Method of Sharing Community across Generations

Education is also a vital tool for tying generations of our population together over time. This includes studying and understanding the past, but does not mean acting as if the past is in fact the present. Universities are supposed to be centers of free speech, dialogue, challenge, and learning about rights and duties. This includes preparing students to protect and preserve the unique ideal of the Western version of the Rule of Law, and a just society in which all people are provided the opportunity to participate and compete.

Universities are key mechanisms for transcending the often overwhelming pressures and factionalism of political immediacy, or what has been referred to as "presentism." Presentism is a strategy aimed at achieving victory in a heated political conflict by forcing a reinterpretation of the past through the lens of the current cultural moment. The use of "presentism" is a fundamental flaw corrupting many of the approaches being used for political purposes in analyzing America's history. John Moses explains the fallacy inherent in "Presentism," one that, while written in relation to Australia's educational and scholarly system, is equally applicable to America's.

> There is a tendency in much Australian historical writing for authors to make judgments about the past that are really formulated out of their concern to advance a particular political agenda in the present. Such writers have fallen into the trap of "presentism." They try to depict the past in the way they would prefer it to have been rather than how it actually was. The fallacy consists in projecting a present political concern backwards towards a past situation in which, of course, the protagonists and decision-makers had different priorities from those of today. Reliable historians try, as far as humanly possible, to re-experience the past through the eyes of the people living at that time. That should have been a methodological tool every student acquired when studying first-year history at university.[10]

Boghossian: Teaching Is About "Creating the Conditions for Students' Rigorous Thoughts and Insisting They Reach Their Own Conclusions."

Former Portland State University faculty member Peter Boghossian has described his sense of the educational mission. In announcing his resignation from the university, he explained his commitment as a teacher, accusing the PSU administration of "creating an environment that imperils dissent." Boghossian put up with a range of insults at the university, and even reports incidents of having been "spit at" and otherwise taunted for his political views. Jack Phillips reports:

> Portland State University professor Peter Boghossian . . . resigned from his position and accused the college administration of creating an environment that imperils dissent. "I never once believed—nor do I now—that the purpose of instruction was to lead my students to a particular conclusion," Boghossian, a philosophy professor, wrote in the letter. "Rather, I sought to create the conditions for rigorous thought; to help them gain the tools to hunt and furrow for their own conclusions. This is why I became a teacher and why I love teaching." But over time, he argued, Portland State University—a publicly-funded college—made "intellectual exploration impossible" and has transformed itself into a "social justice factory" with a primary focus on race, victimhood, and gender.
>
> "Students at Portland State are not being taught to think. Rather, they are being trained to mimic the moral certainty of ideologues," said the letter, which was published on Bari Weiss's Substack page. . . . "Faculty and administrators have abdicated the university's truth-seeking mission and instead drive intolerance of divergent beliefs and opinions," Boghossian added. "This has created a culture of offense where students are now afraid to speak openly and honestly."[11]

The University Ideal as Represented in "The Philadelphia Statement"

Plato remarked that the function of an ideal is not to describe reality in fact, but to offer us standards against which we can judge our behavior. Ideals in their best sense are guides for aspiration. Ideals provide the driving force behind our struggle to achieve a progressively more enlightened political state and community. The fact that the university ideal has multiple meanings, and that it has been used for illegitimate reasons or in a self-interested effort to defend an orthodoxy's position, does not destroy its underlying importance.

The fact is that falling short of perfect attainment of our ideals does not invalidate the critical principles on which they are grounded. It does, however, impose the responsibility to expose the abuses, redouble efforts to eliminate the injustices that were created, and ensure the system strives to prevent future abuses. Rejecting principled methods, values, and ideals, while substituting an extreme degree of subjectivity and personal "voice" for disciplined inquiry, which is what has happened with the Woke and the Crits, denies the university's search for greater understanding. This demeans the ideal of the university and the scholar's search for truth in teaching and research.

Abandonment of a belief in the objectivity of knowledge, or at least to a commitment to coming as close as possible to a full understanding, coupled with the assertion that language, truth, and power are highly malleable at the whims of "victimized" and "historically marginalized" interest groups, has left us with a sense of profound uncertainty and conflict. That sense of uncertainty forces us to struggle over the application of indeterminate rules written in indeterminate language and applied to indeterminate contexts. The challenge is that choices must be made even though there are no clear formulae to guide us. This makes us highly vulnerable to ideologues. It is useful to understand there is at least some emerging pushback against the attacks on freedom of speech, thought, and discourse. One effort of direct relevance to the university is represented by "The Philadelphia Statement." Walter Williams reports:

> More than [twelve thousand] professors, free speech leaders, and conservative-leaning organization leaders have signed "The Philadelphia Statement." The 845-word document says, in part: "Colleges and universities are imposing speech regulations to make students 'safe,' not from physical harm, but from challenges to campus orthodoxy. These policies and regulations assume that we as citizens are unable to think for ourselves and to make independent judgments. Instead of teaching us to engage, they foster conformism ("groupthink") and train us to respond to intellectual challenges with one or another form of censorship. A society that . . . allows people to be shamed or

intimidated into self-censorship of their ideas and considered judgments will not survive for long. "As Americans, we desire a flourishing, open marketplace of ideas, knowing that it is the fairest and most effective way to separate falsehood from truth. Accordingly, dissenting and unpopular voices—be they of the left or the right—must be afforded the opportunity to be heard. They have often guided our society toward more just positions, which is why Frederick Douglass said freedom of speech is the 'great moral renovator of society and government.'"[12]

Chapter Nine

The Mass Formation Psychosis in America's Universities

The Psychology of Totalitarianism

We are experiencing a mass psychosis in which many faculty and administrators in America's university have formed into a single-minded ultra-authoritarian mob whose members consider themselves an "enlightened elite." This is the result of a largely successful fifty-year-long effort by ideological activists to capture the university in America. As with the Communist Party and Maoism in China, the impassioned Marxists of the former Soviet Union, and the murderous fanatics of Nazi Germany, their intention has been to turn the university, and the equivalent of each system's K-12 educational institutions, into instruments of propaganda and systemic transformation.

We are undergoing a more subtle, but still devastating, process in America in which a one-sided political orthodoxy seeks control and, in the process, attempts to silence dissent. We find this silencing in universities and K-12 schools where activist faculty and administrators, along with an increasingly aggressive and intolerant number of students, brook no dissent. They attack, silence, and "cancel" anyone with the audacity to expose or even question their narratives, opinions, theories, arguments, intolerance, and abuses.

The Core Elements of Mass Formation

Belgium's Ghent University professor Mattias Desmet presents a powerful interpretation of what he calls the Mass Formation phenomenon, describing how "mass" systems of belief take over power in society. This includes an emphasis on how a relatively small but well-organized, highly strategic, and very aggressive portion of a population, as low as 20–30 percent, can impose a mass belief system on others. Desmet offers Nazi Germany and Iran as examples, although Russia, China, Venezuela, and others can be added to the list. He also describes the core elements of Mass Formation, which are behaviors congruent with fanaticism and fascism:

> What is mass formation actually? It's a specific kind of group forma-
> tion that makes people radically blind to everything that goes against
> what the group believes in. In this way, they take the most absurd
> beliefs for granted. . . . [I]individuals in mass formation become radi-
> cally intolerant for dissonant voices. In the ultimate stage of the mass
> formation, they will typically commit atrocities toward those who do
> not go along with the masses.[1]

Desmet's ideas of Mass Formation and Mechanist Ideology are also linked to situations where a nation's media collaborate with the mass systems, public and private, functioning as propagandists, censors, and monitors. Media outlets whose core responsibility has long been proclaimed as "speaking truth to power" have become activist systems themselves rather than functioning as objective truth-seekers and purveyors of wisdom and insight.

People Who Lived Through Darkness See More Clearly

I have great admiration for writers in the 1950s and 1960s. They saw the social transformation that was beginning to take place with depressing clarity. Swiss physician and theologian Paul Tournier captured the essence of the cultural forces they were describing when he observed that people have increasingly become "cogs" in our social and economic "machinery": "People have become merely cogs in the machine of production, tools, functions. All that matters is what they do, not what they think or feel. . . . [T]heir thoughts and feelings are . . . moulded by propaganda, press, cinema and radio. They read the same newspaper each day, hear the same slogans, see the same advertisements."[2]

For me, an always startling fact is that the post-WWII period, one that lasted perhaps into the early 1970s as the intellectuals aged, is filled with philosophers and social critics, European and American, along with Canada's Marshall McLuhan, who perceived the world far more deeply and accurately than most of our modern "thinkers." This includes McLuhan, Jacques Ellul, Noam Chomsky, Eric Hoffer, Albert Camus, Buckminster Fuller, Friedrich Hayek, Joseph Schumpeter, Bertrand Russell, Karl Popper, Hannah Arendt, Hans Morgenthau, Max Weber, Alvin Toffler, Thomas Kuhn, Richard Hofstadter, Crane Brinton, Arnold Toynbee, Jean-Paul Sartre, Jurgen Habermas, Jacques Derrida, Michel Foucault, Ayn Rand (Alice O'Connor), Walter Lippmann, Reinhold Niebuhr, and others.

"Adolph and the Aryans," "Mao and the Long Marchers," "Karl and the KGBs"

Most of the individuals listed previously experienced a world in which a Totalitarian mass dictated, controlled, imprisoned, and murdered after power was seized. There should also be no question that those monolithic "masses" imposed a stifling and often deadly "psychosis" on their populations and on others seen as enemies. Hitler and the Nazis, Stalin and the USSR, and Mao Zedong and the Chinese Communist Party destroyed the lives of millions upon millions of innocent people.

It is vital for us to understand that the development of history's most oppressive societies was not instantaneous. In each case, years—even decades—elapsed as the movements planned and implemented their strategies to seize power. Each involved the use of social criticisms about injustice, done by those Eric Hoffer described as the "fault-finding men of words."[3] It also involved the identification of victims and oppressors because "all revolutions require an enemy." This helped to create and recruit a critical mass of revolutionary adherents as the movement gained power through dominance of key institutions.

Those listed previously understood quite well the darkness some people carry within their souls, and the nearly insatiable hunger that drives a portion of the human race in quests for the power to control and dominate others and to feel significant and superior. Anyone forced to endure the impact of a Totalitarian mass is shaped by that experience, whether we are speaking of Maoism, Nazism's National Socialism, or Marxism.

The intellectual and moral leaders who experienced the totalitarian strife of the 1930s and the horrors of the next several decades fully understood why monolithic power should not be given to any of us, and how easy it is to look the other way as the "mass" is acquiring power. They intuitively understood the dangers of the powers provided to governments and propagandists by the internet and social media. This particularly included the understanding that control over such communications "magic" must never be allowed to a few "elites" because, being human, those elites would inevitably seek to impose their visions on all members of society.

We need look no further than the World Economic Forum (WEF)'s "Great Reset" for proof of this reality of the "Alphas" of the human race. The WEF represents a global network of elites intent on remaking global society and nations into a worldwide political system of the network's design. Although it purports to be focused on economics, the truth is that the organization seeks to create a consolidated, overarching political sphere under which all nations are to operate.

The WEF's June 2020 response to the COVID-19 breakout, "Now is the time for a 'great reset,'" helps to understand its true agenda, one the leaders of the organization felt could be advanced more rapidly due to the widespread fear of the pandemic and the willingness of frightened populations to accept a series of Draconian orders issued by governments and faceless bureaucrats who, it turned out in numerous instances, were wrong in their dictates. Here is an excerpt from the WEF's Great Reset plan:

> COVID-19 lockdowns may be gradually easing, but anxiety about the world's social and economic prospects is only intensifying. There is good reason to worry: a sharp economic downturn has already begun, and we could be facing the worst depression since the 1930s. But, while this outcome is likely, it is not unavoidable. To achieve a better outcome, the world must act jointly and swiftly to revamp all aspects of our societies and economies, from education to social

contracts and working conditions. *Every country, from the United States to China, must participate, and every industry, from oil and gas to tech, must be transformed. In short, we need a "Great Reset" of capitalism.*

> *Clearly, the will to build a better society does exist. We must use it to secure the Great Reset that we so badly need. That will require stronger and more effective governments,* though this does not imply an ideological push for *bigger* ones.[4] [Emphasis added]

Most people want security. Others want power. Those who quest for power will do almost anything to obtain and retain it. Failure to understand that irreversible human reality is the ultimate and unbridgeable failure of Marxism. The only solution is the diffusion of power in the way designed in the American Constitution, and that is what the Woke/Crits are trying to reverse in their ongoing strategy to seize control and create a monolithic government in which all participants march to the beat of the same Woke drummer. This brings to mind the mythical musical combos of "Adolph and the Aryans," "Mao and the Long Marchers," and "Karl and the KGBs."

Shutting Off the "Oxygen of Liberty"

All the fundamental institutions and systems by which we communicate, compete, grow, learn, and create are being undermined. The enormous scope of what is occurring on all levels of America's fundamental institutions, including universities and K-12 schools, is what I sought to show in the publication of my book *"Un-Canceling" America*. A more specific focus on education is found in *"No More Excuses!" Parents Defending K-12 Education* from 2022. The role of artificial intelligence (AI) in contributing to the reshaping, benefitting, and plaguing of Western societies was analyzed in the 2019 publication of *The Artificial Intelligence Contagion: Can Democracy Withstand the Imminent Transformation of Work, Wealth, and the Social Order?* in 2019 by Clarity. The unfortunate answer to that titular question is "probably not."

The political censoring and use of the punishment tools of Cancel Culture are consuming our educational systems as well as media, politics, government, business and, strangely enough, America's military. The monitoring, censoring, and shaming of the "heretics," "blasphemers," and "deviants" are being used as weapons to compel agreement and to silence. It is a powerful tactic for those who want to dismantle our nation and recreate it in a darker, bigoted, and repressive political image.

The fact that the Radical Progressives have of late become so obvious in their language control, censorship, and "canceling" is a bad omen. It signals that the "Revolutionary Utopians" have shifted toward the degree of language control and suppression that is characteristic of totalitarian states.

We have reached the stage described by Walter Williams in which he warned: "Once leftists have gained power, as they have in most of our colleges and universities, free speech becomes a liability. It challenges their ideas and agenda and must be suppressed."[5] The Independent Women's Forum's Heather Higgins discusses this in the context of authoritarian societies, warning that it cuts off the "oxygen of liberty" that is vital to healthy democratic societies."[6]

My position is simple. I don't care whether what we are dealing with is propaganda and intimidation arising from cultures of the Left or the Right. My point is that universities lose their central moral reason for being if they suppress the free and independent thought they are responsible for nurturing. Speaking not only as an academic but as an American, when we allow cultures of either hard or soft repression to emerge, in which independent thinking and honest critical discourse are undermined, we have sabotaged our very justification for existing. For many scholars and teachers, this includes the rather amazing privilege of lifetime tenure, although that entitlement is understandably under great duress.

I am not trying to be overly simplistic, but if we continue to "pack" universities with people with agendas and belief systems that reject those basic ideals and mission of progress, and who all think the same, have the same politics, write about the same issues in the same way, and share the same values, we have blinded ourselves to the intellectual richness and diversity of American society. We have tragically turned our educational and political systems into propaganda and indoctrination vectors, seeking to reach back centuries to "fix" every wrong that ever took place. The task of doing so is one that can never be achieved, and beyond a certain level of fairness and justice will only tear the nation apart. We cannot allow this to happen.

Consider what you would call the behavior of hundreds of Stanford University's law students in relation to the Federalist Society's speaking invitation to a US Court of Appeals judge whose presentation was to be on Constitutional law. A report of the debacle appears next.

> A federal judge shouted down by protesters at Stanford Law School ripped the behavior of the student body and administrators, saying they were treating their peers like "dogs**t." Judge Kyle Duncan, who was appointed by former President Donald Trump, was invited to speak at Stanford University Thursday by the school's Federalist Society chapter. However, he was heckled by hundreds of students, who made it impossible for him to deliver his speech. "If enough of these kids get into the legal profession, the rule of law will descend into barbarism," Duncan told the Washington Free Beacon.
>
> Video footage widely shared on social media shows that the school's associate dean of diversity, equity and inclusion (DEI), Tirien Steinbach, did nothing to quell the disruption as protesters hurled verbal abuse at the judge, which appeared to violate Stanford's free speech policies. Instead, Steinbach gave a minutes-long and emotional speech at the event, accusing Duncan of causing "harm" through his work on the U.S. Court of Appeals for the Fifth Circuit. The students were particularly angry at Duncan for a 2020 opinion in which he refused to use a transgender sex offender's preferred pronouns. In comments to the Free Beacon, the judge described the incident as a "bizarre therapy session from hell."[7]

The students and DEI administrator's behavior clearly violated the University's rules on free speech. Tim Rosenberger, who is head of the student Federalist Society at Stanford, compared what occurred to a "train wreck."

> Stanford Law student Tim Rosenberger says the ugly protest against U.S. Circuit Judge Kyle Duncan earlier this month is indicative of a broader problem with speech and culture on campuses, and not just at his own. "There definitely is a problem with speech and with the culture, I don't think it's unique to Stanford," he [said]. . . . "They were just yelling at him," he said. "People are yelling really horrible things about him, about his family members being raped, I assume an allusion to his support for [*Dobbs v. Women's Health*]." Rosenberger said he didn't think the kind of campus disruptions against conservative speakers that have been occurring around the country would happen at Stanford, one of the top law schools in the United States. "We've had hostility, but we haven't had anything like this," he said. "I mean, it was like a train crash, right? It just kept getting worse and continuing."[8]

Both Stanford's president and law dean subsequently offered apologies to Judge Duncan that produced more venom and hate. If we needed a more graphic example of an intolerant mass formation at Stanford, we need look no further than the follow-up by hundreds of masked, black-clad students as they dramatically followed and lined corridors in an effort to intimidate and shame Dean Martinez after she finished teaching her class on Constitutional Law. It brings back images of Nazi "Black" and "Brown Shirts" as brainwashed young fascists facilitated the rise of that murderous and evil political movement. One Stanford student who did not participate in the protest called the experience "eerie."

> Hundreds of student protesters wearing masks and all-black clothing lined the hallways outside Stanford Law School Dean Jenny Martinez's classroom after she apologized to U.S. Circuit Court Judge Kyle Duncan for the disruption of his recent speech. Martinez, who teaches constitutional law, arrived to find her whiteboard covered in fliers ridiculing Duncan and defending those who disrupted

his speech. The fliers echoed the opinion of student activists and some administrators who claimed hecklers derailing Duncan's talk was a form of free speech.

After her class ended, protesters . . . stared at Martinez as she left. The protesters formed a "human corridor" that stretched from the class to the building's exit and contained nearly a third of the school's student body. . . . Approximately [fifty] out of the [sixty] students in Martinez's class also joined the protest and scowled at those who did not join in. "They gave us weird looks if we didn't wear black" and join the crowd, first-year law student Luke Schumacher said. "It didn't feel like the inclusive, belonging atmosphere that the DEI office claims to be creating." Another student, who requested anonymity for fear of retaliation, said the experience was "eerie." "The protesters were silent, staring from behind their masks at everyone who chose not to protest, including the dean," the individual said.[9]

Chapter Ten

Artificial Intelligence Systems Are Creating a "Mass Formation"

AI is particularly good at producing instruments of control that help repressive regimes and endanger open societies.

—George Soros

It feels odd to lead off this chapter with material from George Soros, a man who has done significant damage to American society. But even though I see Soros and his Open Society strategy as ill-considered and counterintuitive, in January 2022 he made a presentation at the Hoover Institute that touched on important points. Several of those are set out in his following comments relating to the impacts of artificial intelligence (AI) and social media, and how they create repressive options for authoritarian societies such as China. We begin with his distinction between "open" societies and "one-party" states.

> In an open society, the role of the state is to protect the freedom of the individual. In a closed society the role of the individual is to serve the rulers of the state. As the founder of the Open Society Foundations, obviously I am on the side of open societies. But the most important question now is, which system is going to prevail? Each has strengths and weaknesses. Open societies unleash the creative and innovative energies of people, closed societies concentrate power in the hands of the one-party state.

Recently, I have asked myself the question, how did the current situation arise? When I embarked on what I call my political philanthropy in the 1980s, American superiority was not in question. That is no longer the case. Why? Part of the answer is to be found in technological progress, most of which is based on artificial intelligence, or AI, which was in its infancy in the 1980s. The development of AI and the rise of social media and tech platforms evolved together. This has produced very profitable companies that have become so powerful that nobody can compete with them, but they can compete with each other. These companies have come to dominate the global economy. They are multinational and their reach extends to every corner of the world. . . . This development has had far-reaching political consequences. It has sharpened the conflict between China and the United States and has given it an entirely new dimension. China has turned its tech platforms into national champions; the U.S. is more hesitant to do so because it worries about their effect on the freedom of the individual. . . . In theory, AI is morally and ethically neutral; it can be used for good or bad. But in practice, its effect is asymmetric. AI is particularly good at producing instruments of control that help repressive regimes and endanger open societies. Interestingly, the Coronavirus reinforced the advantage repressive regimes enjoy by legitimizing the use of personal data for public control purposes.[1]

What Soros describes has more than a grain of truth. But he overstates the alleged dichotomy between a Chinese Communist Party (CCP)-controlled China, and the supposedly "open" democratic republic that he apparently thinks still exists in America. He also fails to understand, or deliberately glosses over that, while Big Tech AI companies in China may be co-opted "champions" of the CCP, Big Tech AI companies in America are not really "champions" of this nation, but willing participants in ongoing attacks on the underpinnings and ideals of the country. Soros also ignores the implications of the fact that Big Tech AI companies operate globally rather than within a single nation's sovereign boundaries. America's Big Tech companies are not truly "American."

At best, America can be described as being a "one and a half" party nation as the Woke/CRT movement takes deeper and deeper hold. There can be no question that the emergence of the hugely powerful AI/internet platforms and social media have already and are still transforming this nation, not as neutral service providing mechanisms, but as willing and active "players" in the process of "destabilizing," "dismantling," and "transforming" America according to the Woke/CRT agenda and vision. What Soros is describing is an ideal America that, if it ever did exist in anything close to reality, no longer fits that supposedly multi-party "sorta" democratic description as we move toward greater and greater control.

Jeffrey Tucker, president of the Brownstone Institute, prolific author, and *Epoch Times* opinion columnist, offers an accurate explanation of what has taken place. He writes:

> The institutions on which we used to depend to defend our liberties and rights—nonprofits, courts, intellectuals, academia, tech, media—have failed spectacularly. We had no idea just how many of them had long ago been already captured. We did not know that feds were deeply embedded at Facebook, Instagram, Twitter, and LinkedIn. We did not know that they had already captured the news pages of the New York Times [*sic*] and so on. We thought that these institutions were merely ideologically biased. We did not know that they had become tools of the regime. . . . When the intellectuals and nonprofits went silent when lockdowns, mask mandates, and vaccine mandates came along, we thought that they were merely afraid to speak. We had not considered that their silence was evidence of a much deeper corruption. They were either being paid for silence or blackmailed into it.[2]

The Platforms Have Shifted from Innovation to Censorship and Propaganda as Tools for Shaping Their Desired System of Political Community

Yoshua Bengio, a professor at the Department of Computer Science and Operations Research at the Université de Montréal and scientific director of the Montreal Institute for Learning Algorithms, is a pioneer in the development of AI. Bengio has warned that the Big Tech companies are too large and powerful, and represent a serious threat to democracy itself. Bengio, like an increasing number of people concerned with the platforms' immense power to control information and messaging, urges that they should be broken up. He explained his position to Axios:

> [T]he concentration of resources, talent and knowledge among giant tech companies is only increasing and governments must act. "We need to create a more level playing field for people and companies," Bengio told Axios at an AI conference in Toronto last week.
>
> . . . [In saying that anti-trust laws need to be enforced, Bengio stated] "Governments have become so meek in front of companies," he said. "AI is a technology that naturally lends itself to a winner take all." . . . "The country and company that dominates the technology will gain more power with time. More data and a larger customer base gives you an advantage that is hard to dislodge. Scientists want to go to the best places. The company with the best research labs will attract the best talent. It becomes a concentration of wealth and power."[3]

Bengio is not alone in warning of the dangers of the powerful information dissemination and control platforms. Edward Snowden has also warned: "We have one company that has the ability to reshape the way we think."[4] Snowden said the degree to which people rely on Facebook for their news is dangerous.

> "When you get a Google in place, a Facebook in place, a Twitter in place, they never seem to leave." . . . "When one service provider makes a bad decision we all suffer for it. . . . The Silicon Valley desire for massive, world-eating services, the scale that takes over not only our country but all others, it's asking us to accept a status quo where we set aside that competition in favor of scale. We should be particularly cautious about embracing this and taking this to be the case."[5]

Part of what must occur is that, at least with the immensely powerful, intrusive, and wealthy media platforms, we must redefine what we think of as "government." A critical part of doing this involves basing our assessments on the degree of power any institution possesses, either in general, or more vital, in specific contexts such as the ability to control our communications, assemble and shape data, skew perception on large scale and subtle levels, and invade privacy.

Excessively concentrated and monopolistic power centers are unhealthy for any political system seeking to act as a democracy or democratic republic. Corporations are not really "people" regardless of legal doctrines. Corporations are "artificial" legal entities that exist only through law. In important ways they are creatures of the state, just as they were when first created as business actors under the authority and permission of the British Crown. They are empowered by the state to generate productive "goods" for the overall community, not to manipulate, undermine, shape, and control the nature of that community.

"Private" sector actors can become too powerful and pervasive to the point that they gain the ability to damage the community they were created to serve. That has happened with the online information control and dissemination platforms. That is what has occurred with Facebook, Amazon, Google, and Twitter. Mark Zuckerberg, Jeff Bezos, Sundar Pichai, and Twitter's (X) former CEO Jack Dorsey have become lost in their "utopian dream" about creating a perfect world. They have not been able to resist abusing the vast power of the online systems and information mechanisms they control. Their power must be limited or removed.

The Demise of the "Free-Floating" Intellectual

Russell Jacoby, in *The End of Utopia*, notes that it is not only a problem of knowing what to communicate but being willing to accept the consequences of our communications should what we say be unpopular. Jacoby writes that Karl Mannheim used the concept of the "free-floating" intellectual during the 1920s to describe individuals of independent mind who possessed the courage to critique power wherever their journey led. In discussing the disappearance of the independent intellectual, Jacoby observes that: "Benda's prescient *Betrayal*, which evoked the philosophes of the Enlightenment, might be seen as summarizing a tradition that was ending."[6]

Jacoby writes that even when first written: "Mannheim's defense of independent intellectuals earned him the ire of both left and right."[7] Truly independent thinking and critique have always been a threat to the preservation and acquisition of power. Honest critique shows the cracks and flaws in rhetoric and propaganda, and penetrates the illusions behind which power seeks to hide. Jacoby goes on to argue that: "Since Mannheim, the structural shifts that affect intellectuals have become so obvious that few can deny them. If Mannheim's analysis of the 'free-floating' intellectuals seemed questionable [even] in the late 1920s, almost 100 years later it is impossible."[8]

We are not dealing with a traditional monolithic aristocracy in modern Western society, but a kaleidoscopic tableau of ideological groups seeking power for themselves and seeking to neutralize or destroy anyone in their way. These movements are empowered by the internet and AI as their primary tool of organizing, communication, and attack on critics who question their agendas and motives.

The AI-enhanced internet has also become an intelligence gathering system. It allows the tracking of "enemies" and has become a potent weapon for attacking those enemies through intimidation, threats, insults, lies, smears, and petitions that create the impression of far greater support than often exists. Anyone seen as an obstacle to a power-seeking movement's actions, or simply those who do not fully agree with identity and interest group agendas, falls into the category of adversary and must be attacked.

Today's "intellectuals" are virtually all "attached" servants of power who have betrayed their purpose and identity. I often ask myself what happened to journalistic integrity. The First Amendment was designed to ensure a free press, and the purpose was so the press could seek the truth and inform us with honest facts and evidence. Instead we have witnessed the development of a communications media that does not provide "true" reports but "stories" that when looked at closely are little more than variations on op-ed essays filled with the individual biases and interpretations of so-called "journalists" serving the market demands of their sites' investors and patrons.

Academics Are Easily Intimidated

Nor is intimidation of scholars and teachers difficult. It occurs in a culture of "soft" extremism where tacit boundaries and taboo areas of inquiry have been established. Scholars and teachers quickly understand where the "no fly zones" of intellectual exploration and critique are located. As Columbia University's John McWhorter writes in *The Atlantic*:

> Our national reckoning on race has brought to the fore a loose but committed assemblage of people given to the idea that social justice must be pursued via attempts to banish from the public sphere, as much as possible, all opinions that they interpret as insufficiently opposed to power differentials. . . . [S]tatements questioning this program constitute a form of "violence" that merits shaming and expulsion.[9]

The campaigns of "canceling" and intimidation are working. McWhorter sums up the results of a survey done by the Heterodox Academy relating to how faculty would feel about expressing their views about controversial issues in front of other colleagues. The results indicate many people are silenced by the fear of possible negative reactions and even "cancelation."

> [T]he Heterodox Academy conducted an internal member survey of 445 academics. "Imagine expressing your views about a controversial issue while at work, at a time when faculty, staff, and/or other colleagues were present. To what extent would you worry about the following consequences?" To the hypothetical "My reputation would be tarnished," 32.68 percent answered "very concerned" and 27.27 percent answered "extremely concerned." To the hypothetical "My career would be hurt," 24.75 percent answered "very concerned" and 28.68 percent answered "extremely concerned." In other words, more

than half the respondents consider expressing views beyond a certain consensus in an academic setting quite dangerous to their career trajectory.[10]

McWhorter adds:

> Our national reckoning on race has brought to the fore a loose but committed assemblage of people given to the idea that social justice must be pursued via attempts to banish from the public sphere, as much as possible, all opinions that they interpret as insufficiently opposed to power differentials. . . . [S]tatements questioning this program constitute a form of "violence" that merits shaming and expulsion. . . . No one should feign surprise or disbelief that academics write to me with great frequency to share their anxieties. In a three-week period early this summer, I counted some 150 of these messages. And what they reveal is a very rational culture of fear among those who dissent, even slightly, with the tenets of the woke left.[11]

A Culture of Fear, Intimidation and Repression

The scope of what is occurring is what I sought to show in the publication of my book *"Un-Canceling" America* in 2021. All of the fundamental institutions and systems by which we communicate, compete, grow, learn, and create are being undermined. The political censoring and punishing tool of Cancel Culture is consuming our educational systems, and it is real. It is being used to compel agreement and silence, and its controllers are expanding its reach and societal penetration. It is a powerful tool for those who want to dismantle our nation and recreate it in a darker, bigoted, and repressive political image. Paul Rossi of the Grace Church School was chastised and shamed for speaking out.

> I was reprimanded for "acting like an independent agent of a set of principles or ideas or beliefs." And I was told that by doing so, I failed to serve the "greater good and the higher truth." The school's director of studies added that my remarks could even constitute harassment.

He further informed me that I had created "dissonance for vulner-able and unformed thinkers" and "neurological disturbance in stu-dents' beings and systems." . . . A few days later, the head of school ordered all high school advisors to read a public reprimand of my conduct out loud to every student in the school. It was a surreal expe-rience, walking the halls alone and hearing the words emitting from each classroom.[12]

This entire episode evokes in me a vision of Jesus dragging the cross on which he was to be crucified through the streets of Jerusalem while being whipped and wearing a "crown of thorns." The malevolence of the type of people who profess compassion and humanity but use their power to shame and torment is always stunning.

Rossi explains:

I raised questions about this ideology at a mandatory, whites-only student and faculty Zoom meeting. (Such racially segregated ses-sions are now commonplace at my school.) It was a bait-and-switch "self-care" seminar that labelled "objectivity," "individualism," "fear of open conflict" and even "a right to comfort" as characteristics of white supremacy. I doubted that these human attributes—many of them virtues reframed as vices—should be racialized in this way . . . when my questions were shared outside this forum, violating the school norm of confidentiality, I was informed by the head of the high school that my philosophical challenges had caused "harm" to students, given that these topics were "life and death matters, about people's flesh and blood and bone."[13]

"What violence is to the totalitarian state, propaganda is to democracy."

Noam Chomsky explains the view that what violence is to the totalitar-ian state, propaganda is to democracy. The point is that in a military or totalitarian state you can control people by force. But "in a democratic state you can't control them by force, so you'd better control them with propaganda—for their own good." The comments appear next and were made in a 1991 interview.

> **Q.** You have said that "propaganda is to democracy what violence is to the totalitarian state," which, of course, relates to what you are saying here.
>
> **A.** [T]here's a very intriguing line of thought in democratic theory that goes back certainly to the seventeenth-century English revolutions—sort of the first major modern democratic revolutions. There's been a recognition which becomes very explicit in the twentieth century, especially in the United States, that as the capacity to control people by force declines, you have to discover other means of control. Harold Lasswell, one of the founders of the modern area of communications in the political sciences, put it this way in the 1930s in an article on propaganda in the International Encyclopedia of Social Sciences: "We should not succumb to democratic dogmatism about men being the best judges of their own interests. They're not. We're the best judges." In a military state or what we would now call a totalitarian state, you can control people by force; in a democratic state you can't control them by force, so you'd better control them with propaganda—for their own good. Now this is a standard view; in fact, I suspect this is the dominant view among intellectuals.[14]

Walter Lippmann's "Specialized Class" and the "Manufacture of Consent"

Chomsky goes on to explain Walter Lippmann's view that a "specialized class" of expert intellectuals in service to power is an essential part of government. The purpose is to protect power and themselves from the dangers of the "mass of people out there who are the bewildered herd" who, left to themselves, would "trample" those in power. The analysis is striking for its description of what today we would think of in hearing Hillary Clinton attack half the population as "deplorable," with Joe Biden and the media savaging anyone they consider to be a populist MAGA supporter.

Q. Walter Lippmann's concept of "the manufacture of consent," is based on the idea that government distrusts the public's ability to make wise decisions and so it reserves real power for a "smart" elite who will make the "right decisions" and then create the illusion of public consensus.

A. Lippmann designed this notion of "manufacture of consent" as progress in the art of democracy, and he believed it was a good thing—and that's important. It's a good thing because, as he put it, "We have to protect ourselves from the rage and trampling of the bewildered herd." There's this mass of people out there who are the bewildered herd, and if we just let them go free—if we allow things like democracy, for example—there's just going to be rage and trampling because they're all totally incapable. The only people who are capable of running anything are we smart guys—what Lippmann called "the specialized class." He didn't add—something, again, which is tacitly understood—that we make it to the specialized class if we serve people with real power. So it's not that we're smarter; it's that we're more submissive. And we, the specialized class, the servants of power, have to save ourselves and our prestige and power from the rage and trampling of the bewildered herd. For that you need manufacture of consent because you can't shoot people down in the streets; you can't control them by force. In that respect, indoctrination is to democracy what a bludgeon is to totalitarianism.[15]

Chapter Eleven

Linguistic "Quicksand" and Linguistic "Cleansing"

Great power is obtained by being able to control the nature of the linguistic "quicksand" of what is deemed offensive at any particular moment and into which the unwary "trespasser" sinks. Daphne Patai argues that, "In feminist circles in particular, academic freedom is under attack by those who advocate and put into effect coercive sexual-harassment policies that are so broad, vague, and all-inclusive that their application routinely violates the due-process rights of the accused."[1]

Feminist scholar Mary Joe Frug explains the strategy of using imagery and shifting word meanings to "appropriate" power to the *Harvard Law Review*:

> "The liberal equality doctrine is often understood as an engine of liberation with respect to sex-specific rules. This imagery suggests the repressive function of law, a function that feminists have inventively sought to appropriate and exploit through critical scholarship, litigation, and legislative campaigns." Frug went on to say that: "This is not a proposal that we try to promote a benevolent and fixed meaning for sex differences. . . . Rather, the argument is that continuous interpretive struggles over the meaning of sex differences can have an impact on patriarchal legal power."[2]

Linguistic Cleansing Through Condemning Purportedly "White Values" Like "Rational Thinking," Intellectual Interaction, Precision, and Rigor

Those who control language control society. One way to control language is to use "open-textured" terms that appear reasonable, fair, and even moral on their face but that in fact have no intrinsic meaning. They are all entirely subjective terms into which the activist pours meaning that advances a specific political end designed to advance an agenda. This process may lack specific meaning but, if successful, replaces other possible meanings and controls the "linguistic field" by blocking other interpretations. "Diversity," "equity," and "inclusion" (DEI) are examples of an Orwellian strategy of linguistic cleansing. This includes "White supremacy," "privilege," "micro-aggression," "insensitivity," and much more.

You can, of course, ask, "Diversity of who and what?," and "What exactly, or even almost, do you mean when you say 'equity,' and being 'inclusive' also covers a lot of ground. Are we talking about full and total inclusivity, or do you have something very specific in mind that excludes other kinds of diversity? Plus, what are the criteria of who is included within the sphere of 'diversity' and who is excluded?"

The problem is that if you ask about such actual meaning and application to real systems of the terms, you are immediately condemned as a "racist" or "phobic bigot" of some sort. A real intent of DEI, CRT, and LGBTQ+ activists, etc. is to control and subjugate the "white" and "toxic male" components of American society. At least in one dimension, this agenda is stripping "people of color" of the skills and values needed for them to do well within our society as proud and skilled members of a system that, for decades, has been striving to be a fairer and more just system. It is also compressing and defining the creative richness of individual humans of whatever mixture into a rigid, narrow, and inevitably antagonistic "identity" that is being artificially created for purposes of gaining political power and control and has nothing to do with justice. Rich Lowry, in his *New York Post* article, "Woke claim that 'rational thinking' is a white male thing is both insulting and absurd," provides a sense of this counter-productive debacle in his analysis of an aspect of the attack on the University of Chicago's Dorian

Abbot for daring to criticize, or more accurately just ask questions about, DEI implementation at his university. Lowry explains:

> The *New York Times* ran a report on the canceling of University of Chicago geophysicist Dorian Abbot for his dissenting views on affirmative action. The paper quoted a Williams College geosciences professor, Phoebe A. Cohen, who supports Abbot's shunning. She explained her dim view of academic freedom thusly: "This idea of intellectual debate and rigor as the pinnacle of intellectualism comes from a world in which white men dominated." Ah, yes, that poisoned fruit of the patriarchy—intellectual debate and rigor.
>
> Of all the faddish notions blighting college campuses and the broader culture, it is among the most indefensible and self-destructive. Start with the fact that to reason is deeply human. Steven Pinker points out in his new book "Rationality" [*sic*] that one of the world's oldest people, the San of the Kalahari Desert in southern Africa, don't survive by happenstance. These hunter-gatherers make closely reasoned, evidence-based judgments about their prey; without the use of logic, they wouldn't be successful. If someone told them they needed to give up all this reasoning and cede it to white males, they'd presumably react with fury and incomprehension. Needless to say, other cultures and civilizations are capable of great intellectual rigor. It doesn't require endorsing the fashionable theories that the West invented nothing and rose to preeminence through colonialism and theft to acknowledge the historic achievements of China, India and the Islamic world.
>
> The implication that women and minorities somehow aren't as capable of rigorous thought as white males, or shouldn't be as interested in it, is deeply insulting. This is taking one of the worst beliefs of the Western past, dressing it up in the rhetoric of diversity and inclusion, and pretending it's somehow a blow for progress. What's the alternative to intellectual debate and rigor? Superstition, personal preference and, ultimately, sheer power. It's the latter that the woke critics of Western reason believe they can wield to crush their enemies, facts and logic be damned.[3]

Forcing Continuous Interpretive Struggles over Language Is a Strategy to Confuse, Make Uncertain, and Keep the "Enemy" Off Balance

Control of the allowable language of discourse is a critical element of political strategy. As part of our calculated political advocacy, we speak in code and false tongues. We shape our words to gain political goals that put power at the center, not truth. Everything becomes goal-oriented, and the goal is neither truth nor understanding, but control and the furtherance of political ends. Outcome is the dominant factor, not intellect, honesty, and insight. This is what the university has become.

Control of the language of discourse not only provides the concepts that can be used but also inhibits the use of disfavored concepts. This is an inevitable process in a general political community, particularly one constructed by postmodernists intent on using their power to construct their own "truths." The question is the degree to which this kind of control is desirable or appropriate in the university. It is not. Universities have a duty not only to the immediate society, but to the past and future. This includes the duty to resist strategies aimed at controlling intellectual freedom and discourse.

Speech suppression, propaganda, and Cancel Culture aren't about truth. They aren't even about taking real offense at what is being said or done by those unfortunate enough to be "canceled." Virtually all of the faux "outrage" screamed by the Woke is tactical. The purpose is to put others on the defensive, uncertain about whether what they said or did was wrong, and still subject to feeling shamed by their accusers. Language manipulation of the kind we are experiencing about such things as discrimination, phobias, micro-aggressions, proper use of pronouns relative to an individual's identity preferences, subconscious bias, etc., are all about power.

Psychological projection is the technique of the day. Truth doesn't matter. The "battle" is everything. The projection strategy of false or grossly overstated accusation is internalized by those who are part of the mass after experiencing continual repetition of propaganda iterations on social media and in the press. Given that studies indicate as many as 86 percent of Americans now obtain their news about what is occurring from social media sources, the often biased and even false reports and links sent around among identity group members and activist journalists offer a one-sided and skewed view of reality.

Wokes and Crits Want to Do Away with the "White Oppressor's" Tools, like "Rationalism, the Rule of Law, and Private Ownership of Property"

The use and abuse of language for political advantage is everywhere. One example, to its everlasting shame and discredit, is offered by the National Education Association (NEA). In endorsing Critical Race Theory in schools, the NEA pledged to fight against anti-CRT speech and to: "issue a study that 'critiques empire, white supremacy, anti-Blackness, anti-Indigeneity, racism, patriarchy, cisheteropatriarchy, capitalism, ableism, anthropocentrism, and other forms of power and oppression at the intersections of our society.'"

You can't make this up, but at least the NEA has company as evidenced by a poster display offered by the Museum of African American History and Culture, part of the Smithsonian Institute. The Museum put up a poster a year or so ago stating that "white culture" includes things like "nuclear family," "self-reliance," "rigid time schedule," and "delayed gratification." One critic responded that the poster was "despicable" and the Museum removed the poster. But the removal does not change the mindset of what we are facing, nor does it change the underlying message that such values are supposedly possessed by a specific ethnic group of "all Whites wherever found." That false racist narrative is designed to create a "revolutionary enemy" to energize "the revolutionary struggle."[4]

Ayaan Hirsi Ali Exposes Wokeism as Seeking "Unchecked and Absolute Power"

In an article that appeared in the *Wall Street Journal* on September 11, 2020, Ayaan Hirsi Ali compared America's Wokeism and Islamic Jihadism through her unique lens created through what occurred in her journey of abandoning Islam, leaving Africa and her family, becoming a member of the Netherlands parliament, while under a death sentence imposed by Muslim fanatics for what they saw as her heresy. She then migrated to America and is serving a prominent role in the Hoover Institute:

> The main goal of the woke is to seek unchecked and absolute power, advancing from the academy and out into other institutions of society," Ali [said]. "In America, and the rest of the English-speaking world, it is no issue of any significance that we can discuss in any meaningful way without running into woke sabotage. One reason why it's difficult to pin down wokeism is that the theories of [philosophical] deconstruction are constantly expanding with grievance after grievance," Ali said. . . . "If you can pin an idea, you can expose it . . . But if its meaning keeps shifting, with the grievance of the day, it becomes elusive. It's not social justice theory. Weirdly, though, it's not a theory at all . . . You can't treat it like other theories that is by taking it through the process of scrutiny for certification or verification." Ali asserted that a "key element" of wokeism is the "contamination of language," pointing to its "lexicon" of terms like "microaggressions, safe spaces" and "equity." And that existing language is "policed" by the woke "to become purified of any perceived bigotry or injustice."[5]

If We "Cave" to the "Pronoun Police" and the "Linguistic Social-Engineers" the Battle Is Over

Linguist Ruth Nanda Anshen offers a vital insight in explaining that humans do not only "use" language but "become" the language they use, even to the extent it defines their identity and sets limits on their ability to perceive and interpret reality. She explains: "man is that being on earth who does not have language. Man is language."[6] When this occurs, particularly with activist collectives, "their" language becomes "their" personal reality, one they zealously seek to impose on the "unenlightened masses." Nicholas Land offers the insight of William Jacobson on this issue.

Cornell Law Professor William A. Jacobson warned that colleges and universities are "manifesting authoritarianism" by removing "problematic" words and firing staff that don't abide by left-wing ideologies. Jacobson said he believes the increase in stories about word-banning on college campuses is a manifestation of what is referred to as "repressive tolerance," wherein tolerance serves to preserve a repressive society by neutralizing opposition to impose forms of authoritarianism. "They monitor your language, they get you to use language that only they approve, and once you've done that with somebody, once you've done that with a campus, that's enormous control," he said.[7]

This may seem subtle, but it represents why the Woke/CRT movement has been continually inventing new language and defining what they consider "correct" contexts for the use of existing language we are supposedly obligated to use. This also applies to language we are required to abandon. The point is multi-faceted. Once you allow an interest group to have control over language, you have granted power to that group. It is being endowed with the power to define the terms of engagement. When that happens, the rest of us are always "walking on eggshells" lest we suffer the "wrath of the Woke" and be condemned as bigoted or phobic.

Another point consistent with Anshen's insight that we "become" the language we use is that our reality, as defined by the language we use, is reshaped into the vision desired by the Woke Identity group. It feels as if we have somehow been drawn into the plot of the 1957 movie *The Three Faces of Eve* in which a woman who is suffering from severe headaches and inexplicable blackouts goes to a psychiatrist to be helped. She amazes the doctor when, under treatment, including hypnosis, she displays dramatic shifts between three fundamentally different personalities. One is a housewife. Another is an extremely sexy woman, and the third is the ultra-practical Jane. The diagnosis was Multiple Personality Disorder, and the plot is based on a real life individual who reportedly displayed twenty-two distinct personalities during her life. With the "language games" being played by the Woke/CRT activists, it seems like we are playing out a larger and more destructive version of "Eve" in our everyday reality.

With all the claims about gender fluidity we are now hearing, it feels like we are "extras" in an incredibly complex cinematic project. Think of the effects of "ne, ve, ze/zie and xe pronouns." Do the same on cisgender, micro-aggressions, White privilege, systemic racism, the they/them, we and like usages. These are not only neutral words. They are control mechanisms, and substantive propositions about "things" that are altering our perception of gender, race interaction, and social and political behavior. Once internalized, they cede control over "us" and our perception of reality to groups that are deliberately using language as a strategic device to advance their political agendas and gain greater power. It is a political strategy—and it works, both offensively to force your agenda into widespread use, and defensively to undermine and degrade any other interpretations.

The "Purity Spiral" and "Virtue Signaling"

Roger Kimball describes what is happening in terms of the "Purity Spiral" and "virtue signaling." He equates the behavior we are experiencing in America with that of China during the Cultural Revolution and the savagery of the Red Guards.

> The journalist Gavin Haynes has a great phrase for a familiar and disturbing phenomenon: the purity spiral. "A purity spiral occurs," he writes, "when a community becomes fixated on implementing a single value that has no upper limit, and no single agreed interpretation. The result is a moral feeding frenzy." In the late 1960s, the Red Guards took to the street to identify and destroy anyone and anything involved with traditional Chinese culture. The result was an orgy of destruction and murder on an industrial scale. . . . The purity spiral is also a search for enemies, a concerted effort to divide the world between the tiny coterie of the blessed and the madding crowd of the damned. The game, Haynes notes, "is always one of purer-than-thou." . . . Writing in the magazine *New York*, the commentator Andrew Sullivan notes the prominent role that language—that is, the effort to police language—plays in the economy of coercion.

"Revolutionaries," he writes, "create new forms of language to dismantle the existing order."[8]

Kimball goes on to provide several examples of how the "dismantling" of the "existing order" and its institutions proceeds. These include "white supremacy," "women," "oppression," and "racism" or "racist," along with "structural racism."

The use of the term 'white supremacy' to mean not the KKK or the antebellum South but American society as a whole in the [twenty-first] century has become routine on the left, as if it were now beyond dispute. The word 'women,' J.K. Rowling had the temerity to point out, is now being replaced by "people who menstruate." The word "oppression" now includes not only being herded into Uighur reeducation camps but also feeling awkward as a sophomore in an Ivy League school. The word 'racist', which was widely understood quite recently to be prejudicial treatment of an individual based on the color of their skin, now requires no intent to be racist in the former sense, just acquiescence in something called 'structural racism' which can mean any difference in outcomes among racial groupings. Being color-blind is therefore now being racist. "[T]here is no escaping this. The woke shift their language all the time, so that words that were one day fine are now utterly reprehensible. You can't keep up—which is the point. . . . The result is an exercise of cultural power through linguistic distortion."[9]

Compelled Sessions on "Sensitivity," "Admit Your Guilt" and "Privilege" Are Clearly Intended As "Re-Programming" and Control

Heather Higgins is chairwoman of the Independent Women's Forum. She suggests pointedly that the various mandated sessions on sensitivity, acceptable, speech, word use, guilt, and Maoist self-flagellation and submission to the Left's narrative is a dishonest move to capture power. Higgins writes:

the left's current narrative of "unity" is coming across to the other side as being asked to "accept guilt" and "shut up." . . . But she said the unity they're talking about is "'you need to accept guilt for anything that we say that you need to accept guilt for,' even if you're not guilty; 'you need to shut up, and you just need to go along with and comply with our point of view.'"[10]

Florida International University's Re-Invention of Allowable Language through DEI Control

As the following analysis indicates, like all good Marxists and followers of Orwell, capturing allowable language is central to gaining control and keeping any opposition off guard. The situation at Florida International University and numerous other institutions demonstrate just how bizarre is a world with a fixation on pronouns to the extent that they mainly suggest a serious emotional problem. Christopher Rufo, a leading critic of Critical Race Theory, discusses this in the context of Florida International University.

> This project of ideological capture begins with language. The university's DEI bureaucrats have published an official "Inclusive Language Guide" that condemns some of the most common words in the English language, such as "husband," "wife," "mother," "father," "Mr.," "Mrs.," "she," and "he" as "non-inclusive." In their place, the university suggests, students should use gender-neutral substitutes such as "partner," "spouse," "parents," and "caregivers," and neologisms such as "Mx." and "they/them" for a singular person. The point is not to generate stable and accurate language, but to undermine the basic grammar of life, thus softening the ground for political change. Next, the DEI administrators create internal cadres by recruiting students into publicly subsidized left-wing activism. To this end, FIU offers various programs, such as the Social Justice Badge Program, which recruit, train, and deploy student activists with the goal of implementing the "redistribution of power" and achieving "equity," or equal outcomes.[11]

The University of Washington's "Language Guide"

There must actually be people who never sleep who are devoting their lives to figuring out and condemning words they can decry as "offensive." My sense is that a significant majority of the people they are supposedly "defending" against perceived insult have no idea they are supposed to be hurt or angry until they are informed of that fact by a bunch of "Woke" students, insulated academics, and activists. There could be no better example of this mindset than that provided by the recent "language guide" prepared at the University of Washington. Adam Sabes reports:

> A University of Washington language guide is calling everyday words used by Americans "problematic." The University of Washington Information Technology department released an "*inclusive language guide*" that lists a number of "problematic words" that are "racist," "sexist," "ageist," or "homophobic." According to the guide, words such as "grandfather," "housekeeping," "minority," "ninja," and "lame" are considered "problematic words." For example, the language guide states that the word "lame" is considered problematic because it's "ableist." "This word is offensive, even when it's used in slang for uncool because it's using a disability in a negative way to imply that the opposite, which would be not lame, to be superior," the guide states.
>
> The guide also states that the term "minority" implies a 'less than' attitude toward a certain community. "When 'minority' is used to refer to other races or abilities, used as a generalized term for 'the other' and implies a 'less than' attitude toward the community or communities being discussed," the guide states. The guide considers "grandfather" a "problematic word" because the term was "used as a way to exempt some people from a change because of conditions that existed before the change." "'Grandfather clause' originated in the American South in the 1890s as a way to defy the 15th Amendment and prevent black Americans from voting," the guide explains. "Housekeeping," is another "problematic" word that the guide recommends should be avoided by others working in the information technology industry because it can "feel gendered."

Phrases with "man" such as "manpower," "man hours," or "man-in-the-middle" are considered "not inclusive" and "thus sexist." The language guide also considers "preferred pronouns" as "problematic" because the term "preferred" suggests that "a person's pronoun is optional." Language such as "no can do," "spirit animal," and separating groups based on certain colors is "racist" or culturally appropriative. According to the language guide, using "red," "white," or "yellow" to separate different teams is based on "racist tropes." "Using colors based as racist tropes—labelling [*sic*] 'white' as good, 'black' as bad, 'red' as attackers, or 'yellow' as excluded third parties—is offensive," the guide states.[12]

Stanford University's "Anti-American" Language Guide

Stanford can't seem to "keep from shooting itself in the foot." What had developed as one of America's top universities is consistently showing it is populated by a bunch of functionally illiterate students, faculty, and administrators from the perspective of awareness, quality of thought, and concern about what is happening to the country that ironically conferred great "privileges" on them simply because they are at "Stanford."

As if Scott Atlas, Jay Bhattacharya, the continuing dislike of the Hoover Institution connection and its collection of real intellects such as Ayaan Hirsi Ali and Victor Davis Hanson, and numerous others does not provide a "seasoning" to the "wokeness" of the overall faculty, we now have the recent effort to "Cancel America" as a part of the nation's language. Bryan Jung offers a description of the initial effort. While the university backed away from that condemnation for political reasons, it provides insight into the administrative and faculty mindset.

Stanford University administrators published a guide to "harmful language" that calls for the elimination of words including "man" and "American." The university created an index of forbidden words that it plans on eliminating from its websites and computer code, with a list of alternative terms to replace them with. The index insists that "pronouns" be used instead of "'preferred' pronouns" because "the word 'preferred' suggests that non-binary gender identity is a choice and a preference." Traditional descriptions like "freshman," "fireman," and "congresswoman" are out the door because of "gender binary language" reasons. Language suggesting violence was also discouraged, including "beating a dead horse," "pull the trigger," "trigger warning," and "killing two birds with one stone." . . . Students and staff are strongly discouraged from calling themselves "American" and are instead told to use the term "U.S. citizen," because it would, according to the index, be an insult to people from the rest of the Americas. The index notes that the Americas comprises [forty-two] countries and that using the term "American," refers only to citizens of the United States, which, according to the index, suggests that other countries in the Western Hemisphere have less merit."[13]

The "Your Words Threatened Me and Made Me Feel 'Unsafe'" Strategy

The mission of the university is being undermined by the heightened sensitivity levels claimed by students, faculty, and administrators. They claim to be hurt, threatened, in fear of their personal safety, or offended by almost anything. While this hyper-sensitivity may be real for some extremely fragile people, imagined by others because they have learned such expressions are "insensitive," part of a "mob mentality," or faked as a political ploy, the "appropriation" and linguistic control movement is remarkable in its scope, effectiveness, and import. (See my online Berkely Electronic Press analysis *Language Control, 'Hyper-Sensitivity' and the Death of True Liberalism* to learn more.)[14]

One of the most powerful and effective ruses being employed is the highly subjective accusation that something an individual says or does produces fear, apprehension, offense, or discomfort in a listener or reader. Most of what is occurring is part of a strategy to control the narrative. We often hear that a person's statements are being condemned because someone alleges they made "them" feel "less safe," "threatened," or "offended." I believe that many of the outraged reactions are strategies done to gain political advantage rather than actual feelings of the complaining persons. "Fake offensiveness"—or "OMG I am so hurt and offended"—occurs because it is the ammunition by which interest groups fight our ongoing political guerrilla war.

Bias Reporting Systems

A serious problem with what are being called "Bias reporting systems" based on subjective perceptions, interest group definitions of what kinds of expressions are seen as offensive or insulting, or are open-textured terms in which the intention and meaning are in the "eye" of the individual perceiver create a situation in which virtually anything can be seen as biased, insensitive, or offensive. This type of system chills speech for many because of the overriding subjectivity involved in human perception, not to mention the ways in which claims of bias can be used as political weapons. The examples offered next demonstrate some of the problems with such systems.

"Stanford Professors Push Back on University-Encouraged Student Informant Culture"

After what the 85 percent Stanford Faculty Senate did in voting to condemn Scott Atlas's positions taken in service to Donald Trump's reaction to the COVID-19 virus, it is absolutely ironic, and contemptible, that many of the university's faculty suddenly realized they could be subject to the same levels of accusation and inquiry. While they had no problem violating Atlas's rights to fair consideration of his views, the Stanford faculty had no problems seeking to protect their own actions. The following report shows this with clarity. It relates to a student and administrative effort to create a complaint system for students to make claims of bias against faculty and other students, even anonymously.

> A group of Stanford professors is calling for an end to a system on campus that allows students to anonymously report on each other for what they perceive to be biased or discriminatory conduct. At least [seventy-seven] professors recently sent a petition to Stanford administrators, arguing that the university's online reporting system, called Protected Identity Harm (PIH) Reporting, threatens free speech on

campus and provides an opportunity for abuse. . . . Stanford Business School professor Ivan Marinovic told the news source that the University's bias-reporting system "reminded him of the way citizens were encouraged to inform on one another" in the communist governments of the Soviet Union, East Germany, and China. "It ignores the whole history," he said. "You're basically going to be reporting people who you find offensive, right? According to your ideology." Ironically, the practice of free speech is what provoked the professors to act. [T]he school's student newspaper, The Stanford Daily, reported about a Snapchat screenshot showing a fellow student reading "Mein Kampf"—the autobiographical manifesto written by Nazi Party leader and orchestrator of the Holocaust, Adolf Hitler—that circulated around campus until finally at least one person reported the incident through the school's PIH reporting system.[15]

Another Example: Bias Reporting at the University of Wisconsin-Milwaukee

The University of Wisconsin-Milwaukee (UWM) updated its bias reporting system (BRS) following a legal demand letter sent by Southeastern Legal Foundation's (SLF) which warned that the university's BRS infringed on students First Amendment freedom of speech. The university's bias reporting system encourages students and faculty who have experienced an incident of bias or hate to submit a report to the institution's Office of Equity/Diversity Services. Previously on its website, UWM did not explain that hate speech and offensive speech are protected by the First Amendment and that students cannot be punished for engaging in so-called hate speech.

Bias reporting systems "unconstitutionally chill freedom of expression because they allow anyone on campus to report students for perceived bias incidents," leading students to self-censor for fear they will be punished for offending other students, SLF wrote. "Bias reporting systems have become a tool to scare conservative students into silence because they are typically the ones engaging in open debate and discourse," SLF General Counsel Kimberly Hermann said. . . . UWM updated its website to clarify that students who are reported for the words that they say, will not be punished.[16]

Chapter Twelve

Orwell and "Protective Stupidity"

We can all wish George Orwell's classic *1984* were merely a work of fiction and political fantasy, but Orwell was a true prophet. He grasped all too well the inherent nature of authoritarian true believers, and the societies they will always create if given power. What is going on has spread throughout America's educational and political society, and is aimed at the shaping of the immature, impressionable, and fertile minds of our children. This is being done through widespread educational strategies introduced to very young kids as early as the beginning of their K-12 formal education.

"Ethnic cleansing" represents tragic situations where a specific ethnic identity group seeks to "cleanse" a territory of competing or different identity groups. We are experiencing language control strategies that are fairly described as "linguistic cleansing." The aim of "linguistic cleansing" is to gain power over others' speech. Done well, this re-engineers a culture into the form desired by the identity groups implementing the strategy.

Language is a mechanism by which a society generates an aura of shared duties and rights. One-sided control of language grants significant power. If I can make or influence you to say whatever I want, or inhibit you from saying or even being able to think about alternatives, then I "own" you. When deployed effectively, the "linguistic weapon" bypasses rational thought and penetrates directly on the levels where we experience emotion, fear, hope, "otherness," and bias.

When you achieve control of language, you are able to dictate how people are able to see the world. "The protective stupidity" in *1984* offers an example of thought control. "Protective stupidity" prevents people from being able to follow any train of thought that could lead them in a heretical direction. Punishing heretics and deviants, as well as anyone who fails to shun them, is an essential part of thought control and the silencing of free and independent thinking. Even if an individual might be able to counter the dominant narrative, at a minimum it sends a powerful message that it would be much safer to go along with the group.

What has taken place in America in the context of Wokeism and Critical Race Theory is that "hyper-sensitive" identity groups have been granted a quasi-governmental power they should never possess. This highly subjective power allows them to define and determine what "insults" or "offends" their members and even what comprises biological and psychological reality. This transfers not only the defensive power to ward off critical attacks, but provides an offensive weapon to acquire greater power.

The coordinated strategies relying on accusations of "hate," "insult," "racism," misogyny, "insensitivity," or one of the other invented "phobias" have produced a society in which hate has intensified, perceived or claimed insult is everywhere, and insensitivity and incivility abound. While we might have thought that this approach was intended to create a more understanding and benign result, the reality is that it has caused enormous divisiveness and generated increasing social friction. Sadly, this was the intention all along.

Linguistic Cleansing, "Protective Stupidity," and "Crimestop"

Once we submit to a system that imposes limits on our speech and minds, we are walking a path that denies the very point of America's existence. That national purpose involves developing ourselves to the highest level of which we are capable, with the belief that through that process of self-awareness and growth we are each contributing to the evolution of an exciting and dynamic community. Becoming obedient drones in a repressive hive controlled by authoritarians totally contradicts that dynamic. "Crimestop" and "protective stupidity" are key factors in tyrants having that control.

Crimestop is "a necessary mental discipline for good party members in *1984*. Good party members have no private emotions; they are in a state of constant enthusiasm about the goals set by the state. Even children can learn to avoid thinking any thoughts deemed dangerous by the state." The first and simplest stage in the discipline, which can be taught even to young children, is called, in Newspeak, "Crimestop." Crimestop means the faculty of stopping short, as though by instinct, at the threshold of any dangerous thought. It includes the power of not grasping analogies, of failing to perceive logical errors, of misunderstanding the simplest arguments if they are inimical to [the approved system], and of being bored or repelled by any train of thought which is capable of leading in a heretical direction. Crimestop, in short, means protective stupidity.[1]

"Hate" speech prohibitions endanger the liberty of discourse that is at the base of our democratic republic. A key element in the "shaping" is the necessity of punishing linguistic deviants until everyone "gets the message." "Canceling" and "political correctness" are important tools for achieving broad control. Central to the ability to control people is the creation of powerful propaganda systems. Universities and K-12 schools are critical mechanisms for spreading the desired message and for suppressing conflicting views.

Christopher Rufo describes to the *Epoch Times* how the Woke/CRT activists are hiding behind a "revolving language system that they use to confuse, that they use to avoid, and that they use to obfuscate":

"There's this revolving language system that they use to confuse, that they use to avoid, and that they use to obfuscate," Rufo said. "They're deploying it because they refuse to defend critical race theory on the merits, because even they know that it's indefensible politically." The presence of critical race theory (CRT) in K-12 education has become a prominent issue in some of the nation's recent high-profile elections. . . . CRT interprets society through a Marxist dichotomy between "oppressor" and "oppressed," but replaces the class categories with racial groups. . . . Parents Defending Education, a parent-led non-profit organization, has documented hundreds of such cases from across the country. For example, a class of third-graders at a San Jose, California, elementary school was instructed to "deconstruct their racial identities," then rank themselves according to the "power and privilege" they supposedly possess.[2]

One result is that the propaganda and thematic framing with which we are being inundated converts us into angry "golem." We surrender our individuality, minds, and soul when we become inextricably tied to an intensive "in" group. We become opposed to anyone our identity group sees as "the other," even to the point that we consider those others to be inferior or the "enemy." This mindset is a predictable and inevitable result of creating "identity groups." Such groups quickly become quasi-religious sects whose members see others as heretics and blasphemers. When that occurs, we no longer have a collaborative community with the ability and willingness to negotiate compromises and mutually beneficial outcomes. Society becomes comprised of fragmented power clusters and "micro-societies" with intractable and competing agendas.

Fragmentation and conflict take place because our own identity group's *language* defines not only *how* we see what we consider reality, but how we are *able* to see the world. Our group's "socially constructed language" no longer translates into the "socially constructed language" being used by our opponents, our enemies, or even by those who simply do not support our agenda and demands.

Social Engineering and Division

The nature of the university as an institution whose intellectual and knowledge ideal is aimed at making the greatest contributions to its community depends on offering the widest and deepest bodies of knowledge across a range of areas, as well as the training required to evaluate and utilize that knowledge with precision and qualitative assessment and interaction. It is folly to tell people in a nation founded on free speech, association, disagreement, debate, and argument to "shut up" lest they be punished and condemned as heretics. Yet that is what is happening. Manipulation of language in ways that I am labeling "linguistic cleansing" has been joined with the tools of Cancel Culture to punish, silence, and control. This is explored at length in my 2021 book, *"Un-Canceling" America*.

The political censoring and use of Cancel Culture and language shaping to ostracize "heretics" is consuming our educational systems, and it is very real. It is being used to compel agreement and to intimidate and silence anyone who doesn't manifest full agreement with the Woke message. Its controllers are steadily expanding their reach and penetration within the university, in the K-12 educational system, and throughout America's other fundamental institutions.

This strategy of creating division and "re-engineering" the individual person and society is being used by identity groups who, in their own words, want to "disrupt," "dismantle," and "transform" our nation and its people. A core part of this dismantling requires that we see America as evil, bigoted, racist, and largely unredeemable.

A significant number of those driving the Woke/Critical Race Theory movement forward are academics, administrators, and impassioned "identity" activists whose population in the universities has grown dramatically. Their ranks are further sustained by strong relationships with private sector organizations in which many of the university activists had worked. The result is that a shared political agenda has been brought into the educational process.

While many of the academics and activists who profess their "wokeness" often have extremely limited experience and knowledge about how to build and construct things, they have exhibited surprising skill at attacking and dismembering what exists. It is like the mid-1920 and 1930s European Deconstructionists that French political philosopher François Furet described as helping assist the Marxist presence in Europe after the creation of the Soviet Union. Their job was to undermine the foundations of Western society by emphasizing their faults and abuses and denigrating their ideals.

"Tearing down" through one-sided critiques of the inevitable imperfections of a complex system is a relatively simple matter. This is what the Woke are doing in America's universities and other institutional systems.

Effective and creative building of strong economic and social systems is far more difficult.

The *Cambridge Dictionary* Redefines the Meaning of Man and Woman

Language is not simply words. Language is the lens through which we perceive and interpret reality. What has been happening over the past twenty-five years or so is not simply a refining of dictionary terms, but an effort to redefine fundamental reality. The problem for any society that has had its own clear reality for centuries is that sudden "tectonic" shifts in the purported meaning of fundamental elements of a society's perceived reality is going to create intense conflict. The fact that a significant majority of a nation's people has trouble with an identity group's fundamental recreations of the reality with which they have always lived does not mean that the "traditionalists" are racist or bigots. It means they don't agree with you. There needs to be legitimate and intelligent interaction on matters of great social importance that various identity groups are forcing all others to accept as "truths." The *Cambridge Dictionary* re-definition of man and woman offers an example.

> *Cambridge Dictionary* is being criticized by conservatives on social media for altering the definitions of the words "man" and "woman" to include people who identify as a gender other than their biological sex. The definition of woman, which previously represented the longstanding view on sex, now states that a woman is "an adult who lives and identifies as female though they may have been said to have a different sex at birth." Similarly, a man is now defined as "an adult who lives and identifies as male though they may have been said to have a different sex at birth."[3]

We Need to Demand that the "Revolutionaries" Clearly Explain What "Higher" Values They Offer to Replace the "Systemically Racist" "White" Values

If such alleged "White values" are keys to "White supremacy" and "White privilege," and we honestly believe those to be bad and oppressive across the board, then we must abandon them and adopt other values. But what are those new values we must adopt? Should we reject the nuclear family, as was stated in Black Lives Matter Global Network Foundation's online organizational statement? Just how "bad" dependence on the nuclear family structure is for healthy societies deserves some discussion. Social and economic data about the advantages strong families create for society and family members routinely show that intact families are stronger economic engines than any alternatives.

Should we not seek to be "self-reliant" and in charge of our lives to the extent of our capability? If neither family structures nor self-reliance are preferred ideals, what replaces them? From where do these presumably "better" replacement values come, and is the proper approach in abandoning the "White" values a search for the opposite? Should we, for example, adopt the value of being heavily reliant on others who are themselves attempting to avoid being "self" reliant? This creates the dilemma that, if you exchange self-reliance for "other reliance" have you not simply created another dependency relationship and, if so, why bother?

It is one thing to attack and quite another to offer legitimate alternatives. Any reasonably intelligent person can shred any society for its imperfections. There is plenty of ammunition to go around. Take a moment to think about what the mantras of "White guilt," "systemic racism," and "White privilege" actually do to the internal dynamics and relationships of a political community. Consider for just a moment what it means to condemn values and ideals such as "Individualism," "being goal oriented," "insisting on reason and rational thought," being "self-confident," "seeking answers," "believing in objectivity," having a "sense of urgency," "prizing reading and writing," "worshipping the written word," saying America is a "land of opportunity," believing that "capability" and "merit" are legitimate factors in who gets jobs, "working hard," or not being "humble." These are all attacked as White Supremacy values and as automatically racist.

It is fair to ask: What are the "non-White" replacement values? Are we to be a "collective" or "hive"? Should we avoid planning for our future well-being, operate according to fully emotional factors rather than logic, or not worry about having evidence for our conclusions? Similarly, should we give up on reason, logic, and objectivity, or be hesitant or insecure in what we do and say—because we are told that self-confidence is a "White value"? Nor should we apparently ever be proud of what we have accomplished, because humility is a virtue.

Similarly, if we are rejecting the concept of being in charge of our lives, just who is supposed to be in charge of our fate and well-being? Within this argument is the barely hidden possibility of being controlled by an authoritarian order whose controllers are totally convinced they know "what is best" for us and compel us to comply with their dictates or suffer the consequences. For revealing histories of this approach, we might look at Hitler's *Mein Kampf*, Mao Zedong's *Little Red Book*, or Xi Jinping's *Thought on Socialism with Chinese Characteristics for a New Era* as precautionary reminders about what happens when fanatical ideologues gain full control.

Demagogues such as Ibram Kendi, who is making a fortune off "anti-racism," are the ultimate racists. What is unfolding is one of the most cynical, intellectually vacant, and morally asinine assertions I have ever encountered. What is amazing is that the "Woke, Crit, Radical Progressive Triumvirate" is getting away with spewing their garbage. We are letting them make incredibly bad faith claims without treating those claims with the contempt they deserve. The tragedy is that most people are refusing to simply come out and say that "the Woke/CRT Emperor has no clothes." They are grifters and scam artists who have successfully used accusations of racism and discrimination to intimidate and shame. The rewards they have gained are secure and lucrative jobs throughout America's entire educational system, including universities, status and prestige, power, and the ability to transform America into a mediocre and divided nation.

Chapter Thirteen

The "Argument Culture"

The Societal Distortions Caused by Fanaticism, Rage, and Hate

Albert Camus described the danger of giving in to rage and hate in his "Defense of Intelligence" speech:

> After four years of continual repression, atrocities, and collaboration by many French with evil, "[w]e were left with the rage that consumes our souls at the memory of certain images and certain faces. The executioners' hatred engendered the victims' hatred. And once the executioners had gone, the French were left with their hatred only partially spent." He concluded, "it is essential that we never let criticism descend to insult; we must grant that our opponent may be right and that in any case his reasons, even though bad, may be disinterested. It is essential, in short, that we remake our political mentality."[1]

A simple formula is that "rage empowers, rage blinds, and rage frightens." The work of activist scholars who see themselves as part of an identity group that has historically been oppressed is a "scholarship of rage" with heightened levels of indignation and resentment. Open and honest discourse is chilled not only by control of language but by the natural desire most of us possess to avoid unpleasant conflict. Scholarship and teaching based on passion and rage at some very real injustices—as well as conditions perceived as unjust but that may or may not be—is not objective. To overcome this obstacle, the Woke and Critical "scholars" have denied the validity of ideas such as objectivity, rationality, the need for clear evidence and data, individualism, and the like. They assert such requirements are nothing more than tools to preserve "White male privilege."

Deep-seated rage, often subconscious and masked even from our-selves, makes us highly subjective. This subjectivity changes the character and tone of the scholar's work and teaching as well as student interaction and participation. While such rage-based work will often be admirable in its eloquence and passion, there are problems with its balance and objec-tivity. This can be a particular problem once the scholar is past the point of stating the depth of the problem with which virtually all of us will agree, such as the absolute evil of slavery wherever found, and moves to issues of causation, accountability, and solutions.

The "Argument Culture" Cares Only About Power and Outcome

The intensity, ideological nature, and passion of the several "righteous" movements—along with the general effects and trends of academic Leftism—have pressed knowledge into the service of increasingly intol-erant political activists. Those activists were only able to gain power through forcefully asserting the compelling need for tolerance. Yet, once that "shaming" of academic traditionalists achieved its goals, tolerance as a virtue disappeared.

For a strong portrayal of modern academic culture as based on dishon-est political argumentation rather than discourse, see Deborah Tannen's *The Argument Culture: Moving From Debate to Dialogue*.[2] Tannen described the argument culture as one where everything is said as part of a struggle to "win" an advocacy interaction rather than to actually understand the subject being discussed and to reach agreement on its truth, validity, prob-ability, or consequences. When Tannen asked an individual she thought had wrongly questioned and misrepresented Tannen's presentation at a conference, the woman did not respond that she disagreed with her. She instead launched an argumentative conflict, saying her critique wasn't about the "rightness" of what Tannen had said but that the individual was making a political argument she thought would produce a desired outcome to fit her agenda.

This, of course, is consistent with the classic Greek idea of rhetoric in which the entire goal is to persuade an audience in order to achieve a desired outcome. For numerous university faculty this is where we are in the "soft disciplines" of academia. A Machiavellian culture has been established in the university world in which the "end" sought is considered by the advocate to justify the "means" used. Ideologically driven academics perceive themselves and their identity groups as fighting for power and their conception of social justice. The "end" is presumed, and their rhetorical tactics are justified.

One of our most intriguing challenges is learning how to build bridges between the two dimensions of theory and immediate reality. Saul Bellow, in his Foreword to Allan Bloom's *The Closing of the American Mind*, observes that:

> The heart of Professor Bloom's argument is that the university, in a society ruled by public opinion, was to have been an island of intellectual freedom where all views were investigated without restriction. Liberal democracy in its generosity made this possible, but by consenting to play an active or "positive," a participatory role in society, the university has become inundated and saturated with the backflow of society's "problems."[3]

The scholar's dilemma, particularly scholars in disciplines such as law that are irreversibly linked to the operation of power and implicit willingness to do violence if necessary, is that societies require shared consensus far more than truth. Political "truths" are myths in many ways, as are the ideals we have long considered fundamental. This does not render them meaningless or even hypocritical, as long as we sincerely strive to come as close to achieving them within our limited human capabilities as is possible. Negative truths about the scientifically unsupportable premises of our fundamental beliefs might interfere with the quality of the operating consensus, at least for those satisfied with their lot. The truth about opportunity, fairness, racial and gender bias, about who receives economic benefits, and so forth would not be knowledge that "sets us free" but "sets us at each other's throats" even if what exists is reasonably close to the ideal.

A one-sided Machiavellian process is the primary source of power and abuse in our growing disputes. This personalized, impassioned, and self-referenced set of movements has tainted the intellectual culture of universities through the politicization of the knowledge the system develops and transmits. Anything that activist "scholars" produce at this point needs to be seen as just another strategic weapon in pursuit of the movement's aims rather than an end in itself. I would include the 1619 Project, Ibram Kendi's (*nee* Henry Rogers) "anti-racism," and Kimberle Crenshaw's "intersectionality" in this critique. They are political tracts intended to have political impacts and support activist agendas rather than honest analyses.

The abuses are not entirely conscious choices. The problem is that many of the emotionally engaged "scholars" and teachers are true believers who don't perceive their own repressive behavior because they are firmly convinced of their cause's rightness. Others' vices are always far easier to detect than our own. It is a human failing that we often see our own our own flaws as virtuous while demonizing those with whom we do not agree, or see as obstacles to gaining what we want. This perceptual blindness means we are unable to communicate with others whose views do not fit neatly into our own agendas and beliefs.

Ironically, those same activists have frequently taken the position that it is fair, reasonable, and just for them to use impassioned and distorted rhetoric. Conversely, that same manipulative latitude is not allowed to those the activists are challenging for power. The reason, they say, is that those in power already have an advantage and would always win if they were allowed to employ the same tactics as their attacking critics. This makes a mockery of the pretense of reasoned discourse that underlies the principles of academic life and free speech. It represents a mantra of "free speech for me but not for thee."

If this sounds familiar, welcome to the twenty-first century, a period in which we have facilely "deconstructed" our fundamental principles, sought to reveal the underlying truths of an unfair social system, and created a political context filled with hollow slogans based on intense propaganda campaigns. These strategies are designed to mask the emptiness into which our "intellectuals" have cast us, and to either retain or obtain power for their advocates.

Factions and Identity Groups Feed Our Hunger for Purpose and Meaning

James Madison explained in the *Federalist Papers #10* (originally published in the *New York Packet* on November 27, 1787) that the "causes of faction are . . . sown in the nature of man, according to the different circumstances of civil society." In warning of the dangers of factions, Madison offered two admittedly impractical "cures" against the "disease." One was to "destroy the liberty" that allows the disputes to bloom, and the other was to give "to every citizen the same opinions, the same passions, and the same interests." Alternatively, adherence to the fundamental principles of the Rule of Law and its Constitutional procedures in which factions worked out their disputes through legal processes and compromise, and worked through those processes to alter rules and decisions they did not like, offered the best means of achieving preferred ends.

Whether we call it factionalism or the rise of competing "identity groups" or "tribes," we are dealing with extremely divisive conflict in American society. A degree of factionalism is unavoidable in any reasonably open society, but in America's vast, diverse, and complex system it has risen to the point that the nation's fundamental ideals and institutions are at risk. The tragedy is that much of the transformation is caused by the intentionally divisive strategies of a host of identity groups possessed by a politically engineered sense of victimhood and desire for power.

In the battle between factions to obtain the greatest share of power and control, one of the main strategies of any movement that hopes to gain the ability to make others conform to its belief and agenda is the acquisition of institutional power. That is what we are now experiencing throughout America's institutions, whether we are talking about the federal, state, or local levels.

In his book *Power*, Adolf Berle explained that gaining and consolidating control of institutions is how people extend their power pervasively and subtly beyond the limited reach of fists or guns.[4] Far too many of us have become narrow and obsessed fanatics who simply cannot—or refuse to—consider others' concerns in comparison to what we want. Hate, contempt, and an intolerant and aggressive rigidity define us. We are increasingly unable to step outside the "cage" in which we and our identity factions have locked ourselves. Anyone who seeks to offer balanced insights is subject to attack, condemned by labels and slogans. Each slogan and label is a preemption of discourse in an effort to acquire or retain power. To the extent we use such tactics, we offend the deepest spirit of our traditions and damage our culture.

"Victimhood" Has Become Our New National Identity

I always (wrongly) assumed diversity and multiculturalism were processes intended by their advocates to create a larger and more interesting national community. America has become an almost unbelievably complex mixture of people with radically differing backgrounds and beliefs. It is a serious problem that, as our political system has become increasingly complex, has become more and more factious. The separation of deliberately created clans and identity "tribes" has fractured the traditional ideal of the American "melting pot" to the extent that long-standing ideal has been decried by political groups who label any expectation of assimilation by new entrants or a desire for a sense of shared community in which members focus not only on their Identity group agendas but understand the need for reasonable compromises about the allocation among differing interest groups. Instead, anyone not willing to automatically accept the assertions and demands of an aggressive political group is condemned as bigoted, "phobic," a "hater," or racist.

Former BLM activist Xaviaer DuRousseau stepped away from the BLM movement and challenges its assertions of "victimhood." He wrote the following column in response to the recent San Francisco demands that Black residents receive $5 million each in reparations payments, free housing, and erasure of any debt they might hold. DuRousseau explains his disagreement with the way victimhood, assertions of systemic racism, and the growing demand for reparations have been used to manipulate

Black Americans into a continuing state of dependency and ultimately a personal and collective tacit sense of inferiority. He explains his views in an analysis presented in the *New York Post*.

> In 2023, we are supposed to believe that our country is still system-ically racist, as if affirmative action, university and occupational diversity quotas, a twice-elected black president, a black vice presi-dent and roughly a dozen black/biracial billionaires do not suffice to debunk the narrative. The cry of systemic racism is exhausted, and the victim cards expired about [sixty] years ago. Nevertheless, the left continues to manipulate black Americans by keeping us depen-dent on a system of handouts. It began with welfare, and the left is continuing its predecessors' work today with the empty promise of reparation proposals. The helpless-victim narrative clouding many black Americans' judgment and perception of reality has hindered our growth as a collective. Instead of directing our focus toward rel-evant issues—such as father absence, crime, illiteracy, and staggering abortion rates—we are told these problems are somehow the result of slavery and Jim Crow and, therefore, not our fault and only curable by someone else bailing us out. I pray to see the day that more black Americans will recognize the way we are being gaslighted [*sic*] for political gain.[5]

The problem with all the intense and complex fragmentation into "iden-tity tribes" is that, without a system of shared principles of the kind rep-resented in the Constitution and philosophical orientation of the nation, no system can function as anything even close to a coherent society. As America's "diversity" grows exponentially, "community" and shared values and perspectives evaporate. This results in a political entity com-prised of a radical array of incompatible interests. Those interests represent politically organized groups whose myriad beliefs, expectations, sense of entitlement, and desires make it impossible for the inhabitants to com-municate or engage in the kinds of interactions necessary to recognize a realistic common ground other than "winner take all." This has resulted in a vicious competition for power and institutional control among distinct interest and identity groups.

New York Post and *Epoch Times* columnist Adam Coleman offers his perspective on a "culture war" in which aggressive and wealthy Black elites seeking power and wealth continually "stir the pot" of racial hate and division for their own advantage by fashioning a narrative that is not consistent with the actual experiences and beliefs of many people who share their skin color. Coleman writes in the *Epoch Times* how this false narrative caused him to become politically involved in "*The Culture War: Recognizing the Battle for Society's Direction.*" He explains:

> One of the reasons I felt like I needed to jump into the trenches was that I felt there was a great narrative being perpetrated by a particular class of people who were attempting to speak for me while perhaps purposely and completely misrepresenting me. After the death of George Floyd, I felt there was an emotional panic attack that was intentionally being induced by a media establishment while elevating a class of black figureheads who shared my complexion but didn't sound like me or any other rational working-class black person that I knew of.[6]

The fact is that our centers of power have become too diverse, too intense, and too divisive. The competing factions are focused exclusively on their own singular concerns. The underlying system of social beliefs, principles, and creeds has become corrupted and attenuated to the extent that at this point it seems there is no turning back from increasingly violent confrontation such as experienced in the 2020 "mostly peaceful" summer riots involving fire bombings, arson, large scale looting and property destruction, murder, and an estimated $2 billion in damage in America's cities. In such an impassioned, hate-filled context, compromise is seen as weakness and betrayal, not as an essential element of interaction and governance in a healthy and complex community. I pray that I am wrong.

"Needing a Sense of Purpose"

The complexity of the modern world is scary. Most of us intuitively know—without actually confronting—that we are fragile grains of sand (or another variant) in a vast and impersonal universe we will never really understand and over which we have absolutely no control. While for millennia we were told that "God" created us and placed us at the center of the universe, that belief did not survive for many people as Western culture went through the travails of the Enlightenment.

There Is a Compelling Human Need to Believe in Something Better Than Ourselves

Former Levi Strauss Director of Marketing Jennifer Sey observes that a lack of faith in something higher and better than ourselves does not mean we do not have a need to feel purpose and mission. She remarks that there remains a "human need for religiosity" to fill a core of emptiness. We seek to fill the emptiness by seeking refuge by membership in some kind of community or movement that provides us with a degree of purpose and meaning. Ella Kietlinska and Jan Jekielek, in "Wokeism Is Costume Elites Wear to 'Signal Virtue' and 'Hide Greed, Corruption': Former Levi's Executive," report on Sey's exit from the "world of Woke" she was experiencing as a senior executive at Levi Strauss.

> Most people want some sort of a moral framework to help them make decisions so that they can feel virtuous and be good people. And in a world where religion is less and less relevant—and I say this as someone who is an atheist—we still look for those constructs and frameworks elsewhere. "It's our desire to believe in something and want to be part of something bigger than ourselves and have this framework for how to make good decisions to be a good person," Sey said. "That's what I think the impetus is." Sey said there is still a human impulse for religiosity.[7]

It should be obvious that the "Woke Culture" as well as socialism and Marxism necessarily recreate a substitute religion complete with prophets,

disciples, and true believers. Sey's observations describe the stark distinction between what "Woke" meant in the 1940s through the 1960s, before
its more recent transmutation into an identity group theology.

> Being "woke" during the 1940s through the beginning of the 1960s
> meant "being awake or alert to the fact that there was racial inequal-
> ity, and being part of the movement to change that," Sey said. "It's
> admirable, I have no issue with that. However, in the last [ten or fif-
> teen] years, and especially in the last three to five years, those beliefs
> have been corrupted and commodified "into an ideology which
> can never be questioned," such as gender ideology, race ideology, or
> body positivity, Sey explained. . . . Wokeism has become religious in
> nature. Woke capitalism is really just an attempt to profit off of this
> ideology and the passion behind this ideology amongst primarily
> Gen Z and millennial consumers," she said.[8]

The result is that we are adrift in a world where for many people the
anchor offered by religious faith has been cut away. Most people find that
frightening, and strive to find a refuge that insulates them from having to
confront the "darkness" of their own irrelevance. Very often that refuge
is created by submitting oneself to a "cause" created by a prophet such as
Marx, Mao Zedong, or Hitler, who claims to possess a vision of such a
nature that if we follow and obey we are "saved." This provides us with
a purpose that creates an identity and elevates us to a special status that
allows us to feel "meaningful." The "cause" of imposing accountability
for "victimhood" is described by Vivek Ramaswamy as America's "new
national identity" in a report in *The Epoch Times* by Masooma Haq and
Jan Jekielek. They write:

> Vivek Ramaswamy, 2024 presidential candidate and author of the
> 2021 book, *Woke, Inc.: Inside Corporate America's Social Justice Scam*,
> and its sequel, *Nation of Victims*, said the country is suffering from a
> national identity crisis that has left a void for victimhood to fill and
> that national policies that have tried to address grievances are the true

cause of systemic racism. "Victimhood has become our new national identity," said Ramaswamy. Americans need to get from victimhood to empowered, patriotic Americans pursuing excellence, but the path to empowerment "is a complicated one that runs through some uncomfortable terrain," he said. Ramaswamy said during a recent interview with Epoch TV "American Thought Leaders" program. "The affirmative action is the systemic racism that is still here in America today, and I'm sorry to say, it will then create the new kind of racist, anti-black racism that we had spent so many decades moving on from."

"It's also a disservice to even the qualified members of those minority groups who do get those positions because of merit, because no one can tell the difference," said Ramaswamy. . . . "It's an assault on merit, it's an assault on excellence."

This massive gap must be filled with purpose, and affirmative American values including "unapologetic pursuit of excellence, individual self-actualization," said Ramaswamy, otherwise people will be left in the perpetual state of victimhood. "The truth that people don't like to hear is that 'a culture committed to excellence demands inequality of results, demands inequity of results,'" said Ramaswamy. . . . The system is suffering from a lack of excellence, which in turn has at least weakened if not destroyed the merit-based system and for this reason, most people don't trust institutions," said Ramaswamy. Those in charge of the "institutions are behaving not only in ways that dilute the purpose of those institutions, but are also put in those positions in ways that betray the principles of merit."[9]

The "Digital Nation" Isn't Working Out All That Well

These themes of purpose, meaning, and alienation were set out by BuzzFeed News reporter Joseph Bernstein in a December 2019 analysis titled: "Alienated, Alone And Angry: What The Digital Revolution Really Did To Us: We were promised community, civics, and convenience. Instead, we found ourselves dislocated, distrustful, and disengaged."

Bernstein describes our descent from a nirvana of naive belief in what the internet and its applications offered us, and the eventual realization that the technology was generating a society directly opposite to what was intended. Bernstein writes:

In April 1997, *Wired* magazine published a feature with the grand and regrettable title "Birth of a Digital Nation." It was a good time to make sweeping, sunny pronouncements about the future of the United States and technology. . . . [T]he journalist Jon Katz argued the country was on the verge of something even greater than prosperity and progress—something that would change the course of world history. Led by the Digital Nation, "a new social class" of "young, educated, affluent" urbanites whose "business, social and cultural lives increasingly revolve around" the internet, a revolution was at hand, which would produce unprecedented levels of civic engagement and freedom. The tools of this revolution were facts, with which the Digital Nation was obsessed, and with which they would destroy—or at least neuter—partisan politics.

"I saw . . . the formation of a new post-political philosophy," Katz wrote. "This nascent ideology, fuzzy and difficult to define, suggests a blend of some of the best values rescued from the tired old dogmas—the humanism of liberalism, the economic opportunity of conservatism, plus a strong sense of personal responsibility and a passion for freedom." Comparing the coming changes to the Enlightenment, Katz lauded an "interactivity" that "could bring a new kind of community, new ways of holding political conversations"—"a media and political culture in which people could amass factual material, voice their perspectives, confront other points of view, and discuss issues in a rational way." Such a sensible, iterative American public life contained, Katz wrote, "the . . . tantalizing . . . possibility that technology could fuse with politics to create a more civil society."[10]

"It Hasn't Tamed Politics. It Sent Them Berserk."

Bernstein's article continued:

> Looking back . . . it's clear that the past [ten] years saw many
> Americans snap out of this dream, shaken awake by a brutal series of
> shocks and dislocations from the very changes that were supposed to
> "create a civilization of the Mind in Cyberspace." When they opened
> their eyes, they did indeed see that the Digital Nation had been born.
> Only it hadn't set them free. They were being ruled by it. It hadn't
> tamed politics. It sent them berserk.
>
> And it hadn't brought people closer together. It had alienated
> them. . . . I've come to see conditions of disconnection and frus-
> tration everywhere the Digital Nation touches: on social media, in
> search algorithms, in the digital economy. The feelings of power-
> lessness, estrangement, loneliness, and anger created or exacerbated
> by the information age are so general it can be easy to think they
> are just a state of nature, like an ache that persists until you for-
> get it's there. But then sometimes it suddenly gets much worse. . . .
> Cynicism and powerlessness are the hallmarks of another form of
> digital life, an authoritarian one Americans should badly want to
> avoid. . . . Alienated people are especially vulnerable to the destruc-
> tive forms of belonging promised by nationalism and racism.[11]

Chapter Fourteen

Education's Rejection
of the Search for Truth

"MY Truth Is the ONLY Truth"

A scholar who is critical of aspects of postmodernism argues:

> Truth, among postmodernists, is whatever you can get away with saying in whatever specific context you find yourself. Power lies in the context (the prevailing mentality) and, thus, power becomes truth. Obviously, then, this movement influences our concern for the future of academic freedom. Indeed, if there is no truth but only power, the need for academic freedom ceases to exist.[1]

It is far too easy for politicized scholars to mistake or substitute their personal beliefs for more valid and truth-filled insights. In that context, one becomes convinced that anything said by use of their personal "voice" is a form of irrefutable "truth." The problem is that true believers are trapped within the closed system of their own circular logic. This cage of assumption and identity agenda renders them unable to hear or comprehend other viewpoints, except to consider them heresy or the voices of the opposition.

This closed-mindedness is a danger even for an individual activist-intellectual without ties to a group, but the risk expands by orders of magnitude when someone becomes part of a political collective. This results in a substantively sterile—though impassioned—form of discourse that offers little beyond the speakers' prejudices. It traps and blinds by the extreme personalization of reality and the pursuit of political ends.

Ironically, or perhaps prophetically, the "anti-truth" phenomenon of the Woke is starkly revealed in a cartoon describing "The Dogma Day Parade." Wiley Miller's 2002 cartoon captures our dilemma perfectly. The panel describes "The opening ceremony of the annual dogma day parade," and depicts an urban intersection at which four men stand. Each is poised to march in a different direction, and each man is carrying an identical sign proclaiming "Follow me to the truth."[2]

Since that cartoon appeared two decades ago, the situation has only become worse. We are trapped in a Dickensian *A Tale of Two Cities* scenario involving the "best of times" and the "worst of times." The "worst of times" political conflict that is ruining the American university and degrading the American society is driven in significant part by the emergence of Big Tech social media outlets.

The unfortunate fact is that these Big Tech systems are controlled by deeply political and almost uniformly Woke staff and proud of it. Although it is an almost amusing and seemingly trivial development, Elon Musk, when he moved into Twitter (now X) headquarters after buying the company, found T-shirts stored in closets with the message "STAY WOKE" emblazoned on them.

Bill Maher: "In today's world, when truth conflicts with narrative, it's the truth that has to apologize."

One of our last "true Liberals," Bill Maher, has been a strong voice against the repressive behaviors of the Woke and Crits. His motives are not aimed at supporting the political agendas of the Right, but at defending the fundamental values and behaviors essential to Liberalism and a healthy democratic community. Fox News reporter Charles Creitz writes:

> Liberal comedian Bill Maher roasted the woke concept of "presentism," where historical figures and events are judged in the prism of the present—further arguing against the oft-claimed leftist position that White people are usually to blame for history's lesser moments. "New rule: You can get creative with a novel, a TV show or a movie, but history books—that's not supposed to be fan fiction," Maher said

on "Real Time." . . . "But in today's world, when truth conflicts with narrative, it's the truth that has to apologize—Being woke is like a magic moral time machine where you judge everybody against what you imagine you would have done in 1066: And you always win."[3]

Miyamoto Musashi: "Truth is not what you want it to be; it is what it is. And you must bend to its power or live a lie."

In my book, *The Warrior Lawyer*, a significant part of the focus was on Sun Tzu's *Art of War* and Miyamoto Musashi's *Book of Five Rings*.[4] The point of using those classics of strategic thought and action was to take my students outside the boundaries of Western thought and vocabulary in order to open their minds and actions to alternative systems. It was always satisfying as a teacher to see their awareness grow to the point that, for most students, somewhere about halfway through the semester, you could see "the light" coming on and the ways in which they planned, perceived, thought, and acted was expanded.

One fundamental goal of the course was to end up with what Musashi called "All things with no teacher" when describing his purpose. The concept stands for seeking to allow the students to "go beyond" the teacher, and for teachers to supply their students with a system that continues to "grow" them into a way of perception and thought that begins with what the teacher offers, but understands that the teacher's knowledge, beliefs, values, and perceptions are only that person's and therefore inherently subjective, and that the students must be given the ability and responsibility to "become" who they are through the power of their thought and experience.

This creates a methodology that no longer depends on a teacher because the point is that the teacher creates a dynamic in which the student becomes his or her own teacher throughout life. The point is to facilitate creation of the student's unique system with understanding derived from within their evolving personal system, capability, and experience. Imparting "All things with no teacher" is the teacher's function. The sacred duty of the teacher is not to inculcate, intimidate, or indoctrinate in the teacher's values and frames of reference. Yet, too often, "truth-obstructing" indoctrination is what is being produced by our educational systems. We seem too often to be refusing to honor a teacher's duty and are refusing, or incapable of teaching, our students the richness of independent thought and analysis. As the educational system moves even further in the direction of "Your truth must be MY truth" we face totalitarian domination."

Two decades ago, in "A Chilling of Discourse," I wrote:

> A key consequence of the collectives of multiculturalists, postmodernists, radical feminists, critical race activists, sexuality advocates, and others working for radical change is not only the politicization of knowledge in what is after all a realm of politics we call law, but the incoherence of knowledge and the loss of the quality and integrity of our pursuit of knowledge through scholarship. One result is that much of the scholarship and teaching found in the humane and political or noncumulative disciplines such as law are forms of self-interested propaganda in which honesty is muted or excluded and truth-seeking and balance are subordinated to predetermined political agendas."[5]

The Erosion of the Ideal of Truth

The erosion of the ideal of truth as a guiding force for what we do dishonors the tradition of the truth-seeking function of scholars and teachers, and the responsibility that we teach our students how to differentiate truth from falsity. For the university-based intellectual, the problem with commitments to ends other than truth-seeking, is that once we accept a mission distinct from the pursuit of truth, evidence, and honest discourse, the remaining options are suspect. These alternative paths are those of falseness, hypocrisy, power, self-deception, subordination of self to a collective, profit and greed, dogmatism, indoctrination, intimidation, and propaganda.

The dominant internet and social media systems have created tools of sweeping power to which groups intent on undermining the American political system would never otherwise have had access. We are experiencing a historical "Gutenberg Moment" in which the emergence of a transformational technology has facilitated the creation of interactive communications and monitoring networks. These capabilities are far beyond anything previously available. With the full cooperation of Big Tech, and our dominant legacy media systems, this has given governments and single-minded activist groups powers they would never otherwise have had, and that they should not possess.

What we intend by the idea of truth—legal, scientific, political, and otherwise—is obviously subtle, wide-ranging, functionally disparate according to the area of inquiry, and perhaps impossible to make entirely concrete in many instances. But a society without commitment to the ideal of truth pursued with integrity and honesty (even if not entirely real or provable) is not a community. It is only a collection of disparate people and controlling factions seeking to take advantage of each other while never being able to trust the validity of anyone or anything. That is what we are creating in America.

A society without the ability to negotiate reliable terms of what will be considered true, and thus authoritative, is one in which promises are meaningless, nothing is reliable, and betrayal is a predictable and even inevitable condition of relationships. Western societies cannot afford to surrender such a basic principle without devolving into a system operating on the increasingly prevalent use of force and Machiavellian machinations under the control of powerful political cliques committed to seizing power.

The Honest Search for Truth Is the Loser

Martha Nussbaum explains that some elements of the political movements now taking place are concentrating their attacks on principles long seen as fundamental. One of those is rejection of the search for truth itself. She explains the attack strategy of activist university faculty who deny even the validity of the rational search for truth, characterizing their argument as follows:

> "The very pretense that one is engaged in the disinterested pursuit of truth can be a handy screen for prejudice." [Conversely] the

independent scholar's task is to test and question everything, not to accept convenient assumptions—no matter how attractive or comfortable. But conflict and "truths" that don't conform to the dominant assumptions make people uncomfortable, and scholars tend to be easily discomfited.[6]

In the same vein, Albert Camus also tells us, while warning about the onset of what he calls "the black night of dictatorship":

> If you merely make an effort to understand without preconceptions, if you merely talk of objectivity, you will be accused of sophistry and criticized for having pretensions. . . . I know as well as anyone the excesses of intelligence, and I know as well as anyone that the intellectual is a dangerous animal ever ready to betray. But that is not the right kind of intelligence. We are speaking of the kind that is backed by courage, the kind that for four years paid whatever was necessary to have the right to respect. When that intelligence is snuffed out, the black night of dictatorship begins. . . . [T]here is no freedom without intelligence or without mutual understanding.[7]

Chapter Fifteen

The Neo-Marxist Revolution in Universities

A Little History

The current conflict over the extent to which Marxism and socialism have infiltrated our universities and K-12 educational systems is close to a surreal phenomenon for those of us who grew up during the Cold War between Russia and the United States. The "Reds" or Communists were the enemy. Socialism was bad and evil. For my generation, we had regular air raid drills in our schools in the 1950s that included hiding beneath our flimsy wooden student desks protected by their black-painted cast iron frames. Unsurprisingly, even though we were naive kids in grade school and junior high school, we weren't entirely stupid. Crouching beneath the potential deadly shrapnel of our desks didn't instill a sense of safety if the H-bombs actually came.

While nuclear war was always lurking in the background, for a two-week period it was imminent. From October 16, 1962, until late in the day on October 29, the Cuban Missile Crisis standoff between the United States and Soviet Union over Russian ships at sea carrying nuclear tipped missiles to Cuba dominated everything. In my college's dining hall on the last day of the standoff, when the declared deadline was imminent and the two countries played their game of "chicken," we toyed with our dinners as we stood, sat, and milled around, wondering whether our world was going to be gone in a nuclear flash. Then the news that the Soviet ships had turned around was broadcast, and we all exhaled a loud collective breath because the world did not end and we got to live another day.

We also experienced the Korean War against North Korea and China. Then there was the rise of communism in Cuba after Castro took

over—complete with mass killings and imprisonment of dissidents or enemies of the state. We all understood the socialist/Marxist states were our
enemies and those forms of repressive government still would be if they
actually existed. Instead, even though the Soviet Union "morphed" into
the Russian Federation and the others kept their same names, we have
moved on from the ideological states to one of oppressive military dicta-
torships. Russia, China, Iran, and Venezuela aren't "revolutionary icons."
They are criminal gangs of thugs who seized power under the rhetoric of
"the people" and "justice" but never gave up power after seizing it.

The key message to be taken from what any serious examination of the
Marxian/socialist state reveals instantly is that the state never withers away
in such systems, and there is no "proletarian paradise." I taught several
times in St. Petersburg, Russia after the collapse of the Soviet Union, and
there was a significant degree of hope among the young Russians that the
nation would become a true democracy. But even though the alleged form
of government changed, the Party never really surrendered power, and
remained just as corrupt and power-driven as ever.

Those who naively or cynically rage on about the evils of America,
Western Europe, and similar political systems as oppressors are either
stupid or "blowing smoke" for political and financial gain. It was a very
serious matter to discover during the COVID-19 pandemic just how
widespread the Woke/Critical Race Theory movement is being driven by
self-admitted Marxists, with allies using the "softer" socialist label in an
effort to mask what they are doing to create a political system that history
shows us never works. Marxism/socialism is always a quest for centralized
power, and the Woke/CRT movement is no different.

The oft-stated denials of Marxist and socialist beliefs at the base of
Critical Legal Studies, Critical Race Theory, and Wokeism should not
be believed. Marxist principles have been a dominant part of the Woke/
CRT effort since the beginning. When I began my career as a law professor after several years of representing poor and minority clients as a Legal
Services and civil rights lawyer in Colorado, and then receiving a Master
of Law degree from Harvard and teaching Harvard's clinical students, I
was contacted by people with whom I had interacted while helping create

the law school's first real clinical program representing low-income clients who otherwise had no access to lawyers.

I was invited to join the nascent Critical Legal Studies (CLS) movement. Our discussion included description of the goals of social justice and equality for which I have always worked, still advocate, and support. But as the discussion progressed, I was informed, almost breathlessly by the individual to whom I was talking, that CLS was dedicated to socialism and European Marxist political philosophy. At that point I stated, "I'm sorry, I don't do 'Ism's' and can't be part of what you are doing." That was the end of the attempt to recruit me, and I lost some friends who remained steadfast members of the CLS movement. My experience with many "Crits" through the years validated my decision.

"All liberation depends on the consciousness of servitude."

One of my basic questions relates to prominent Marxist scholar of the Frankfurt School, Herbert Marcuse's assertion that "all liberation depends upon a consciousness of servitude." The question that demands to be raised is, *"OK, now that they are in control, what do our newly conscious band of previously victimized Marxist/socialist brothers and sisters do?"* The answer is not nearly as obvious as is seemingly assumed. The Woke and revolutionaries do not really have a clue about "what works" after they destroy the existing order. The question to be asked the Woke at this point in their "transformative revolution" is, "What do we do if you win?"

It is no accident that the Woke and CRT movements convert virtually everything they attack into unjust "exploitation" of, or "victimhood" imposed on, those in their identity group. The "exploiters" are demonic capitalists rather than humans. That accusation and interpretation provides the base for Marxist social critique. The idea is that individually, and as part of a community based on the altruistic belief of "from each according to his abilities, to each according to their needs," the "freed" and no-longer-exploited humans would, by their very inherent nature, act in ways that realized the greatest qualities of the human race once they were no longer deterred by the devilish evils of exploitation and capitalist greed.

Ella Kietlinska and Joshua Philipp describe aspects of Marcuse's philosophy in the *Epoch Times*. They write:

> People need to be conscious of their servitude first, of being oppressed before they can react through revolution. . . . Taking responsibility for one's own life and dealing with one's problems individually is not what Marxists advocate. They admit that a person can succeed individually but claim that by doing so the person joins a bad system, [Mike Gonzalez, the Angeles T. Arredondo E Pluribus Unum Senior Fellow at the Heritage Foundation] explained. . . . In order to dismantle the system, according to Marxist thought, [Marcuse said] "you need to be upset," he said, to feel victimized by the system, and only then will people act collectively.[1]

Marcuse, Marx, Lenin, and many others were delusional if the interpretations and intentions they proclaim are taken at face value, as opposed to being cynical polemical devices employed to justify the seizure of power and control. As we see through the stark examples provided by the behavior of Russia, China, Guatemala and Venezuela, the glorious evolution of the human race always claimed to be the result of the Marxist political philosophy has not occurred. Instead, those who are successful in removing deity-based religion from the equation on which their social order is founded simply recreate a substitute system of faith with themselves as the priesthood and laity.

America's "Progressives" Are "Soft Marxists"

Although there were innovative thinkers such as Derrick Bell, Duncan Kennedy, Roberto Unger, and others in the early days of Critical Legal Studies (CLS), many of the new faculty and administrators who entered the university during the 1960s and 1970s Civil Rights movement weren't necessarily intellectuals in the traditional sense of that concept, or even necessarily teachers, researchers, or scholars due to the intrusion of their political agendas into their teaching and scholarship. They were activists on a mission and possessed of a specific agenda and worldview. They "knew" the "Truth."

They treated subjective interpretations of their own "lived" experiences and European Marxist treatises as objectively valid. They worshipped the big words and almost impenetrable language that they read in books written by European leftists and Marxist deconstructionists and decided they had undergone an "epiphany" presenting incontrovertible and sacred "truths." They did this even while paradoxically asserting, like the European deconstructionists and Marxists they were parroting, that "objective truths" did not exist. What was really going on was the invention of a new religion, "Wokeism"—which to a disturbing degree was a "stealth" paraphrasing of Marx, Lenin, and European Marxist/socialists such as Herbert Marcuse.

Heather Mac Donald exposes a form of Marxism and the pursuit of centralization of power. She writes:

> The core claim of both critical race theory and feminist jurisprudence is that law is merely a mask for white male power relations. . . . But the Crits' real gripe was not with law but with liberal society. They berated liberalism's emphasis on individual freedom and limited state power. Many called for a world without distinct public and private spheres, in which the individual would not be "alienated" from the collectivity. The Crits were particularly scornful of "illegitimate hierarchies," a phrase that included every possible type of ranking or distinction among individuals. Harvard's Duncan Kennedy . . . infamously called for breaking down law school hierarchies by rotating all law school jobs from dean to janitor on a regular basis and paying all employees the same salary.[2]

Bruce Abramson and Robert Chernin argue that American progressivism already follows a soft form of the Chinese model. In that model, an enlightened, elite oligarchy broadcasts official facts, beliefs, and values that none may question.

> In a China-dominant world . . . Human rights, civil liberties, rule of law, and representative government will be greatly diminished. More

than the world order will change. National governance, including our own, will follow suit. . . . American progressivism already follows a soft form of the Chinese model. An enlightened, elite oligarchy broadcasts official facts, beliefs, and values that none may question. Those who fall in line are allowed to prosper in ways that serve the oligarchy's conception of the public interest. . . . An America without the fundamental rights and liberties that have always defined our national soul is an America fertile for an era of Chinese dominance. Nearly every trend in contemporary American life appears to be heading in that direction.[3]

Alan Dershowitz, a professor of Law emeritus at Harvard, is demonstrating courage and integrity in opposing the rapidly unfolding corruption of the university as institution, and the dangers this creates for American society. Jan Jekielek and Masooma Haq interviewed Dershowitz about the state of the American university system and the fact that a considerable element of the Woke and Critical Race Theory movements derive from the political philosophy of Herbert Marcuse. Marcuse developed a system of thought that began as anti-Nazism, but ultimately became a fascist repressive system that Dershowitz argues provided the philosophical base for the Woke movement.

> Dershowitz agreed that the left has been heavily influenced by Herbert Marcuse, a German-American philosopher and political theorist associated with the Frankfurt School of critical theory, who advocated for "liberating tolerance," which consists of intolerance of right-wing movements and toleration of left-wing movements. [He explains] "[Marcuse's philosophy] is interesting because although it grew out of anti-Nazism, it turned into its own form of fascism, so Marcuse was kind of the godfather of the woke repressionist movement," said Dershowitz.[4]

A False Identity Politics Is Using Marcuse's "Oppressed" and "Oppressor" as a Strategy to Undermine and Dismantle America and Create Hate

The struggle to develop our fullest humanity depends on being able to utilize our minds to perceive as broadly and deeply as possible. The Woke's cancel culture and conversion of the fundamental role of human individuality into a kind of collectivist submission is part of a deliberate effort to suppress our minds and block the range and depth of our insights. This strategy is done to create the energized base of adherents who become convinced they are unfairly victimized and those who are responsible for their plight. This is an essential step by which the "enemy" is created, blamed, and targeted in order to generate the needed "revolutionary fervor." We see this clearly in the inventions of "White supremacy," "White privilege" and "White guilt." Mike Gonzalez, the Angeles T. Arredondo E Pluribus Unum Senior Fellow at the Heritage Foundation who specializes in analysis of Critical Race Theory, explains the connection between identity group politics and the creation of the revolutionary split between what is labeled as "oppressor" and the "oppressed" victims.

> Identity politics is the reimagining of America as not a united country or a united nation but as a confederation of identity groups. . . . "Some of these groups are considered to be oppressed and then one of these groups is the oppressor," Mike Gonzalez said. These groups have been created synthetically by activists on the left for the purpose of instilling the members of the oppressed groups with a sense of victimhood and grievances so they would act as a catalyst to change the society and to change America, Gonzalez said. This is consistent with the archetypal Marxist conflicts between "the oppressor" and "the oppressed."[5]

Simply put, money, power, ideology, and control have major roles to play in the concealment and denial that accompany the implementation of the "Woke agenda" in our universities. We are well into a second generation of individuals who have been mis-educated as students and as teachers in an intellectually deficient educational system. That system has ignored the teaching of fundamental concepts, skills, methods, civic duty, and collective and individual responsibilities of the kind necessary to sustain the ideals of the American political community.

What is missing includes a rapidly growing lack of respect for the spirit of the Rule of Law. Along with this destructive mind set is the absence of civic awareness concerning the terms of membership in a healthy democratic community, and not being taught how to think. Along with these deficiencies is a dramatic lack of learning the essential foundations of data and unbiased knowledge on which rich and legitimate "thinking" must operate. The human mind may well be understood as a kind of "organic computer," but without the best quality of data created by educational and experiential inputs, as well as the creative and methodological conceptual structures by which those inputs are processed and interpreted the "computer" can't function at any real levels of quality.

Even that is only a part of the problem. Our educational systems also fail in teaching the skills needed to resolve disputes, and being able or willing to engage in the political and intergroup compromises needed to maintain the health of an incredibly complex democratic republic such as exists in America. As the shifting systemic demographics rapidly change the cultural identity of the nation, and identity group tribalism undermines the traditions of individualism that are at the foundation of democracy, it becomes even more vital that we learn how to mitigate conflicts between collective groups that are seeking greater shares of America's social goods.

Part of the problem is that "identity" and "diversity" are not obvious concrete standards. They are being used as open-textured terms being applied to give special advantage to "favored groups." In many instances, while seemingly benign and obvious, such concepts are being used to suppress true and wide-ranging diversity and identity across the total national population. It is not that the concepts themselves are inherently bad conceptually and morally. It is that they are being used as weapons to gain power for specific political interests. Bob Zeidman is the president of Zeidman Consulting, a contract research and development firm in Silicon

Valley, and president of Software Analysis and Forensic Engineering Corporation. He writes:

> Our irrational emphasis on diversity is creating the problem that it's intended to eliminate. Instead, let us try to enact the color-blind society envisioned by Martin Luther King and strive to live up to the philosophy inscribed in our Declaration of Independence that all people are created equal and should be treated equally.[6]

Marxism and Socialism Always Fail Because They Contradict the Reality of Human Nature

When I was teaching law at the University of Westminster in London and serving as a Senior Research Fellow with the University of London's Institute of Advanced Legal Studies (IALS), I lived a block away from the British Museum. I would frequently wander over to the museum and visualize Karl Marx bent over his books while seeking to decipher political reality. *Das Kapital* emerged from his efforts. While I have long considered Marx as a brilliant analyst and critic of the unfair conditions of social reality as it existed in his historical moment, I simultaneously see him as someone who was so dedicated to one vision or interpretation that he was blind to the actual motivations and darker behaviors of humans.

Marx, while researching and writing on social conditions in *Das Kapital* in the British Museum's Reading Room, never was willing to accept the reality of human nature. Or, perhaps even worse, Marx may have understood the falsity of his analysis of human nature and the supposed inevitability of the state "withering away," yet deliberately presented a duplicitous "truth" to justify his political theory and advance the "revolution" he desired.

Due to the power, pettiness, and competitive and jealousy realities of human nature that contradict Marxian dreams of human goodness, such systems *never* manage to move beyond and heavy-handed control and centralized authoritarian power. Marxism's fatal flaw is that humans differ naturally in the degree of their goodness and evil, and in the lack of altruistic impulses, egomania, physical and intellectual abilities, resentment and jealousy, and in their drive toward creating the wealth, opportunities, and goods required to provide for the overall community versus for themselves and their allies. The fact is that few people who possess power ever willingly surrender that control. John Stuart Mill understood this essential point about humans, a point Chief Justice William Rehnquist emphasized in his opinion on the imposition of capital punishment. Mill wrote:

> The disposition of mankind, whether as rulers or as fellow-citizens, to impose their own opinions and inclinations as a rule of conduct on others, is so energetically supported by some of the best and by some of the worst feelings incident to human nature, that it is hardly ever kept under restraint by anything but want of power.[7]

Wanting human reality and behavior to fit into an ideal of innate human goodness does not make it so. Differences in talent, merit, good and bad fortune, and the distribution of social goods are inevitable. While excessive extremes in opportunity and outcomes can be destructive to the social order, there is no viable system in which perfect equality or perfect "equity" is possible. We can and should act decently with an eye toward advancing the overall human good, but we can never achieve a perfect system. Taken too far, the attempt to do so will *always* produce repressive authoritarian systems, resentment, and violence.

Marx also asserted that a main function of religion was preventing people from demanding social change. He argued it did this by reducing the sense of oppression. The idea was that, by promising a heaven, organized religion gave people something to look forward to even as they endured the darkness of earthly existence. The thought was that you were better able to put up with misery now if you have the promise of a life of "eternal bliss" to look forward to after earthly death. This can be seen in the devotion to "spiritual" songs and music among enslaved Blacks, and in Black churches even today. Of course, the system worked even better if there was a hell in which the "bad guys" suffered eternal pain and despair. At least you could look forward to your tormentors "getting their just desert."

The Reality of Socialism in Practice: All Power to the Government

North Korean defector Yeonmi Park offers an honest critique of the inevitable nature of socialism in real communities as opposed to academic or propagandized constructs woven by activists in advancing political theories in order to undermine the systems they attack to acquire power for their movements. Park captures the reality of socialism under the operational control of humans:

> The definition of socialism means giving all the power to the government—they decide the means of production. They despise every aspect of our lives . . . In North Korea, they say, 'Okay, we're going to make sure everybody is equal . . . So give us all your land.' So we gave the regime all the land, so they abolish[ed] private property. Nobody could own anything. State owns it. And that is when they took everything, did not give anything back to us. And then when we gave all our rights, they didn't give anything back . . . That's a reality of socialism.

Park added that those who promote the Marxian ideology fail to study history.

> "That's why we keep repeating it. We have seen how this plays a role, a playbook for dictators. There is a playbook for this elite . . . to seize power from people. And this brainwashing is a seed of that like making sure that everybody [is] . . . brainwash[ed] to believe this is a way to get to that paradise. And the paradise doesn't exist," she said.[8]

The Marxist "Pseudo-Religion" Oozes Onto the Scene

As suggested, we are experiencing the birth of a new religion, a "Progressive Theocracy." It may lack a deity figure, but is nonetheless a powerful form of belief and social control. A primary tool by which that Progressive Theocracy achieves its goals is by creating the system we are calling Cancel

Culture. Those who deviate or refuse to accept its legitimacy are "blasphemers" or "counter-revolutionaries."

While Karl Marx described religion as "the sigh of the oppressed creature, the sentiment of a heartless world and the soul of soulless conditions. it is the opium of the people"[9] he actually created a new secular religion through Marxism. Marx made the error of thinking that if it were possible to free people from the effects of deistic religious faith, they would ultimately create a purely humanistic and benign secular system. The belief was that this state of being could be achieved, and that it would deliver us to a Marxian version of the Garden of Eden where we would live perfect and content lives at peace with one another. Marxism demands the elimination of religion, but Marxism is a religion in itself.

> Marx believed that the 'objective' truth was that the proletariat (i.e. most people) suffer deprivations because of their exploitation by the Bourgeois (namely the extraction of surplus value empowers the minority Bourgeois class and leaves the majority of the proletariat with insufficient money to lead a decent quality of life), however, people fail to realise this because religion teaches them that all of the misery in life is God's will. Religion is only necessary under exploitative systems where the majority of men do not control the conditions under which they labour, under systems where men work for someone else rather than for themselves. Under communism, where man controls the conditions of his labour, he is essentially 'for himself', and thus will have no need of religion. Under communism, where reality is 'fair' religion will not be required, and so will simply wither away.[10]

Marx, like Socrates and the philosophical activists of the French Enlightenment, claimed to believe in the essential goodness of the human species. He, and they, failed to understand that many, if not most, people required a source of guiding authority and that, if the divine was denied to them, they would seek alternatives and create other mechanisms. The flawed Marxist belief, however, like that of the Enlightenment, was that once humans were provided with knowledge through education, and freed from the oppression of their "exploiters," they would blossom into their presumed natural state of compassionate and benign entities.

"Deconstructionists" and "Fault-Finding Men of Words" Have Subverted the University

What we have been dealing with is a still-growing generation of "deconstructionists" aimed at subverting the American system of government and culture. They have masked their strategy through seizing and corrupting what I consider to be the deeply moral "high ground" of justice, race, and gender equality. This capture took place while the progressive activists were attacking the core principles of America in an effort to shock and destabilize the system. They weren't trying to fix the system but to dismantle it. This strategy is taken directly from Marxist scholar Herbert Marcuse.

> According to Marcuse, the American worker was never going to overthrow the system because the American worker was too content and too happy with capitalism, Gonzalez said. Marcuse posited that there would be people of different races and colors who would be the revolutionary base that would rise up and overthrow the so-called oppressive system, but they must be instructed first about their oppression and servitude.[11]

A key part of the strategy involved using strong moral-message code words such as multiculturalism, diversity, racism, phobia, justice, fair, equal, equity, and numerous other terms whose meaning and application I am still trying to figure out. These have provided a powerful motivating force of moral condemnation crafted to advance the Woke agenda. The power of such terms is not because they are anchored in evidence or logic. The power is derived from the fact that, as with any effective propaganda slogan, they bypass rational thought and penetrate to our emotive core. Once they are internalized, those who invented them can change their scope and meaning at will because they are all open-textured concepts. As such, the assertions are capable of meaning whatever their advocates claim because they do not operate on the level of rational assessment. Wokeness and Diversity, Equity, and Inclusion (DEI) offer prime examples of this strategy.

Abraham Maslow offers several insights into our current state of knowledge and describes the major premises of European existential psychology. One has an obvious connection to the extreme insistence on "identity" politics that is at the base of the Woke/CRT movement. Maslow describes "a radical stress on the concept of identity and the experience of identity as a sine qua non [an essential condition] of human nature and of any philosophy or science of human nature."[12] Another element relates to the "lived experience" strategy in which an "identity" activist's declaration of what they claim has been undergone or observed must be accepted as valid and generalizable throughout the system.

Maslow describes this as an approach that "lays great stress on starting from experiential knowledge rather than from systems of concepts or abstract categories or a priori's. . . . Existentialism rests on phenomenology, i.e., it uses personal, subjective experience as the foundation upon which abstract knowledge is built."[13] This, of course, conveniently leaves out the subjective effects on how one's experiences are interpreted through the lens produced by a fanatic's quasi-religious fervor.

Noam Chomsky Echoes Abraham Maslow in Describing the Two Paths to Power Taken by Twentieth Century "Intellectuals"

Chomsky explains:

> In the nineteenth and twentieth centuries, intellectuals have rather typically taken one or another of two very similar paths. One is basically the Marxist/Leninist path, and that's very appealing for intellectuals because it provides them with the moral authority to control people. The essence of Marxism/Leninism is that there's a vanguard role and that is played by the radical intellectuals who whip the stupid masses forward into a future they're too dumb to understand for themselves. That's a very appealing idea for intellectuals.

There's even a method: you achieve this position on the backs of people who are carrying out a popular struggle. So there's a popular struggle, you identify yourself as a leader, you take power, and then you lead the stupid masses forward. That basically captures the essence of Marxism/Leninism—a tremendous appeal to the intellectuals for obvious reasons, and that's why that's one major direction in which they've gone all over the world. There's another direction which is not all that different: a recognition that there's not going to be any popular revolution; there's a given system of power that's more or less going to stay, I'm going to serve it, I'm going to be the expert who helps the people with real power achieve their ends. That's the Henry Kissinger phenomenon or the state capitalist intellectual.[14]

Chomsky and "The God That Failed Phenomenon"
Chomsky continues:

Those two conceptions of the intellectual are very similar. In fact I think it's a striking fact that people find it very easy to shift from one to the other. That's called "the god that failed phenomenon." You see there isn't going to be a popular revolution and you're not going to make it as the vanguard driving the masses forward, so you undergo this conversion and you become a servant of "state capitalism." . . . I think the ease of that transition in part reflects the fact that there isn't very much difference. There's a difference in the assessment of where power lies, but there's a kind of commonality of the conception of the intellectual's role. [M]y point is that the people we call intellectuals are people who have passed the filters, gone through the gates, picked up these roles for themselves, and decided to play them. Those are the people we call intellectuals. If you ask why intellectuals are submissive, the answer is they wouldn't be intellectuals otherwise. Again, this is not one-hundred percent, but it's a large part.[15]

Former US secretary of Defense, CIA director, chair of the Atomic Energy Commission (AEC), and more, James Schlesinger commented on the responsibility of the modem intellectual as understood by Hans Morgenthau. Morgenthau described four ways for intellectuals to proceed. There is the irrelevance created by being an academic in the "Ivory Tower." But beyond that are the roles of being an "expert servant" to those in power and an "agent and apologist" for those in power. The final option for the intellectual is to engage in "prophetic confrontation" by speaking "truth to power." An interesting fact is that by bringing activist power into the university, and overall education, the Woke have at least escaped irrelevance. The destructive fact, however, is that the university world is no longer populated by scholars and honest teachers, but by "politicians" who see "dismantling" and "transforming" as their mission, and a significantly larger host of administrators committed to being "agents and apologists" for those who have seized power and control over our educational institutions. These administrators want to keep the "best job they will ever have." Schlesinger comments:

> The intellectual . . . seeks truth; the politician, power. And the intellectual . . . can deal with power in four ways: by retreat into the ivory tower, which makes him irrelevant; by offering expert advice, which makes him a servant; by absorption into the machinery, which makes him an agent and apologist; or by 'prophetic confrontation.'[16]

Chapter Sixteen

The Repressive "Mass" Formed by Wokeism, Genderism, and Critical Race Theory

The Constitutional Terms of America's Federalist Republic Were Designed as a Safeguard Against Extreme Factional Control and Insurrection by Diffusing Power

The deliberate and planned diffusion of power that lies at the base of the US Constitution and its federalist system, the compelling idea of the founders, was to ensure that power must be shared between the states and the central government. This concept is the greatest design achievement of the American political system, one without which the nation's political enterprise would fail. Unfortunately, the risk of failure is increasing rapidly as identity politics and divisiveness dominate and suppress discourse and cooperation at all levels of society and throughout our most fundamental institutions, including our entire system of education.

A vital part of educational processes at both the university and K-12 levels is to impart the knowledge needed to keep a complex and diverse national community linked across generations. Another, equivalent, goal is to provide knowledge and skills applicable to a present-day context. But a community fails if its members do not understand and respect the historical ideals that tie culture and community together. Education is a kind of "trans-generational glue."

Part of America's essential trans-generational learning in the university and K-12 systems is the importance of what James Madison, writing as Publius in *Federalist No. 10*, described as dealing with the inevitability of competing factions in society. *Federalist No. 10* is titled *The Union as a Safeguard Against Domestic Faction and Insurrection*. In any political community, but particularly one of the enormous scale, diversity, and complexity of the American Republic, the inevitably fractious factions need to learn how to achieve compromise through education and political discourse. If the education a population receives focuses on and indoctrinates students with only one side of an issue or belief system without recognizing the obvious fact that people do not necessarily share the same perspectives and values, or by trying to transform the system to one that represents only their own faction's desires, there can be no productive discourse and no compromise. The result is fragmentation, division, and strife. Sound familiar in the devolving society we are currently experiencing?

Madison wrote in *Federalist No. 10*:

> The latent causes of faction are thus sown in the nature of man; and we see them everywhere brought into different degrees of activity, according to the different circumstances of civil society. A zeal for different opinions concerning religion, concerning government, and many other points, as well of speculation as of practice; an attachment to different leaders ambitiously contending for pre-eminence and power; or to persons of other descriptions whose fortunes have been interesting to the human passions, have, in turn, divided mankind into parties, inflamed them with mutual animosity, and rendered them much more disposed to vex and oppress each other than to co-operate for their common good. So strong is this propensity of mankind to fall into mutual animosities, that where no substantial occasion presents itself, the most frivolous and fanciful distinctions have been sufficient to kindle their unfriendly passions and excite their most violent conflicts.[1]

Madison explains that the aim of a true democratic republic is to diffuse power and create mechanisms that allow and facilitate the continuing health of a society. Echoing John Locke, Madison observes the importance of making certain that a nation's populace understands and is governed by awareness of the need to resolve factional disputes through the willingness to respect established Rule of Law processes. These include accepting that the legitimate path to achieving what you desire involves using the operational procedures of the system to gain desired outcomes if you do not initially "get your way." Violence and sabotage are not the "solution" in a Rule of Law system. Yet, that is what we are now experiencing.

Shortly before his death, George Mason University economics professor Walter Williams decried the suppression of free speech and traced much of it to universities.

> The violence, looting, and mayhem that this nation has seen over the past several months has much of its roots in academia, where leftist faculty teach immature young people all manner of nonsense that contradicts common sense and the principles of liberty. Chief among their lessons is a need to attack free speech in the form of prohibitions against so-called hate speech and micro-aggressions. Here are examples of several of those *terrible* micro-aggressions: "You are a credit to your race." "Wow! How did you become so good in math?" "There is only one race, the human race." "I'm not racist. I have several black friends." [or] "As a woman, I know what you go through as a racial minority."[2]

The Goals and Strategies of the Woke/Critical Race Theory Movement

Critical Race Theory (CRT) faculty gained significant presence in multiple university disciplines in the late 1970s and throughout the 1980s and 1990s. CRT, Sexuality and Genderism, LGBTQ+, and Wokeism represent an intensely ideological and identity politics–driven collection of aggressive advocates seeking to advance their groups' specific agendas. One key distinction between the Woke/CRT movement and the university up to that point is that Woke/CRT represents an intense infusion of extreme subjectivity into the classrooms, as well as faculty research, and ultimately the administrative structures of academia. The university as institution was captured and fundamentally changed through this takeover. The agendas of the activists required "destabilizing" and "transforming" the existing system and that is what has taken place in an increasingly corrupted process of expanding institutional control.

The primary tools being used to destabilize and weaken the existing system, and to intimidate and terrorize its participants into complicity and silence, include accusations of racism, sexism, of "White men" trying to hold onto their presumed and total systemic privilege, and a convenient invention of what is referred to as an ideology of "White Supremacy," a psychological affliction claimed to infect the minds of everyone unfortunate enough to be covered by white skin. Everything is now being viewed and interpreted through a clouded racial and "genderist" lens that is blurred by the politics, ideology, ignorance, and particularly, the significant financial benefits that have been gained by the beneficiaries and promoters of the "Woke/CRT industry."

One of the main devices being employed has involved strategic reliance on the university institution's cachet of legitimacy, truth, and wisdom conveyed by the institution's historically perceived integrity and historical commitment to the pursuit of truth. This has involved not only legitimate criticisms of societal issues and concerns, but the use of a distorted view of history and politics along with the assignment of sweeping accountability for other's past wrongs. This has been done most recently with the overly broad assertions of Critical Race Theory and the 1619 Project, and at this point, these represent the "end game" of a social revolution begun decades earlier.

We are now confronted by the harsh reality of how we preserve true social justice—honestly defined. As James Madison warned, this includes the need to resist the inevitable emergence of dominant factions that seek to aggressively capture power over others and use that power to the advantage of the specific faction to which they owe allegiance and from which they benefit. A strategic tactic of this approach in the ongoing cultural conflict is to create a system that mirrors the biblical morality play represented in the doctrine of "Original Sin." The strategic device tars all "White" people now alive, holding them accountable for the real and imagined "sins" of dead "White Guys" committed throughout history.

What is being asserted and accepted as "gospel" at this point is transparently vapid and socially destructive. But the infusion of uncertainty and the looming sense of guilt for things you never did are intentional and strategic. That is why the Woke/CRT "scholars" created things like "White privilege," subconscious racial bias, "micro aggressions" of which the purported violator is not even aware, and an all-encompassing "Systemic Racism" that envelops the entire social system and seeks to justify tearing down our society and transforming it into "something else."

Collectively, these assertions of the Woke/CRT movement are linked to condemnation of the fundamental ideals, methods, and values of the American community. This includes rejection of foundational assumptions of the desirability of rationality, truth, individuality, merit, equality, opportunity, and many other assumptions that provided the foundation of the American system of education, knowledge, philosophy, government, and society. Such values are now being derided as nothing more than tools of exploitation and power by the white male–dominated system, because otherwise their power and tradition would block the strategies of the "revolutionaries." That is also why the Woke/CRT movement is being driven by university "elites" who, as described by philosopher Eric Hoffer, operate as "fault-finding men of words" skilled in the use of high-sounding words and phrases that undermine the foundations of an established society in order to ultimately take power and control for themselves and their new "vision." John Patrick Diggins explains how the process unfolded through use of Marcusian political theory.

> [I]n the late seventies and eighties a substantial number of former New Left students found themselves comfortably inside the very institution they had once assaulted as part of the corrupt "system" that must be destroyed—the college and university of the "higher learning." Here, [Herbert] Marcuse's idea of "critical theory" would flourish, as would a development he failed to anticipate, the women's revolution, perhaps the single most important social movement to emerge from the sixties.[3]

In "The Culture War: Recognizing the Battle for Society's Direction," Adam Coleman, author and columnist for the *New York Post* and *Epoch Times*, voices a similar perspective on what is occurring.

> The education foot soldiers who are pushing ideological absurdities on your children come from elite education institutions that have been groomed to believe they know what's best because they were taught by the best. This is a clash for control over society. The culture will be the sacrificial lamb to gain the power some people have always been aiming for; they just needed a highly distracted population to pull off the great heist. . . . Our class adversaries are focused on the long game in this conflict: You should be too. It's worth fighting for what you want to uphold, but it's best not to get caught in the weeds searching for small wins from insignificant battles when you're still losing the war.[4]

America's universities first allowed the inclusion of ideas and the teachings of social justice courses that helped to initiate, create, and then drive the rapid expansion of Wokeness and Critical Race Theory. The problem we now face is that the movements went too far. The new academic activists who entered the ranks of academia "flipped" the social discourse from accurate social critiques of America's history of discrimination, to sweeping and vastly overstated "systemic" condemnations and psychological interpretations of subconscious discrimination and biases that the targeted individuals would never be able to disprove.

These accusations and assertions were not intended to provide honest perspectives and discourse. Their purpose was to support the activists' acquisition of power through the imposition of guilt, moral condemnation, and trumpeting the legitimacy of unproven and unprovable assertions. As authoritative intellectual centers, universities initially helped create the arguments, analyses, and slogans that imbued the movement with its substantial moral power. As the civil rights and Woke movements took hold, the new generation of Woke and critical academics being brought into the university sphere as faculty and administrators progressively filled their ranks with political activists who were part of identity groups possessed of anti-democratic agendas. They then increasingly sent cadres of radically shaped graduates into the world of K–12 education as teachers and administrators.

It was an important fact that even though the traditional scholarly standards were largely not applied to the work of the Woke faculty members, universities provided enhanced legitimacy to the existence and assertions of Critical Race Theory. Universities possessed presumed institutional commitments to truth, full intellectual discourse, interactive challenge, and insistence on supposedly rational and rigorous thought and valid data rather than assumption and assertion. The Woke/Crits were provided *carte blanche* when their production was assessed to a degree not granted other academics.

Many of the Woke/CRT "scholars" used very large, seemingly benign, and open-textured and malleable words they borrowed from European Marxist Deconstructionists intent on destabilizing their own Continental systems. The "Supercalifragilisticexpialidocious" Disney-fantasy words being thrown about were terms no one really understood with any clarity, but they "sounded smart." No one ever really asked the activists what they meant because neither potential questioners nor Woke/Crit activists actually understood what they were talking about. But the terms sounded impressive. The movement's faculty members tossed these words back and forth with each other, and praised and cited each other's work while no one on the outside of the movement really understood what was going on as the intense and divisive fault-finding polemic it was.

Even then, if we had not experienced the incredible rise of internet communications systems over the past twenty years, the Woke and Critical Race Theory activists would not exist on any level of consequence. This is because they would not have had a sufficient audience accessible through the "web" or "net" and would have been limited to the academic system of communications and publication, essentially journals read by a very limited audience, along with workshops and conferences. They would never have been able to create the interactive networks and linkages that have been essential for their success.

An Overview of the Critical Race Theory Movement

Richard Delgado and Jean Stefancic, currently professors of law at Seattle University, offered what they considered a favorable overview of the Critical Race Theory movement in *Critical Race Theory: An Annotated Bibliography*. It is a useful representation. The authors identify ten primary strands as part of Critical Race Theory. Delgado is considered one of the founders of the Critical Race Theory movement. Although I disagree with them politically, I commend the accuracy with which they describe the movement's key strategies. These are:

1. critique of liberalism
2. storytelling/counterstorytelling and "naming one's own reality"
3. revisionist interpretations of American civil rights law and progress
4. a greater understanding of the underpinnings of race and racism
5. structural determinism
6. race, sex, class, and their intersections
7. essentialism and anti-essentialism
8. cultural nationalism/separatism
9. legal institutions, Critical pedagogy, and minorities in the bar
10. criticism and self-criticism; responses.[5]

The activists in the ranks of the Woke/CRT movement not only include faculty and administrators within our universities, but K–12 power-brokers and teachers unions whose ranks have been seeded over the past thirty-five or so years by university schools of education that provided the "transformational" politics, slogans, and agendas of the Woke/Crit activists. The organized teachers unions and their leadership, along with school boards, administrators, state boards of education, and the US Department of Education, are seeking to supplant parents as the controlling guide in shaping the children under their "revolutionary" command. The aim is to turn America's youth into revolutionaries who will follow the leaders' dictates. They also flood the messaging of social and legacy media outlets.

What is occurring is a comprehensive strategy to transform all of our fundamental systems. The strategy aims at gaining and consolidating power, and using that power to shut down and punish all opposition wherever found. It is working. The classic depiction of the university as a detached "Ivory Tower" is dead, just as are the institutions of journalism, free speech, and K–12 education.

"Dirty Filthy Oppressor": A More Honest Picture of Critical Race Theory

Lance Izumi, senior director of Education Studies at the Pacific Research Institute, writes in the *New York Post* about the experience of a Black family living in Las Vegas. The example involves the mother's reaction to what her mixed race son was experiencing in his school that was imposing a Critical Race Theory agenda on students to the point that her son was decried as a "dirty, filthy oppressor." Izumi cited a new book he co-authored detailing the reaction of many parents to this highly questionable educational agenda.

> Gabs Clark [is] a widowed low-income African-American mother of five children who had been living in a motel in Las Vegas. Her high school-aged son, William, was in a local charter school which required a course called *Sociology of Change*. According to Clark, the course included an assignment that asked students "to list your identities, your race, your gender, your sexual orientation, your religion." William, who is mixed race with blonde hair and blue eyes, refused to complete the assignment and was given a failing grade for the class, which kept him from graduating. According to Clark, because of his fair complexion, the class viewed her son as "a dirty filthy oppressor." Clark filed a federal lawsuit charging the school with violating William's First Amendment free speech rights, Fourteenth Amendment equal protection rights, and federal anti-discrimination rights for compelling him to complete the race-based assignment. The case has since been settled out of court.
>
> Critical Race Theory (CRT) is among the most divisive doctrines to ever threaten America's schoolchildren, and it has sparked an unprecedented grassroots uprising of parents whose stories of

ideological resistance have been detailed in our new book The Great Parent Revolt. A multidisciplinary education philosophy that places race at the center of American history and culture, CRT is akin to racial Marxism—with whites viewed as oppressors and non-whites framed as the oppressed. The philosophy is at the center of high-profile intellectual efforts, such as The New York Times' controversial 1619 Project, which claims that slavery and anti-black racism are at the core of the entire American experience."[6]

Contrary to Woke/CRT Claims, "We are a systemically anti-racist country."

In describing how universities have become "propaganda mills" rather than serious intellectual and educational centers, Alan Dershowitz, Felix Frankfurter professor of Law, emeritus, at Harvard University, provides significant insight into the strategy being used. It is centered on creating powerful narratives and then using them to justify actions that go far beyond the event or fact used as a "trigger."

> "I think left, radical people, from the communists in the 1930s and '40s to today's woke generation, look for opportunities, they find events, and therefore they can use it to project their narrative and to project their agenda," Dershowitz said. The left, including the Biden administration, has declared the United States "systemically racist," but Dershowitz disagrees. "We are not a systemically racist country. We're a systemically anti-racist country," he said.

Dershowitz further explains:

> The left's attempt to solve racism and give an advantage to one group is disadvantaging others, Dershowitz said. "Look at the Harvard case. Who's suing Harvard? Asian students, because they're being discriminated against because of quotas for black students." Students for Fair Admissions (SFFA) has a lawsuit against Harvard University alleging it treats white and Asian-American students with stricter admissions

standards—a practice some call reverse discrimination. . . . "And the result is not equality. The result is to introduce a new kind of inequality and an anti-meritocratic approach," said Dershowitz."[7]

Identity politics is, inevitably, brainwashing. Jan Jekielek and Masooma Haq go on to describe Dershowitz's view that the corruption of mind is caused by one-sided analysis and the "true believers'" fanatical adherence to a preconceived answer.

"Dershowitz said while he often agrees with liberals' "substantive points of view," he does not agree with the means they use. "They don't care about means. They think the ends justify the means, their utopia is going to be achieved," said Dershowitz. The left has started to believe you don't need free speech or due process, he added. "Why do you need free speech if you know the truth with a capital 'T'? What do you need due process [for] if you already know that a man who was accused by a woman of course is guilty? Why do we need to have a trial?" said Dershowitz. . . . "How dare they call themselves progressives," Dershowitz said. "They are regressives. They are reactionaries. They are repressors. They want to stop due process and free speech and equal protection."[8]

John Nolte describes a situation that calls the motives of various advocates into question and explains how the issue of race and racism has been twisted by leading Woke/CRT activists to their own benefit and profit. This includes actions that are disgusting hoaxes that are then exploited to intensify the claim that America is an overwhelmingly racist society. Nolte writes:

"On Wednesday, as I watched MSNBC race hustler Al Sharpton, NBC's Willie Geist, and NASCAR driver Bubba Wallace make horse's asses of themselves with the claim that a loop tied (in 2019) at the end of a rope used to pull down a garage door was in fact a noose "placed" there to racially terrorize Bubba in 2020 (even

though Bubba was randomly assigned that garage for a single race). .
. . When Sharpton, Geist, and Wallace are so desperate to exploit an
act of racism that they are willing to look that ridiculous inventing
one, what we have here is a demand for racism that far exceeds the
supply. There is proof of this supply problem all over the place. For
instance . . . Did you know that the NASCAR "noose" is the ninth
noose hoax in as many years? This is the ninth time the media and
the left have invented a noose hoax to frame America as racist. As far
as overall hate hoaxes, we are now in *the hundreds* . . . That's right, in
just a few years, there have literally been over a hundred hate hoaxes
perpetrated by the media and the left to frame America as racist.

But it's not just the hoaxes that prove the left has a supply problem. Look at what the left now defines as *racism*. The left's demand
for racism so far exceeds the supply that . . .

- It is now racist to demand action to stop the violence in Chicago.
- It is now racist to say "All Lives Matter."
- It is now racist to be colorblind.
- It is now racist to *not* acknowledge the color of someone else's skin
  and *not* treat them different because their experiences are differ-
  ent, or something.
- Abraham Lincoln is racist.
- Ulysses S. Grant is racist.
- Criticizing the burning and looting of predominantly black neigh-
  borhoods is racist.
- Criticizing Barack Obama for anything is racist.

There's so little racism in America that whenever the media happen upon an actual act of racism, it's the biggest story in the world for
days, sometimes weeks. And here's my favorite . . . The left's demand
for racism so exceeds the supply, they have invented the coloring
book of "unconscious racism" or "unconscious bias." How great is
that? What I mean is that there is so little actual racism out there, the
left have been forced to resort to *mind reading* . . . And after they're
done reading our racist minds, they have been forced to resort to
framing us using the crimes of ThoughtCrime and WrongThink. [9]

New York City Imposes Mandatory Critical Race Theory Training on All City Employees

While *Conformity Colleges* is primarily about what is going on with Wokeism and Critical Race Theory activism in universities and how that ideological activity has spread throughout the American system of education, it is also important to understand that it is an anti-intellectual "virus" that has infected politics, government, business, our media, and more. An example is found in New York Mayor Eric Adams's mandate that all the city's employees must undergo Critical Race Theory training. This parallels a similar mandate imposed on all federal agencies and employees by the Biden Administration. The New York action is reported next.

> Mayor Eric Adams' New York City forced all of its employees into a radical critical race theory-inspired training, according to a copy of the training. . . . The "mandatory" training was sent to all New York City employees with a March 6 deadline. "The training provides all NYC employees with a framework to understand . . . the importance of racial equity . . . in the workplace," the email said. The controversial lens expressed in the training is called critical race theory, which holds that America is and was always structurally racist; CRT adds that the U.S. was designed from its start to systematically oppress minority groups in order to uphold systems of power for the dominant culture or White racial group. CRT also maintains an oppressor versus oppressed lens of society and classifies people into groups based on supposed "privilege."[10]

Chapter Seventeen

Heroes, False Prophets, and Demagogues

In 1959, I listened to the nightly news reports on a little pink transistor radio as Fidel Castro and his heroic "revolutionaries" came down from the Cuban mountains to confront Batista's evil people who suppressed the population. I "knew" they were heroes fighting against injustice and evil. To my unsophisticated young boy's ears, Castro was a combination of Tonto and the Lone Ranger, or Superman bringing a version of "Truth, Justice, and the American Way." A hero like Davy Crockett, George Washington, and Abraham Lincoln. Castro was bringing freedom to the oppressed people of Cuba. My beloved grandfather, who worked in "the mill" for almost forty years and was active in helping to organize the Steelworkers Union in Youngstown, Ohio, had always told me to protect the "common man," and that commitment made Castro a hero to me, until it became clear he was allied with the USSR and hated America.

It also became clear that Cuba's overthrown dictator Juan Batista and American criminal syndicates had been running the country for their own benefit, so there was reason for many Cubans to not like the United States. Then Che Guevara took the revolution's message of justice to Africa and South America, and for a brief time he was a hero to me, and still is for some people. Tragically, however, as almost inevitably occurs, it quickly became obvious that Cuba had simply changed dictators through Castro and was enforcing an oppressive system through secret police, military power and the imprisonment or execution of dissidents.

But while there are false prophets and demagogues everywhere, there are also real heroes. Martin Luther King Jr., Jesse Jackson, Rosa Parks, Cesar Chavez, and Cassius Clay (Muhammad Ali) come to mind. Another person

I respect immensely is a fantastic civil rights leader I worked with in Colorado named Elizabeth Patterson. She was an incredible Black woman possessed of rare courage that allowed her to face whatever came up. These are all people whose courage inspired me. John F. Kennedy and Bobby Kennedy offered a beacon for many of us to follow. There were numerous times when I was working in Washington, DC that I would walk across the bridge over the Potomac and go into Arlington National Cemetery to visit JFK's grave.

We all need heroes, guides, and people with vision who fight against injustice. For me, as a matter of reading and my own educational experience, I can add Patrick Henry, Nathan Hale, the "Green Mountain Boys," Jeanne d'Arc, Horatio at the Bridge, the three hundred Greeks who held back the Persians, and the Arthurian Knights of the Round Table. Much of it myth, of course, but our myths are often more important as guiding ideals than our common reality. I don't care, for example, if George Washington didn't chop down a cherry tree or refused to tell a lie. Nor do I care if Abe Lincoln actually walked miles barefoot to return some pennies when he realized the store owner had miscalculated.

These myths are taught to children in order to create ideals about honesty and good behavior. That is why it is so important that our youngest children, at home and in their earliest school years, experience the ideals and moral lessons we feel strongly they should have as individuals and contributing members of society. The duty to challenge the evils of racism and unjust treatment are prominent among the goals of education.

The strange thing, to me, is that contrary to the assertions of the Woke who parade about as if they created awareness of social justice and injustice, in my own educational processes the schools I attended—K-12 and college—did provide such perspectives six decades ago. The modern "Woke" are actually "late to the party" and many of them are unwelcome guests because their often absurd and overblown claims have risked causing damage to the decades of achievement experienced since the 1960s by generating a new kind of racism and discrimination in their overweening search for power and control.

There are other heroes. George Washington as the Father of Our Country and Abraham Lincoln as the "Great Emancipator." My mythic heroes, all with the inevitable "feet of clay" that afflict all humans, include Ethan Allen, Daniel Boone, Davy Crockett, Geronimo, Martin Luther King Jr., Nelson Mandela, whose courage was "off the charts," and numerous others. Sitting Bull and other Sioux agreed to a treaty with the US Government in 1868, but after gold was discovered in the tribal lands the treaty was breached. Sitting Bull allied the Great Plains tribes and resisted the unjust white settler takeover of the areas that had been granted by treaty. Heroes can be found everywhere, but they do not always win.

On a more personal level, our family has a great, great, grandfather John Barnhizer who fought on the American side in the Revolutionary War; another Yankee descendant who fought to free slaves on the Union's side in the Civil War; my father who, like hundreds of thousands of other Americans, fought against the Nazis; my uncle, Bob Bradley, who spent time as a prisoner of war in WWII; and my grandfather, Thomas Seth Jones, who served in the Army Air Corps in WWI. Along with the above, my younger brother, Bret Barnhizer, served two tours of duty in Vietnam, spanning the years between his eighteenth and twenty-first birthdays. He was an Army medic and was assigned to two different infantry brigades and a separate Military Advisory Team working in dangerous territory to determine and counter North Vietnamese deployments.

We Need to Aspire and Be Inspired, and That Makes Us Vulnerable

We need to aspire and be inspired by something we perceive as "higher" and "better" than us. This need makes us susceptible to "prophets" who seem to understand something of universal importance that is better than us. Our "prophets" are masters at manipulating others who are searching for "the way" to have something meaningful and majestic in which to believe and be part of. The prophets weave spells and we fall prey to their "magic."

In the deep dark space we all have within ourselves but from which we seek to hide, we humans know how little we actually understand. We also know that most of us have a "mean and spiteful little person" living inside us. Our deep-felt need for meaning creates a void many of us try to fill. We silently "whistle in the dark" in the face of our own ignorance, as I did at night in grade school when walking past the graveyard located next to the path I took on my way home. It was even scarier when I was thirteen, after I watched Bela Lugosi in *Dracula* for the first time by myself on Halloween Night. After weeks spent whistling even more loudly and walking really fast on my journey home to safety, I snuck out of my parents' house at midnight and made myself walk through the cemetery to challenge my fear. It actually worked. I wasn't attacked by a vampire intent on sucking my blood.

Our fears and needs, including the need to feel we are part of something significant, make us susceptible to impassioned and powerful people who persuade us they have great insight. Sorting out the real prophets from the hustlers, manipulators, demagogues, and "snake oil salesmen" has always been a difficult task, and we seem to fail more often than we succeed. It becomes even more difficult when movements such as Wokeism, Marxism, Maoism, Fascism, or Nazism are successful in building a larger and larger membership whose impassioned "believers" tell us how great it is and offer benefits for being part of the collective. Of course, as their power increases, it is made clear that there are consequences if we do not "get in line."

Noam Chomsky argues that "intellectuals are the most indoctrinated part of the population . . . the ones most susceptible to propaganda."

Noam Chomsky is a public intellectual known for his work in linguistics, political activism, and social criticism. He is sometimes called "the father of modern linguistics." Chomsky is Institute Professor and professor of Linguistics Emeritus at MIT and Laureate Professor in the Department of Linguistics at the University of Arizona, where he is also the Agnese Nelms Haury Chair in Environment and Social Justice. He is the author of *Aspects of the Theory of Syntax* and *The Minimalist Program*, both published by MIT Press.

I remember the time I staged a significant international conference on sustainable economic and social strategies for national and global societies.

Noam Chomsky, who I found to be a delightful man, was about to make his presentation, and my responsibility as the host was to introduce the brilliant linguist and philosopher. I started telling people all the technical stuff about his background, but all of a sudden something came over me and I said, "You all know who he is and the incredible analytical and political things he stands for, so, HERE'S NOAM!"

Entirely distinct from my inadequate introduction, Noam Chomsky offers significant and honest insight as to how intellectuals function. In a 1991 interview, Chomsky offered a damning opinion about how many intellectuals function. This included describing intellectuals' almost automatic submission to those in power to preserve their own power, privilege, status, and reputations. The following Q & A from Chomsky's 1991 interview capture the reality of the motivations and behavior of the "special class" of intellectuals.

Q. You have suggested that "intellectuals are the most indoctrinated part of the population . . . the ones most susceptible to propaganda." You have explained that the educated classes are "ideological managers," complicit in "controlling all the organized flow of information." How and why is this so? What can be done to change this situation?

A. Now, my point is that the people we call intellectuals are those who have passed through various gates and filters and have made it into positions in which they can serve as cultural managers. There are plenty of other people just as smart, smarter, more independent, more thoughtful, who didn't pass through those gates and we just don't call them intellectuals. In fact, this is a process that starts in elementary school. Let's be concrete about it. You and I went to good graduate schools and teach in fancy universities, and the reason we did this is because we're obedient. That is, you and I, and typically people like us, got to the positions we're in because from childhood we were willing to follow orders. If the teacher in third grade told us to do some stupid thing, we didn't say, "Look, that's ridiculous. I'm not going to do it." We did it because we wanted to get on to fourth grade. We came from the kind of background where we'd say, "Look, do it, forget about it, so the teacher's a fool, do it, you'll get ahead, don't worry about it." That goes on all through school, and it goes on through your professional career. You're told in graduate school, "Look, don't work on that; it's a wrong idea. Why not work on this? You'll get ahead."

[Y]ou allow yourself to be shaped by the system of authority that exists out there and is trying to shape you. Well, some people do this. They're submissive and obedient, and they accept it and make it through; they end up being people in the high places—economic managers, cultural managers, political managers. There are other people who were in your class and in my class who didn't do it. When the teacher told them in the third grade to do x, they said, "That's stupid, and I'm not going to do it." Those are people who are more independent minded, for example, and there's a name for them: they're called "behavior problems." . . . In fact, the whole educational system involves a good deal of filtering of this sort, and it's a kind of filtering towards submissiveness and obedience."[1]

What Happens when the "Submissive and Obedient" Intellectuals Chomsky Describes Are Controlled by Rabid Activists and Demagogues?

The university is, as Marshall McLuhan explained through the "medium is the message" concept, an overarching and penetrating medium through which power can be obtained and society shaped. In his classic 1964 book *Understanding Media: The Extensions of Man*, McLuhan argues in Chapter One, "The Medium Is the Message," that a "message" is "the change of scale or pace or pattern" that a new invention or innovation "introduces into human affairs."[2] In *Conformity Colleges*, among the points being made is that the university system, and the entire educational system as structured, is a critical medium that contains and energizes "the message."

That capture of the "medium" of the university, the overall educational system, and the institutions of communication on nearly all levels, is why the takeover of the educational system being described here is such a vital element of the social and political transformation. Institutional capture lies at the center of the Woke/Crit agenda. That takeover of the university and the K–12 system grants the Woke/CRT activists free rein to use the techniques of propaganda to instill their "transformative" agenda in the hearts and minds of students and make them "social justice warriors" in their cause. This provides the presumptively "educated" mass of true believers a sense of meaning and significance. This outcome, however, is not achieved through the quality of their vision but by propaganda, intimidation, and indoctrination.

French Natural Law philosopher Jacques Ellul speaks of stereotypes, propaganda, and symbols. He writes:

> Propaganda gives the individual the stereotypes he no longer takes the trouble to work out for himself; it furnishes these in the form of labels, slogans, ready-made judgments. It transforms ideas into slogans, and by giving the "word," convinces the individual that he has an opinion. The stereotype, which is stable, helps man to avoid thinking, to take a personal position, to form his own opinion.[3]

How this works has been explained by Thomas Green in his book, *The Activities of Teaching.*

> Every mind is fettered at some point, ridden with presuppositions and stereotypes that stand in the way of mental freedom. . . . [A] person may hold a belief because it is supported by the evidence, or . . . may accept the evidence because it happens to support a belief he already holds. It is possible to hold conflicting sets of beliefs as psychologically central because we tend to order our beliefs in little clusters encrusted about, as it were, with a protective shield that prevents any cross-fertilization among them or any confrontation between them.[4]

Propaganda, True Believers, and "Gangs"

As my wonderful mother, who lived to be a hundred and was "sharp as a tack" to the end, always told me, "all propaganda begins with a grain of truth" and then builds a distorted message on that initial assertion. This is what we are now experiencing. Intellectuals, or perhaps more accurately, "pseudo-intellectuals," are at the core of those twisting us with their message aimed at gaining power for themselves.

The problem, as Yale professor Robert Dahl has written, is that special interest groups, "gangs," and the like, always end up as closed systems. Others are "outsiders." In his *Dilemmas of Pluralist Democracy*, Dahl describes how organizational behavior and formal and informal identity groups and "gangs" are organizations that define us, limit our focus, and control how we view others in terms of their relationship to our own "organization."

> Organizations . . . are not mere relay stations that receive and send signals from their members about their interests. Organizations amplify the signals and generate new ones. Often they sharpen particularistic demands at the expense of broader needs, and short-run against long-run needs. . . . Leaders therefore play down potential cleavages and conflicts among their own members and exaggerate the salience of conflicts with outsiders. Organizations thereby strengthen both solidarity and division, cohesion and conflict; they reinforce solidarity among members and conflicts with nonmembers. Because associations help to fragment the concerns of citizens, interests that many citizens might share—latent ones perhaps—may be slighted.[5]

Those who teach, research, and study in the "soft" or noncumulative disciplines become easy prey for demagogues, false prophets, and others seeking power. Some, like Ibram Kendi and Nikole Hannah-Jones, are the manipulators and the profiteers making many thousands from their proclamations and accusations. They, like Lenin, Marcuse, Mao, Chavez, Castro, and other demagogues, entice others into their "web." Once their targets are seduced, they enrage their revolutionary base of true believers and sycophants who seek power and ego gratification by proclaiming their "victimhood" and how their followers have been unfairly exploited. This identifies and defines an "enemy" who must then be held accountable for their own supposedly associated "systemic sins" or, if that doesn't work all that well, to convince people they are morally and financially responsible for the alleged sins of their historical forebears. If that scam doesn't produce the required results because of a lack of "guilty" forebears, they are told they are accountable for the actions of all people, whenever born, whose identity characteristics, i.e. skin color, are similar to those now being condemned.

When those pursuing such esoteric and intellectually strained topics and disciplines are not willing or able to employ the abilities of reason, testing, critique, and utilization of the full range of honest data, it is extraordinarily easy for demagogues such as Marx, Lenin, Hitler, Ibram X. Kendi (née Henry Rogers), Hannah-Jones, and others to convince their "disciples" that their proclamations are true. This has become even more common due to the politically driven identity collectives that now dominate American politics. Most people want to be part of something significant. Their need to identify with something a mass of people consider significant and meaningful makes them easy victims of those who offer "certainty," a sense of purpose, and faith in a cause.

The problem is that this becomes destructive when collectives committed to specific organizational agendas, identity preferences, and pursuits of political transformations to advance their members' interests are allowed to gain control. Such situations cannot be resolved through rational discourse. That inability to interact through rational discourse based on evidence creates a serious threat to the well-being of an overarching and complex political community of the kind that had existed in America but is now corrupted through attacks by the "prophetic" leaders of "the tribes."

Chapter Eighteen

All Revolutions Need an "Enemy"

"Thinking People" Are "Dangerous Obstacles" for Revolutionary Narratives: Just Ask Mao Zedong

There are consequences to what is taking place. One is the assault on rationality, logic, and evidence as being tools of White Supremacy and White Privilege. Why, you might ask, would the Woke/CRT elites make such attacks? The answer is that people capable of thinking clearly, critically, and analytically, who insist on factual proof for what is claimed, are serious threats to revolutionaries. Mao Zedong understood this threat, and in his 1937 tract described the dangers Liberalism posed to a revolution. This was because "thinking people" get in the way of revolutionary narratives. They question orders and assertions and must be silenced through fear, brainwashing, or more severe forms of "canceling." The result is a shift toward tyranny and authoritarianism, and that is where "Wokeism" leads.[1]

"Educating" students in K–12 systems and universities in ways that indoctrinate sabotages our young by undermining their ability to engage in legitimate critical thinking on vital issues. Since such inadequately educated individuals lack the full range of knowledge and are unable or unwilling to think with balance, depth, and precision, such "mis-education" condemns anyone who challenges the controlling movement's dominant narrative to be condemned as an enemy and bigot. This is what is happening throughout our educational systems, and is the cause and effect of our rapidly splintering society.

Attacks on critics or people who simply do not agree with an aggressive movement's aims and tactics provide the "lifeblood" of revolutionary movements. This is because all successful "revolutions" require an "enemy," a "moral cause" that generates hate and envy among the revolutionary base, and a system by which slogans and propaganda can be transmitted to true believers and "social justice warriors."

This is what was done in creating the Soviet Revolution, the terrors of Maoist control in China using the young fanatics of the Red Guard, and in Nazi Germany where the Jews, Communists, and Gypsies were all portrayed as "demons" and murdered in the millions. To this, we can add the "Death to America" mantra of the Iranian Ayatollahs, the class warfare championed by Chavez and Maduro in Venezuela, the same for Castro's Cuba and Ortega's Nicaragua, and numerous others. This is what is taking place today in America with the "Whites"—particularly White males—being relegated to the demonic "enemy" class.

Attacking an existing system and seizing the control needed to weaken those they wanted to displace in a quest for power demands the identification of an "oppressor." The oppressor needs to be something distinct and readily identifiable. The "oppressor's" alleged sins have to be grounded on something awful. From my personal perspective, nothing is worse than slavery, racial discrimination, and the unwillingness to value another person based on that individual's actual self and behavior. These issues penetrate directly to how I interact with the world and to what I value. What I detest is that the Woke and Crits have warped and twisted these values for their own political purposes. They have painted their extreme interpretations of reality with an extremely broad and sloppy brush. They needed an "enemy" and so they created one.

The problem with creating an "enemy" sufficient to motivate and enrage a revolutionary movement is that the hate and division can't simply be turned off with a magical political "button." A revolutionary movement does not mobilize its adherents through reason and logic. Nor does it rely on fact or reality in its depictions of those chosen as the evil oppressors. Hyperbole, emotion, overstatement, false claims, and overblown narratives are the devices of energizing the "soldiers" of the movement. Once accomplished, that hate and division and blame does not go away but corrupts and taints the entire system. It is expiated, if at all, through the victorious participants in the struggle taking their rage and hate out on the defeated. This is what is occurring with the Woke/CRT movement, and it is likely to get worse.

Once you initiate the "enemy" cycle, how do you stop the hyperbole and hate once you win? "They" are not simply people who disagreed with you. "They" are "demons," "foul" beings, "users," exploiters, abusers, and more. The enemy must be identified and specifically identifiable. The six-point yellow star that was required to be worn visibly in Nazi Germany labeled Jews as the hated "enemy" so that the revolutionary mantra of some imagined guilt was constantly before the revolutionaries.

Ramping up the revolutionary "mob" against the "enemy" is some-thing Lenin, Mao, Hitler, Chavez, Castro, Mussolini, Franco, the Iranian Ayatollahs, and every other "revolutionary" does on the way to taking control and becoming a dictator. The "victimized" mob they created to win their "war" must be energized, fed, and given the "spoils" of vic-tory. The "vanquished losers" must be made to pay and atone publicly for their "crimes" or the actions of prior generations who share some similar identity characteristics. This is done in the spirit of "Original Sin" and "Collective Guilt."

Like those who are being described as America's "Neo-Marxists," the Soviets and Maoists deliberately broke down the family structure. This was to make the "Party" the only valid unit to which loyalty was owed. In China and the Soviet Union, the "true believers" were encouraged to con-demn their own parents and friends. The need for a "revolutionary mass" loyal only to the "leader" controls all successful mass movements. That is why, to the committed Marxist, it isn't enough to simply ignore issues of family. The family's structure must be undermined and destroyed. The revolutionary's sole loyalty must be to the "revolution." Family allegiance, love, and loyalty get in the way.

It is no accident that the Woke/Crit movement in America seeks to collectivize their "believers," and tries to make parents of K–12 children appear as "domestic terrorists" if they oppose Critical Race Theory's flawed and sweeping assertions. Those ideological activists are doing vir-tually nothing to enhance real educational opportunities in major urban areas. They are ignoring the crisis of the disintegration of Black families in our cities as well as the abysmal public education being provided by urban school systems to those described as "previously marginalized" communities who find themselves unfortunate to be under the control of Woke/Crit true believers and opportunists. The urban and "progressive" leaders in control of the metropolitan areas that make up a majority of the US population lack the ability, or willingness, to take honest and effective actions to fix what they created during their multiple decades of control. Instead, they stoke and feed on the rage, the riots, the mantra of victimhood, and the invention of micro-aggressions and subconscious biases.

At this moment, we are caught in a highly stressful and divisive period in which identity groups under the control of aggressive political activists are seeking to define the world in ways that serve their specific political agendas but betray the communities of which they are a part. John McWhorter, Columbia University professor and author of *The Power of Babel: A Natural History of Language* and *Losing the Race: Self-Sabotage in Black America* condemns much of what is taking place about race in America. He describes the "anti-whiteness" movement as a new form of racism that is sabotaging the growth and dignity of blacks in the United States. McWhorter indicates this is demonstrated in Robin DiAngelo's *White Fragility: Why Is It So Hard for White People to Talk About Race?* arguing there are three ways in which the sabotage is taking place. These are based on a mindset of defeatism that he says has infected those of Black ethnicity in America. That mindset is being driven by three elements. McWhorter describes them as:

- cults of victimology,
- separatism,
- anti-intellectualism, making blacks their own worst enemies in their struggle for success.[2]

Most recently, McWhorter made a vital observation in warning that "White Fragility" is both patronizing and racist. He argues that what is going on "dehumanizes" and "infantilizes" Black people by creating a "cult" of "white guilt." Sam Dorman writes:

> McWhorter . . . charged . . . that "White Fragility" is "about how to make certain educated white readers feel better about themselves." [He explained] . . . DiAngelo's outlook rests upon a depiction of Black people as endlessly delicate poster children within this self-gratifying fantasy about how [W]hite America needs to think," McWhorter wrote. "Or, better, stop thinking. Her answer to [W]hite fragility . . . entails an elaborate and pitilessly dehumanizing condescension toward Black people." McWhorter further concludes.
>
> "The very assumption is deeply condescending to all proud Black people." . . . "The sad truth . . . is that anyone falling under the sway of this blinkered, self-satisfied, punitive stunt of a primer has been taught . . . how to be racist in a whole new way."[3]

The cracks are beginning to show. This is reflected in the recent criticisms of the Progressive Left by the traditional Liberal Bill Maher who stated during an interview that the Left has become like the Ku Klux Klan because rather than adopting MLK's dream of people being seen through the lens of their character, the Woke perceive everything through race.[4] Longtime Democratic political strategist James Carville stated recently that Far Left democrats were the "most stupid, naive people you could imagine."[5] I would add to these two criticisms that quite a few of the leaders are not naive or stupid as opposed to greedy and power-driven.

The Woke/Crits versus the "Toxic Male, White-Skinned Enemy Guys"

The extremely aggressive attack on history and what we call "Western thought" is all part of a strategy, one equivalent to the role of medieval "sappers" besieging fortified towns and castles. Ideals and history are the foundations of the fortress idea that "the enemy" hides behind the walls of power. This means that a revolution or siege fails if the enemy's foundations are not undermined and walls breached. The job of the "sappers" was to tunnel beneath otherwise impenetrable walls in order to weaken the foundations and plant destructive charges. The attackers blew up the charges, destroyed the foundations, breached the walls, and conquered the citadel.

This is what is now occurring. It is why the "social justice warriors" and activists of today are rewriting history to fit their "narrative" and rejecting fundamental ideals. Those ideals serve as the "foundational building blocks" of Western society and their ongoing loss to a regressive and Neo-Marxist political bloc is sapping the spirit and integrity from American society. The primary tactic being used is the redefinition of what is perceived as reality, done through control of language and the use of thematic constructs that reshape our view of history and assign blame for anything that runs counter to the Left's narrative.

The revision of history is a key element. This is aimed at making people feel guilty about what was done a century or more before they personally even existed. The idea is to create a strategic version of "Original Sin" by which all people of a specific strategically invented identity are tainted and for which they—and they alone—must atone. What we now see with the flawed and overblown 1619 Project advanced by the *New York Times* is the assertion that *all* "Whites" are bad, racist to the core, and continuing oppressors of Blacks and People of Color! When you think about such assertions even a little, they represent a disgusting and politically-driven form of new racism being immorally advanced by those billing themselves as "Anti-Racists."

A Woke political movement that always claimed to pride itself on a dizzying range of "diversity" has used a strategic lie to gain power. In doing so, that movement created a single, non-diverse, monolithic cultural identity of "White." There is really no such category, and those who may biologically fit into an extremely loose category of "whiteness" represent an incredible range and diversity of characteristics, just as are those fitting loosely within the "skin" of Black, Asian, Latino, Native American, and the increasingly large ethnic and biological mixtures that characterize the healthy expansion of human relationships. To those committed to the all-encompassing political mantra, "People of Color Good. White people Bad!" it doesn't matter where those "Whites" were born, how they were raised, what language they speak, what values and experiences they have, their differing cultures and languages, or the economic and social conditions under which they live. They are "White" and "They" are the "enemy" of the "revolution."

There Are No "Off" Buttons for the Hate

When you create this kind of intense revolutionary hate there are no "off" buttons. In the *Twilight Zone* dimension in which the Crits and Woke reside, *all* those they tar with the label "Whiteness" to generate rage and pursue power for themselves are the same. *All* Whites are condemned to live their lives under the burdens of "Original Sin" and "Collective Guilt" imposed by the Critical Race Theory and Woke narrative. *All* are tainted, evil, guilty, and whatever else the revolutionary leaders accuse them of being. *All* deserve to be sentenced to "Woke/Crit Hell." Once you stir up those emotions, you can't just push a button to shut off the hate and accusations. You can't get more racist than that, and the "New Racism" created by the left's extreme ideologists will be very difficult to reverse.

The Left also likes to accuse people of "being on the wrong side of history." This, of course, means that the activists and critics of the Left invariably consider themselves to be "on the right side." Nothing could be more wrong. Consistent with history, one thing that is guaranteed is that if the Woke/Crit movement is ultimately successful, they will recreate an America that is darker, irreversibly torn, bigoted, and repressive.

"History" shows us that divisiveness and hate cannot be easily backed off from after you fill a society with the "poison" such attitudes and beliefs represent. This is the trap Woke/Crit activists have created for all of us, including themselves. The Woke/Crits are "destroyers," not "creators." We are already discovering there is no "off button" for the hate.

A longtime, very close friend, who personally endured the racism of the 1950s and 1960s with "Colored" water fountains, "Colored" restrooms, "Colored" schools, "Colored" restaurants and hotels, and other deeply racist divisions in the South, recently conveyed to me an important point about the existing Critical Race Theorists. He said that virtually none of the Woke/Crit activists who came of age in 1981 or later actually know much of anything about "racism" other than what they read in books and keep repeating endlessly to sell their agenda. Doing so makes them feel "special" and creates a space of "lived experience" they claim provides them knowledge only they can access, and provides status and a sense of legitimacy and power they would otherwise not have. Is this understandable? Yes. Is it morally, intellectually, or socially legitimate and a path America can afford to follow? No.

The fact that overt and provable discrimination has become thankfully rare over the last sixty years is one reason we see so much reliance on "invisible" manifestations of discrimination. Micro-aggressions, subconscious biases, systemic bias, hyper-subjective interpretations of what a person not only said but must have meant according to the subjective Woke interpreter. "Original Sin" and "Collective Guilt" systemic analyses are the weapons being used to silence anyone who dares to challenge the accusations. *Time* magazine just published an analysis claiming that a commitment to regular physical exercise was racist and a form of "White supremacy."[6] A female university professor reported that, based on her "research" into TikTok postings, white women who were proud of their neat kitchens and pantries were "racist."[7] Such bizarre claims are integral to the Woke/Crit movement. They continually invent new forms alleged to be a form of racism in order to keep the "fire" burning in the Movement and the "enemy" off balance.

The truth is that the leaders of the Woke/Crit movements thirst after power. They are willing to say and do almost anything to obtain and keep it. Some are convinced they know what they are doing, and that they are morally superior beings filled with "virtue." Others are opportunists seizing the moment to harvest financial benefits and status. Booker T. Washington called such people the "Trickster Figures" who profited from stirring up racial dissension.

Other progressive leftists and the Woke may not be greedy "Tricksters," but they are fanatics and/or "virtue signalers." The fanatics see the turmoil we are going through as a "holy war" in which they, as committed "revolutionaries," are entitled to do whatever is needed to overcome an "evil" enemy. As the increasingly wealthy Socialist Bernie Sanders uttered after the 2016 Democratic Convention, they must use the Machiavellian strategy of "by any means necessary" to achieve victory against the Republicans and Donald Trump. That is what they did and are still doing.

Everlasting Collective Guilt and Original Sin

The current "transformative" struggle being driven by the "revolutionaries" is not about the invented "enemies'" individual actions. This is a deliberate strategic choice. The levels of overt discriminatory behavior had largely evaporated in a society that accepted the moral tragedy of its prior behaviors and was striving to correct the harms that had been created. This represented great progress on eliminating and suppressing racism. But it produced consequences the Woke and CRT movements could not accept if they were to become dominant. This was because the 1960s Civil Rights Movement had increasingly transitioned Americans away from our discriminatory past by creating strategies for achieving social equality that obstructed the quest for power of those whose entire political and moral leverage derived from playing the "race card" to "trump" the existing system.

As real racism diminished dramatically after the 1960s, the language and concepts that had been used to attack actual, specific, disgusting, and overt racism had to be redefined and expanded, and that is what occurred. Micro-aggressions, subconscious biases, "systemic" structures, "privilege," and other devices to redefine racism were developed as part of a strategy to maintain power in the Woke/CRT movement.

The advantage of having an "oppressor" identity group is that their "Original Sin" and "White Guilt" no longer have the protection of due process or fair consideration of its members' individual actions, as persons. Everything is focused on making the "enemy" appear to be a faceless and soulless oppressor. That is, in fact, why the claims of systemic racism, "White supremacy," and "White privilege" were invented by those seeking to dismantle the existing political community and seize power. "Systems" can have harmful effects without requiring the identification of specific individual actions. Guilt then becomes a collective, almost subconscious phenomenon that imposes an associational responsibility and accountability without requiring the direct condemnation of individuals who did nothing wrong.

Innocent individuals found guilty of amorphous "Original Sin" accusations simply because they allegedly benefitted from "White privilege" or "White supremacy" become the unwitting victims of a past culture, rather than actual "doers" of racism or bigotry. They are allowed to partially escape the moral stigma created by dead people they never knew, and with whom they share no connection other than the superficiality of skin as long as they behave in a proper manner of public obeisance and atonement. They become a new "lesser and subservient" class based solely on the color of their skin. Some redemption and partial atonement is allowed as long as the individual admits his or her receipt of undeserved benefits and expiates the sins of white forebears by genuflecting and supporting the agendas and demands of the new racists.

Adam Coleman, *New York Post* columnist and author of *Black Victim To Black Victor: Identifying the ideologies, behavioral patterns and cultural norms that encourage a victimhood complex,* offers an example that very recently played out in the context of longtime radical racial activist and Marxist figure Angela Davis. He writes:

> Leftists hurl rocks at America, claiming it is an irredeemably racist nation. But what happens when they discover they live in a glass house, and are as much a part of that messy, flawed history? Activist, communist and former fugitive Angela Davis was shocked to learn she is a Mayflower descendent on Tuesday's "Finding Your Roots" episode. Now 79, Davis was the latest to appear on the PBS show where celebrities and public figures learn about their ancestry. Near the episode's end, after discussing multiple members of her family, the former Black Panther learned she's descended from William Brewster, one of the 101 people who came to the colonies in 1620 aboard the Mayflower. "No, I can't believe this," Davis replied, laughing. "No, my ancestors did not come here on the Mayflower." She continued to protest while Gates confirmed the findings, then responded, "Oof. That's a little bit too much to deal with right now."

"Would you ever in your wildest dreams think that you may have been descended from the people who laid the foundation of this country?" he asked. "Never, never, never, never, never," she said."[8]

Coleman adds:

Activists like Angela Davis have spent their entire careers excoriating America's ancestors for their supposed participation in or benefiting from a system of white supremacy since the first Europeans landed here—and now Davis has realized she descends, at least partly, from those very villains. As horrified as Davis may be at finding out this information about her lineage, she shouldn't be. Even if she were right about her interpretation of "old America," she has nothing to do with it and she has nothing to be ashamed of. The sins of the father shouldn't be paid by the son; likewise, we shouldn't judge Davis' grandchildren for having a commie as a grandmother. Leftists have a hard time understanding that we shouldn't encourage people to behave like the communist regime in North Korea, which punishes all descendants with imprisonment for up to three generations for a single action of someone who happens to be in their bloodline whom they may never have met. . . . History is complex because people are complex. We should stop being overly critical and simplistic about the behavior of our ancestors, who were people of their time, by comparing it to our present-day norms and social expectations.[9]

Such "logic" of justifying "collateral damage" imposed on people who did nothing to deserve it is one of the tragedies of Groupthink and identity group extremism. The powerful moral condemnation and twisted invention of new forms of "racism" and "racist" is being used as a weapon to obtain power and to control target groups. The upshot of several decades of such Neo-Racist propaganda is that we now have been led to understand that a more evil and sinister group of people than whites has never before lived on Earth. This is particularly true in the case of Paul Rossi, whose example appears next.

Paul Rossi, the Grace Church School, and the Degradation of the Individual

We have already seen that the Woke/CRT movement is strategically and ideologically committed to undermining the fundamental ideals of Western society. Individualism is one of the most important to be weakened and scorned as a "racist" tool of exploitation because it demands intellectual integrity, analysis, critical thinking, and refusal to submit to "the mass" or the collective. Unless the Woke/Crits can shame us from being the "best we can be" as individuals fully committed to the overall well-being of our community and refusing to be submerged in a power-driven collective, it will ultimately fail.

Examples of the Woke seeking to achieve that end are everywhere. Paul Rossi's experience offers one. Rossi was fired from the Grace Church School for challenging the shift to Critical Race Theory–based teaching. He brings out the ways in which it undermines a student's individualism, warning that CRT is "cheapening, it's warping, it's diminishing the individual." *Epoch Times* reporters Masooma Haq and Jan Jekielek offer the following analysis of what Rossi faced.

Paul Rossi says some level of societal indoctrination is inevitable in education, but when students are taught an explicit political ideology and prohibited from questioning those teachings, the results are damaging, the former teacher said. Rossi, who taught high school mathematics and persuasion at Grace Church School in Manhattan for 10 years, left the school in 2021 after publishing an essay titled "I Refuse to Stand By While My Students Are Indoctrinated" on the blog of former *New York Times* editor Bari Weiss.

"What was happening was explicitly a political indoctrination that was based around the idea of a moral imperative . . . a collective morality, which focused on certain maxims like 'impact regardless of intent,'" Rossi said. Students and faculty at Grace Church School were taught, and expected to abide by, the tenets of critical race theory (CRT). Rossi explained that white students and faculty were considered the "oppressor" group while nonwhite students and faculty were considered the "oppressed" group, and the oppressed had the moral high ground. The people in the oppressed group were allowed to say whatever they wanted to the so-called oppressors, but the oppressors were expected to remain silent, he said. This type of ideology is causing damage to students "because it's cheapening, it's warping, it's diminishing the individual," he said.

Rossi . . . said he initially embraced the school's equity and diversity training as benevolent, but that he soon saw how destructive this type of indoctrination was and how it lacked objectivity and truth-seeking. He said there was an understanding that you could traumatize and harm someone else merely by sharing an opinion that was unwelcome or provocative. . . . Rossi provided an example of how CRT might be discussed. "So, you [a white person] could profess to say that, 'You know, no, I really try to treat people equally based on their personality or interactions,'" Rossi said. "And an anti-racist moral schema [would presuppose] 'But no, actually your biases prevent you from behaving that way, and furthermore, you don't even know what your biases are. You need to rely on the diversity, equity, and inclusion experts to tell you what those are, or for a person of color to 'school' you or call you out in certain situations that you may not be aware of.'"[10]

Propaganda and Indoctrination Reject Insight and Understanding

C. G. Jung warned that reason and critical thought vanish whenever we allow hate and rage to dominate. Rage and hate are now found everywhere throughout education, politics, and our social media interactions. The irrational and divisive impact of these emotions is making us nasty, intolerant, condemnatory, and stupid. In that context we can "feel," but we can't "think" with clarity and precision. Jung explains:

> The gift of reason and critical reflection is not one of man's outstanding peculiarities, and even where it exists it proves to be wavering and inconstant, the more so, as a rule, the bigger the political groups are.

The mass crushes out the insight and reflection that are still possible with the individual, and this necessarily leads to doctrinaire and authoritarian tyranny . . . .[11]

This problem of one-sided ideological perspective emerges in any system that delegates the authority to predetermine the conditions of allowable discourse to a self-interested group. The result of such a delegation is a pattern of thinking that is intellectually circular, superficial, and destructive. Careless, vindictive, and strategic indictments of speech as sexist, racist, homophobic, or Islamophobic have become far too commonplace. These terms are gross and oversimplified accusations. But they are a very effective means to consolidate a collective movement's political power through attack and intimidation.

Unfortunately, one of the goals of the Woke/Crits is to shift power and the burden of proof from the attacker to the persons being attacked. This forces the target to try to prove a negative, i.e., "No. I'm not a bigot, racist, sexist, homophobe, Islamophobe" and so forth. A phobia is part of a dialectical opposition. If there is a "phobia" there must be a state of "normalcy" against which that phobia is evaluated and compared. But consider the various "phobias" or similarly weighted terms that have made their way into our political life. For each condition, ask who decides the standards, and whose interests are served by possessing that power?

Once we are past the margins where extreme bias exists, who determines what behavior or statements indicate Islamophobia or homophobia? Past the obvious margins, who decides when someone is acting in a sexist or racist way? There are reasonable ways to inhibit or sanction that behavior at the margins without shutting off the richness of social discourse on critical issues.

Slogans and labels—regardless of the user's political orientation—are very often a deliberate preemption of discourse. It is done to acquire power or protect an existing power base rather than an attempt to make an intellectual contribution. To the extent we give credence to such labels and behavior, we offend the most fundamental intellectual spirit of our tradition. This exchanges our culture of the aspiration to truth—however flawed and limited our methods—for service to a culture of one-sided power and politics operating solely in its group's own interests. No one can stop the choices from being made, but at least we can be honest about what is occurring. Our responsibility is to condemn the use of cant and diatribe as a substitute for honest inquiry and intellectual challenge.

My position is that granting a self-interested group the power to label anything said by another as harassment is an unwise delegation of authority. Such a transfer of authority, whether overtly through codes or covertly by not requiring those who make such accusations to provide specific proof and justifications, makes it inevitable that there will be a dearth of fully honest discourse. This is so for several reasons—few of them intellectual—and many immoral and malicious. Several examples of malicious and moral attempts to intimidate and punish those who do not automatically conform to the Woke/Crit narrative appear next.

Michael Rectenwald and His "Cancellation by NYU's 'Liberal Studies Diversity, Equity, and Inclusion Working Group'"

Michael Rectenwald's experience at NYU captures the fundamentally anti-intellectual insanity of the Woke movement. It demonstrates the actors will do almost anything to excise the "cancer" of a free thinking faculty member from their own "diseased" bodies and minds.

An NYU professor posting on Twitter and criticizing political correctness and student coddling was booted from the classroom after his colleagues complained about his "incivility." Liberal studies professor Michael Rectenwald stated he had to go on paid leave from NYU based on the organized reactions to his criticisms. He claimed: "They are actually pushing me out the door for having a different perspective." Rectenwald posted on an anonymous Twitter account called Deplorable NYU Prof, arguing against campus trends like "safe spaces," "trigger warnings," policing of Halloween costumes, and academia's growing culture of Political Correctness. "It's an alarming curtailment of free expression to the point where you can't even pretend to be something without authorities coming down on you in the universities," Rectenwald [said]. . . .

A 12-person committee calling itself the *Liberal Studies Diversity, Equity and Inclusion Working Group*, that included two deans, several faculty members and multiple students, published a letter to the editor in the same NYU paper [in which Rectenwald admitted he had written the posts]. The Deans and "Committee" stated: "As long as he airs his views with so little appeal to evidence and civility, we must find him guilty of illogic and incivility in a community that predicates its work in great part on rational thought and the civil exchange of ideas," they wrote. "We seek to create a dynamic community that values full participation."[12]

A truly reprehensible element that nonetheless exposes the kind of people Rectenwald was dealing with is that the DEI "committee" suggested publicly that Rectenwald was in need of mental health assistance due to his views.

"Canceling" the University of Chicago's Dorian Abbot for Questioning "Diversity, Equity, and Inclusion" Efforts

Dorian Abbot's "sin" was simply that he raised several questions about how DEI was being implemented at the University of Chicago. The result included the usual "we feel so frightened" petition by an instantly mobilized horde of graduate students, demands for sanctions, and the cancelation of a scheduled presentation at a suddenly cowardly MIT. A brief report appears next.

> Dorian Abbot, a tenured faculty member in the Department of Geophysical Sciences at the University of Chicago, has recently come under attack from students and postdocs for a series of videos he posted to YouTube expressing his reservations about the way Diversity, Equity, and Inclusion (DEI) efforts have been discussed and implemented on campus. In these videos Prof. Abbot raised several misgivings about DEI efforts and expressed concern that a climate

of fear is "making it extremely difficult for people with dissenting viewpoints to voice their opinions." . . . Nowhere in these materials does Prof. Abbot offer any opinion that a reasonable observer would consider to be hateful or otherwise offensive.

Shortly after uploading the videos, Abbot's concerns were confirmed when 58 students and postdocs of the Department of Geophysical Sciences, and 71 other graduate students and postdocs from other University of Chicago departments, posted a *letter* containing the claim that Prof. Abbot's opinions "threaten the safety and belonging of all underrepresented groups within the [Geophysical Sciences] department" and "represent an aggressive act" towards research and teaching communities. The letter also issued 11 demands, many of which would serve to ostracize and shame Prof. Abbot, while stripping him of departmental titles, courses, and privileges. The signatories further demand that the Department of Geophysical Sciences formally and publicly denounce Prof. Abbot's views, and change hiring and promotion procedures so as to prioritize DEI.[13]

Eliezer Gafni, UCLA

As if the Abbot situation does not raise enough concerns about an out-of-control system based on subjectivity and "witch hunts," Eliezer Gafni, a highly regarded computer professor at UCLA, was the victim of a student petition as indicated in the following report. It parallels the experience of the Syracuse University distinguished faculty member who was suspended from teaching for offending all Chinese people and all Asian-Americans of any background for having described COVID-19 as the "Wuhan" flu. Gafni made the same mistake. In each case I find it odd that no one is mentioning that the Chinese Communist Party (CCP) has engaged in a massive international campaign to attack anyone who makes such a claim.

Students at the University of California Los Angeles are calling for the replacement of a computer science department chair appointed just weeks earlier, claiming he is "unfit to serve" in the role. . . . Petition signers said Gafni told a student that [the student's] calling the term "Wuhan virus" offensive politicized the issue. Wuhan is the city in China where COVID-19 was first discovered late last year. An online petition they started accuses Professor Eliezer Gafni of showing "disregard for the racialized experiences of people of color in the United States" and "disinterest in open communication between all students and UCLA Computer Science administration." Although the petition commends him for his "exceptional professional achievements and excellence in his academic work," signers claim that he has not exhibited a "strong sense of ethical and societal responsibilities or the collaborative skills—especially with regard to clear communication and inclusivity—that are essential for this role."[14]

Gordon Klein's "Online Mass Cancelation" at UCLA

Twenty thousand "people" allegedly signed an online petition against UCLA's Gordon Klein. That is extremely hard to believe. What is far easier and more likely, is that several computer whizzes launched "bots" as pretend petition signees.

> A California college professor reportedly is being investigated for discrimination and under police protection after refusing a request to exempt black students from final exams in the wake of George Floyd's death. The Los Angeles County Sheriff's Department reportedly has an increased police presence outside Klein's home after multiple threats. At least 20,000 people signed a petition calling for Klein's removal after a student who wasn't in the class posted the email exchange on social media. Klein was asked for a "no-harm" final exam, shortened exams, and extended deadlines for final assignments and projects due to "traumas" that put students in the class "in a position where we must choose between actively supporting our black classmates or focusing on finishing up our spring quarter," according to screenshots obtained by Inside Higher Ed.[15]

If twenty thousand people in this situation had the time to check out what happened, determine whether UCLA had issued a policy consistent with what Klein stated about what he and other faculty were required to do, obtain other relevant background information on the situation, and think about what they really thought about the facts uncovered, then I could at least respect the efforts. This is the danger and casual viciousness of the Cancel Culture stupidity. "Knee jerk" responses to online petitions, virtue signaling, mean spiritedness, peer pressure, feeling significant, and the power of "taking action" are all contributing factors. It still, however, would not be enough to produce twenty thousand human "cancellers."

New Zealand Academic, Anne-Marie Brady, Attacked for Writing Report Criticizing the CCP's Actions in New Zealand

The CCP's effort to suppress being criticized or otherwise held accountable for the 2020 pandemic and the release of the COVID-19 virus was global, spreading far beyond Europe and the United States. Anne-Marie Brady offers another example.

> New Zealand academic Anne-Marie Brady said Friday that there was nothing to justify the "complaints," "gagging order," and suppression of academic freedom she faced for months after she coauthored a report documenting the Chinese regime's influence operations. An internal review of Brady's report titled "Holding a Pen in One Hand, and a Gun in the Other" was ordered by the University of Canterbury (UC) after she presented the paper to New Zealand's parliament in the summer. . . . The paper is an investigation by the professor into how China's People's Liberation Army (PLA) exploited civilian channels for military purposes in New Zealand. Brady, who specializes in Chinese domestic and foreign politics at UC, wrote in her latest paper that the Chinese Communist Party (CCP) "is preparing China for what the Chinese leadership believes is an inevitable war." Anders Corr, principal of Corr Analytics, [stated] "Let's hope [the complaint's dismissal] serves as a lesson to other universities not to try and squelch the freedom of speech of their academics with bogus investigations into their work."[16]

Chapter Nineteen

What Happens When the Revolutionaries Win?

Walter Williams, professor of Economics at George Mason University, has warned:

> Tyrants everywhere, from the Nazis to the communists, started out supporting free speech rights. Why? Because speech is important for the realization of leftist goals of command and control. People must be propagandized, proselytized, and convinced. Once leftists have gained power, as they have in most of our colleges and universities, free speech becomes a liability. It challenges their ideas and agenda and must be suppressed.[1]

The result of the ultra-politicization of our approach to knowledge, intellect, and understanding is that we have established a culture of argument, condemnation, and pressure within our academic institutions that is "chilling" honest discourse about fundamental social concerns in ways that destroy the ideal of the university as a center of open communication in which freedom of discourse in teaching and scholarship are paramount. Academia—which ought to provide solutions and linkages—has itself become a primary vehicle of intolerance. I challenged such behavior when it was being done by an orthodoxy that used its power to inhibit free thought when I first came into the law school world, and I challenge it here when the identity and ideology of the actors have been reversed and a newly dominant orthodoxy is imposing its will on others.

Paul Rossi further described his experience of being chastised and shamed for speaking out at his former place of employment, the elite Grace Church School. This helps explain what is occurring to many innocent people being subjected to the Woke/Crit agenda.

> I was reprimanded for "acting like an independent agent of a set of principles or ideas or beliefs." And I was told that by doing so, I failed to serve the "greater good and the higher truth." The school's director of studies added that my remarks could even constitute harassment. He further informed me that I had created "dissonance for vulnerable and unformed thinkers" and "neurological disturbance in students' beings and systems." . . . A few days later, the head of school ordered all high school advisors to read a public reprimand of my conduct out loud to every student in the school. It was a surreal experience, walking the halls alone and hearing the words emitting from each classroom.[2]

The Woke Victors of 1970–2000 Have Become "Ideological Dictators"

Charles Axelrod described how existing idea systems become rigid to the point that a new language of discourse eventually emerges to challenge the stagnating system. His description is essential to understanding the impact a generation of activist university faculty and administrators have had on the university, as well as on the K–12 educational systems to which universities supply teachers and administrators. Axelrod writes:

> Ideas do not float freely among people; they become rooted in commitments, ossified and sustained within intellectual communities; they are cradled among avid sponsors and defenders whose work relies on their stability. Thus the tension of discourse refers not merely to the presence of one language addressing (and straining) another, but to the presence of one language addressing the inertia of another.[3]

Robert Wolff warned about what happens when a monolithic orthodoxy or Mass ideological system is allowed to gain control. We see this already taking place in universities and K–12 educational systems. It also dominates our increasingly strident and often false political "discourse," permeates social media, and shapes our once respected institutions of legacy journalism such as the *New York Times, Washington Post*, the *Los Angeles Times*, and other news sources on which we relied previously for information. Wolff writes about what occurs in educational systems: "The received doctrine is taught in the schools, its expounders are awarded positions, fellowships, honors, and public acclaim. . . . [D]issenting doctrines . . . are excluded from places of instruction, denied easy access to media of communication, officially ridiculed."[4]

In Axelrod's terms, the newly arrived faculty moving into universities and K–12 systems created a "language of discourse" that challenged the "frozen language" possessed by an aging academic orthodoxy seeking to protect the interpretations on which their careers and legacies were grounded. The real crisis is that, once the new faculty and administrators speaking what they considered "truth to power" came to dominate the university institution, they implemented a system like what has been done by victorious "revolutionaries" and created means to protect and extend their own orthodoxy. John Patrick Diggins describes what has occurred.

> Once inside academe, the New Left gave up all pretense of reaching "the people" to whom "all power" was supposed to belong. Unlike veterans of the Lyrical Left and Old Left, or true public intellectuals who carried on as editors or journalists for widely circulating magazines, New Left veterans regrouped as a professoriate and wrote primarily for each other in small, arcane academic journals.[5]

Many members of the conflicting identity collectives or factions never depart from the "dramas" of their own belief systems and political agendas. As academics and scholars they consequently fail to achieve the essential distance that would allow them the degree of objectivity needed to understand the full context they are critiquing. One result of the ever-present and often overwhelming subjectivity is that many groups of collectivist-scholars were and are speaking almost exclusively to each other in support of political agendas directly related to characteristics and issues in which they are immersed. They are a mutual support and admiration "society."

Unfortunately, even while containing some important insights, the new academic authoritarians are heavily politicized and are consumed with advancing intensely held identity group agendas. The adherents brook no alternative interpretations that, if accepted, could interfere with their perceived interests. One problem with open-textured "soft" categories of inquiry is that they are highly vulnerable to infusions of opinion and political interpretation. The subjectivity and malleability of the material represented by such "soft" and political areas of study is at the center of the issue of the quality and validity of what is being asserted by teachers, scholars, administrators, and others. Much of what is offered in such contexts is a "matter of opinion" and, in the university at least, one's opinion should always be tested and critiqued to the highest levels possible to limit the effects of extremist subjectivity.

The Easily Politicized "Soft Disciplines" Are Providing the Ideologues a Path to Power

Social and "soft" knowledge is inevitably Hegelian and is developed, refined, and critiqued through the dynamics of synthesis and opposition. The problem is when the attackers go too far in shifting from the pursuit of intellectual validity and insight to a path of power acquisition for their own identity group. This corrupts the fundamental mission of the university. This is precisely what has occurred and, as Mark Bauerlein lamented, "they have ruined the university."

In doing so, they have shut off open discourse, hired people "like them" to the exclusion of all others, and punish, marginalize, or exile those who disagree with their agendas. They also have created a kind of "thought police" or "Red Guard" in the form of Diversity, Equity, and Inclusion (DEI) administrators who, in a very real sense, are in effective control of the university. Formal and informal mechanisms such as these are also found in K–12 systems, large corporations, the media, and federal, state, and local government.

The chilling of intellectual freedom through a combination of "carrot and stick" is one where the incentives and disincentives come from several sources. If a scholar is part of an identity collective and accepts the "party line" or set of issues and political "truths" that represent the dogma of the particular sect, then that person's work will be shaped by that allegiance and, at least in part, be a product of a closed perspective. Intellectual independence is lost.

But for the scholar's career, such arrangements can be positive. This is because there is a clearly defined research agenda and a ready-made audience to approve and cite the work as long as it fits within the collective's aims and needs. The "carrot" is that rewards are offered for becoming part of the collective in the form of having a dedicated support group committed to advancing work of that particular kind due to their own self-interest in legitimating the collective's perspective as a field of study. New scholars are therefore drawn into membership in a collective as a result of career self-interest. Not to do so risks being condemned or made irrelevant for taking a different stance. Faculty simply assess the potential costs before speaking out.

Ayaan Hirsi Ali Sees the Truth of What Is Happening

Few people have achieved the quality of understanding and scope of experience possessed by Ayaan Hirsi Ali. She was born in Somalia and left behind her family after she broke away from traditional Islam. She has received death threats from Islamic fanatics. She became a member of the Netherlands parliament and then experienced her friends being murdered in the Netherlands by radical Islamists. Hirsi Ali then moved to the United States. She is in a perfect "lived experience" position to voice warnings about the "Cancel Culture" and "Wokeism" as well as the ideology of Critical Race Theory. Here are some of the thoughts she offered on the September 11, 2020 anniversary of the attack on the World Trade Center in New York:

> For two decades, I have opposed the fanatical illiberalism of those strands of Islam that gave rise to Al Qaeda. I broke with my Somali

family and ultimately with their faith because I believed that it is human freedom that should be sacrosanct, not antiquated doctrines that demand submission by the individual. So implacable are the proponents of Shariah that I have faced repeated death threats. Yet I have always consoled myself that, in the U.S., freedom of conscience and expression rank above any set of religious beliefs. It was partly for this reason that I moved here and became a citizen in 2013. . . . But the power of the illiberal elements in the American left has grown, not just on campus but in the media and many corporations. They have inculcated in a generation of students an ideology that has much more in common with the intolerant doctrines of a religious cult than with the secular political thought I studied at Holland's Leiden University. . . . Their ideology goes by many names: cancel culture, social justice, critical race theory, intersectionality. For simplicity, I call it all Wokeism.

The adherents of each [Wokeism and Islamism] constantly pursue ideological purity, certain of their own rectitude. Neither Islamists nor the Woke will engage in debate; both prefer indoctrination of the submissive and damnation of those who resist. . . . Both believe that those who refuse conversion may be harassed, or worse. Both take offense at every opportunity and seek not just apologies but concessions. Islamism inveighs against "blasphemy"; Wokeism wants to outlaw "hate speech." Islamists use the word "Islamophobia" to silence critics; the Woke do the same with "racism." Both ideologies aim to tear down the existing system and replace it with utopias that always turn out to be hellish anarchies: . . . Both are collectivist: Group identity trumps the individual. Both tolerate—and often glorify—violence carried out by zealots.[6]

Chapter Twenty

America's "New Red Guard" and the Reincarnation of Mao Zedong

In 1998, when I was first teaching in St. Petersburg, Russia, I stood on the same little second story balcony from which Lenin launched the Revolution. A Russian woman in her early nineties described what it was like in the 1920s when she was a little girl. She described how, once it became night, the Russians of St. Petersburg huddled in their apartments with the lights out as they heard cars speeding around with screeching brakes when they reached target locations. The Secret Police jumped out, broke down doors, and dragged helpless people away, never to be seen again. This is the behavior of power-driven mass groups who create an enemy—Jews, Gypsies, Blacks, Whites, Asians, or any other targeted group. I fear strongly that we are moving toward such a tragic time in America. Rather than challenging such behavior, universities are feeding into the mindsets that produce it.

Xi Van Fleet Describes Mao's Red Guard

Think back to the "mostly peaceful" riots in summer 2020. Murders, Molotov cocktails, arson of police headquarters—as well as stores and vehicles—assaults, widespread looting, beatings, defacing buildings, and tearing down of historic statues and monuments all occurred. Estimates of the financial damage inflicted go as high as $2 billion. But this doesn't begin to take into account the full impact on America, on our belief in the Rule of Law, the losses suffered by many citizens, as well as the large number of businesses, many owned by Black entrepreneurs, that were burned and looted. What we experienced in 2020, and are still enduring with frequent mindless and deadly random violence against police and ordinary people, is the behavior of fanatical mobs and thugs. This is what was experienced in China under Mao's Red Guard, in Germany with the Hitler Youth, and in the Soviet Union.

Xi Van Fleet endured Maoism and the Red Guard as a child. Like Yeonmi Park, who escaped North Korea's oppressive regime and ultimately made her way to America, she is fully aware of what such systems look like and how being controlled feels. Van Fleet explains that what she sees occurring in America's K–12 schools and universities is far too similar to what she witnessed in China under Mao.

> Critical race theory (CRT) aims to indoctrinate students and turn them into "Red Guards," akin to those during the Cultural Revolution in China, warned Xi Van Fleet, a Chinese-American living in northern Virginia's Loudoun County, at a "Rally to Save Our Schools" event on Sept. 8. She called CRT "communist race tactics" with the goal of "indoctrinating our kids, dividing Americans, and controlling Americans." . . . She said that upon taking over China in 1949, the first thing the CCP did was to indoctrinate teachers with Marxist ideology so they could teach it to students. Red Guards were the "full display" of what indoctrinated children could do, she said. The Red Guards were communist youth led by then-CCP leader Mao Zedong to persecute those identified as the CCP's "class enemies" during the Cultural Revolution from 1966 to 1976. They beat up their teachers in public and tore down temples and statues. . . . CRT adherents believe America is systemically racist, that racial oppression exists in every institution, and that an individual is either an oppressor or oppressed based on the color of their skin.[1]

America needs to pay close attention to what is going on in China, as well as what the Chinese Communist Party (CCP) is doing throughout the world. China is a strange place. The Chinese leadership is instinctively paranoid, frightened of dissent, intolerant of criticism, and subject to misinterpretation and overreaction even to the point of military conflict. This is an important reason why China suppresses criticism, stifles any dissent, and why a seemingly innocent movement such as the Falun Gong is banned and criminalized.[2]

It is why Xi Jinping is now requiring the suppression of free thought within China's universities, is requiring the teaching of approved political thought as part of the curriculum, and is keeping watch on Chinese students studying abroad to ensure they are not "corrupted" by Western values. See my book, *The Artificial Intelligence Contagion: Can Democracies Withstand the Imminent Transformation of Work, Wealth, and the Social Order?*[3] and the online analysis *"Something Wicked This Way Comes": Political Correctness and the Reincarnation of Chairman Mao* published on Berkeley Electronic Press.[4] The interesting thing is that while the *Artificial Intelligence Contagion* was published in China, the chapter criticizing the CCP's extensive abuses of AI, the Uyghurs, and so forth were deleted by the Chinese publisher.

If the malevolence of the Red Guards doesn't offer enough satisfaction, we can add the feeling evoked by a 1983 Disney movie titled *Something Wicked This Way Comes* based on a 1962 Ray Bradbury novel of the same name. *Something Wicked* reflects an inchoate fear of a dark and evil force moving steadily but invisibly toward a group of young innocents in a small town. It is my position that in America today, and Europe for that matter, something wicked is coming our way. The wickedness is masked by hidden agendas and even what the activists consider good intentions.

Part of that developing evil is represented in the campaigns by many groups to not only label any view other than their own as hate speech, vile, reprehensible, and so forth, but to savagely pursue and punish anyone who fails to give obeisance to their positions. This is being done by heckling, seeking to destroy the careers of those who don't cave in to their demands, issuing threats, labeling individuals and institutions with powerful accusations which are largely impossible to disprove, demanding resignations or firings, and other contemptible behavior that is claimed to "offend" or denies the censors their "safe spaces." What is occurring is not new, but it is gaining in sophistication, scope, viciousness, and intensity as fanatics learn how to use the internet as a weapon.

China is not making any pretense about the role of universities and its total educational system. The indoctrination of China's students with acceptable political attitudes has become a key part of China's brainwashing of its people. Xi Jinping has declared that the Party must dominate the curriculum of the nation's universities. His order requires that the educational system put the Party and its aims at the center of the educational process. The stated purpose is to ensure that what is learned is all in the interest of preserving the Communist Party's supremacy and control. A report explains:

> Chinese authorities must intensify ideological controls on academia and turn universities into Communist party "strongholds," President Xi Jinping has declared in a major address. "Higher education . . . must adhere to correct political orientation," Xi said in a high-profile speech to top party leaders and university chiefs that was delivered at a two-day congress on "ideological and political work" in Beijing. According to Xinhua, China's official news agency, Xi's goal is that universities must be transformed into "strongholds that adhere to party leadership" and political education should be made "more appealing." Xi elevated his political authority by removing term limits and being declared the party's "core leader." In presenting his order he said teachers needed to be both "disseminators of advanced ideology" and "staunch supporters of [party] governance."[5]

Rage Mobs, Book Burning, and Destroying the Past

David Kopel has, along with several co-authors, vividly described what occurred during Mao's Cultural Revolution and the predations of the Red Guard.

> At the beginning, the violence of the Cultural Revolution was only on campus. The student mobs began to call themselves "Red Guards," since they were acting to guard Chairman Mao. Under communism, there was supposed to be no civil society; no organization should exist outside the state. . . . The "red" class already were organized,

thanks to military training at summer camps and rifle clubs at home. Mao's constant exhortation was "Never forget class struggle." . . . At first, adult political cadres and others resisted, attempting to suppress the violent upstarts . . . "without the support of the gun barrel, their cause was doomed," writes historian Fang Zhu, in *Gun Barrel Politics: Party-Army Relations in Mao's China*.

. . . Street names that referenced the past were replaced with communist names. Historic artifacts, public monuments, non-communist historic sites, religious buildings, tombs, and non-communist art were destroyed. . . . Libraries were pillaged, including rare historic manuscripts. "Entire sections of libraries—the Chinese, Western, and Russian classics—were often put to the torch in huge outdoor bonfires," writes Anne F. Thurston, in *Enemies of the People: The Ordeal of the Intellectuals in China's Great Cultural Revolution*. Great Cultural RevolutionOrdeal of the Intellectuals in Chinaist names. Historic f loud knocks on the door, objects breaking, students shouting and children crying. But most ordinary people had no idea when the Red Guards would appear, and what harmless possessions might be seen as suspicious. They lived in fear.[6]

Rejecting the Constitution at the University of New Mexico and Northern Arizona University

Charlie Kirk, the young director of a politically conservative organization, Turning Point USA, was invited to speak about freedom of speech at the University of New Mexico. When he arrived, he was met with aggressive and outraged protesters intent on stopping anyone from being able to listen to Kirk's presentation. He stated that it is not conservatives who are doing such things, but organized extremes on the Left, including college students who don't want other students to hear voices that present alternative views to those of the protesters. Charles Creitz describes what happened.

"I wonder if they're paid—and why they were spending their evening to protest me and our Turning Point USA chapter just to talk about the U.S. Constitution and freedom of speech," [Kirk] said. "It's really interesting when you try to show up on a college campus and do an optional voluntary event how angry the other side gets."

"But this is a very important moment for people to recognize and understand that the other side—the left, the radical left—they're acting like the very same domestic violent extremists that the entire federal government is now organized to go after," Kirk added.

"Go look at that footage [from the University of New Mexico]— Is that the Proud Boys? Is that the American Right; are those conservatives? No, those people are on the left," Kirk said, wondering aloud who is paying the angry young objectors to hurl slurs, curses . . . adding that the Albuquerque protesters appeared to have pre-made signs: which could undermine the supposition the protests were organic. "I went there last evening to send a message to every one of these people, to send a message, one that's watching that we're going to stand for free speech. And you are not going to be able to disrupt our events or bully our students with force."[7]

We can wish such contemptible behavior on the part of student protestors were rare. But it didn't take long for Charlie Kirk to experience its continuing reality. Visiting Northern Arizona University to speak, he was confronted by another group of incredibly intolerant and childish students, as reported next. Given the frequency with which such confrontations are taking place, anyone who thinks we haven't see the reincarnation of the "Red Guard" simply does not want to face reality.

Right-wing activist Charlie Kirk was drowned out by protesters chanting "Fuck you, fascist!" during an appearance at Northern Arizona University. Mediaite reported that the Turning Point USA founder visited the university on Tuesday for a debate entitled "Prove Me Wrong: The Government is Lying to You." Awaiting Kirk was a swarm of rowdy protesters carrying signs including "Facists [sic] fuck off!" "Charlie Kirk has a small face," "Trans rights = human rights," and "Charlie K. is a piss baby." Mediaite said Kirk set up a booth to debate students only to be "drowned out by screaming students, bullhorns, and even a brass band."[8]

Antifa, Some Teachers, and Incredibly Immature Student Protestors are the American Version of the "New Red Guard"

Although there are many who raise the specter of the Proud Boys being a violent and even terroristic group, far more violence has been committed by Antifa, who in their black uniforms and masks, have regularly traveled throughout the United States and launched serious attacks on individuals and groups considered threats to progressive extremists. The threat Antifa presents is indicated by several reports offered next that reveal not only violent actions but efforts to recruit new young members during what is supposed to be education.

> A free speech rally organized by conservatives was overrun by several hundred counterprotesters—some holding Antifa flags—on Saturday in downtown San Francisco. A number of individuals from the counterprotester group physically attacked conservatives, including event organizer Philip Anderson, who lost a front tooth after he was punched in the mouth, while one man wearing a Trump T-shirt had to be taken away in an ambulance after being attacked. A police officer also had to be taken to the hospital. . . . Anderson took the stage at about 1 p.m. and was greeted by chants and plastic water bottles and glass bottles thrown over police barricades. . . . The San Francisco Police Department said three officers suffered non life-threatening injuries when they were assaulted with pepper spray and caustic chemicals. One officer was taken to a local hospital for treatment, the department said. No arrests were made, the department said.[9]

A pro-Antifa teacher in California bragged about turning his students into far-left "revolutionaries." He said:

> "I have 180 days to turn them into revolutionaries . . . scare the f—k out of them." The teacher also said he tracks his students political leanings throughout the course of the year and that "every year, they get further and further left."
>
> "I've met so many people in my life who, when they met me, thought I was off the wall, and now they're all Marxists," he said. "Like why can't we, you know, take up arms against the state?"[10]

Another California teacher hung "F—the Police, F—Amerikkka" posters in a classroom. "A parent at Alexander Hamilton High School slamming the 'disgusting brainwashing of students with taxpayer dollars' shared photos with Parents Defending Education, a national nonprofit, that were taken inside his child's classroom. The photo shows a Palestinian flag, a transgender flag, a Black Lives Matter flag and a Pride flag prominently displayed on the blackboard."[11]

A Florida University journalism student described her educational experience as one in which she felt she was being bullied and brainwashed. Mia, asking to remain anonymous for obvious reasons, explains:

> She felt bullied by a professor who forced students to parrot her scorn for America's "systemic racism" and affirm "progressive talking points" on immigration, gender-identity issues, "queer theory," intersectionality, transgenderism, religious faith, and the ideas of Karl Marx, author of "The Communist Manifesto."
>
> "I can't write what I truly believe" about these issues, Mia said. "When I did that, I got an F. In order to pass a class, I have to affirm leftist ideas I don't believe in. When I repeat all the talking points and present them as ideas I believe wholeheartedly, I get As."
>
> "It feels like being brainwashed when they reward you for repeating their ideas and punish you for saying things that go against their beliefs." At the core of the students' struggle is the university's

apparent glorification of CRT, a Marxist-derived ideology that substitutes race or gender for class struggle. . . . Antiracism practices often are taught in classes and employer trainings that promote "diversity, equity, and inclusion" (DEI).

Journalism major Mia spoke of a required class in which the professor emphatically spoke about "white privilege" and "systemic racism" as fact. If students wrote about views contrary to the professor's anti-white, anti-establishment positions, their grades suffered, she said. Classmates indicated they were afraid to ask questions or assert their true beliefs, she said. One professor, who lauded the teachings of Marx, warned students on the first day of class that "hate speech," which the professor didn't define, would be reported to the dean, Mia said. It had a chilling effect. The professor also warned students not to get "too comfortable" in writing about their beliefs in a journaling assignment, Mia said. That could lead to students being reported and punished, the professor promised, indicating she'd lodged formal complaints against students for such violations. The professor praised students who acknowledged, with apparent regret, that their parents had not raised them to hold views similar to the professor's but were thankful to finally be learning about progressive beliefs, Mia said.[12]

"Gray Lady" Down: The Journalistic Decay of the *New York Times*

They came for the decaying *New York Times*, and the *Times* willingly "canceled" its own integrity. Like many, I once greatly admired the *New York Times*. I still subscribe and read it in hopes it will regain its independence and journalistic soul. It was the center of thought and truth and could be trusted above all else. Now, like many, I see the *Times* as an unreliable and biased political instrument whose reporters I do not trust. My sadness is in fact "legion." Such capitulations should strike fear in the heart of the rapidly dwindling supply of legitimate journalists. The transition has proceeded rapidly. I still read the *Times* and am dismayed at the fact that a very disturbing number of the paper's supposedly hard news reports have the feel of substantially skewed op-eds. The same can be said for the *Washington Post*, which was once under the direction of Katherine Graham and Ben Bradlee, and now is being ruined by Jeff Bezos.

Intolerant Groupthink and repression of views seen as incompatible with the emergent ideology has infected our entire culture, not only the American system of higher education, but journalists whose legitimacy is founded on the duty to pursue truth and report based on honest evidence and reasoned analysis. Journalism has been transformed into one-sided propaganda diatribes that would make the Chinese Communist Party's propaganda operatives envious.

Reports indicate that the CCP has paid news outlets such as the *Washington Post* and *New York Times* very large sums of money to publish favorable stories on China as part of that nation's global propaganda strategy. We seem to find out almost daily about being betrayed by a significant proportion of academics, biased journalists, and other "intellectuals" who are being compensated by China. According to the *Times* of India, the payments as reported to the US government as $700,000 to *Time* magazine and *Foreign Policy* combined, $371,577 to the *Financial Times*, $272,000 to the *LA Times*, $4.6 million to the *Washington Post*, and $6 million to the *Wall Street Journal*.[13]

New York Times writer Bari Weiss resigned her position at the *Times* and went on to establish Substack. She explains that "standing up for principle at the [*New York Times*] does not win plaudits. It puts a target on your back." Judith Miller describes the situation.

> Weiss wrote a powerful resignation letter to *Times* publisher A. G. Sulzberger. In it Weiss stated the reasons she was resigning. These included being called a Nazi and a racist by colleagues and what she considered management's "failure to defend her against internal and external bullying; senior editors' abandonment of the paper's ostensible commitment to publishing news and opinion that stray from an ideological orthodoxy; and the capitulation of many *Times* reporters and senior editors to the prevailing intolerance of far-left mobs on Twitter, which she called the paper's 'ultimate editor. . . . Weiss added that the rise of online mobs seeking to suppress views with which

they disagreed has become "a potent and possibly destructive force." At the heart of the problem was American liberals' growing "intolerance of opposing views, a vogue for public shaming and ostracism, and the tendency to dissolve complex policy issues in a blinding moral certainty."[14]

The *New York Times* completed its transformation from world leader in honest and balanced journalism to propaganda rag with the July 22, 2020 publication of an op-ed by a Chinese scientist at Beijing University. Yi Rao aggressively criticized the US handling of the COVID-19 epidemic. A neuromolecular biologist at Peking University, he claimed China's strategy to deal with COVID was clearly superior to that being implemented in America. The op-ed by Yi Rao appeared weeks after one by Arkansas Senator Tom Cotton that led to a staff revolt in the *Times*. That revolt led quickly to the forced resignation of James Bennet, longtime Senior Editor of the *Times* who had dared to publish Senator Tom Cotton's op-ed dealing with the possible use of force against the Summer of 2020 rioters who were of course, "mostly peaceful" when you ignore inflicting $2 billion in damages on innocent businesses, causing a number of deaths, committing arson and firebombing, and attacking people who did not automatically accept their actions or were simply dining at sidewalk cafes. While the *Times* felt entirely comfortable publishing a transparently propagandistic op-ed by Yi Rao, Bennet violated the secret but intense "code" of the paper's Woke/Crit staff. Zachary Evans writes in the *National Review*.

> The staff revolt at the *Times* produced the forced resignation of Senior Editor, James Bennet. The reason for Bennet being forced out after years of serving as a positive force at the *Times*? It was that Cotton's point of view did not fit the political beliefs of the *Times*' journalists and purportedly even made some "feel unsafe" and threatened. So they "came" for Bennet and in doing so exposed the world-famous newspaper's ultimate degradation.[15]

New York Times columnist Bret Stephens attacked his own paper's decision to disavow Senator Tom Cotton's op-ed about the possible use of the Insurrection Act against the violent unrest across the United States that followed George Floyd's horrific death and overwhelmed city police forces. Stephens described the *Times'* behavior as "an invitation to intellectual cowardice," writing "as the paper dismisses distinguished journalists along with controversial opinions, it's an invitation to intellectual cowardice."[16]

The *New York Times'* certainly has a divided newsroom:

> The announcement Friday of the departure of two high-profile journalists from *The Times* has spurred what some staffers have described as unprecedented levels of divisiveness and controversy inside the newsroom, with staffers warring with each other in private, on Facebook, and even in public on Twitter. The sequence of events led many inside and outside *The Times* to believe that management had been pressured to take the action it did by what several staffers characterized as a "vocal minority." "I hate to say this, but inside *The Times* there is a 'cancel culture,'" one staffer at *The Times* commented to CNN Business. The staffer, echoing what several other *Times* journalists told CNN Business in separate conversations, described a dynamic where "there is not much infighting, but there is a small group of people who are very vocal" and who, this staffer said, do not appear to be satisfied until "heads roll."[17]

The in-fighting continued:

> Former *New York Times* reporter Alex Berenson slammed the mainstream media and Big Tech for its continued attempts to censor and "deplatform" views it does not like or does not want to debate, during his speech at the Conservative Political Action Conference in Orlando, Fla. . . . "I'm honestly surprised as any of you that I'm here—if you knew my voting record you'd think I should be speaking at the ACLU, not CPAC," he said at the conference. . . . Berenson said that he and other classical liberals have not changed their views

on freedom of expression or open public discourse: "It's not me, it's the *Times*," he said adding that columnists at liberal mainstream papers like the Grey Lady have pivoted to routinely call for censorship of their political opponents. . . . The pro-censorship crowd is frustrated, he said, because they are recognizing their inability to control public narratives as easily as they want, given the diaspora of media and technology in recent years. . . . "This censorship is still happening—a lot of people still can't get their stuff published on Amazon."[18]

The *New York Times* chalks this all up to a needed "culture change":

> The *New York Times* says it needs a culture change to become a better place to work, particularly for people of color. The newspaper told its employees in a report Wednesday that it will take steps to be more inclusive and welcoming, saying its study of the workplace culture represents a "call to action." . . . The report also said that a workplace culture that celebrates individual achievement and often relies on "unwritten rules" for advancement can be uncomfortable for many, but particularly people of color. . . . Carolyn Ryan, deputy managing editor and one of three authors of the report [stated] "It was our culture, this kind of 'sink or swim' ethos." . . . But the report found that while the *Times* was building a more diverse staff, it concentrated less on fostering an inclusive culture."[19]

New York Times' "Woke" Staff Demands "Sensitivity Reads" Before Publishing

Apparently the management of the *Times* is serious about its capitulation to what can be called "political commissars." Joseph Wulfsohn reports:

> The *New York Times* Guild raised eyebrows on Friday for recommending "sensitivity reads" as part of the paper's publication process. The group of unionized journalists revealed they have met with Times leadership earlier in the month, stressing that the paper needs

"a top-to-bottom resetting of priorities to improve the working conditions of our colleagues of color." The guild urged its employer to
diversify its workforce to 24 percent Black employees and over 50
percent people of color by 2025 as an apparent reflection of the New
York City population. They also called for a minimum of job applicants to be people of color and that staff of color should be added
to the Standards team as well as investing in mentorship programs.
However, one particular request sparked some confusion on social
media. "Get it right from the beginning: sensitivity reads should happen at the beginning of the publication process, with compensation
for those who do them," the *Times* Guild wrote.[20]

Andrew Sullivan: "We all live on campus now."

Andrew Sullivan explains what caused his termination from *New York*
magazine. It involves an explosion of speech and thought suppression that
is undermining the fundamental values of American society:

> Sullivan reiterated thoughts he made years ago about how "we all live
> on campus now," noting the increasingly limited exchange of ideas on
> college campuses has spilled into everyday life and pointed to a survey
> that showed only 1.46 percent of the faculty at Harvard University
> identify as "conservative." "But that's probably higher than the pro-
> portion of journalists who call themselves conservative at the *New
> York Times* or CNN or *New York Magazine*," Sullivan wrote.
>
> "A critical mass of the staff and management at *New York
> Magazine* and Vox Media no longer want to associate with me." . . .
> "They seem to believe, and this is increasingly the orthodoxy in main-
> stream media, that any writer not actively committed to critical
> theory in questions of race, gender, sexual orientation, and gender
> identity is actively, physically harming co-workers merely by existing
> in the same virtual space. Actually attacking, and even mocking,
> critical theory's ideas and methods, as I have done continually in this
> space, is therefore out of sync with the values of Vox Media. That, to
> the best of my understanding, is why I'm out of here."[21]

Matthew Yglesias at VOX

Yglesias challenged the "dominant sensibility" in the "young-college-graduate bubble" that had emerged at VOX and now is no longer working there. He is a columnist at Bloomberg Opinion and Substack.

> Yglesias felt that he could no longer speak his mind without riling his colleagues. . . . [A]s a relative moderate at the publication, he felt at times that it was important to challenge what he called the "dominant sensibility" in the "young-college-graduate bubble" that now sets the tone at many digital-media organizations." Vox journalist Matthew Yglesias . . . was one of 150 signatories including other liberal writers, professors, and activists who came together to defend civil debate in hopes of ending the ongoing efforts by the viral mob to silence dissenters. . . . Vox contributor Emily VanDerWeff told the editors that Yglesias' signature on the letter "makes me feel less safe at Vox" and claimed that it makes her job "slightly more difficult."[22]

Glenn Greenwald

Longtime independent journalist Glenn Greenwald, when writing for *The Guardian*, helped bring Edward Snowden's revelations on the unconstitutional behavior of America's intelligence agencies to light. He left that behind to be a co-founder of *The Intercept* in 2020. As described next, Greenwald left *The Intercept* because, in his mind, the new activity had been taken over in ways that changed its character radically.

> Glenn Greenwald is walking away from *The Intercept*, citing widespread "repression, censorship and ideological homogeneity" from liberal editors who support Joe Biden as the reason he resigned from the media outlet he co-founded. . . . He called the current iteration of The Intercept "completely unrecognizable when compared to that original vision" because it no longer offers a venue for airing dissent, marginalized voices and unheard perspectives. [Greenwald then added in a Tweet] "The same trends of repression, censorship and ideological homogeneity plaguing the national press generally have

engulfed the media outlet I co-founded, culminating in censorship of my own articles."[23]

Guardian Columnist Suzanne Moore

Long-time Guardian writer Suzanne Moore left that paper saying: "I was bullied by 338 colleagues." Heralding the death of traditional journalism, what Moore experienced is akin to the experiences of Bari Weiss, Stan Wischnowski, Matthew Yglesias, James Bennet, and Andrew Sullivan,

> The exodus of traditional journalists from major news organizations due to the suppression of ideas and growing tension with colleagues is also occurring across the pond. Suzanne Moore announced her departure as a columnist for *The Guardian* after writing for the British newspaper for roughly three decades. . . . Moore argued that journalism has been "in a strange place lately" and that it was "unsure of itself and what it should be doing. . . . " The columnist wondered why she was treated "so appallingly" at *The Guardian*, writing, "So what did I do that was so terrible? I stepped outside the orthodoxy." . . . "The fact is the so-called mainstream media has turned into leftist propaganda rags. They do not deserve constitutional protection in the US. They ignore the crimes of the left and demand persecution for alleged crimes of Republicans and conservatives. Unlike the Democrats of the 1860's, these are nothing but cowards."[24]

Stan Wischnowski Forced Out By Young "Journalists"

Philadelphia Inquirer editor Stan Wischnowski was forced out by young "journalists" who said, "We're tired of being told to show both sides of issues there are no two sides of":

> A top editor at *The Philadelphia Inquirer*, Stan Wischnowski, lost his job because he published an article by the paper's architecture critic entitled "Buildings Matter, Too." The *Inquirer's* staff was predictably "outraged." Forty-four mostly young "journalists of color"

sent a letter to the paper's "leadership" indicating their disgust that the headline appeared. Soon after, Stan Wischnowski was gone.

The most chilling line in the letter from the self-styled "journalists of color" read: "We're tired of being told to show both sides of issues there are no two sides of." It is clear those who composed it reject balanced reporting. But this is how far too many young people increasingly seem to think. The belief is that there is only one "right view" and all others should be suppressed. There is no nuance, or alternative interpretations, only their point of view. While this is not healthy, it is at the heart of how Cancel Culture is being approached."[25]

Noam Chomsky Describes How the Media Actually Operates

In examining the media's role in indoctrination, Chomsky says that "the media's institutional structure gives them the same kind of purpose that the educational system has: to turn people into submissive, atomized individuals who don't interfere with the structures of power and authority." Similarly, democratic governments use propaganda and "the manufacture of consent" in place of violence and force to control the masses. "Indoctrination is to democracy what a bludgeon is to totalitarianism," he said. This atomization of individuals, this breakdown of independent thought, and this general depoliticizing of society together create the perfect environment, in Chomsky's view, for a charismatic, fascist dictator to seize power.[26]

Q. You have written repeatedly that the state and the media collaborate to support and sustain the interests and values of the establishment. Are our media victims of ideological indoctrination, or are they willing conspirators in suppressing truth?

A. They're not victims and they're not conspirators. Suppose, for example, you were to ask a similar question about, say, General Motors. General Motors tries to maximize profit on market share; are they victims of our system or are they conspirators in our system?

Neither. They are *components of the system* which act in certain ways for well-understood institutional reasons. If they didn't act that way they would not be in the game any longer.

The media have a particular institutional role. We have a free press, meaning it's not state controlled but corporate controlled; that's what we call freedom. What we call freedom is corporate control. We have a free press because it's corporate monopoly, or oligopoly, and that's called freedom. . . . The terms *freedom* and *democracy,* as used in our Orwellian political discourse, are based on the assumption that a particular form of domination—namely, by owners, by business elements—is freedom. If *they* run things, it's free, and the playing field's level.

Coming back to the free press: yes, our press is free. It's fundamentally a narrow corporate structure, deeply interconnected with big conglomerates. Like other corporations, it has a product which it sells to the market, and the market is advertisers, other businesses. The product, especially for the elite press, the press that sets the agenda for others that follow, is privileged audiences. That's the way to sell things to advertisers. So you have an institutional structure of major corporations selling privileged elite audiences to other corporations; now it plays a certain institutional role: it presents the version of the world which reflects the interests and needs of the sellers and buyers. That's not terribly surprising, and there are a lot of other factors that push it in the same direction. Well, that's not a conspiracy, any more than G.M.'s making profit is a conspiracy. It's not that they're victims; they're part of the system. In fact, if any segment of the media, say the *New York Times,* began to deviate from that role, they'd simply go out of business. Why should the stockholders or the advertisers want to allow them to continue if they're not serving that role?

Similarly, if some journalist from the *New York Times* decided to expose the truth, let's say started writing accurate and honest articles about the way power is being exercised, the editors would be crazy to allow that journalist to continue. That journalist is undermining authority and domination and getting people to think for themselves, and that's exactly a function you don't want the media to pursue. It's not that it's a conspiracy; it's just that the media's institutional structure gives them the same kind of purpose that the educational system has: to turn people into submissive, atomized individuals who don't interfere with the structures of power and authority but rather serve those structures. That's the way the system is set up and if you started deviating from that, those with real power, the institutions with real power, would interfere to prevent that deviation. Now that's the way institutions work, so it seems to me almost predictable that the media will serve the role of a kind of indoctrination.[27]

Chapter Twenty-One

China's Strategy of Propaganda and Division Harms America's Universities

China, Xi Jinping, and the "Long Game"

The Chinese Communist Party has eliminated term limits on the office of president so that Xi Jinping can continue in office. Xi is now China's "president-for-life," and this allows him to take the long view strategically and wait out the West's constantly shifting and largely incoherent policy approaches. Xi's strategy aimed at creating a dominant global empire can now be implemented over time as he plays the strategic "long game."

China's ability to develop and implement a focused, consistent, and coherent strategy over a lengthy period takes advantage of the fact that Western nations are blinded by internal short-term "democratic" and identity group contradictions, political bickering, and jockeying for power. In the United States, European Union, and United Kingdom, this includes frequent regime changes, the fear of Islamic terrorism and Middle Eastern military clashes, intense internal identity group schisms, and paternalistic cultural arrogance toward other nations. Dominant Western nations continue to make the mistake of viewing China as a powerful but still backward force.

Even though Xi seeks to portray himself and China in a benign light through superficially humanistic speeches, such as his 2017 presentation at the World Economic Forum in Davos, and as a partner in interest with Western nations, including the United States and European Union, the reality is that China is a threat to the nations of Asia and many others. Xi Jinping, in fact, has set a path toward the creation of a new Chinese empire aimed at becoming the world's dominant superpower.[1]

Xi Jinping's Suppression of Free Thought in China's Universities

The Chinese, and here we mean those with political, economic, and military power within the national system and totally dominant political organism of the Chinese Communist Party, are ambitious to a fault, arrogant due to their multi-millennial existence relative to "upstart" nations such as the United States, resentful that they do not receive what they consider the respect due a five-thousand-year-old nation, and simultaneously defensive after centuries of Mongol and Western dominance. This resentment and defensiveness creates a unique and dangerous mix of motivations that could easily become explosive.

The Chinese Communist Party is also understandably terrified of what could happen if enough among the nation's 1.3 billion population become exceedingly dissatisfied at the Party's leadership and that dissension spreads. Mao's "Long March" civil war, the disastrous Cultural Revolution of the 1960s, and the democratic movement that led to the 1989 Tiananmen Square massacre of thousands of university students are never far from the Party's collective mind. According to Xinhua, China's official news agency, the goal is that universities must be transformed into "strongholds that adhere to party leadership" and political education should be made "more appealing." Xi consolidated and elevated his political authority by removing term limits and being declared the party's "core leader." In presenting his order he said teachers needed to be both "disseminators of advanced ideology" and "staunch supporters of [party] governance."[2]

The Suicidal Ignorance of Allowing the Chinese Communist Party Open Entry Into America's Universities and K–12 Schools

Take the CCP's approach to university and elementary and secondary education, where what is now known as "Xi Jinping Thought" is progressively inculcated in China's youth, and project that frame of mind to more than a hundred Confucius Institutes in our universities and 519 K–12 affiliations called "Confucius Classrooms" funded by the CCP in

US schools. The following reports discuss those issues. The first is by a Senate Subcommittee on "China's Impact on the U.S. Education System" and the second is an analysis from *Politico:* "How China Infiltrated U.S. Classrooms: Even as they face criticism, Chinese government-run educational institutes have continued their forward march on college campuses across the United States."

CHINA'S IMPACT ON THE U.S. EDUCATION SYSTEM, STAFF REPORT, "United States Senate, PERMANENT SUBCOMMITTEE ON INVESTIGATIONS, Committee on Homeland Security and Governmental Affairs," Rob Portman, Chairman, Tom Carper, Ranking Member

When China sought to market itself to students around the world, it looked to its past. Confucius, the ancient Chinese philosopher, is synonymous with morality, justice, and honesty. The Chinese government capitalized on this rich legacy and began establishing Confucius Institutes on college campuses around the world in 2004, including the first in the United States at the University of Maryland. Today, there are more than 100 Confucius Institutes in the United States, the most of any country. The Chinese government funds Confucius Institutes and provides Chinese teachers to teach language classes to students and non-student community members. In addition to Chinese language classes, Confucius Institutes host cultural events, including Chinese New Year celebrations, cooking classes, speakers, and dance and music performances. These selective events depict China as approachable and compassionate; rarely are events critical or controversial. The Chinese government also funds and provides language instructors for Confucius Classrooms, which offer classes for kindergarten through 12th grade students. Confucius Classrooms are currently in 519 elementary, middle, and high schools in the United States. Continued expansion of the program is a priority for China.

Confucius Institute funding comes with strings that can compromise academic freedom. The Chinese government approves all teachers, events, and speakers. The Chinese teachers sign contracts with the Chinese government pledging they will not damage the national interests of China. Such limitations attempt to export China's censorship of political debate and prevent discussion of potentially politically sensitive topics. Indeed, U.S. school officials told the Subcommittee that Confucius Institutes were not the place to discuss controversial topics like the independence of Taiwan or the Tiananmen Square massacre in 1989. As one U.S. school administrator explained to the Subcommittee, when something is "funded by the Chinese government, you know what you're getting."

Confucius Institutes exist as one part of China's broader, long-term strategy. Through Confucius Institutes, the Chinese government is attempting to change the impression in the United States and around the world that China is an economic and security threat. Confucius Institutes' power encourages complacency towards China's pervasive, long-term initiatives against both government critics at home and businesses and academic institutions abroad. . . . The Thousand Talents program is another state-run initiative designed to recruit Chinese researchers in the United States to return to China for significant financial gain—bringing with them the knowledge gained at U.S. universities and companies.

China did not stop at expanding at university and college campuses. The next phase of Confucius Institutes involved funding teachers for Confucius Classrooms in K–12 grade school. There are currently 519 Confucius Classrooms operating in the United States with expansion of this program a top priority for China. In the United States, a Confucius Institute receives funding and instructors directly from Hanban and passes it to the K–12 grade school to support affiliated Confucius Classrooms.[3]

Findings of Fact and Recommendations in the Senate Staff Report

1. In the last 15 years, the Chinese government has opened over 100 Confucius Institutes on college and university campuses in the United States. While there are currently more than 500

Confucius Institutes worldwide, the United States has more Confucius Institutes than any other country. Recently, ten U.S. colleges and universities have decided to close Confucius Institutes.

2. The Chinese government also funds teachers for Confucius Classrooms in the United States, which teach Chinese language and culture in kindergarten through 12th grade schools. There are over 1,000 Confucius Classrooms worldwide and more than 500 in the United States. Expanding the Confucius Classroom program is a priority for the Chinese government. A document obtained by the Subcommittee details a sophisticated plan to expand Confucius Classrooms by seeking the "top-down policy support from the state government, legislative and educational institutions, with a particular emphasis on access to the support from school district superintendents and principals."

3. U.S. government officials have expressed concerns about Confucius Institutes. FBI Director Chris Wray testified that the FBI is "watching warily" Confucius Institutes and "in certain instances have developed appropriate investigative steps." Bill Priestap, the FBI's Assistant Director for the Counterintelligence Division, testified that Confucius Institutes "are not strictly a cultural institute [and that] they're ultimately beholden to the Chinese government."

4. The Chinese government controls nearly every aspect of Confucius Institutes at U.S. schools. Confucius Institutes report to the Chinese government's Ministry of Education Office of Chinese Language Council International, known as "Hanban." Confucius Institutes are funded, controlled, and mostly staffed by Hanban to present Chinese-government approved pro-gramming to students at U.S. schools. Hanban approves each Confucius Institutes' annual budget and has veto authority over events and speakers.

Seeing Confucius Institutes Through the Eyes of a Ranking Chinese Propaganda Officer

In *Politico*, Ethan Epstein, associate editor of the *Weekly Standard*, offers a troubling analysis of the Chinese Communist Party's strategy for exerting significant influence over America's educational systems—universities and K–12 elements alike—continuing the strategy of "get them while they are young and highly impressionable" in order to build cadres of supporters. Epstein explains:

> [T]he Confucius Institutes' goals are a little less wholesome and edifying than they sound—and this is by the Chinese government's own account. A 2011 speech by a standing member of the Politburo in Beijing laid out the case: "The Confucius Institute is an appealing brand for expanding our culture abroad," Li Changchun [Propaganda Minister] said. "It has made an important contribution toward improving our soft power. The 'Confucius' brand has a natural attractiveness. Using the excuse of teaching Chinese language, everything looks reasonable and logical."
>
> Li, it now seems, was right to exult. More than a decade after they were created, Confucius Institutes have sprouted up at more than 500 college campuses worldwide, with more than 100 of them in the United States—including at The George Washington University, the University of Michigan and the University of Iowa. Overseen by a branch of the Chinese Ministry of Education known colloquially as Hanban, the institutes are part of a broader propaganda initiative that the Chinese government is pumping an estimated $10 billion into annually, and they have only been bolstered by growing interest in China among American college students.
>
> Yet along with their growth have come consistent questions about whether the institutes belong on campuses that profess to promote free inquiry. Confucius Institutes teach a very particular, Beijing-approved version of Chinese culture and history: one that ignores concerns over human rights, for example, and teaches that Taiwan and Tibet indisputably belong to Mainland China. Take it

from the aforementioned Li, who also said in 2009 that Confucius Institutes are an "important part of China's overseas propaganda set-up." Critics also charge that the centers have led to a climate of self-censorship on campuses that play host to them.[4]

"Mind Dominance," *The Art of War*, and Winning Without Fighting

To this point, the US struggle with China has not involved direct military confrontation, although threats and provocations in the air and at sea by Chinese forces have been frequent. The Chinese have also uttered numerous threats of an impending military conflict, and even stated the strong likelihood of nuclear war. In 2005, a senior Chinese general stated that China would use nuclear weapons against the United States if it interfered with any attempt by the Mainland to recapture Taiwan: "China should use nuclear weapons against the United States if the American military intervenes in any conflict over Taiwan, a senior Chinese military official said."[5]

In 2012, another very senior and well-placed Chinese major-general warned that future conflict was coming as a result of America's "containment" policies directed at China.

A Chinese general recently offered an alarming assessment that a future conflict with the United States is coming as a result of U.S. "containment" policies. The release last week of a transcribed speech by People's Liberation Army (PLA) Maj. Gen. Peng Guangqian revealed the harsh words toward the United States and those in China he regards as muddle-headed peacenik intellectuals. Gen. Peng, a well-known PLA strategist, has a hawkish reputation and a large following in China. . . . "The United States has been exhausting all its resources to establish a strategic containment system specifically targeting China," Gen. Peng said. "The contradictions between China and the United States are structural, not to be changed by any individual, whether it is G.H.W. Bush, G.W. Bush or Barack Obama, it will not make a difference to these contradictions."[6]

In 2017, a high-ranking Chinese officer stated:

> China is preparing for a potential military clash with the United
> States, according to an article on the Chinese army's website. "The
> possibility of war increases" as tensions around North Korea and the
> South China Sea heat up, Liu Guoshun, a member of the national
> defense mobilization unit of China's Central Military Commission,
> wrote on Jan. 20.[7]

Tensions and saber rattling have continued with China's efforts to take
over the South China Sea, and its continuing support of North Korea as a
useful diversion. It would be wise for the United States and others to take
the Chinese military leaders' intentions seriously because China is devoting massive sums to the expansion of its military power, including in space
and communications. This is demonstrated clearly when we look at the
various strategic maneuvers in which that nation is engaged strategically
and technologically.

The possibility of a military explosion driven by China's paranoia was
voiced by Admiral Harry B. Harris Jr. Harris, who has served as head of
the US Navy's Pacific Command, says Beijing intends to control the South
China Sea, a conflict zone China is now claiming as its own regardless of
the rights of neighboring countries and the clear strictures of international
law. Admiral Harris recently told the House Armed Services Committee
that: "China's intent is crystal clear. We ignore it at our peril." Harris
added: "I'm concerned China will now work to undermine the international rules-based order."[8] Former US Secretary of Defense James Mattis
has challenged China's aggressive moves in the South China Sea, stating
during a speech in Singapore that "despite China's claims to the contrary,
the placement of these weapons systems is tied directly to military use for
the purposes of intimidation and coercion."[9]

Chapter Twenty-Two

Real Diversity and Multiculturalism Contribute to Our Society

What began as a laudable effort to expand true diversity within universities and education has turned into a one-sided tool for political recruitment and power. The concept of "one way to think," "one way to act," and one preset series of "progressive" values to adopt, is an absolute denial of "real diversity." It is "tribalism," pure and simple, and deliberately pits one group or tribe against another. Bob Zeidman explains quite clearly what has happened. Zeidman is the president of Zeidman Consulting, a premiere contract research and development firm in Silicon Valley, and president of Software Analysis and Forensic Engineering Corporation, the leading provider of software intellectual property analysis tools. Zeidman is a pioneer in analyzing and synthesizing software source code. He said:

> I'm a computer scientist. I haven't been able to open a single engineering or science journal in the past two years without seeing multiple articles about diversity. Many issues of these magazines are devoted entirely to diversity rather than, for example, scientific research or engineering accomplishments. . . . I recently attended a presentation by the Association for Computing Machinery, the foremost international organization for computer scientists. Titled, "Language Matters: DEI and the Question of URM," it was a one-hour discussion by three black women computer science professors alternately angry at white people and Asians for holding back intellectually superior black women. In fact, they held the most animosity toward

white women who "pretended" to be disadvantaged when they were actually part of the "white supremacy" of our society. In years past, such bigotry was disguised and discussed quietly in private. Now, these bigots are public, loud, and given credibility and acknowledgment by international associations.[1]

Zeidman goes on to describe how the "new" definition of diversity being forced on our society by the Woke/Crits is tearing the system apart and seeking to create a "color-divided society" rather than Martin Luther King Jr.'s "color-blind society."

> For many years, and accelerating since the Black Lives Matter riots, "diversity" has been a buzzword, a demand, a goal, and an obsession of government, business, religion, and almost every organization in America. . . . Diversity is currently defined by society as diversity of skin color, sexual behavior, and gender identity. In the days of the civil rights movement of the 1960s, we demanded a "color-blind society." Now we demand a *"color-divided society."* What would Martin Luther King Jr. think of all this? He dreamed that his children would one day *"live in a nation where they will not be judged by the color of their skin but by the content of their character."* And yet, these days we seem to judge people solely by the color of their skin in addition to their sexual behaviors and gender identity. Would the Reverend King approve? I think clearly he would not. But probably the woke include him among the immoral old leaders whose statues they topple and whose "old-white-men" philosophies they disdain.[2] [Emphasis added]

The Woke are bullies high on the narcotic of power provided by a society that has been attempting in good faith for over sixty years to deal with the darker parts of its history. In far too many instances, that newly acquired power is being abused through shaming, bullying, and punishing. This is being done not only to those who dare to disagree, but to those who fail to "shun" the miscreant or to affirmatively support the ideologues.

Think, for example, of the implications of the chant that "Silence Is Violence!" The meaning is that you are not only "with" us but are required to publicly endorse what the Woke/Crits say and do. Otherwise you are a "bigot," a "racist," and ultimately an "enemy." If "silence" is "violence" and overt allegiance to a specific agenda—even if not real—must be demonstrated, anything other than such overt and public allegiance justifies condemnation. Daring to question the ideologues' agenda is a form of heresy, or moral treachery that deserves unrelenting punishment.

As the demographic group we lump into the ethnic stew being referred to as "White" declines in terms of population share, Whites will expand already existing political strategies with other ethnic groups. This is already occurring with many mixed ethnicity families coming into being. This will make it increasingly difficult for the Woke to know who to blame for historical wrongs, and there are early signs that the Woke/Crit movement is having an early sense that inter-relationships are undermining their core message. In addition to a significant growth in mixed ethnicity among individuals and families, there will be an expansion of alliances that will include Asians, Latinos, and those referred to as "White" Hispanics, as well as many Blacks. Before you know it, we will all be "people of color."

The reality is that regardless of the hostile and racist rhetoric being delivered by the Woke and CRT activists, there is no monolithic overarching "Brotherhood" or "Sisterhood" of ethnic groups. The People of Color "alliance" exists only in relation to its opposition to what I guess should be referred to as "Colorless People." The reality is that the POC aggregation is only a strategic tactic. It contains no substantive or moral core shared amongst its alleged membership. It is sustainable only in the moment. It is dominated by a limited but extremely vocal cadre of "power-mongers," and it is being used as an oppositional power-oriented strategy to stir up hate and justify demands. Fortunately, the political system will change in many of its characteristics, but that shift is not going to be along the lines of exclusive and rigid ethnicity that current identity groups anticipate, particularly ones centered on "Blackness" and a relentless attack on "Whiteness."

As They Are Being Applied, Diversity and Multiculturalism Are Strategic Ploys to Divide America

The primary strategies used to gain advantage and control include the use of open-textured words such as "diversity" and "multiculturalism." Like all propaganda slogans, they are designed to generate positive reactions in the abstract and within us at emotive levels that bypass evidence and rationality. This is because the terms implicitly suggest fairness, tolerance, acceptance, and other virtuous orientations, but as applied in narrow and one-sided ways that serve only their advocates' true agendas, they are wedges used to break up an existing system.

The quest for power is the most common element underlying the use of terms with powerful moral impacts. Unfortunately, this is a strategy to manipulate rather than an honest moral quest. Not only are the activists themselves using the university as a base of operations, but many of the university-based academics are part of political collectives that are intimately linked with the external activists. Taken together, the identity coalitions that emerged blur and even eliminate the lines between scholar, teacher, and militant activist. This creates a confusing kaleidoscope of divergent beliefs, goals, and ideologies operating under the entirely artificial "People of Color" mantra. The participants in this alleged coalition cooperate in some areas because, until the goals of power are achieved, it is in their interest to do so.

Roger Kimball is the editor and publisher of the *New Criterion* and publisher of Encounter Books. A recent book is *Where Next? Western Civilization at the Crossroads.*[3] Kimball describes how the positive ideals of diversity have been betrayed in the reality of America's universities and other institutional systems, even to the point of representing Antonio Gramsci's strategy of the "long march through the institutions." Kimball writes:

> [We are experiencing] what the Italian Marxist Antonio Gramsci called "the long march through the institutions." The institutions in question ran the gamut from the family and the churches through schools, colleges, the media, and, finally, corporate and governmental

bureaucracies. That "long march" began on the fringes of culture in the late 1950s before moving to the center in the 1960s and 1970s. It proceeded like Johnny Appleseed, dropping fertile if poisonous seeds that took years to germinate and sprout. Now they have fully blossomed, as phrases like "drag queen story hour," "transsexual bathrooms," and "white supremacy" remind us.[4]

As to the hypocrisy of the diversity movement in its takeover of our educational institutions, Kimball accurately explains that it has produced exactly what it actually intended behind the moral screen of fairness, anti-discrimination, and justice—a conformist, narrow, ideological, and homogenous culture.

It's one of the great ironies of our time that the word "diversity" is repeated everywhere while the opposite, a stultifying homogeneity, is the reality that's enforced "on the ground." Our educational institutions offer the classic example. Is there any self-respecting college or university that doesn't tout its commitment to "diversity" these days? You can't peruse a college's promotional literature, let alone set foot on its campus, without being inundated by assurances that diversity is its most cherished value, the cynosure to which every other pursuit is subordinated. But when you look at what they actually teach and preach it turns out that a rigid conformity is the order of the day.

We used to titter that there were people whose title was some variation on "Dean of diversity." "You're kidding, right?" was the response. No one is laughing now. On an increasingly wide range of subjects, only one opinion is granted the patent of diversity. Those deans are there not to invigilate academic excellence but to enforce social and moral conformity. . . . Just so, if you hear an academic or an academic administrator (or, for that matter, a government bureaucrat) proclaim his commitment to diversity, you can be sure that he means his commitment to "diversity," i.e., conformity masquerading as diversity. We all know this. It's part of what Anthony Trollope called "the way we live now."[5]

The irony is that militant collectives such as the POC movement have little in common. They exist due to the perceived need to fight what is professed to be a common political enemy. That "enemy of the moment" is comprised of those already occupying coveted positions of power and those who question the legitimacy and agendas of the newly emergent movements. After that "enemy" is weakened sufficiently and power is available for redistribution, the collectives will start aggressively "negotiating" with each other to acquire their "rightful" shares of the "spoils of war."

It is, for example, deliberately political, or simply ignorant, to argue that Blacks are a monolithic group whose members possess identical interests. Nothing could be more wrong. It is also an error to ignore the fact that relationships and marriages between diverse ranges of people of differing ethnic groups—Black, White, Asian, and Hispanic/Latino—are growing in number and producing many children of mixed ethnicities. The situation is already changing more toward what I think of as a healthy "mongrelization." I love that fact and hope that we are able to survive the insanity that currently exists on the way to actually becoming a fully integrated "human race."

Along with this goes the fact that the categories used in the previous paragraph lack any real specificity or utility as ethnic generalizations. Within each of the greatly "collapsed" categories referred to by the political activists as POC or BIPOC is an amazing range of diversity and difference in culture, language, world view, historical relations, and more. I have taught, worked in, or traveled with some degree of intensity to at least thirty-five countries and worked with people from twenty or thirty more. Anyone who thinks, for example, that the collective term "Asian" stands for a unified cultural or "skin color" ethnicity for four billion people spread around the world is operating under a delusion.

While, for example, the CCP defines most Chinese as of Han ethnicity, that designation is a deliberate political device mandated by the CCP to indicate a far greater ethnic harmony among China's 1.4 billion people than actually exists. China is home to a significant array of diverse cultures and groups. The same exists for India, Bangladesh, Indonesia, Thailand, Malaysia, the Koreas, Japan, Singapore, the Philippines, Mongolia, etc.

Each represents a collection of differences that make it an insult to lump them all together under a singular label. And of course the same can be said for Africa and Latin America, not to mention Europe. We need to understand that the Woke are "running a game" on us, and that "us" includes not only people they are trying to force into a "white" box for reasons of power, but many, many of the "people of color" who are "people" rather than political pawns.

This strikes me as something less than a formula for achieving equality. It seems more like a strategy for reversing ethnic dominance in a way that benefits a small group of aggressive political actors who have designed a way to seize power and a greater share of social goods for themselves rather than a much larger and diverse set of people. Some of that reversal will temporarily shift some power to the politically invented identity groupings of Latin American and Native American as part of the People of Color coalition. But virtually all of the power shift will be going to a cluster of African American identity groups that do not represent the full diversity or cultures of those they purport to represent.

Asians may technically be listed as a People of Color class, because it would be too obvious to exclude them from that rhetorical "umbrella." But Asians are not really part of that POC political force because, from the perspective of credentials and education, they would be entitled to a share of the benefits of power considerably beyond other political groupings. Advantages are not simply ones of financial status. There is no question that having an intact and supportive family structure, as well as members who value education, has significant impacts on educational and work performances.

Our New University "Identity Monoculture" Rejects True Diversity and Compels "Identity Conformity"

The ideological monoculture that has emerged throughout our key institutions is almost surely a more-or-less temporary phenomenon. At the present moment it brings to mind Lord Acton's telling reminder that "all power corrupts and absolute power corrupts absolutely." My position is that too much power has already flowed to the ideological cliques that comprise the new university monoculture. They intimidate the rest of the system to the extent there is no real discourse or debate on many of the issues at the center of concern in American society. This intimidation is not only an informal consequence of ideologically driven identity collectives. It has also been built into the institutional system that governs universities.

But, the Woke/CRT/DEI movement has "overplayed its hand" and a countering system is "waking" up and developing strategies to respond to those who have dramatically abused their new powers. That reaction of what I guess many of the Woke/Crits would understand as a manifestation of the Marxist Dialectic will take a decade to work its way through the processes and struggles of resistance and transformation of what has been wrought over the past forty years, and it will be a bitter experience for many.

Academic hiring over the past four decades has concentrated on people who possess superficially diverse characteristics, but share homogenous politics, agendas, and value systems. The result is that a critical mass of ideologically committed faculty has been created that works together to further expand their numbers and to inhibit challenges to their emergent hegemony. In such a context it is unsurprising that a member of the Critical Legal Studies (CLS) movement would not be able to perceive the intellectual and political cultures of law schools as repressive. This reaction is generated because the individual in question is no longer an outsider challenging the abuses of power by a repressive orthodoxy, but an insider who figures prominently within the power and ideological structure of the new orthodoxy.

Many members of the original CLS movement that began in the 1970s made significant intellectual contributions to the analysis of law. Their leftist politics had effects on individual analysis, but the infusion of their ideas and methods into what was, at the time, a largely stagnant system of doctrinal explication was a breath of fresh air. That original form of CLS has disappeared as a coherent political movement. It has been replaced by political movements dedicated to divisive identity politics. As the original CLS scholars moved into the mainstream of the law school world, many of their ideas were reinterpreted and made part of general academic discourse.

The CLS movement—whatever its Marxist and European Deconstructionist ideological flaws and intellectual pretensions—offered an important vehicle for challenging and opening up a self-satisfied system of rigid doctrinal analysis. While the basic CLS movement was always political, and its politics clearly those of the European Left, it was a more intellectualized and generic sort of ideology. The neo-Crits, the Critical Race Theory activists, on the other hand, as they emerged in the late 1970s and 1980s, represented an ideological and identity-politics driven set of aggressive advocates pushing for their specific identity groups' agenda no matter what.

The argument is not that activism or even collective organization within the university is illegitimate. My concerns are those of balance versus extremism. Activism and collective organization can be means for scholars in emerging or cutting edge areas of knowledge to defend themselves from retaliation by the high priests of a discipline's controlling orthodoxy. It also increases the likelihood that their ideas are heard and taken into account.

The mantra of the multiculturalists is "all's fair in love and war." It doesn't even matter if the group or persons being attacked, "chilled," or condemned were historical oppressors. The real issue is whether they are obstacles or competitors for power. Multiculturalism of the variety Martha Nussbaum and Russell Jacoby describe is a political tool. The quest for power is the most common element in an otherwise loose and shifting alliance of interests. The academic political collectives represent a kaleidoscope of divergent beliefs, goals, and ideologies. They cooperate because it is in their interest to do so, and their mission is political power, not the attainment of intellectual growth.

Ironically, the loosely allied collectives have little in common other than the need to fight what is perceived to be a common political enemy, i.e., those already entrenched in coveted positions of power and those who might question the legitimacy and agendas of the newly emergent movements. There is a critical distinction between what I have come to think of as the "new" scholars and their collectivist strategies and "old" activist scholars who were driven by a commitment to advancing comprehensive social good across the board. The "new collectivist scholars" possess visions driven by specific issues with which they personally identify. Those issues are subjectively and inseparably a psychological and emotional part of the persons seeking their implementation.

The "old activist scholars" of the 1960s and 1970s—of which I am proudly a member—operated according to a broader commitment to justice and the advancement of society as a general matter, recognizing that they were themselves fortunate and privileged, or simply that seeking justice and fair treatment for those who had been denied opportunities was simply "the right thing to do" and a moral mission. I know I still feel this way and so do many others who came to the social justice movement in that moment.

Whether this attitude is approved as a moral position based on the desire to do "good works" for those who have been denied fair opportunity, or scorned as some kind of elitist *noblesse oblige*, the cultural value of giving to others, rather than seeking for oneself and those like you, represents a fundamental break between the "old" and "new" scholars. Since my own background was that I came from a blue collar family of steelworkers and farmers, delivered eighty-six newspapers as a paperboy each day when I was in junior high school, "ran crane" in Republic Steel's mill, picked up trash for a summer job, and was the first in my family to go to college, I really don't think that *noblesse oblige* had much to do with my decision making.

As the Civil Rights era unfolded and bared the reality of racial discrimination's denial to minority humans of their human right to be treated as individuals and provided the rights and opportunities all people most people "woke" up to the historic tragedy of racial discrimination. Denying to all the opportunity to "be the best you can be"—was increasingly understood as unacceptable even to the point of evil, or as I have long felt, a form of emotional or mental illness.

That is one of my main concerns with the condemnations being thrown about by the "Progressive," "Woke," and Critical Race Theory ideologues. By seeking to undermine and deny value and integrity to the traditional cultures of the West including justice, equality, opportunity, individualism, reason and the like, values that are the only systems that have actually allowed such radically self-critical democratic dynamics aimed at growing society closer and closer to attaining full justice, fairness, equality and opportunity to be attained, the excessive focus on multiculturalism and as non-diverse "diversity" is a corrosive social acid. Over time it destroys the internal coherence of cultures and societies and that is exactly what is happening to America.

In *The End of Utopia: Politics and Culture in an Age of Apathy*, Russell Jacoby criticizes the application of the phenomenon of multiculturalism, observing:

> The ideas of multiculturalism, cultural pluralism and diversity turn sacrosanct. They become blank checks payable to anyone in any amount, lacking meaning or content. They not only suggest a politics, but often replace politics. However, even with adjectives like radical or transformative attached, what politics do they designate? Apart from the wish to include more voices in the curriculum or different faces at the office, no vision drives multiculturalism. The rise of multiculturalism correlates with the decline of utopia, an index of the exhaustion of political thinking."[6]

The Orwellian Narrative of the Woke/Crits

The way the core narrative thematic language is being used as a political weapon, labels such as multiculturalism, diversity, inclusion, equity, justice, fairness and the like are key parts of political tactics rather than intellectual or moral conceptions. The narrative fashioned by the weaving together of such open-textured and emotionally based terminology creates a system that resonates deeply within us on non-rational emotive levels but that can be easily manipulated to achieve strategic ends and made to mean whatever those in power assert.

Consider the "diversity" narrative that has increasingly dominated the academic and political culture over the past five decades. Claiming the United States lacks diversity is a cynically unfair characterization of America. The nation is in reality the most diverse and multicultural country in the world. Estimates are that Africa is home to three thousand distinct tribal groupings with two thousand different languages being spoken. This creates a kind of "diversity," but in fact what exists is a very large number of tribal "identity groups" that are often in competition for power for their own tribes rather than for an integrated national community. While Asia has six primary ethnic groups—listed as East Asian, South Asian, Southeast Asian, Southwest Asian, Central Asian, and Oceanian/Pacific Islander—that generalized list of six primary groups doesn't begin to reveal the numerous ethnic groups, religions, and cultures existing within those six extremely large and diverse demographic compositions. Abby Budimn and Neil G. Ruiz report for the Pew Foundation:

> Asian Americans are the fastest-growing major racial or ethnic group in the United States. More than 22 million Asians live in the U.S., and almost all trace their roots to specific countries or populations from East and Southeast Asia and the Indian subcontinent, according to a Pew Research Center analysis of U.S. Census Bureau data. The largest Asian origin groups in the U.S. differ significantly by income, education and other characteristics. These differences highlight the wide diversity of the nation's Asian population and provide a counterpoint to the "model minority" myth and the description of the population as monolithic. Highlighting these differences within the Asian population has been central to debates about how data about the group should be collected by governments, colleges and universities and other organizations, and how it can be used to shape policies impacting the diverse U.S. Asian population.[7]

Multiculturalism requires no coherent intellectual vision. This is because it is political rather than moral or even philosophical. For the Woke it is a key part of a strategy to acquire power for the groups' asserting moral superiority. Cloaked in its claim of representing a higher social morality based on its deconstructive critique of the biases inherent within the existing political order it is seeking to overthrow, multiculturalism is a device to gain power from those who have traditionally possessed it. How this works is described next by John Fonte, a senior fellow and director of the Center for American Common Culture at the Hudson Institute, when he writes about what he calls *Ill Liberalism*. By claiming the higher moral ground, the burden of justifying existing power relationships and entitlements is shifted from the multiculturalists to the existing society they seek to undermine and supplant.

As Russell Jacoby indicates in asserting that multiculturalism signals the exhaustion of political language, the rhetoric of unbounded diversity and multiculturalism represents a nihilistic doctrine to which the democratic republics of Western societies and their "intellectuals" have succumbed. The argument underlying the diversity and multicultural movement is that it is virtuous to accept anyone's beliefs or values as not subject to criticism because—the claim is made—no one has the moral right to judge themselves as "better" or another's practices as "worse."

This is itself a moral judgment, and was always a one-way "principle." It emerged as part of a period in which it was *de rigueur* among activists and intellectuals to denounce the dominant culture of the West with great vitriol. This approach is a cynical tool. It is aimed at undermining a community's base of authority through elevating an overarching a form of one-sided extreme individuality that trumps core systemic values. The irony is that those employing the individualistic strategy in which the perceptions of individual "marginalized" people are made paramount is being advanced aggressively by a political movement committed to producing their own collective community that speaks and thinks with one voice.

John Fonte also writes in *Ill Liberalism* about the dangers of identity politics, multiculturalism, and diversity when they are done in ways that overwhelm a culture's ability to adapt to the radical changes coming from outside the culture itself.

> Sidney Hook forcefully restated the liberal-democratic concept of civic assimilation, declaring that "precisely because" American liberal democracy is a "pluralistic, multiethnic, and uncoordinated society" all citizens need a "prolonged schooling in the history of our

free society, its martyrology, and its national tradition." Today, the traditional idea of assimilating immigrants into a national identity is officially rejected by the governments of Canada and Australia, and is under constant attack by elites in the United States. The leading organization of American civic educators declares that national assimilation is often "neither democratic nor humane." Suggestions that liberal-democratic regimes should limit immigration to levels consistent with steady civic assimilation are fiercely denounced as both impossible and immoral. Put bluntly, cultural democrats are saying that traditional liberal democracies do not have the moral right to reproduce themselves, either by fostering civic assimilation, by limiting immigration, or by some combination of the two.[8]

The University of Chicago's Martha Nussbaum, the Ernst Freund Distinguished Service Professor who has also taught at Harvard, Brown, and Oxford universities, echoes Fonte in her book, *Cultivating Humanity: A Classical Defense of Reform in Liberal Education*:

> Under the label "multiculturalism"—which can refer to the appropriate recognition of human diversity and cultural complexity—a new antihumanist view has sometimes emerged, one that celebrates difference in an uncritical way and denies the very possibility of common interests and understandings, even of dialogue and debate, that take place outside one's own group. [She adds the vital point that] [t]his view denies the possibility of the task [Ralph] Ellison set himself: of revealing the human universals hidden within the plight of one who was both black and American.[9]

Pitting "Black against White and the Asian against Latino"

Winsome Sears, lieutenant governor and the first Black woman elected to statewide office in Virginia, is among the growing number of people condemning what they see as a divisive, dangerous, and bad faith "Woke" and Critical Race Theory movement. She proclaims her profound disagreement with a movement that she says is pitting "Black against White and the Asian against Latino." She is not alone in her condemnation.

> Winsome Sears . . . attributed her victory to voters being sick of seeing Black and White people pitted against each other. "They're tired of the Black against White and the Asian against Latino," Winsome said. "They're tired of it, and they're tired of politicians who won't let the wounds of the past heal."
>
> "I've just always assumed whatever room I'm in, I belong. Whatever I want to pursue, it's mine for the taking," she said. "Nobody is denying that we don't want to hear all the history, least of all me. I certainly don't want the sins of the past to be repeated. [But] We don't have to tear one person down in order to build another up. That's no way to be. That's not America."[10]

Zeidman Asks the Taboo Questions about "New Racism" and the Danger of Emphasizing Differences rather than Human Similarities

Exaggerated identity politics and faux tribalism aimed at gaining power are smothering the very essence of America's Democratic Republic. With all the Woke/Crit condemnations of what they define over broadly as racism and genderism, the terrible reality is that it is their policies, false analyses, and behaviors that is rapidly worsening racial attitudes in America between Blacks, Whites, Asians, Latinos, Jews, Muslims and more. Bob Zeidman offers important insight into the fact that we are avoiding real discourse over numerous fundamental matters. He writes on that failure in terms of claims to diversity:

> So why are all these diversity efforts not just failing, but actually exacerbating the problem? The answer is simple. Most people know the answer, but few are willing to say it publicly. But I'll say it here. As our society emphasizes our differences and places us into groups of oppressors and oppressed, resentment is growing. People see those in other groups getting special privileges and accommodations, and

they want those privileges and accommodations, too. Our nation's diversity efforts are causing competition for resources. And they're causing resentment. This is human nature. That other group is getting attention, money, and special privileges, why shouldn't my group? And if I don't belong to a victimized group, I'll create one.

I feel these ugly emotions inside me, and I consider myself a good person who would never purposely discriminate against a person because of their innate and immutable characteristics. I'm certain that others feel this way too. Since I was young, I was taught to respect all people equally. Yet today, I see a person of color and immediately wonder if that person is qualified for their job or got there through affirmative action. I worry that if I "misgender" a person, even as an honest mistake, that I could lose my job. If I "misappropriate" someone's culture by . . . I don't even know . . . ordering Mexican food or wearing the jacket I bought in Tijuana, then I will be accused and ostracized. . . . I find myself associating less and less with people outside my own group for fear that an unintentional "racist" or "phobic" interaction could negatively affect the rest of my life."

Let me be clear. There's definitely racism, antisemitism, and other forms of group-hate in our nation; it's increasing and needs to be stopped. But the solution isn't to further divide people into victim groups. The solution isn't to compensate certain groups for past, perceived, and even real incidents of hatred. The solution isn't to create a victimhood Olympics with each group competing for the most attention and reparations. The solution to reducing hate crimes is simple. Stop emphasizing our differences. Stop dividing people into groups and assigning them behaviors based on those groups. Not all white people are oppressors. Not all black people are victims. Not all Jews are rich and powerful. Not all Hispanics are illegal. Not all gay people are good and worthy of respect. Stop telling kids that a white person can't be a role model for a black person, or a man can't be a role model for a woman, or that someone outside your group can't be your role model. I'm a white male. As a kid, two brilliant female math teachers encouraged me to pursue math, science, and engineering. I dreamed of meeting and training with Bruce Lee. Sidney Poitier was my vision of an educated gentleman. And my goal was to obtain not one, but two Nobel Prizes like Marie Curie.[11]

Showing K–12 Children Images of Whites as Blood-Sucking "Cartoon Mosquitos" Being Destroyed by Non-Whites Wielding Flamethrowers

Carrie Sheffield is a columnist and broadcaster in Washington, DC and a senior policy analyst at Independent Women's Forum. She has a master's degree in public policy from Harvard University with a business policy concentration and a BA in communications from Brigham Young University. In her article, "Critical race theory is teaching kids to hate each other," Sheffield offers an extremely troubling analysis of the truth of the effects of Critical Race Theory in contrast with elevated rhetoric about its "healing" vision. She writes:

> When parents reject public-schools teaching critical race theory, a common retort from the left is that it's a university graduate-level analytical framework that's incomprehensible by children and therefore incapable of being taught in K-12 schools. This attempted gaslighting of parents—nothing to see here!—through such false claims is destructive. In fact, we're already seeing the horrifying results on our kids. The truth is union-controlled public schools are teaching kids to be racist—paid for by your tax dollars—and it's making schools more dangerous and disharmonious. Instead of the promised racial reckoning blossoming into racial utopia, the CRT crowd is fracturing America. Dr. Martin Luther King Jr. dreamed of a country where children are judged by their character, not skin color. But in January, school officials forced students at Virginia's West Springfield High School to watch a racist, dehumanizing video about micro-aggressions. It depicts white people as blood-sucking, cartoon mosquitos who must be destroyed by nonwhite people wielding flamethrowers. . . . And in Springfield, Ohio, police reported an incident at

Kenwood Elementary School, where a group of black students on the playground rounded up white students "and forced them to state, 'Black Lives Matter,' against their will."[12]

Chapter Twenty-Three

A DEI Victim's Cautionary Narrative

The "Diversity, Equity, and Inclusion" System as Described by a University's "Canceling" Victim

What follows is a description of a university teacher's personal experience with the machinations of his institution's DEI system. He had been attacked after referring to COVID-19 in his syllabus as the "Wuhan Virus." This was immediately targeted by a student who complained that it had the sound of anti-Chinese racism, and the university's provost—with extensive working ties to China—immediately condemned him and suspended him from teaching. Somehow, the fact that, like numerous others, his belief that the COVID-19 virus had leaked from a research lab in Wuhan was "morphed" into an accusation that the use of that term indicated a racist attitude toward all people of Chinese origin or ancestry wherever found in the world. His description of what he was forced to deal with is set out next. He wrote the following in response to an earlier draft of my previous book, *No More Excuses! Parents Defending K–12 Education.*

By Any Means Necessary

You are quite right to point out that "Progressive Theocracy" comprised of the Crits, Wokies, and Radical Progressives—has been allowed to gain control, with the result that a "received doctrine" dominates the mindset of those seeking and abusing power. This is the sort of orthodoxy I ran into in my own struggles at my university. It is most significant that the final chapter of *Defending K–12* proposes avenues for counterattacks, and possible remedies for this moral and intellectual sickness. What strikes me is that much of the pushback comes from Loudoun County, VA, a most progressive neighborhood indeed. This illustrates the old adage that everyone is conservative about what they know best (or what directly affects themselves or their children). One critical problem is that we continue to be on the defensive and out-maneuvered by our opponents. Their uncivilized mob operating according to the malicious mantra of "by any means necessary" attacks some fundamental institution and we are invariably caught flat-footed and defensive. It is time to take the battle to these guys and in the words of a progressive icon "get in their faces."

Universities Have Sold Their Souls

Universities have sold their souls to the diversity, equity, and inclusion crowd. Every university now has an extravagantly funded office dedicated to DEI and appended alphabet soup nuttiness. My experience with this Stasi-inspired bureaucracy suggests that, if your function is to ferret out and punish bias, you will find bias everywhere. Hence, they invent garbage like micro-aggressions. All faculty at my university were compelled to view a two-hour presentation by the DEI activists on such topics. The high point of this charade was some joker introducing himself as "a scholar of micro-aggression." Good grief! Another fellow then gave a spiel about the "importance of proper pronouns." This is because, as you point out, part of the strategy of seizing and maintaining power is to destroy language itself and replace it with Orwellian "newspeak."

The university dropped its phony "case" against me, "curiously" as soon as I retained legal counsel. By then I had been physically and emotionally exhausted by the ordeal, so I was quite content to let the situation simply die away without further recriminations or press involvement. I was so disgusted with the whole system that I decided to retire within two or three years. As I told the Dean: "You guys have pretty much won, just leave me alone to go in peace."

An Undergraduate Student Is Appointed to Monitor a Professor's Class

However, our associate provost for Faculty just had to devise some sort of additional punishment or humiliation in direct contradiction of my agreement with the college. Her initial diktat was that some woke undergrad attend my classes to critique my inclusiveness and attentiveness to students' emotional needs. I said "Sure, if you think that some kid majoring in gender studies will have anything useful to say to me about space group theory or advanced solid state chemistry."

OK, Then Let's Do a Mandatory "Sensitivity Seminar," Instead!

She backed off on that idea and then demanded that I do some sensitivity seminar that all faculty would eventually have to do. Just to put an end to my interactions with administrators, and since everyone was going to have to do it eventually, I said "fine." Well, this turned out to be something right out of the Marxist struggle session handbook. Three moderators took us through absolutely egregious and over-the-top examples of bias in class. These were situations involving such extreme examples of the Woke fever swamp imagination that I have not encountered anything remotely like them in fifty years as an academic.

The culprits in the moderators' examples were always white, and the fragile sensitivities of the oppressed snowflake students were to be protected at all costs. The most obnoxious part of this was the assumption of absolute moral authority by a bunch of bureaucrats and "studies" professors. The most absurd of the moderators was a white woman with a preposterous spiky hairdo desperately proclaiming her intersectionality. At least I got a good laugh out of this total clown show.

Chapter Twenty-Four

The Split Between Woke and Traditional University Faculty

Just or unjust, the Woke/CRT agenda is about gaining and exercising power. The search for what each competing group would consider distributional and corrective justice for its members versus that for other organizations is always political. Efforts are always directed toward obtaining the power required to achieve desired ends. Organized strategies in service of these power-directed agendas have been brought into the heart of the university.

The Woke Are Hiring Their Own: What a Surprise

John Leo argues the university is being corrupted and that the freedom and diversity of thought that is essential to a healthy democratic republic undermined. He states: "When leftists take over a department, they almost always hire their own, so except in some technical fields, non-leftists tend to disappear."[1]

As the data presented next shows quite clearly, that one-sided hiring process is what has been and is still occurring. The result is that America's universities are being shifted dramatically from a primarily neutral intellectual system to a politically oriented system that is left or progressive. Harvard offers one example.

Only 1 Percent of Harvard Faculty Respondents Stated They Are "Conservative"

In the 2022 annual survey conducted at Harvard concerning faculty political affiliations, only 1 percent of Harvard faculty respondents stated they are "conservative" and no respondents identified as "very conservative." Meimei Xu reports in the *Harvard Crimson*:

> More than 80 percent of Harvard faculty respondents characterized their political leanings as "liberal" or "very liberal" . . . A little over 37 percent of faculty respondents identified as "very liberal"—a nearly 8 percent jump from last year. Only 1 percent of respondents stated they are "conservative," and no respondents identified as "very conservative." Moreover, only 16 percent of Harvard faculty members classify their political views as "moderate." . . . Harvard is hardly alone in its political bias. University faculty identifying as "liberal" consistently outnumber their "conservative" colleagues. This trend has accelerated in recent years, with left-leaning professors rapidly displacing their right-leaning counterparts on college campuses nationwide.[2]

The Political Orientations of University Faculty

The Higher Education Research Institute (HERI) has published the results of its survey indicating the trends in university academics' political affiliations. Various studies focus on political party affiliation and, while that can be a useful indicator, it doesn't necessarily measure the intensity of an individual's political ideology. The material offered next uses party affiliation to some extent, but other indicators, taken together, provide deeper insight into the dramatic shift toward the more radical and progressive Left among university faculty and administrators.

As the reports indicate, "non-leftists" have almost completely disappeared in many of the "soft" or non-technical disciplines. The "soft" knowledge disciplines are where the Left and progressives dominate. These are also the areas in which opinions, assertions, and political biases shape the discourse. The startling fact is that numerous university departments have no faculty who identified as conservative.

Frank Luntz published a 2002 survey suggesting that the figures on political diversity were extreme twenty years ago. They have become even more so since. Luntz wrote in 2002: "[T]hose on the conservative side of the political spectrum don't have much of a place in the Ivy League faculty lounges. Just 6 percent of Ivy League professors would describe themselves as either conservative or somewhat conservative, and only 3 percent consider themselves to be Republicans."[3]

John Leo commented on Luntz: "Frank Luntz's survey [of the political party affiliations of university faculty] may not prove anything, [but] his comment on the poll seems fitting:"I think universities should insist on the same diversity in their faculty that they look for in their students. I have a problem when these faculties have no Republican or conservative representation at all."[4]

The National Communication Association's (NCA) 2017 analysis of faculty political affiliation shows Democrat-aligned faculty to outnumber Republicans by 8.5:1, and even more telling is that: "The ratio of registered Democrats to Republicans has increased in the past decade and is highest among young professors."[5] The undeniable fact is that younger faculty are expanding their numbers and as they increasingly widen the political gap are widening the "viewpoint" schism on university campuses to the point of no return. An NCA report, "Political Party Affiliation Among Academic Faculty," demonstrates the continuing trend, including the fact that "60 [percent] of both History and Journalism/ Communication departments report employing no registered Republicans."[6]

> A recent article in Econ Journal Watch examined faculty voter registration at 40 leading US universities. Authors looked at the ratio of Democrats to Republicans among tenure-track faculty in five academic disciplines: economics, history, journalism/communication, law, and psychology. The report found 3,623 of the 7,243 professors registered as Democrats and only 314 registered as Republicans. The ratio of registered Democrats to Republicans has increased in the past decade and is highest among young professors. The report also finds that Journalism/Communication and History are among the most liberal departments. In fact, 60 [percent] of both History and Journalism/Communication departments report employing no registered Republicans.[7]

Such conditions do not occur by accident. Instead, they are the inevitable product of members of a political and cultural group deliberately "reproducing" themselves, and in doing so, reinforcing their own power base while overwhelming any opposition.

Abrams and Khalid: 2020 Faculty and Administrator Analysis

Samuel Abrams is a professor of politics and social science at Sarah Lawrence College, a faculty fellow with New York University's Center for Advanced Social Science Research, and a senior fellow at the American Enterprise Institute,. Amna Kalid is an associate professor in history at Carleton College. She specializes in modern South Asian history and the history of medicine. Abrams and Khalid have analyzed the significant split among university faculty and staff, finding a substantial majority of university academics are very politically liberal. They report:

> The HERI [Higher Education Research Institute] approach that asks how faculty members self-identify across the political spectrum gives us a better sense of the ideological leanings among the professoriate. . . . In 1989–1990, when HERI first fielded this survey, 42 [percent] of faculty identified as being on the left, 40 [percent] were moderate, and another 18 [percent] were on the right. This is not a normal curve—it is a clear lean to the left. Almost three decades later in 2016–2017, HERI found that 60 [percent] of the faculty identified as either far left or liberal compared to just 12 [percent] being conservative or far right. In 1989, the liberal:conservative ratio of faculty was 2.3:1.
>
> In less than 30 years the ratio of liberal identifying faculty to conservative faculty had more than doubled to 5:1.[8]

Part of the study involved looking at faculty from the perspective of gender, academic rank, and the faculty members' academic discipline. Faculty political affiliation overwhelmingly leaned left, even to the point of some departments in numerous universities having no conservative-identifying faculty or, given the disdain in which activist faculty hold anyone not of their identity affiliation, no faculty willing to "out" themselves as conservative.

An additional factor of significance is that the imbalance in faculty was by far the greatest with women leaning left relative to male faculty at a sixteen to one ratio. Women tend to cluster in interdisciplinary areas involving noncumulative or "soft" knowledge such as women's and gender studies, Interdisciplinary subjects, LGBTQ+, discrimination, race, ethnic studies, and similar areas of inquiry. As teachers, researchers, and activists, it is highly likely that teachers in such programs communicate strongly political messages to students. There is clear evidence, even admissions, that, in women's and gender studies programs, external activist groups and agendas have been implicitly and consciously infused into the curriculum. This is done by faculty who hold strong views centered around issues that, for them, "hit close to home" and have come to represent unquestionable "truths" that they themselves define.

Since the beginning of the modern Civil Rights movement in the late 1960s, critical social issues have been infused into the university culture in both teaching and research. Courses on social issues proliferated and were taught by faculty who took the issues "personally" because, as the Identity Group divisions in America grew and intensified, the teachers were in a sense teaching about themselves and their "lived experiences." Many factionalized activist academics pursue agendas that are a subjective part of the characteristics they share with a personal identity group that sees the world through a predetermined lens. Their subjective experiences and highly politicized ideology make it difficult for many to maintain objectivity of the kind that demands the fullness of the core issues with which they are concerned because "they" and others in their Identity collective "know" all the issues of causation and accountability.

Mary Margaret Fonow and Judith Cook offer an explanation in *Back to the Future: A Look at the Second Wave of Feminist Epistemology and Methodology*. The book is a collection of independent chapters looking at the connections between university scholarship and the promotion of feminism. The challenge this orientation creates is the fact that subjectivity is driven by a combination of an individual's personal experience and the power of the movement's identity group agenda and collective interpretations. In a chapter titled "Objectivity and truth: problems in doing feminist research," Joan Acker, Kate Barry, and Johanna Esseveld write:

> "[T]he women's movement outside of academia posed new questions and new formulations of women's situation which then could be taken up in the academic setting. Women researchers, in addition, were usually members of the women's movement and had, and still have, a political commitment to ending women's oppression."[9]

Although I dread even mentioning the point, the above authors are correct in asserting that many women who have entered faculty ranks in the past decades have done so with coordinated and highly focused agendas in mind. Those agendas oddly enough bear significant parallels in methodology and substance to Critical Race Theory. I don't often rely on *Wikipedia*, but the capsule description that source provides demonstrates my point of a very substantial and aggressive political movement existing within the university, one that was initiated in the late 1960s and has grown very rapidly to have courses and programs at over 900 US colleges and universities. *Wikipedia* reports:

> Women's studies is an academic field that draws on feminist and interdisciplinary methods to place women's lives and experiences at the center of study, while examining social and cultural constructs of gender; systems of privilege and oppression; and the relationships between power and gender as they intersect with other identities and social locations such as race, sexual orientation, socio-economic class, and disability.
>
> Popular concepts that are related to the field of women's studies include feminist theory, standpoint theory, intersectionality, multiculturalism, transnational feminism, social justice, affect studies, agency, bio-politics, materialism, and embodiment. Research practices and methodologies associated with women's studies include

ethnography, autoethnography, focus groups, surveys, communi-
ty-based research, discourse analysis, and reading practices associated with critical theory, post-structuralism, and queer theory. The
field researches and critiques different societal norms of gender, race,
class, sexuality, and other social inequalities.

Women's studies is related to the fields of gender studies, feminist
studies, and sexuality studies, and more broadly related to the fields
of cultural studies, ethnic studies, and African-American studies.[10]

Another analysis in the *Encyclopedia of History* offers the following definition,
with the overarching fact that the program of studies is political, operates
according to a specific set of narratives, and sees "white, caucasian males" as
the source of women's ills. The *Encyclopedia* description is as follows:

WOMEN'S STUDIES

In its short history (from the late 1960s in the United States) women's
studies has moved around the world as an idea, a concept, a practice, and finally a field or *Fach* (German for specialty or field). . . .
Women's studies is the study of women and gender in every field. *Its
basic premise is that traditional education is based on a study of men—
usually upper-class, Caucasian, educated men—while other groups of
men and all different groups of women are erroneously subsumed under
the category "mankind." [emphasis added]* Early on courses drew especially on history, literature, and sociology, but they quickly expanded
to the other humanities (philosophy, religious studies, comparative
literature, art, music) and the social sciences (anthropology, political
science, economics, psychology, geography). Science and technology
have been slower to embrace women's studies, but biology, math,
technology, computer science, chemistry, physics, and medicine have
all begun to examine their assumptions for sexist bias, and courses
in "gender and physics," "women geologists," or "sexism and science"
are de rigueur in most programs.

Over the years the term itself and the naming of the enterprise have
been contested and changing. The first name was "female studies,"

but "women's studies" quickly found more adherents. . . . Some programs have changed their names to "gender studies," "women and gender studies," or "feminist studies." . . . It is safe to say, however, that all permutations share some commonalities—that women matter and that their own assessment of their experiences is the starting point for description and analysis; that the history of women's subordination is differently experienced but commonly shared; that the elimination of that subordination is a common goal. The concept of gender as a social construction that reflects and determines differences in power and opportunity is employed as the primary analytic category.[11]

I am not going to replicate them here, but a look at the Women's Studies menus offered by the sample represented by the University of Pennsylvania and University of Wyoming provide a detailed look at what is an undeniably political "transformative" agenda. Given that the movement has grown to over nine hundred universities since its development in the late 1960s, there should be little question that it has brought a strong and unrelenting identity group into academia that is not going away and is very proud of its political focus and intensity as it seeks to restructure an American society it feels has oppressed them.

The irony is that when you compare the narratives and analytical "methods" of the Critical Race Theory and Feminist movements, they utilize the same "frames" and strategies in describing how they have been victimized and denied opportunity on a systemic "push button" basis. It is as if they are operating from the same "playbook" and implementing that strategy against the "team" they are trying to defeat. All you need to do is read the various course and curriculum descriptions of what Women's Studies and Gender Studies programs assert to be their mission and core substance. There can be no doubt that it is the oppression, relegation of women to subservient status, and denial of opportunity by a hierarchy of men who are accused of abusing their power and victimized women in virtually every societal activity. Just as is found in Critical Race Theory, complete systemic victimization and oppression lie at the heart of Women's and Gender Studies programs. This inevitably creates and feeds a mindset of suspicion, and division. Along with this perspective goes the need to tear down the institutional university and rebuild it in a more Feminist image.

The message from all this is that there is intensive infusion of politics and ideology into education that is not insignificant. We do not have to praise the state of affairs in the world of university teaching and scholarship in order to recognize that the rapid and large scale introduction of identity interests in the form of previously marginalized or underrepresented segments of the population has been radically transformed. The shift took place at a fairly slow pace in the late 1960s and early to mid-1970s, but it accelerated once a critical mass was created and Civil Rights laws pushed the hiring of women and minorities in teaching and administrative positions.

During that multi-decade period, many new faculty and staff came into the university institution holding strong political agendas that in dominated their approaches to teaching and research. I remember the point when law school hiring announcements began to uniformly carry the obviously preferential statement that "Women and minorities are strongly urged to apply." The second wave of highly focused hiring signals was pushed in the 1980s and 1990s when Gays and Lesbians were added to the preferential mix of faculty candidates. There can be no real question that such an affirmative hiring preference conferred a significant selection advantage over another group who, viewed subliminally, were the "bad guys," i.e. "white males."

Gender: Democratic Women Faculty Outnumber Republican Male Faculty at a 16.4:1 Ratio

In terms of academic rank, Abrams and Khalid found that, at the lower tier of the tenure track represented by Assistant to Full Professor, the political split was widening, with the left-leaning ratio being 10.5:1 at the Assistant level versus 8.2:1 at the Full Professor level. This supports the argument that universities are increasingly hiring progressively more liberal/left faculty than those with other political leanings, with the result being an increasingly dramatic shift to the agendas of the political left.

Finally, the Abrams/Khalid data show a dramatic differentiation in political affiliation by discipline that very heavily tilts leftward. In Anthropology, it was 42.2:1, English 26.8:1, and Sociology 27:1. This is in stark contrast to disciplines with hard data and tested methodology at their core. In Mathematics, the ratio was 5.5:1, Chemistry 4.6:1, and Economics 3:1.

"According to research conducted by the National Association of Scholars, Democratic professors outnumber their Republican colleagues by a ratio of 8.5 to 1 on top college campuses. Additionally, researchers found that the disparities in political affiliation vary greatly by gender, tenure status, and academic discipline. Women were significantly more likely to identify as Democrats when compared to their male colleagues, with female Democratic-leaning professors outnumbering Republicans by a ratio of 16.4 to 1 and male Democratic-leaning leaning professors outnumbering Republicans by a ratio of 6.4 to 1."

Academic Rank:

For Assistant Professors the Democrat/Republican ratio was 10.5:1
For Associate Professors the ratio was 8.7:1,
For Full Professors 8.2:1.

"The partisan affiliation ratio among professors varied by professorial rank. According to their findings, the Democrat to Republican ratio was highest among nontenured assistant professors, at 10.5 to 1, followed by associate professors, at 8.7 to 1, and full professors 8.2 to 1. While Democrats outnumber Republicans at each stage, the significant decrease in the ratio at each career stage poses a question as to whether many assistant professors feel the need to promote Democratic ideas and viewpoints in order to advance their careers."

Academic Disciplines: All ratios favored Democratic aligned faculty. There were significant variations by discipline as follows.

English 26.8:1
Sociology 27:1
Anthropology 42.2:1

Mathematics 5.5:1
Chemistry 4.6:1
Economics 3:1

"When comparing the ratio by academic discipline, it is worth noting that despite having stark differences in political affiliation among different subjects taught, Democratic-leaning professors outweigh their Republican counterparts across each academic discipline. That being said, the most drastic differences in the ratio were reported among professors of English, at 26.8 to 1, sociology at 27 to 1, and anthropology 42.2 to 1.

When it comes to the more academically rigorous and well-respected disciplines of mathematics, at 5.5 to 1, chemistry, at 4.6 to 1, and economics at 3 to 1, a much smaller ratio was observed. "Between 1989 and 1998, the survey showed negligible change in the number of professors who described themselves as far left or liberal, approximately 45%. As of 2014, surveying 16,112 professors, the percentage of liberal/far left had increased to 60%."[12]

"Homogenous: The Political Affiliations of Elite Liberal Arts College Faculty"

A study by Mitchell Langbert, Associate Professor of Management, Marketing and Entrepreneurship at Brooklyn College, CUNY, also found a wide range between Democratic and Republican faculty—defined as D:R Ratios. Langbert's 2018 study of faculty at "elite" universities found a Democrat/Republican split of "D:R 1.6:1 in engineering faculty, and an amazing 56:0 in communications and 108:0 in interdisciplinary studies": Unsurprisingly, it is in the areas of Interdisciplinary Studies and Communications where the educational strategies and interpretations consistent with Critical theories of race and gender are found. Langbert reports:

> The STEM subjects, such as chemistry, economics, mathematics, and physics, have lower D:R ratios than the social sciences and humanities. The highest D:R ratio of all is for the most ideological field: interdisciplinary studies. I could not find a single Republican with an exclusive appointment to fields like gender studies, Africana studies, and peace studies. As Fabio Rojas describes with respect to Africana or Black studies, these fields had their roots in ideologically motivated political movements that crystallized in the 1960s and 1970s.[13]

This suggests strongly that, as John Leo and others argue, faculty engaged in political areas of study attract and recruit faculty who share their ideological perspectives on issues of political and personal consequence to those hiring new faculty and key administrative staff. This has much to do with the fact that, as discussed in Chapter Twenty-Five, DEI administrators and faculty with strong political agendas in "Woke/Crit" subject matter areas have taken control of the institutional university.

Chapter Twenty-Five

DEI Administrators Are in Control of the University

The Extremely Rapid Growth of DEI and Associated Staff at America's Universities

A recent study examined the presence of DEI staff at major universities. DEI has constructed an overarching and dominant bureaucracy. The power to do so stems from the fact that the DEI actors have the ability to condemn anyone for alleged racist or "insensitive," "offensive," or implicit "micro-aggressions." We should add "sub-conscious biases" to the mix because many "bigots" clearly don't realize just how bigoted they really are. They need to "be brought to the Light" and that is what DEI officers and programs seek to do.

One might initially think that there were relatively limited numbers of people employed in DEI activities. That is far from the truth. For example, as of 2021, the top ten universities in terms of DEI employment were the University of Michigan, Virginia University, Ohio State University, the University of California, Virginia Tech, Stanford University, the University of Maryland, University of Illinois, Syracuse University, and the University of Colorado. Together, these ten universities have 851 DEI staff with Michigan leading by far with 163. The top twenty-five universities in terms of DEI staff total 1687 people.[1]

Although these numbers with an average of forty-five or so DEI staff per university seem substantial, the actual totals are much higher. There are approximately 5300 colleges and universities in the United States. While the total number of formally designated DEI personnel is unclear, as is the number of administrators who have diversity, equity, inclusion matters in their area of responsibility, the fact is that there are thousands of university and college administrators engaged in DEI-type activities. University DEI employment is big business, and the growth in their ranks in the last decade or so has been amazing. These employees need to justify their continuing employment and expanding their areas of concern and responsibility has been vital in that regard. This has had what many faculty consider—of course largely silently—to be a negative impact on the quality of education. The same has been said about DEI administrators in K–12 educational systems.

As the ranks of DEI officers grow, the power and influence they wield over universities has increased dramatically. In a very real sense, they are now the "power majority" regardless of their actual numbers. They represent a highly organized political movement, some of whose members are engaged in the creation of what they see as a form of social justice that includes atonement, as well as what they see as the implementation of complete and comprehensive corrective and compensatory justice at every level of American society. They see themselves as "fighting the good fight" against the sources of darkness and discrimination wherever found. Many activists have also discovered that the Woke/ CRT agenda is a pathway to power, status, employment security, and money.

The DEI System's Pay, Power, Perks, and Privilege Will Not Be Surrendered Willingly

Those who wish to resist or reverse what is happening need to understand that there are too many people serving as DEI officers, too many consultants depending on the public and private revenues associated with "feeding" the system, and too many publishers and others who are profiting from the "industry" that has been created. They will fight to prevent any change in the recently created system that provides them with status, high pay, security, and a taste of power. For many Woke faculty, DEI personnel, and external consultants, what now exists is the best and most lucrative job they are likely to ever have. Without the DEI, Woke, and Genderism systems, they would lose the "fatted cow" and have nowhere to go that would offer equivalent status and benefits.

Just how desirable and potentially profitable is the work of the Woke and DEI staff? This, along with the salaries and costs of the system, is suggested by the following analysis of the numbers of people engaged in these activities. This recent report demonstrates the advantages offered DEI officers.

> [S]alary data shows that the universities of Michigan, Maryland, Virginia and Illinois, plus Virginia Tech, boast some of the highest-paid DEI staffers at public universities. . . . These institutions' top diversity employees earn salaries ranging from $329,000 to $430,000—vastly eclipsing the average pay for the schools' full-time tenured professors. . . . [Jay Greene states] "the effective purpose of diversity, equity and inclusion is to create a political orthodoxy and enforce that political orthodoxy, which fundamentally distorts the intellectual and political life on campus."
>
> "It's becoming almost an all-consuming priority where even large numbers of staff who don't have official responsibilities for DEI—don't have it in their job titles—are nonetheless working on it and see it as one of their top priorities."
>
> Mark Perry, a senior fellow at the American Enterprise Institute and a professor emeritus of economics at the University of Michigan . . . said diversity staff has expanded outside of DEI departments. "What's happened over the last five to 10 years is its spread out in decentralized ways," Perry told Fox News. "At the University of Michigan, each college, school, or department on campus will have a diversity officer, including the library, the arboretum, school of nursing—the college of engineering at Michigan has about 10 diversity officers. Greene said it's "shocking," given the large scale of investments, that there is "no evidence to show it's achieving its ostensible purposes of helping improve racial climate, tolerance and welfare of students."
>
> He added that a university with an average DEI staff of 45 people—along with the costs of diversity initiatives—can involve tens of

millions of dollars per year. Greene said that's a "severe undercount" since it doesn't include "all of the other efforts made by people who don't have this in their job titles." . . . Greene's study shows that the University of Michigan has the most DEI personnel out of the universities, with 163 individuals working on such efforts as of 2021. Michigan's vice provost for equity and inclusion and chief diversity officer, is also the highest-paid DEI official from the top 15 colleges on their list. . . . [He] earns an annual salary of nearly $431,000.

Other schools with massive staff devoted to DEI initiatives also dish out handsome paychecks to their top equity personnel. [T]he vice president at the office of diversity and inclusion at the University of Maryland, which employs 71 DEI personnel, makes $358,000 a year, a database of Maryland public employees shows. . . . [The] vice provost for inclusion and diversity at Virginia Tech, which has 83 DEI personnel, earns over $351,000 annually. . . . [The] vice president for diversity, equity and inclusion at the University of Virginia, which has 94 employees devoted to DEI, makes $340,000 a year. . . . [The] vice chancellor for diversity, equity and inclusion at the University of Illinois, which has 71 DEI employees, earns nearly $330,000 annually, salary disclosures show.[2]

Even though many educational institutions repeatedly claim that they do not teach Critical Race Theory and that it, at worst, is only taught as an elective in some American law schools and universities, that claim is a gross mischaracterization. CRT programs exist in many forms throughout both university and K–12 education. There are numerous examples presented in my book *"Un-Canceling" America* that reflect "flat out" lies about what is being done, and not only in Critical Race Theory, Ethnic Studies, and Gender and Sexuality elements in the curricula. Darlene McCormick Sanchez reported on one dramatic example in an *Epoch Times* analysis:

A University of Florida insider released a report exclusively to *The Epoch Times* showing that the university underreported its Diversity, Equity and Inclusion (DEI) programs, even as the governor's office confirmed universities across the state have spent millions of dollars promoting DEI. The insider, who spoke to The Epoch Times on condition of anonymity, said the University of Florida (UF) funding numbers turned in at the direction of Florida Gov. Ron DeSantis did not disclose a vast network of personnel and programs pushing DEI, which includes Critical Race Theory (CRT). He pointed out that as many as 33 DEI liaisons at UF fell under the radar when the university self-reported its DEI programs to the governor's office.

Key findings by the governor's office released to the media . . . showed that taxpayers had financed a chief diversity officer at the UF for $750,000 per year, and another $445,000 for the University of Central Florida's vice president for DEI and their assistants. The Center for Environmental Equity and Justice at Florida A&M University cost $1.8 million in tax dollars per year, according to the news release. The DEI offices at the University of South Florida and Florida International University cost taxpayers another $2 million dollars.[3]

Anti-Woke critic Christopher Rufo, senior fellow at the Manhattan Institute, strongly condemns what he considers the distorted ideology of Wokeism and Critical Race Theory. He explains his position in a critique of the extent to which it dominates Florida International University:

Florida International University [FIU], a public institution, has adopted a radical "diversity, equity, and inclusion" program that condemns the United States as a system of "white supremacy," segregates scholarships and student programs by race, and trains students for participation in left-wing protests and political activism. I have obtained a collection of documents through Sunshine Law requests that reveal a stunning bureaucratic transformation. Diversity, Equity, and Inclusion (DEI) officials at FIU, who serve a population of more than 40,000 undergraduate students, have steadily operationalized the principles of critical race theory and created a vast web of programming that wraps this ideology into nearly every process of academic life.

Following the [2020] summer of protest, the ideological programs at FIU intensified. The university's DEI officials implemented a heavy mass of programming designed to control language, thought, behavior, hiring, curriculum, and the distribution of resources according to the dictates of left-wing racialism. If left unchecked, the DEI bureaucracies will swallow universities whole. They will gradually re-segregate higher education according to the dictates of intersectionality and turn the principle of individual rights on its head.[4]

Dr. Tabia Lee, herself a Black woman and now former faculty director of the Office of Equity, Social Justice, and Education at De Anza College in Cupertino, California, was denied tenure and fired for questioning some aspects of the DEI agenda at De Anza. Lee has criticized the DEI movement as being done in ways that create and intensify racial division in a socially undesirable way. Rikki Schlott, *New York Post* columnist and researcher for the Foundation for Individual Rights and Expression (FIRE), reported on the situation:

> Dr. Tabia Lee says DEI professionals with the "wrong" vision can be bullied out of the industry. "The default here in America especially is [a type of DEI] that focuses on racial division and perpetual strife around racialized identity," she said. "I think that that's something that's very toxic for everyone. I don't think anyone benefits from that."
>
> Lee—who formerly served as faculty director of the Office of Equity, Social Justice, and Education at De Anza College in Cupertino, California—said the industry squeezes out those who disagree with a singular, politicized vision of what diversity, equity, and inclusion is supposed to look like.
>
> In a recent lawsuit filed against De Anza College, Lee alleges she was wrongfully denied tenure . . . after she pushed back against DEI messaging she saw as divisive. She says her vision of true diversity—one which includes promoting diversity of opinion—made her an "instant pariah" on campus. Questioning land acknowledgement

practices [based on historical unjust "takings" of land from Native Americans] and suggesting the school capitalize both "black" and "white" in official communications saw Lee accused of being a white supremacist. And ultimately, she claims, asking those questions left her out of a job. "The companies are starting to notice that there's not much accountability in the field," Lee said. "They've allowed consultants to come in without any accountability measures attached to the work that they're doing."[5]

It is truly fascinating that the Woke/CRT DEI movement would in any way claim with a straight face that they are producing understanding, benevolence, and social harmony through many of their actions. Consider the almost certain results of staging a mandatory workshop or training program in which people defined as being "White" are confronted with accusations of being subconsciously racist, "micro-aggressors" for reasons they don't understand, "privileged" beneficiaries of an alleged system of total "whiteness" in which they are unfairly taking advantage of "historically marginalized" identity groups due to inherent "white" characteristics and behaviors. In that context, think about the normal human reaction that would be produced to being told you are racist due to the kinds of factors listed next, ones that were part of a mandatory Coca-Cola employee sensitivity program. This list could make any reasonable person ask "Are you kidding me?" The arrogance and intellectual hypocrisy are truly unbelievable.

Since the summer of 2020, corporations have sparked controversy over divisive DEI lessons. [An example is provided by Coca-Cola.] In early 2021, Coca-Cola famously hosted a diversity training which taught employees how to be "less white," urging them to be more humble, less ignorant, and less oppressive. Coca-Cola was criticized for a divisive diversity presentation that included a slide about how to be less white.

To be less white is to:

-be less oppressive

-be less arrogant

-be less certain

-be less defensive

-be less ignorant

-be more humble

-listen

-believe

-break with apathy

-break with white solidarity.[6]

2017: Administrative Staff Ideological Skewing is at a 12:1 Ratio Favoring Liberal/Left

The number and power of university administrative staff have increased dramatically. In 2021, data reveal that 66.2 percent of college administrators were women and 33.8 percent were men.[7] A 2017 survey by Abrams and Khalid of a nationally representative sample of about nine hundred "student-facing" administrators found:

> that liberal staff members outnumber their conservative counterparts by the astonishing ratio of 12:1. Only 6 [percent]of campus administrators identified as conservative to some degree, while 71 [percent] classified themselves as liberal or very liberal. Of the three constituencies on campus, the political skew of administrators is the most marked. . . . With the rapid growth of the administrative positions on campuses it is hard to find an area of campus where this professional class does not play a role. . . .
>
> Administrators, intentionally or unintentionally, are signaling to students which topics are open to debate and identify which questions should simply be overlooked for fear of negative consequences. The irony is that those who are purportedly working to increase diversity are often the ones who are responsible for limiting the scope for diversity of viewpoints.[8]

The power of the DEI system has grown to the point that no one in universities, or many other locations, dares dispute the DEI movement's assertions for fear of being labeled a bigot, a "phobe" of some kind, or a racist. This applies to the realm of political viewpoint discrimination, one that has changed a previously free-thinking university intellectual culture into one where faculty, many students, and even administrators are afraid to say anything on a range of critical issues. It is taboo to question the assertions and assumptions voiced by the Woke/Crits.

The career implications of getting on the wrong side of DEI and Woke activists and organizations are significant. This applies to social media consequences, as well as potential job opportunities because your "online reputation" is not under your control and critical posts condemning and labeling anyone who steps out of line are timeless, non-contextual, and very often anonymous or concealed behind the mask of a radical group.

What happened at the Dalton School offers a clear understanding of the fact that DEI has gone far beyond the university world and has spread through private and public K–12 school administrations, as well as governmental and corporate cultures, as revealed in the Coca Cola program on how to be "less white." The Dalton School isn't quite a university, but many of its graduates end up at Ivy universities and go on to play a significant role in the social system. It is helpful to see the list of demands Dalton's faculty made in 2020 concerning actions they insisted the school's administrators take. Note that significant expansion of administrative staff is at the core, as are propaganda and monitoring and control of what is taught to ensure no deviation from approved language and concepts. Here are some of the demands made by Dalton's faculty.

- The hiring of twelve full time diversity officers
- Hiring an additional full time employee whose "entire role is to support Black students who come forward with complaints."
- Hiring multiple psychologists with "specialization on the psychological issues affecting ethnic minority populations."
- Paying off the student debt of incoming black faculty.
- Re-routing 50 percent of all donations to NYC public schools.

- Elimination of AP courses if black students don't score as high as white.
- Required courses on "Black liberation."
- Public "anti-racism" statements required from all employees.
- Mandatory "Community and Diversity Days" to be held "throughout the year."
- Required anti-bias training to be conducted every year for all staff and parent volunteers.
- Mandatory minority representation in (otherwise elective) student leadership roles.
- Mandatory diversity plot lines in school plays.
- Overhaul of entire curriculum to reflect diversity narratives.[9]

The steadily widening size of the split between the young faculty and aspiring faculty who have flooded into the university ranks versus established and longer term faculty who dare to challenge the Woke/Crit agenda is demonstrated by the experience of University of Chicago faculty member Dorian Abbot that was described previously. What was Abbot's sin in the eyes of the younger faculty, and those seeking advanced degrees while aspiring to become university faculty members? Abbot expressed several concerns about "the way Diversity, Equity, and Inclusion (DEI) efforts have been discussed and implemented on campus." There were immediate demands for discipline and, to the eternal shame of the Massachusetts Institute of Technology (MIT), MIT canceled a scheduled presentation previously set for Abbot for daring to raise even moderate questions about the "Sacred Cow" of DEI.

Such reactions have been disturbingly common in America's universities. One rather dramatic example, perhaps "garish" would be a better description, is offered in the following report. To me, Professor Emily Drew of Willamette University, a self-proclaimed academic "expert on racism," might possibly consider the fact that she has become that which she so vehemently criticizes. And, what the hell is an "Inner Becky"?

A professor in Salem, Oregon,—who is a self-described expert in "racism . . . and social change"—derided White people for showing up as "damaging" to people of color. Professor Emily Drew of Willamette University works for a consulting company called Crossroads which charges tens of thousands of dollars for critical race theory-related development sessions. . . . Drew will be using her academic expertise on "racism" in a training of how White people can become "less damaging" to people of color. Previous events she hosted were titled, "Working on our Whiteness" and "Challenging Our Inner Becky: Interventions of White Women-ness in Our Community."[10]

The Revealing Agenda of the American Association of Colleges and Universities 2022 Conference on Diversity, Equity, and Inclusion Reveals a Strategy

What is going on with the DEI movement goes well beyond financial considerations. DEI is not just a job. It is an organized and coordinated industry and a social justice mission. That, however, does not automatically make all its aims, strategies, and behaviors legitimate. The DEI system's activities include a wide range of university and corporate conferences, symposia, and workshops aimed at bringing together DEI-engaged university staff to ensure they are focused on a shared and coordinated mission. That mission involves, and to a significant degree is centered on, the tenets and assertions of Critical Race Theory, Genderism, and Wokeism.

DEI has penetrated deeply into the politics and behaviors of students, other administrators, and faculty at America's universities. DEI staffs conduct training programs, do "deep interrogations" and "equity audits," monitor classes and communications, and take complaints against others from students who, in some instances, seem similar to Mao Zedong's youthful Red Guard. They are also obviously intent on "transforming" the university's culture in a comprehensive way according to what they desire. In the main, this is also being done by administrative bureaucrats and ideologues rather than an engaged faculty. Of course, for university faculty to engage with this reform effort in any full and critical way would most likely cost those individuals their careers.

Given that in many instances the DEI staff are conducting orientation seminars and workshops and counseling sessions for students that emphasize the types of overt and subliminal or "micro" speech they are supposed to consider "wrong," it is unsurprising that students empowered to monitor teachers are making many of the complaints against faculty. In the very few examples offered earlier of faculty being subjected to suspensions or disciplinary review, the cases were based on student complaints against faculty members in connection with Abbot, Zubieta, Gafni, Klein, Patton, Ferguson, Rectenwald, Sullivan, Vermuele, Jacobson, and Neal-Boylan. Empowering students to spearhead the complaint process rather than Woke faculty and administrators is an effective strategy. In that way, the faculty and administrators become mediators of conflict rather than instigators, and the appearance of a false neutrality can be maintained.

The Program, Assumptions, and Goals of the 2022 Diversity, Equity, and Inclusion Conference Show Where This Is Going

The 2022 American Association of Colleges and Universities (AAC&U) offers an online description of its 2022 conference on Diversity, Equity, and Inclusion. The description sets out the AAC&U's goals and the strong sense on the part of its DEI component that they have *only begun* the work of transforming the internal culture and structures of colleges and universities. The language of the organizers is set out next. I have italicized particular characterizations that—to me at least—provide insight into the movement's intent. It is truly illuminating as to the motivations and agenda of the Woke/Crit DEI movement. The program description states:

> Nearly half of higher education professionals believe that recognizing and overcoming persistent inequities is among the most significant challenges now facing colleges and universities. More than a third believe that building capacity for institutional transformation is also a significant challenge.
>
> Over the past year many institutions have *released statements* condemning the racial and social injustices in our communities, and institutional leaders have acknowledged that strategic reform is urgently needed to address structural racism and inequities in higher

education. Making real progress toward sustainable transformation will take more than just words. The reality is that most institutions continue to struggle with identifying a process for engaging in the deep interrogation of practices, policies, and structures needed to achieve the goals outlined in these statements.

AAC&U invites you to join us for a conference that will go beyond the rhetoric and prioritize campus strategies, institutional culture, and accountability in operationalizing the values of equity and diversity.

Conference sessions will:

- explore the experiences of institutional and community participants;
- identify barriers that are hindering our progress; and
- promote discussion of the privileges, the biases, and the false belief in a hierarchy of human value that are embedded in our systems, structures, and policies.

It is imperative that we stay focused on making progress towards transformation that can be achieved and sustained, and the efforts that represent more than just our words. 2022 Conference on Diversity, Equity, and Student Success. This conference will go beyond the rhetoric and prioritize campus strategies, institutional culture, and accountability in operationalizing the values of equity and diversity."[11]

"Deep Interrogation?" Even My Non-Existent Shrink Can't Do That!

The mission and purposes statement set out previously indicates it is desirable to engage in a "deep interrogation" of the practices, policies, and structures underlying DEI's agenda. Translating the language of the AAC&U DEI Conference agenda into real operational terms suggests that it is a combination of "framing" key strategic language along with the weaving together of an appealing "narrative" with a powerful message that, on the surface, cannot be denied as to legitimacy and desirability. As with any vital issue, however, "the Devil is in the details" and in the real-world applications.

The continual use of phrases such as needing to "go beyond the rhetoric" and needing "more than just words," "institutional culture," "identifying barriers," "deep interrogation," "privileges," "biases," "false belief in a hierarchy of human value," "capacity for institutional transformation," and "accountability in operationalizing the values of equity and diversity" is actually kind of scary. It is a deliberate act of "linguistic framing" of the kind that Stanford's George Lakoff analyzed in terms of how specific narrative language carries within it the ability to go beyond fact and logic and penetrate our "deep" levels of emotive interpretation.[12] The "frames" are all extremely open-textured terms into which those in control of discourse can pour nearly any content they desire. That is the special power of the activist and ideologue. Spend a moment thinking about what the following assertions contained within the AAC&U 2022 Conference mission mean. I have added italics to various points.

- *Building capacity* for institutional transformation.
- Making real progress toward *sustainable transformation* will take more than just words.
- Most institutions continue to struggle with identifying a process for engaging in the *deep interrogation* of practices, policies, and structures needed to achieve the goals.
- Go beyond the rhetoric and prioritize campus strategies, institutional culture, and accountability in *operationalizing the values of equity and diversity.*
- Staying focused on making progress towards *transformation.*
- *Identify barriers* that are hindering our progress;
- Promote discussion of the *privileges*, the *biases*, and the *false belief in a hierarchy* of human value that are *embedded* in our *systems*, *structures*, and *policies.*

My background is diverse. I have had an extensive array of "lived experiences." One thing I have learned after representing several thousand clients, mostly ones that would be described as "marginalized," taught thousands of law and other university students, created workshops and conferences in America and around the world, worked with fellow activists and advocates from over thirty countries typically labeled Third or even Fourth World, is that a fair number of the people in those contexts are "running a scam" in the sense that they may or may not be representing their intentions and interests, but they learn how to benefit from the interactions and processes.

Knowledge certainly is power, and control of allowed knowledge and permissible language is a vital part of acquiring and maintaining power. We can talk about justice, fairness, discrimination, micro-aggressions, and the like all you want—and there are certainly threads of legitimacy in various of the assertions and formulations—but at the heart of the current ongoing movement is an aggressive drive for power. Control of language, emotional narratives, education and critical institutions are "the Game" for the Woke/Crits, and they are winning.

Heritage Foundation Study: Learning Gaps Grow Worse Between Black, Latino, and White Students in School Districts with "Diversity" Officers

More in depth study needs to be done given the critical nature of the issues involved, but the Heritage Foundation study's data and analysis demand a close look. The problem with doing such a deep inquiry, however, is that everything about such matters has been "racialized" and the educational establishment does not want to see its main points and accusations about what is going on looked at closely.

The unfortunate truth is that a national "educational bureaucracy" exists whose competence and motivations need to be examined. The Woke and Critical Race Theorists and activists have taken over that educational bureaucracy, including accreditation systems, administrative controls, curriculum, state and local school boards, and teacher organizations. The problem is that the Woke have little interest in developing or dealing with facts that could potentially challenge their political, ideological, and narrative interpretations asserting that all problems are the fault of institutional or "systemic" racism or gender bias of various kinds. This makes it unlikely honest analysis will be done, at least by those who are the primary beneficiaries of controlling what is occurring.

A significant, but largely unstated aspect of our dilemma is that, as the following report suggests, schools and the K–12 and university educational bureaucracies are now part of a lucrative employment, materials development and purchasing contracting center, and consultancy industry. This economic activity has penetrated our entire educational establishment and is distributing extremely large amounts of money to DEI administrators, consultants, and businesses.

An amazing array of racial and gender "experts" are feeding on the billions of dollars being spent on educational materials and training programs. They also enjoy basking in the ego gratification of being in power. Anyone seeking to interfere with that financially lucrative system, or suggest that the host of "diversity coordinator" jobs that have been created have effectively captured the K–12 and university systems of education, will be subjected to aggressive attacks. Kyle Smith, Jay Greene, and James Paul suggest there are problems with the results being achieved in that system.

> A new study says that putting a high-paid diversity bureaucrat on the school payroll may actually make things *worse* for black and Latino students. . . . An empirical study by the Heritage Foundation that analyzed data in 554 districts teaching 22.5 million students found that, now that chief diversity officers (CDOs) have been hired by virtually every college campus, 79 percent of the largest K-12 districts have hired such officers as well, and even rural districts are taking them on at a fast clip. Okay, so how is that working out? Districts with CDOs have greater achievement gaps between rich and poor, between white and black, and between white and Latino students. "In districts without a CDO," reports Heritage, "the average black student is 1.9 grade levels behind the average white student on standardized test results." With CDOs, that gap grows to 2.4

grade levels. The same pattern emerges when comparing white and Latino students, although the gaps are smaller.

What if this is merely downstream from poverty, though? Districts with CDOs, which are concentrated in cities, have a higher percentage of students who qualify for free lunches. Suburban and exurban districts are wealthier. To address that question, Heritage's researchers looked at test scores over time. Over a decade ending in 2018, "the white-black achievement gap grew by 0.03 grade levels each year in districts with CDOs relative to districts without that position." Between whites and Latinos, the gap grew by 0.02 grade levels per year in districts with CDOs vs. those without them. The Heritage Foundation found that in school districts with CDOs, the average black student is 2.4 grade levels behind the average white student on standardized test results. Heritage ran regression analyses to control for other factors (such as school budgets, racial composition, baseline levels of student achievement and so on) and found the same outcomes: CDOs are associated with worse performance by minorities, and the gaps are growing larger in those districts.[13]

The Heritage Foundation report's Summary of Findings continues next.

An analysis of student test-score data shows that employing a chief diversity officer (CDO) in K–12 school districts does not contribute to closing achievement gaps and is even likely to exacerbate those gaps. If CDOs are not accomplishing their stated goals, what is accomplished by creating these positions? CDOs may be best understood as political activists who articulate and enforce an ideological orthodoxy within school districts. They help to mobilize and strengthen the political influence of one side. The creation of CDOs tilts the political playing field against parent and teacher efforts to remove the radical ideology of critical race theory and other illiberal ideals from school curricula and practices.[14]

Resisting the Indoctrination of Students by Teachers, Diversity, Equity, and Inclusion Administrators (DEI's), and Well-Paid "Equity" Consultants

When everything is made of internalized propaganda slogans, there is no possibility of rational understanding or openness to data. Minds are exceedingly difficult to be changed when the consequences include malicious attacks and ostracism by those in power, or loss of lucrative employment and job security on the part of those being challenged. Evidence doesn't matter because with the use of powerful morality-based narratives and "frames," as described by George Lakoff's powerful work on linguistics, we are operating on an emotional level designed to bypass rational analysis. That emotive process unfolds through an entirely different channel of communication and perception than is involved with our rational minds that are supposed to screen, assess, and question what we are told. The narrative power is created because effective propaganda is shaped to penetrate and seize us on the levels of emotion, urges, and biases—not reason and evidence.

This explains why those on the left condemn the "evils" of rationalism, individualism, reading and writing, mathematics, logic, and the like. Such terrible "White values" challenge those of the "collective" they have been trying to create through social and emotional learning, hypersensitivity, micro-aggressions, "White Supremacy," and "White Privilege" narratives, etc. This strategy is aimed at replacing fundamental tools of the mind by subordinating rationality to emotion. This is creating a form of hyper-sensitivity that is allowed to be interpreted solely and subjectively by the recipient (rather than the speaker) as insensitive, "micro-aggressive," or racist speech.

Booker T. Washington Warned Us to Watch Out for the "Trickster Figures"

Booker T. Washington wrote in 1911:

> There is a class of colored people who make a business of keeping the troubles, the wrongs, and the hardships of the Negro race before the

public. Having learned that they are able to make a living out of their troubles, they have grown into the settled habit of advertising their wrongs—partly because they want sympathy and partly because it pays. Some of these people do not want the Negro to lose his grievances, because they do not want to lose their jobs.[15]

Think about the tragedy reflected in the somber, morally stark, and painful message voiced by Booker T. Washington in that preceding paragraph. Chicago Reverend Corey Brooks applied Booker T. Washington's view on the behavior of "Trickster Figures" to what he sees happening in the Black Lives Matter movement. Reverend Brooks recently spent more than one hundred nights camped out on the roof of a Chicago building to bring attention to the plight of Black Americans in areas of education, opportunity, poverty alleviation, crime, and other areas. Nor does he absolve Chicago's minority leaders of responsibility.

> I just read a report that said millions are unaccounted for after all of the original three Black Lives Matter leaders quit. The amount given was $60 million. $60 million. I believe it was far more. [BLM admits the organization received over $90 million in contributions. The organization is under investigation in numerous states for failing to provide required reports on what happened to the funds.] If there is no accountability with the BLM board, and if there is such shadiness within the organization over all this money, then you can bet there's even more money that's being hid. When Booker T. Washington wrote these words over 100 years ago, he was [essentially] describing BLM. What makes me especially mad is that we have had blacks like these who milked black pain for money ever since we came out of slavery. We called them trickster figures . . .
>
> [Brooks adds] Let me repeat: "Some of these people do not want the Negro to lose his grievances." Let that sink in, folks. You know who they are talking about? The folks right here. Right here in these streets. They want these folks to stay beaten down and downtrodden. They want to hold up the very people whose lives I've been trying to

improve everyday for the last 20 years, and they want to hold these people up to Americans and say, see how bad you treat us, give us money.[16]

The Tragic Example of BLM Confirms Booker T. Washington's Insight

Epoch Times reporter Isabel Van Brugen provides a disturbing example of the financial abuses. She explained:

The national arm of Black Lives Matter (BLM) on Feb. 2 shut down all of its online fundraising streams, shortly after California's Department of Justice threatened to hold the organization to account over its "lack of financial transparency," which includes at least $60 million in undisclosed donations. California and Washington states had recently prohibited BLM from collecting donations due to transparency issues, but it did not comply with those orders, the Washington Examiner reported. The news outlet found last week that the charity appeared to have no known leader in charge of its $60 million bankroll since BLM co-founder Patrisse Cullors resigned in May 2021. Cullors had been at the helm of the Black Lives Matter Global Network Foundation (BLMGNF), the legal entity that represents the national BLM movement, for nearly six years. Cullors came under fire when it was discovered that in a very short period she went from owing hundreds of thousands of dollars to being able to purchase four expensive houses. After that fact was reported, Cullors soon resigned from heading BLM.

Shortly before the organization cut off its online fundraising streams, Indiana Attorney General Todd Rokita described Black Lives Matter as a falling "house of cards" and compared it to an "illegal enterprise." "It appears that the house of cards may be falling, and this happens eventually with nearly every scam, scheme, or illegal enterprise," Rokita [stated]. "I see patterns that scams kind of universally take: failure to provide board members, failure to provide even executive directors, failure to make your filings available. It all leads to suspicion."

"Accordingly, directors, trustees, officers and return preparers responsible for failure to timely file the above-described report(s) are personally liable for payment of all penalties, interest and other costs incurred to restore exempt status," the letter said.[17]

Xaviaer DuRousseau, a former BLM activist and member, turned more conservative following his experiences with the Movement's divisive rhetoric and echoed Booker T. Washington's warning. He wrote:

> San Francisco's Board of Supervisors "voiced enthusiastic support" after hearing 111 recommendations from the African American Reparations Advisory Committee. The proposal includes giving every eligible black resident $5 million and the elimination of their personal debt and tax burdens. . . . This campaign for reparations is led by leftist grifters looking to sell their latest lucrative book about being oppressed and progressives who expect a gold medal for their virtue signaling.[18]

Adam Coleman offers his perspective on the "culture war" in which aggressive and wealthy elites seeking power and wealth continually "stir the pot" of racial hate and division for their own advantage while fashioning a narrative that is not consistent with the actual experiences and beliefs of many people who share their skin color. Coleman wrote in his article "The Culture War: Recognizing the Battle for Society's Direction":

> One of the reasons I felt like I needed to jump into the trenches was that I felt there was a great narrative being perpetrated by a particular class of people who were attempting to speak for me while perhaps purposely and completely misrepresenting me. After the death of George Floyd, I felt there was an emotional panic attack that was intentionally being induced by a media establishment while elevating a class of black figureheads who shared my complexion but didn't sound like me or any other rational working-class black person that I knew of.

The microphone was consistently given to wealthy civil rights activists, flashy civil rights lawyers, and snooty black intelligentsia to repeat narratives of fear, victimhood, and ideological fallacies of the life experience of every black person in America. A sports star says to the media that we worry about if a cop is going to wake up on the wrong side of the bed and want to shoot a black person, while simultaneously living a life of being protected by the police daily while traveling around the country: Something doesn't add up here.

This was when I realized that the culture war isn't just about fighting to protect our society from being reimagined into a perverted version of what we used to love but about recognizing who was on the offensive and why. Our culture is simply a means for dividing, demoralizing, and conquering the masses so that the most powerful malevolent people in our society can seize control easier. While we're boycotting a beer company and complaining about the Barbie movie, the perpetrators of the great narrative are finding ways to dissolve our civil liberties and corrupt our political institutions to solidify their stranglehold on the working class.[19]

It is also useful to consider the reality of Ibram X. Kendi, the exotically named "Prophet of Anti-Racism" who has made a fortune on his writing and speaking on the need for a new form of racism imposed on white people in order to atone for any and all discrimination people with similar-colored skin might have done in the past, no matter how distant. Kendi, born Henry Rogers, but now taking a name with far greater "street cred" has made a very large amount of money from lecturers around the country, from sale of his books on anti-racism, salary from Boston University where he teaches, directing a center on race and racism he established at BU in 2020 along with a $10 million grant from former Twitter heads Jack Dorsey. Unfortunately, things don't appear to be going so well at the Center for Antiracist Research. This is captured in the following news report, "Fed-up staff seethe over Boston U's antiracist center: 'Colossal waste of millions of dollars': Ibram Kendi's Center for Antiracist Research accused of mismanagement amid layoffs":

> Current and former staff at Boston University's Center for Antiracist Research, gave a scathing assessment of its leadership, fiscal management and inability to meet goals, in Thursday's student newspaper. "The Center has very, very much failed to deliver on its promise. It's been a colossal waste of millions of dollars," Spencer Piston told the student newspaper, The Daily Free Press. Piston is an associate professor of political science, who works as the faculty lead in the Policy office at the Center for Antiracist Research "CAR."
>
> Piston claimed the center operated within a "culture of secrecy" and had never been transparent about how it managed the millions of dollars in grants and gifts it received since its inception in 2020. "It's pretty hard for me to imagine they blew through $30 million in two years," he told the student newspaper. "There's been a lack of transparency about how much money comes in and how it's spent from the beginning, which comports with a larger culture of secrecy." . . . The Daily Free Press described how the center had failed to produce promised research, despite Kendi touting data science as a "pillar" of his center in 2020. "The Racial Data Lab and the Antiracist Tech Initiative make up the extent of the Center's data-based output under their Research category, according to CAR's website," the newspaper said. However, the Racial Data Lab's only project was a "Covid Racial Data Tracker" which is now-defunct.
>
> Staff also complained that Kendi wasn't fit to serve as a leader and claimed his standing as a public figure took prominence over their center's research. "It was mostly about him, rather than the work, and it was just very difficult to highlight the work over the founder," an anonymous former manager in the policy office said in the report.[20]

Simply put—money, power, ideology, and control have major roles to play in the concealment and denial that is prevalent concerning the implementation of the "Woke agenda" in our universities and K–12 educational systems. It is not only an intellectual and ideological warping; it is an industry and a "gravy train" for those advancing and profiting from the Woke/Crit system. We are now well into a second generation of individuals who have been mis-educated as students and teachers in an intellectually deficient educational system implemented by our K–12 systems and the corps of teachers "educated" by many universities.

That system has ignored the teaching of essential concepts, skills, and the collective and individual responsibilities of the kind necessary to sustain the ideals of the American political community. What is missing includes an absence of civics, lack of respect for the spirit of the Rule of Law, not being taught how to think or how to resolve disputes, as well as not being able or willing to engage in the political and intergroup compromises long considered essential to maintain the health of a complex democratic republic such as America.

Chapter Twenty-Six

What Kind of Faculty Are DEI Systems Allowing Universities to Hire?

In Chapter Twenty-Five, containing the results of a 2017 study by Samuel Abrams and Amna Khalid, one of the important data points brought out was the dramatic and growing shift toward a left/liberal political affiliation based on faculty rank, with the more liberal expansion being the 10.5:1 ratio at the Assistant Professor—or newer and not yet tenured—level. There is also the even more fluid issue of the very significant shift from tenure track faculty appointments to non-tenure track, term contract faculty with renewal options controlled by administrative officers and deans, as well as the increased use of adjunct faculty who serve at the whim of Woke/Crit university administrators. The result is the probability of an even wider split between traditional faculty and politicized "Woke" faculty even greater than the full-tenure track data represent. This is because the non-tenure track teacher variations are under even greater pressure to conform to the clearly defined values of the Woke/CRT groups now in control of universities if they want to be hired in the first place or have renewed contracts.

Given the data concerning the dramatic left/liberal v. conservative split in America's university faculty and administrators, the expanded control that DEI systems have over faculty hiring on the tenure track to adjunct levels will only make the situation worse. It is reasonable to conclude that in the very near future something approximating an absolute monopoly over the intellectual content and focus of teaching and research in the "soft" political disciplines will be totally one-sided and fully politicized.

A Report on the Situation in Arizona's Universities

The fact that the Woke/CRT/DEI system that now dominates universities is using both overt and tacit mandates in which individuals are required to demonstrate their commitment and loyalty to the movement's ideals and assertions, or suffer the consequences. The requirements are mandated through diversity pledges and statements, and for showing how much you have done to advance the aims of the DEI/Woke system as well as what an individual would do to advance that mission if hired. An example is offered in the case of the University of Arizona.

American universities are increasingly requiring students and faculty to pledge support for equity and inclusion efforts through "diversity statements," which in turn suppress the hiring of independent or conservative faculty and student applicants, according to a report from the Goldwater Institute. At Arizona's public universities, diversity statements are mandated in 28 percent of job postings at the University of Arizona, 73 percent of job postings at Northern Arizona University (NAU) and 81 percent of job postings at Arizona State University (ASU) as of fall 2022, according to the Goldwater Institute report.

"DEI [diversity, equity and inclusion] programs and 'statements' do not produce free expression nor more diversity of thought, equal opportunities, and a culture that includes everyone in school activities because DEI's guiding principles are rooted in the racially discriminatory worldview known as critical race theory," Jonathan Butcher wrote in the report. Faculty registered as Democrats now outnumber Republicans by more than 7 to 1 at the University of Arizona and 12 to 1 at ASU, according to a report by the National Association of Scholars.

Diversity statements sometimes required applicants to replace the traditional cover letter with a DEI statement, which forced candidates to provide "up to two full pages detailing their activism or commitment to the DEI regime," asking them to endorse what the Goldwater Institute refers to as "CRT-based concepts" like "intersectional personal identities." At NAU, applicants were encouraged to use "CRT-based terminology" like "intersectional personal identities" in their required DEI responses, the report found. Kimberlé Crenshaw developed the framework for Critical Race Theory and coined the term "intersectionality," according to the Association of American Law Schools. Even for a technical position at ASA, like a research fellow for "ultra-bright nano-structured photoemission electron sources," required applicants to submit a statement on their commitment to DEI.[1]

FIRE's Statement on the Use of Diversity, Equity, and Inclusion Criteria in Faculty Hiring and Evaluation

The following report by the FIRE organization, the Foundation for Individual Rights and Expression, one highly critical of the impact of Diversity, Equity, and Inclusion administrations on America's universities, outlines the problems with what is happening. This report dares to challenge the otherwise taboo assertions and agendas of the Woke and DEI movements and, whether the reader agrees or disagrees with its analysis, creates the opportunity to question and challenge, which, after all, should be the duty of any critic in a democracy.

A recent AAUP [American Association of University Professors] survey of hundreds of colleges and universities found that more than one-fifth of them include DEI criteria in tenure standards, including 45.6 [percent] of large institutions (those with more than 5,000 students). Of the institutions that do not include DEI criteria for tenure, nearly half indicated they are considering adding such criteria in the future. . . . In many cases, these policies threaten to restrict employment or advancement opportunities for faculty who dissent from the prevailing consensus on DEI-related issues of public and academic interest. These policies may even negatively impact faculty who broadly agree with their institution's DEI values but disagree on some of the specifics, or who simply cherish the right to speak without compulsion.

The First Amendment prohibits public universities from compelling faculty to assent to specific ideological views or to embed those views in academic activities. . . . Such colleges and universities educate and employ the overwhelming majority of America's students and faculty members, and this document is intended to address DEI policies at those institutions. . . . The law hasn't changed. But adverse consequences for those who hold or voice dissenting, minority, or simply unpopular opinions are increasingly common on campus.[2]

The Reproduction of Hierarchy

It is now a situation where, in the words of Harvard's Duncan Kennedy, who is one of the early figures in the Critical Legal Studies movement that advanced the birth of Critical Race Theory, those in control of universities and other critical social institutions, inevitably engage in the "reproduction of hierarchy."[3]

America's universities and K–12 educational establishments have in fact produced a "New Hierarchy" and keep adding to the numbers of activist "clones" that have been brought into the system. In the American universities of the past four decades, they have increasingly hired people as faculty and administrators who are "like them." As is dismayingly obvious in the material dealing with DEI hiring guides and behavior, for an individual seeking to have any chance of being hired as a faculty member or administrator, candidates must demonstrate a full commitment to the total system of Diversity, Equity, and Inclusion as set out in great detail in the hiring guides.

DEI officers are effectively in control of the university institution, even though that control is more informal than officially admitted. DEI faculty hiring guides show quite clearly that the process of identifying and ranking potential faculty hires depends heavily on candidates establishing their full commitment to the tenets of Diversity, Equity, and Inclusion. The problem is not simply one of numbers, but of the collective and self-validating politicization the new "diverse" faculty have brought into the university. It isn't only an issue of a shared collective perspective, but one of ruthless suppression of anyone who does not follow the agendas and dictates of the political activists who now control the institution.

The asserted preference for attracting and incorporating a more diverse community of faculty and administrators has long been voiced in the announcements of academic vacancies. Initially, the preferences were for minorities and women, and as the "gender" movement expanded, LGBTQ+ preferences came into play. This system of clearly articulated formalized preferences for non-traditional candidates with specific and often personal reform agendas resulted in a massive change in the characteristics of university faculty and administrators. Subsequent chapters offered here on the shift in faculty and the increase in university administrators in DEI positions demonstrate the scale and nature of what occurred.

There Is No "Safe Space" for Non-Woke/Crit University Faculty

The AAUP recently released a study that shows the dramatic shift from tenure track faculty positions toward non-tenure and contingent forms. This makes faculty even more hesitant to offend the vocal and aggressive political activists now dominating university power structures. Even for the declining number of faculty who are on tenure-track appointments, the "land mines" represented by political issues centered on DEI and diversity have become a dangerous part of the process. *Insight Into Diversity* magazine reported on the AAUP's findings:

> The American Association of University Professors (AAUP) has released its first major study in nearly 20 years on tenure policies at U.S. institutions of higher education. The findings reveal significant changes in faculty career pathways over the last two decades, aligning with previous research that showed the decline in tenure at U.S. colleges and universities. The 2022 report shows that 53.5 percent of higher education institutions have replaced tenure-eligible positions with contingent faculty appointments, compared with only 17.2 percent of colleges in 2004. In 2019, just 10.5 percent of faculty positions in the U.S. were tenure-track and 26.5 percent were tenured, according to the AAUP. Nearly 45 percent were contingent part-time, or adjunct, roles. One in five were full-time, non-tenure-track positions.

The study also assesses how DEI goals and standards play a role in tenure decisions, an aspect that has been overlooked in previous research, according to the AAUP. The association found that 21.5 percent of colleges and universities currently include DEI criteria in their tenure standards. Nearly 39 percent of respondents said they are considering adding such criteria. Furthermore, nearly 40 percent of institutions reported that their tenure criteria had been evaluated for implicit bias within the last five years. An equal number said that their promotion and tenure review committees must participate in implicit bias training.[4]

The following examples further demonstrate the difficulty of being an academic in the modern DEI-controlled university of 2023. Whether the system is operating through student complaints or administrative actions pursuant to complaints and observations, we can recognize that criticizing DEI systems for excessive subjectivity and scope is a "no go" area. This was touched on earlier in the context of language control and manipulation, and that is used as a basis for the most serious judgments and conclusions. A university that allows and facilitates such actions and processes is no longer legitimate. It is a propaganda machine and a political device in service of power.

University DEI Guides for Diversifying Faculty Searches and Hiring at Brown University and Columbia University

I condensed the following examples taken from two university websites as much as possible. There were numerous other universities with such recommended guidelines but they are almost all identical in their thrust even to the point of asking the same questions and using the same evaluation scoring. What comes through in the DEI guidelines is that the DEI staffs of many universities have created an extremely vague, highly malleable, entirely subjective, and easily abused or biased system of evaluation that is being imposed on hiring committees. At the same time, university faculties have become so one-sided in their politics it is not as if they are not themselves in agreement with the candidate evaluation "standards." Many of the examples can be easily found online and have been essentially copied by DEI staffs from a template created by the University of California Berkeley, one of the most ultra-left universities in America.

The staffs of DEI bureaucracies are shaping and controlling universities. An honest examination of the standards and type of inquiries hiring committees are now expected to use in evaluating and testing candidates' political orientation leads to the conclusion that the Woke/Crits are making certain only those who think like them and share their political agenda are allowed inside the walls and lecture halls. As already indicated, there is an extreme political skewing in the views and politics of university faculty, and the immediate realization gained from reading the interview mandates and "rubrics" to be used by university hiring committees and DEI offices is that, in evaluating potential faculty candidates, many universities are continuing to expand their already heavily left orientation and, as the already reduced ranks of a limited number of more politically conservative faculty retire or otherwise leave, the newly hired faculty members are almost exclusively skewed to the highly "progressive" left.

The reality is that current university faculty and administrators are hiring "clones" of themselves. The standards make it obvious that new faculty won't be hired unless they demonstrate a complete commitment to DEI. In looking at the DEI guidelines excerpts set out next, think about what is being described. Consider the vagueness of what is being asked in many instances. Then identify the automatic assumptions contained in the guidelines about bias, privilege, and the like. There is clear "group-think" going on, and it is to the great advantage of Woke university faculty and administrators. It is extremely clear that the individuals being interviewed for faculty positions are expected to fully share the assumptions, commitments, interpretations, and definitions of their university's DEI department. This includes being committed to advancing DEI's solutions.

This whole thing gives me the chills, and I believe deeply in the issues of social justice that are purportedly at the heart of the DEI movement. But what I read in such DEI statements is lock-step political propaganda. This will further polarize us and shut down honest and essential debate.

Brown University: Guide to Diversifying Faculty Searches

A diversity statement provides the search committee with relevant, useful information about a candidate's qualifications and potential for future success, similar to a candidate's CV, research statement, or teaching statement. The diversity statement should not request identity information of candidates as the statements are to asses all candidates regardless of their backgrounds. Specifically, a diversity statement invites applicants to describe their past contributions, current engagements, and/or future aspirations to promote diversity, equity, and inclusion in their careers as researchers and educators within their departments, institutions, and disciplines. It is important for search committees to consider and specify several factors. . . . Without specific criteria to guide decision-making, evaluators may favor applicants that look like themselves or remind them of themselves or others they are accustomed to being around, which increases the potential of implicit or unconscious biases.

Examples of Evidence Demonstrating Contributions to Diversity

Knowledge and Understanding
- Knowledge of, experience with, and interest in dimensions of diversity that result from different identities, such as ethnic, socioeconomic, racial, gender, sexual orientation, disability, and cultural differences.
- Familiarity with demographic data related to diversity in higher education.
- Comfort discussing diversity-related issues.
- Understanding of mentorship power dynamics and personal-professional boundaries between faculty and students.
- Understanding of the challenges faced by underrepresented individuals, and the need to identify and eliminate barriers to their full and equitable participation and advancement.

Teaching
- Strategies to create inclusive and welcoming teaching environments for all students—particularly students who are underrepresented and/or experience marginalization.
- Strategies to encourage both critical thinking and respectful dialogue in the classroom.
- Using new pedagogies and classroom strategies to advance equity and inclusion.

Research
- Inclusive research environments that foster respect and equitable advancement (of graduate students if applicable).
- Mentoring and supporting the advancement and professional development of underrepresented students or postdocs.
- Research focused on underserved communities. Service/Professional Activities
- Outreach activities designed to remove barriers and to increase the participation of individuals from underrepresented groups. Strategies to create inclusive and welcoming teaching environments for all underrepresented students.
- Participation in workshops and activities that help build multicultural competencies and create inclusive climates.
- Supporting student organizations that serve underrepresented groups.
- Participation with professional or scientific associations or meetings that aim to increase diversity or address the needs of underrepresented students, staff, or faculty.
- Serving on university or college committees related to equity and inclusion, or preventing sexual harassment and sexual violence.

Assessing Diversity Statements
Define "excellence" in each area of the rubric. Weaker statements [by candidates] tend to be brief, vague, and lack evidence of impact whereas excellent statements have breadth, depth, and impact. Below are sample criteria for excellence.

- Awareness of, and ability to, articulate understanding diversity broadly conceived, and historical, social, and economic factors that influence the underrepresentation of particular groups in academia. Life experience may be, but is not necessarily, an important aspect of this understanding.
- A track record, calibrated to career stage, of engagement and activity related to diversity, equity, and inclusion. Demonstration requires specific details about these activities, including goals, strategies, and outcomes, as well as information about the role played. Strong evidence typically consists of multiple past and current examples of action from classrooms, labs, campuses, or communities.
- Specific, concrete goals, plans, and priorities, calibrated to career stage, for engagement on diversity, equity, and inclusion in one's teaching, research and service as a potential faculty member at Brown University. Ideally these plans involve an awareness of current programs and initiatives already taking place on campus.[5]

Columbia University:
"Evaluating Faculty Candidates' Diversity, Equity, and Inclusion Statements"

Rating Criteria

1. Awareness of and ability to articulate understanding regarding diversity, equity, and inclusion broadly conceived, and historical, social, and economic factors that influence the underrepresentation of particular groups in academia, as well as their experiences of inclusion and belonging. Life experience may or may not be an important aspect of this understanding.
2. A track record, calibrated to career stage, of engagement and activity on diversity, equity, and inclusion, and creation of a respectful community. Demonstration requires specific details about these activities, including goals, strategies, and outcomes, as well as information about the role played. Strong evidence typically consists of multiple examples of action from

undergraduate through graduate (and postdoctoral if relevant) studies.

3. Specific, concrete goals, plans, and priorities, calibrated to career stage, for engagement on diversity, equity, and inclusion as a potential staff member at Columbia. Ideally these plans involve an understanding of current programs and initiatives already taking place on campus.

Knowledge and understanding:

- Knowledge of, experience with, and interest in dimensions of diversity that result from different identities, such as ethnic, socioeconomic, racial, gender, sexual orientation, disability, and cultural differences.
- Familiarity with demographic data related to diversity in higher education.
- Understanding of the challenges faced by underrepresented individuals, and the need to identify and eliminate barriers to their full and equitable participation and advancement.
- Comfort discussing diversity-related issues.
- Understanding of mentorship power dynamics and personal-professional boundaries between faculty and students.
- Understanding of the impact of bullying, microaggressions, and harassment.

These materials were developed based on the work of UC Berkeley and other institutions that have created resources for Faculty Search Committees and Faculty Candidates.[6]

Chapter Twenty-Seven

Regime Change: Repelling the DEI Assault on Higher Education

While the political rhetoric being used by that "Progressive" effort is powerful, and utilizes the language of fairness and justice, the strategies being implemented present a tragically different form of DEI, one that can be more accurately restated as "Division, Enmity, and Intimidation/Indoctrination." That corrupt form of DEI is tearing the nation apart. The real tragedy is that many of the activists who are advancing the political strategy do intend to "divide and conquer" to gain power for themselves. It must be stopped.

Finally: "Regime Change: Repelling the DEI Assault on Higher Education"

There is absolutely no way the integrity and quality of the institutional university can be saved if the determination is left in the hands of the university by itself. The transformation has come upon us too fast, and those in control of the institutions have too much to lose if meaningful adjustments are to be made. This does not mean the activists are evil, but does mean they have exchanged insight and honest interactions for the seductions of power, status, and financial rewards. Anyone who criticizes what is going on is a racist, bigot, "transphobic," "homophobic," or some other condemnatory slur of the moment. Such attacks are weapons, and they hurt. The responses by nearly anyone within the system is to be silent, or to jump on the Woke/Crit bandwagon because, if you don't, your teaching, research, or administrative career is pretty much "toast."

If the previous observations are even close to accurate, then the pressures for change to an honest university must at this point come from outside the institution. Anyone who has spent a significant amount of time as a faculty or administrative staff member in one of America's universities understands that while words and eloquent rhetoric on the core political ideas of the academic culture of the moment are found virtually anywhere, courage is in very short supply. That means the courage required to advance the needed rebirth of the universities integrity must come from the outside.

The sources of courage include state legislatures, parental, and other groups who understand how serious the destructive ideological changes experienced over the past several decades have been while academics have been "asleep at the wheel." The sources also include lawyers and courts willing to hold the often repressive behaviors of Woke/Crit actors financially and otherwise liable when they deny basic rights to people—faculty, administrators, and students—seeking to exercise their right to speech and reasonable Constitutional action. This must occur because "educating" millions of America's youth in universities and K-12 systems who cannot think with precision, understand only what an ideologically focused curriculum has indoctrinated them with, and learned that to survive you must either believe what you have been told or act as if you do.

I could write more about what is going on and what is needed to understand and address this dangerous moment that is dividing and "dumbing down" America. But a deep and comprehensive analysis has been done by Peter Wood, President of the National Association of Scholars (NAS). He offers a critique of the effects of DEI and Woke/Critical Race Theory on universities. Wood organizes his assessment under four primary headings. They are:

1. How words and key concepts are being used to manipulate, and extend the impact and reach of the Woke/Crit strategy well beyond any rational interpretation. As we have seen throughout the analysis contained in *Conformity Colleges*, control of language is a core element of the Woke/CRT strategy through shifting

definitions, overarching narratives such as "white supremacy" and privilege, and linguistic "framing."

2. The impact of the educational takeover on America's key interests, both foreign and domestic. Of course this includes National Security and declining economic competitiveness as our young people are being "dumbed down" relative to rising nations.

3. A series of specific recommendations.

4. The starting place for taking action aimed at mitigating and reversing what has occurred.

Peter Wood's complete analysis is well worth a close reading. I edited the piece as much as possible and while it still retains its strength and clarity, I strongly recommend going to the full document itself to capture its full detail and richness. Peter Wood has given permission for use here. Any italicized words and phrases were added by me, as well as statements in boldface. Wood's analysis is set out immediately below.

In this essay I intend to address the critique of America on racial grounds mainly at the college and university level, but problems in K-12 schools will necessarily come into the picture.

Words Matter

America's racial critics often disarm their opponents by using a vocabulary whose unassuming or technical demeanor hides radical meanings. Because many of these words and phrases are ambiguous, I will start by setting out these terms as I shall use them.

Anti-racism is a word contrived by Boston University professor Ibram X. Kendi. It looks as if it means "opposed to racism," but Kendi and his followers use it to mean racial favoritism toward blacks, deliberate discrimination against whites aimed at compensating for "systemic" racial injustice, and the suppression of all speech and action opposed to their preferred policies.

Systemic racism refers to the supposedly omnipresent racially disparate treatment built into institutions such as law, the real estate market, medical practice, and education. Proponents of the concept

of systemic racism argue that it generally operates outside the awareness of white people or other beneficiaries of the privileges it confers
on one group at the expense of another. Even individuals who decry
racism and are free from any personal racial animus are thus part of
systemically racist institutions.

Critical Race Theory ("CRT") is a branch of neo-Marxist social
analysis formulated by Harvard Law School professor Derrick Bell
in the late 1970s and further developed by his colleague, Kimberlé
Crenshaw. Bell and Crenshaw argued that the Civil Rights Movement
had failed to reform American society in any fundamental way and
that, rightly seen, all American institutions are systemically racist. .
. . Most consequentially, CRT achieved substantial influence among
scholars focusing on education, and in the curricula of education
schools.

Diversity was a doctrine first articulated by U.S. Supreme Court
Justice Lewis Powell in a 1978 decision. Powell argued that colleges
and universities might engage in some racial favoritism toward
black students if the schools could show that this would advance
the "intellectual diversity" of college classes and thus benefit all students regardless of race. Powell's opinion was not supported by any
other Justice at the time and thus lacked the force of law, but colleges
and universities soon began to justify racial preferences in admissions by citing diversity. In time, the idea that racial "diversity" was a
means to achieve "intellectual diversity" gave way to the widespread
assumption that racial diversity is an end in itself.

Diversity, Equity, and Inclusion ("DEI") is the contemporary
expansion of the diversity doctrine. "Equity" replaces the older idea
of individual equality under the law with the idea that all social goods
should be distributed in proportion to each ethnic group's size relative to the total population. "Inclusion," which violates the principles
of freedom of association and individual merit, requires the extension
of group-identity quotas to every part of society, public and private.
This fixation on group-identity extends beyond race, as the proponents of DEI increasingly write "gender identity" into institutional

policy. DEI ideologues share with their "anti-racist" peers the habit of suppressing their critics rather than answering their criticisms.

National Peril

The rise of the anti-racist, DEI, CRT agenda in American education had been decried by many on the grounds that it poses a peril to the nation. . . . All the criticisms have enough weight to bear consideration. Still, it may be useful to lay out the chief concerns of critics of DEI, etc. These are:

- **Ethnic division and strife.** DEI is an incitement to racial resentment, primarily of blacks against whites, and at another level of whites against blacks.
- **Political opportunism.** DEI in schools and colleges is aimed at recruiting students through emotional manipulation into durable loyalty to progressive political ideologies.
- **Cultural impoverishment.** DEI displaces from the curriculum and disparages study of the great achievements of western civilization and the American past. DEI imposes ruthless hostility toward Western values and falsely romantic views of other traditions.
- **Historical amnesia.** DEI amplifies accounts of injustices in American history and minimizes American accomplishments. Sometimes, as in *The 1619 Project*, it sets forth grossly inaccurate accounts of the American past as if they were true, and it provides students with no basis to recognize that there are other accounts better grounded in the facts.
- **Professional incompetence.** Because it lowers academic standards and diverts attention from well-established facts, DEI leaves graduates with an inferior education. . . .
- **International competitiveness.** Other nations are not handicapping generations of students by providing them with inferior DEI-inflected educations and false maps of the world in which we live. . . .

- **Destructive orientation.** DEI is an essential piece of indoctrination in the social justice ideology that is now taking hold in the American economy as the "ESG" movement (Environmental, Social, and Governance investing). . . . The perils posed by DEI no doubt vary from time to time and place to place. The factor on this list that is ubiquitous is ethnic division and strife. In all contexts, DEI fosters racial conflict.

Recommendations: The National Association of Scholars (NAS)

What then do we advise?

First, we advise that lawmakers gather hard data on how CRT, DEI, and anti-racism are being incorporated into higher education. Some of this is directly through the classroom, but the classroom is the least troubling of the insertion points. The more powerful ones include:

- **Pronouncements from on high.** College presidents, deans, and other high-ranking officials issue encompassing statements, often in the form of confessions of systemic racism in the institution coupled with declarations that the leaders will pursue radical reformations and all-encompassing anti-racist agendas. These declarations always impose extensive financial commitments on their institutions.
- **Mission statements.** These are important not only for enunciating institutional mission but as the frameworks employed by accreditors. They are being rewritten in DEI language.
- **Diversity action plans.** Many institutions codify their commitment to DEI in the form of strategic plans, which offer a vast array of institutional policies devoted to increasing diversity and equity. Activists frequently call for such plans, and at times they are even recruited to help develop them. Often, various departments within universities will issue their own unit-level plans, compounding the number of DEI policies within a given university.

- **Accreditation requirements.** Higher education accreditors impose DEI requirements on colleges and universities, which they must follow if they wish to be eligible to receive federal student loans and grants. DEI ideologues within colleges and universities use the accreditation system to pretend to lawmakers and citizens that they are imposing DEI only because they must. This is a transparent subterfuge, since the colleges and universities are voluntary members of the accrediting organizations, and themselves authorize the accreditors to impose these requirements.
- **Research incentives.** Colleges and universities increasingly incentivize research that focuses on DEI. Often such research compounds DEI-policies by creating the perception that more DEI measures are needed.
- **Expanding bureaucracy.** Every college and university that is serious about CRT/DEI has already extensively employed specialized personnel in newly created offices. These officials are not faculty members, although they are sometimes disguised with faculty titles and inserted into departments in which they have no relevant qualifications.
- **Diversity commitments.** Applicants for faculty positions are increasingly required to submit statements in which they affirm their commitments to advancing DEI.
- **Diversity reviews.** Faculty members are increasingly required to submit annual statements explaining their recent contributions to DEI.
- **Performance evaluations.** Increasingly DEI criteria are added to the performance evaluations of all university faculty and staff.
- **Tenure Criteria.** More and more universities have added DEI criteria explicitly to the factors weighed in granting tenure to faculty members. A recent study by the American Association of University Professors (AAUP) reported that 21.5 percent of all colleges and universities in a survey already have DEI criteria embedded in tenure standards, and another 38.9 percent have

such criteria "under consideration." At large universities the trend is even more pronounced, with 45.6 percent already imposing such standards and another 35.5 percent considering them—a total of 81.1 percent.

- **College bylaws.** College and departmental bylaws are being rewritten to redefine faculty rank and performance expectations in light of DEI goals.

- **DEI applicant set asides.** These are illegal racial quotas, no matter how they are named. Faculty are told that they must achieve a certain percentage of minority hires in all areas of employment and regardless of qualifications.

- **Learning outcomes.** The success of teachers is often measured according to prescribed "learning outcomes," and these are now evaluated through a DEI filter.

- **DEI redefinitions.** Under the heading of "inclusion," DEI proponents often redefine key terms to expedite the success of minority candidates. Academic qualifications, for example, are redefined to include "lived experience." Evidence is redefined to include "trauma-informed" opinions. Expository English prose is redefined for black students to include the grammar and vocabulary of a black dialect. The definition of academic "success" in every discipline is redefined to include mastery of the contributions of blacks and women, even when these are historically minimal.

- **De-Testing.** Colleges and universities are widely eliminating standardized tests and professional entry requirements that they judge to be barriers to minority advancement.

- **De-ranking.** This means not tracking student performance in any way that would allow comprehensive comparison of students' relative accomplishments or academic success.

- **Distributive funding.** This means allocating resources for faculty hires, research, student financial aid, and other line items according to the race of the recipients rather than the importance or merit of their contributions.

As a result of these multiple insertion points of the CRT / DEI agenda, an individual faculty member may reject CRT or DEI but find himself in an institution that advances these ideologies at every turn.

The Starting Place

Once a reliable audit has been performed, the next steps are to weed out these institutional impositions and to replace the individuals who put them in place. While this is not the place to present a detailed plan for this reformation, we have a general idea of what that would entail. The DEI agenda entails violations of three Constitutional provisions: parts of the First, Fourth, and Fourteenth Amendments. DEI impositions involve coerced and prohibited speech in violation of First Amendment freedoms of speech; intrusion into matters of personal conviction that violate Fourth Amendment privacy protections; and racially discriminatory rules that violate the Equal Protection Clause of the Fourteenth Amendment. State legislatures have abundant authority over public colleges and universities in their states and considerable authority over private or independent colleges and universities as well that operate with state charters, public subsidies, and tax exemptions. There is no reason that legislatures could not responsibly exercise their existing powers to end the un-Constitutional and illegal actions colleges and universities have put in place to advance "anti-racism."

Granted, colleges and universities are not accustomed to this sort of oversight and would doubtless complain that it is unwelcome and illegitimate. And doubtless some legislators would be intimidated by those claims. But the truth is that state legislatures are well within their rights to act. As one law professor recently put it, "The fight against Critical Race Theory is a fight for national survival."

To these ends, in addition to institutional audits, state legislatures should consider:

- **Banning mandatory DEI training.** This training imposes on faculty members and staff indoctrination on matters of personal belief. Often it is in violation of the conscience of individuals who must submit to falsehoods about their personal identities as well as misrepresentations of history and society. Seldom does such training bear in any constructive way on professional competence or job responsibilities that are appropriately part of the individual's employment.

- **Banning all forms of DEI evaluation.** Evaluation tools embedding DEI ideology are a form of coerced conformity to doctrinal falsehoods.

- **Requiring transparency.** This should apply to all course syllabi, optional training sessions, and DEI committee meetings. Keeping DEI off the record or out of sight is a way that DEI advocates evade accountability.

- **Creating a counter-bureaucracy.** Institutional bureaucracies have been created as the enforcement arm of the DEI movement. Ideally, these positions should be abolished. The people holding them cannot be expected to assist in the dismantling of the DEI apparatus, to which they are beholden for their employment and which they fervently support. To weed out the DEI administrative state, a state legislature needs a counter-bureaucracy of appointees whose mandate comes from outside the control of the DEI establishment. . . .

- **Establishing vigilance.** Universities that have embedded DEI in their admissions, hiring, evaluation, tenure, and curricular criteria are not stopping there. Some of the frontiers of expansion are the use of Title IX to evade due process restrictions on arbitrary punishments; the advancement of the transgender agenda; and the effort to alter the terms of bequests and restricted gifts. Legislatures should establish independent bodies to report on such developments. This is a responsivity that cannot be entrusted to the state's educational boards or professional bodies that have long since proven their loyalty to the higher education establishment at the expense of the public interest.

- **Encourage vocational schools and post-secondary education.** One of the driving forces behind DEI is the overuse of the college degree as a credential for employment. Many individuals who lack the ability, the preparation, or the commitment to undertake rigorous college instruction pursue admission to college anyway out of the belief that the college credential is necessary for career success. Colleges then lower standards and dilute the substance of their programs to accommodate these students. . . .

- **Terminate funding to institutions that refuse to mend their ways.** Higher education is in the midst of a large-scale transformation as the number of students who wish to attend college continues to decline. Another significant fraction of college-age students has chosen to pursue degrees through remote learning, further eroding the traditional base of colleges and universities. Faced with these realities, some colleges have already closed or merged, and competent observers predict more will follow.

The National Association of Scholars has detailed recommendations and policy proposals along these lines and stands ready to share them with elected leaders who wish to pursue them.[1]

About the Author

David **Barnhizer** is professor of Law Emeritus at Cleveland State University. He received a BA degree from Muskingum University where he majored in Psychology and minored in History. He earned law degrees from The Ohio State University where he was an editor of the law review and member of the Order of the Coif national honorary, graduating *summa cum laude.* He also earned a Master of Law degree from Harvard University where he was a Ford Foundation Urban Law Fellow and a CLEPR Clinical Teaching Fellow. He is a *Diplomate* of the National Institute of Trial Advocacy, and was the "Special Consultant on Clinical Education" for the ABA/AALS Guidelines Study on Clinical Education.

My Teaching Experiences

While working as a lawyer in the federal Legal Services program in Colorado Springs representing lower income and minority clients, I also taught at the University of Colorado, Colorado Springs. As an adjunct, I designed and taught an "Economics of Poverty" course dealing with the impact of economic systems on poor and minority people and the limiting of opportunity and social justice for Blacks, Latinos (or Chicanos), and other minorities. I have been a multi-year Senior Research Fellow at the University of London's Institute of Advanced Legal Studies (IALS), and on three separate occasions served as Visiting Professor at the Westminster University School of Law in London. In that role I taught seminars on Comparative Law to a mixture of diverse law students from the United Kingdom, Africa, Asia, the Middle East, Latin America, and Europe. I also taught human rights and international environmental law classes in St. Petersburg, Russia in a joint program with St. Petersburg State University.

As part of my work at Harvard while a Ford Foundation Urban Law Fellow, I helped to establish the Law School's expansive clinical program and represented indigent clients with law students working under my supervision at the Cambridge Legal Assistance Office. After leaving Harvard, I created and directed the nationally recognized Clinical Law program at Cleveland State University. We provided civil and criminal representation to minority and economically disadvantaged individuals in the Greater Cleveland area. My work included teaching seminars on social and racial justice concerns, as well as individualized instruction and supervision of law students who represented marginalized clients. The work also involved such activities as suing police who violated the civil rights of Blacks and other minorities and serving as counsel for the Cleveland area's Black on Black Crime Committee—a group of minority citizens seeking to come to grips with crime in their urban neighborhoods.

I established the Street Law Program at CSU, the second such program in the United States, working in conjunction with Cleveland Public Schools. This followed the model that had been created at Georgetown University. The Street Law Project was an educational vehicle in which law students were trained to teach a range of legal knowledge and dispute resolution techniques to high school students in the heavily minority Cleveland public schools. The teaching program was conducted as part of CSU's clinical program for more than a decade. Along with this I worked with the University's innovative Center for Effective Learning.

My other areas of teaching and research involve Jurisprudence and the Philosophy of Law, Strategy, Environmental Law (US and International), Ethics and Professional Responsibility, Human Rights, Trial Advocacy, Pre-trial skills such as negotiation, counseling, investigation, and strategy, plus Criminal Law and Procedure. While at Cleveland State University, I designed and conducted the training program for the area's Public Defender's Office, created and directed the Environmental Law Clinic, and founded and supervised the law school's externship semester in Washington, DC that placed law students with Congressional subcommittees, the Department of Justice, and non-governmental organizations. I also worked in conjunction with the US Legal Services Corporation, training civil rights lawyers throughout the United States in critical counseling, negotiation, and trial advocacy skills essential for their representation of minority individuals and groups. Along with this I was a consultant with the US Department of Education, a member of the Editorial Board of the *Journal of Legal Education*, a three-time chair of the Association of American Law Schools Section of Clinical Education as voted by Clinical Faculty at America's law schools, the Special Consultant to the ABA/AALS Guidelines Study, and recipient of the first AALS "Pincus Award" given annually by the AALS to outstanding clinical teachers. At CSU, I also received the "Oleck Award" for outstanding law teaching. In addition, I created, planned, and coordinated the first two Association of American Law Schools (AALS) National Clinical Education conferences. Hundreds of US clinical law teachers were trained to excel in educational methodologies, one in which small group and individualized teaching strategies were fundamental approaches, augmented by larger class sessions.

The range of my experience is diverse. I served in a government ministry in Mongolia as the Special International Consultant on sustainable development. Another activity was being a member of the governing board for the NGO group ISA Net, a non-governmental organization with more than twenty member groups from Latin America, the US and Canada, Europe, Asia and Africa. ISA Net focused on confronting the abuses created by large-scale agri-business in developing countries that were displacing local communities and economies through shrimp aquaculture. Along with this I worked in the International Program of the Natural Resources Defense Council in Washington, DC, with the World Wildlife Fund, as Executive Director of the Year 2000 Committee, and with technology startup companies. I also served as Rapporteur for a high-level conference on Foresight Capability conducted by the Energy and Commerce Committee of the US House of Representatives, and as a consultant for the President's Council on Environmental Quality (CEQ) developing reports on Climate Change and large corporate reactions to the federal government's *Global 2000 Report to the President* concerning critical emerging issues. Something about which I am very proud is my involvement with the Fairmount Fine Arts Center, where my wife was a member of the Spanish Dance Touring Group. I served as President of the Fairmount Board of Trustees for several years.

Books by David Barnhizer

No More Excuses!": *Parents Defending K-12 Education* (Amazon, 2022)

"Un-Canceling" America (Amazon, 2021)

The Artificial Intelligence Contagion: *Can Democracy Withstand the Imminent Transformation of Work, Wealth, and the Social Order?* (with Daniel Barnhizer, Clarity Press, 2019)

Hypocrisy & Myth: *The Hidden Order of the Rule of Law* (with Daniel Barnhizer, Van de Plas Publishing, 2009)

The Blues of a Revolution: *The Damaging Impacts of Shrimp Farming* (David Barnhizer and Isabel de la Torre, ISA Net, 2003)

Effective Strategies for Protecting Human Rights: *Economic Sanctions, Use of National Courts and International Fora, and Coercive Power* (Ashgate, 2001)

Effective Strategies for Protecting Human Rights: *Prevention and Intervention, Trade, and Education* (Ashgate, 2001)

The Warrior Lawyer (Transnational, 1997) [This book applies the strategic work of Sun Tzu and Musashi to the practice of law]

Symposium Editor, *The Justice Mission of American Law Schools*, 40 Cleveland State Law Review, No. 2 & 3 (1992)

Editor, *Strategies For Sustainable Societies* (Global Tomorrow Coalition, 1988)

Some Relevant University-Focused Articles

David Barnhizer, "Freedom to Do What? Institutional Neutrality, Academic Freedom and Academic Responsibility," 43 J. Legal Education. 346 (1993);

David Barnhizer, "The Justice Mission of American Law Schools," 40 Cleveland St. L. Rev. 285 (1992);

David Barnhizer, "The Purposes of the University in the First Quarter of the Twenty-first Century," 22 Seton Hall L. Rev. 1124 (1992);

David Barnhizer, "The University Ideal and Clinical Legal Education," 35 N.Y.L. School L. Rev. 87, 88 (1990);

David Barnhizer, "The Revolution in American Law Schools," 37 Cleveland St. L. Rev. 227 (1989);

David Barnhizer, "The University Ideal and the American Law School," 42 Rutgers L. Rev. 109,(1989);

David Barnhizer, "Prophets, Priests and Power Blockers: Three Fundamental Roles of Judges and Legal Scholars in America," 50 U. Pitt. L. Rev. 127 (1988).

Notes

Chapter One

1 Mark Bauerlein, "The Strange Obedience of the Professorate," *Epoch Times*, October 20, 2021, https://www.theepochtimes.com/the-strange-obedience-of-the-professorate_4055973.html.

2 Oliver Tearle, "A Short Analysis of Yeats's 'The Second Coming', A summary and analysis of one of W. B. Yeats's most famous poems by Dr Oliver Tearle" (Interesting Literature, 2016). https://interestingliterature.com/2016/01/a-short-analysis-of-yeatss-the-second-coming/.

3 Walter E. Williams, "The Fight for Free Speech," *Epoch Times*, October 7, 2020, https://www.theepochtimes.com/the-fight-for-free-speech_3528032.html. Schmidt, Benno C., Jr. "The University in Search of Itself." *Yale Alumni Magazine* 54, no. 8 (1991):at 67.

4 Garrett Sheldon, "The Decline and Fall of the University," *Epoch Times*, February 9, 2023, https://www.theepochtimes.com/the-decline-and-fall-of-the-university_5046082.html.

5 FIRE, "FIRE Statement on the Use of Diversity, Equity, and Inclusion Criteria in Faculty Hiring and Evaluation," June 2, 2022. https://www.thefire.org/research-learn/fire-statement-use-diversity-equity-and-inclusion-criteria-faculty-hiring-and

6 Mattias Desmet, *The Psychology of Totalitarianism* (2022). Chelsea Green Publishing, Vermont and London.

7 Albert Camus, *The Wager of Our Generation, in Resistance, Rebellion, and Death*, trans. Justin O'Brien (New York: Alfred A. Knopf, 1960), 237, 238–39.

8 Albert Camus, *The Rebel: An Essay on Man in Revolt*, trans. Anthony Bower (New York: Random House, 1956), 30.

9 Albert Camus, "Defense of Intelligence," in *Resistance, Rebellion, and Death*, trans. Justin O' Brien (New York: Alfred A. Knopf, 1961), 38.

10 Hunter Lewis "Political Debate Sweeps Campus," *Herald-Sun*, February 13, 2004, A1.

11 Ivan Petropoulos, "Stand up for Duke's conservative voices," *Duke Chronicle*, February 17, 2021, https://www.dukechronicle.com/article/2021/02/stand-up-for-dukes-conservative-voices.

12 Ibid.

13 Ibid.

14 Emma Colton, "Stanford professor who challenged lockdowns and 'scientific clerisy' declares academic freedom 'dead': Stanford's Dr. Jay Bhattacharya says his life became a 'living hell' when he challenged Dr. Fauci over 2020 COVID lockdowns," Fox News. November 21, 2022. https://www.foxnews.com/us/stanford-professor-challenged-lockdowns-scientific-clerisy-declares-academic-freedom-dead.

15 Joshua Q. Nelson, "University of Alabama professor leaves due to 'obsession' to push equity in science: 'Rise of illiberalism': 'These are no longer places that embrace the freedom of exchanging ideas,' the professor said," Fox News. January 24, 2023, https://www.foxnews.com/media/university-alabama-professor-leaves-due-obsession-push-equity-science-rise-illiberalism.

16 Philip Carl Salzman, "Hate and Fear Are Now Major Motivators on Campus," *Epoch Times*, October 11, 2022, https://www.theepochtimes.com/hate-and-fear-are-now-major-motivators-on-campus_4785439.html.

17 Hans Yeung, "From Cultural to Educational Desert," *Epoch Times*, December 23, 2022, https://www.theepochtimes.com/from-cultural-to-educational-desert_4941932.html.

Chapter Two

1 Marshall McLuhan, *Understanding Media: The Extensions of Man* (New York: McGraw-Hill, 1964).

2 Liz Peek, "Intolerance threatens US—here's who to blame for 'cancel culture,'" Fox News, June 22, 2020, https://www.foxnews.com/opinion/intolerance-threatens-us-cancel-culture-blame-liz-peek.

3 Peter Drucker, *The New Realities* (Harper Business, 1989), 76.

4 Martin Buber, "What Is Common to All," *The Knowledge of Man* (Maurice Friedman ed., Maurice Friedman & Ronald Gregor Smith trans., Harper & Row 1965), 69 and 108.

5 Ibid.

6 Bret Stephens, "The 1619 Chronicles: Journalism does better when it writes the first rough draft of history, not the last word on it," *New York Times*, Oct. 9, 2020. https://www.nytimes.com/2020/10/09/opinion/nyt-1619-project-criticisms.html.

7 On this topic, see David Barnhizer's *"No More Excuses!": Parents Defending K-12 Education* (Amazon, 2022).

8 Jeffrey A. Tucker, "Leviathan Must Be Stopped," *Epoch Times*, February 3, 2023, https://www.theepochtimes.com/leviathan-must-be-stopped_5032634.html.

9 Victor Davis Hanson, "The woke university implosion—and what comes next," *New York Post*, December 25, 2022, https://nypost.com/2022/12/25/the-woke-university-implosion-and-what-comes-next/.

10 Mark Bauerlein, "The Strange Obedience of the Professorate."

11 Walter E. Williams, "The Fight for Free Speech," *Epoch Times*, October 7, 2020, https://www.theepochtimes.com/the-fight-for-free-speech_3528032.html.

12 Bauerlein, "The Strange Obedience of the Professorate."

13 FIRE, 2023 College Free Speech Rankings, https://www.thefire.org/college-free-speech-rankings.

14 Rikki Schlott, "Columbia University is worst college in nation for free speech: report," *New York Post*, September 7, 2022, https://nypost.com/2022/09/07/columbia-is-worst-college-in-nation-for-free-speech-report/.

15 Victor Davis Hanson, "The woke university implosion—and what comes next," *New York Post*, December 25, 2022, https://nypost.com/2022/12/25/the-woke-university-implosion-and-what-comes-next/.

Chapter Three

1 "'US similar to North Korea': Defector slams 'woke' US schools," *New Zealand Herald*, June 14, 2021, https://www.nzherald.co.nz/world/us-similar-to-north-korea-defector-slams-woke-us-schools/GSXLIC4TAQNJ7GZF4TIBLLAJEE/.

2 Ibid.

3 Ibid.

4 Rikki Schlott, "More than half of college professors bite their tongues over cancel culture fears," *New York Post*, February 28, 2023, https://nypost.com/2023/02/28/new-survey-reveals -college-professors-fear-of-being-canceled/.

5 Brianna McKee, "Universities Need to Stop Being the Enablers of Social Activism," *Epoch Times*, September 20, 2022, https://www.theepochtimes.com/universities-need-to-stop-being -the-enablers-of-social-activism_4741527.html.

6 Charles Creitz, "Leftist mob riots after Charlie Kirk shows up at campus, tries to shut down free speech event," Fox News, December 2, 2022. https://www.foxnews.com/media /leftist-mob-riots-charlie-kirk-shows-campus-tries-shut-free-speech-event.

7 Anthony J. Diekema, *Academic Freedom and Christian Scholarship* (Grand Rapids, MI and Cambridge, UK: Wm. B. Eerdmans-Lightning Source: 2000), 34.

8 Noah Carl, "Threats to Free Speech at University, and How to Deal with Them—Part 1," *Areo Magazine*, December 10, 2019, https://areomagazine.com/2019/12/10/threats-to-free-speech -at-university-and-how-to-deal-with-them-part-1/.

9 Ibid.

10 Masooma Haq and Jan Jekielek, "Americans Self-Censoring at Higher Rates Than During McCarthy Era: Jewish Institute for Liberal Values CEO: Cancel culture has gone unopposed for too long, says David Bernstein," *Epoch Times*, December 28, 2022, https://www.theepochtimes. com/americans-self-censoring-at-higher-rates-than-during-mccarthy-era-jewish-institute-for -liberal-values-ceo_4949349.html.

11 Russell Jacoby, *The End of Utopia: Politics and Culture in an Age of Apathy* (New York: Basic Books, 1999), 33.

12 Hermann Hesse, *Beneath the Wheel* (S. Fisherman, Germany, 1906).

Chapter Four

1 Jacques Ellul, *The Technological Society*, 1964 (Vintage/Random House, Toronto); Jacques Ellul, Konrad Kellen & Jean Lerner Translators, *Propaganda: The Formation of Men's Attitudes* (1965, Vintage Books, New York).

2 Ibid.

3 Ibid, 349.

4 Greg Lukianoff and Jonathan Haidt, "The Coddling of the American Mind," *The Atlantic*, September 2015, https://www.theatlantic.com/magazine/archive/2015/09/the-coddling-of-the -american-mind/399356/.

5 Ibid.

6 Ibid.

7 "'US similar to North Korea': Defector slams 'woke' US schools," *New Zealand Herald*, June 14, 2021, https://www.nzherald.co.nz/world/us-similar-to-north-korea-defector-slams-woke-us -schools/GSXLIC4TAQNJ7GZF4TIBLLAJEE/.

8 Ibid.

9 Deborah Tannen, *The Argument Culture: Stopping America's War of Words* (Ballentine, New York 1999).

10 Gabriel Marcel, *Man Against Mass Society*, trans. G.S. Fraser (London: A Gateway, 1962), 135–136.

11 Aaron Kheriaty, "Technocracy and Totalitarianism," *Epoch Times*, November 21, 2022, https: //www.theepochtimes.com/technocracy-and-totalitarianism_4876998.html.

12   Nassim Nicholas Taleb, "The Most Intolerant Wins: The Dictatorship of the Small Minority," INCERTO 8/14/2016, https://medium.com/incerto/the-most-intolerant-wins-the-dictatorship-of -the-small-minority-3f1f83ce4e15.

13   Aaron Kheriaty, "Technocracy and Totalitarianism," *The Epoch Times*, 11/21/22, https://www .theepochtimes.com/technocracy-and-totalitarianism_4876998.html.

14   Ella Kietlinska and Joshua Philipp, "'Silent Majority' Must Speak Up When Vocal Minority Imposes Views on Society: Rapper and Commentator," *Epoch Times*, September 22, 2022, https: //www.theepochtimes.com/silent-majority-must-speak-up-when-vocal-minority-imposes -views-on-society-rapper-and-commentator_4746906.html.

15   Ibid.

16   Ibid.

17   Ella Kietlinska and Jan Jekielek, "Wokeism Is Costume Elites Wear to 'Signal Virtue' and 'Hide Greed, Corruption': Former Levi's Executive," *Epoch Times*, December 2, 2022, https: //www.theepochtimes.com/wokeism-is-costume-elites-wear-to-signal-virtue-and-hide-greed -corruption-former-levis-executive_4899644.html.

Chapter Five

1   Roger Kimball, "Political Correctness, or, the Perils of Benevolence," *National Interest*, Winter 2003/2004, 159–160.

2   Hannah Grossman, "North Korean defector: I am terrified of the 'massive indoctrination coming from the left' in public schools: North Korean defector Yeonmi Park draws a parallel between Nazi ideology and the left-wing indoctrination," Fox News, June 6, 2022, https://www .foxnews.com/media/north-korean-defector-i-am-terrified-of-the-massive-indoctrination -coming-from-the-left-in-public-schools.

3   Mark Hendrickson, "Escaping Weaponized Schools," *Epoch Times*, January 31, 2023, https: //www.theepochtimes.com/escaping-weaponized-schools_5023284.html.

4   Whitney v. California, 274 U.S. 357 (1927).

5   Ibid.

6   Edward W. Younkins, "Aristotle: Ayn Rand's Acknowledged Teacher," *The Autonomist*, April 25, 2004, http://usabig.com/autonomist/articles/aristotle.html.

7   John W. Gardner, *Excellence: Can We Be Equal and Excellent Too?*, New York, Harper (New York, Harper & Row, 1961), 180.

8   Eric Hoffer, *The True Believer: Thoughts on the Nature of Mass Movements* (New York: Harper & Row, 1951), 127.

9   Ibid, 121–128.

10   Elizabeth Mitchell, "What Happened to America's Public Intellectuals?," *Smithsonian*, July 2017, https://www.smithsonianmag.com/history/what-happened-americas-public-intellectuals -180963668/.

11   Ibid.

12   Ibid.

13   James Martin, *The Wired Society* (Englewood Cliffs NJ: Prentice-Hall, 1978).

14   Rose Eveleth, "Academics Write Papers Arguing Over How Many People Read (And Cite) Their Papers," *Smithsonian Magazine*, March 25, 2014, https://www.smithsonianmag.com /smart-news/half-academic-studies-are-never-read-more-three-people-180950222/.

[15] Robert Marquand, "'In search of 'public intellectuals'. A growing number of writers and critics looking at the American scholarly landscape see few signs of a new generation of 'nonacademic' thinkers," *Christian Science Monitor*, December 14, 1987, https://www.csmonitor.com/1987/1214/dintel.html.

[16] Robert Schmuhl, "Where Have All the Thinkers Gone?" *Notre Dame Magazine*, Summer 2002, https://magazine.nd.edu/stories/where-have-all-the-thinkers-gone/.

Chapter Six

[1] Alice Dembner, "Silber Says New Theories Can Put Limit on Freedom," *Boston Globe*, November 30, 1993, Metro/Region, page 1.

[2] See "Stanford Professors Push Back on University-Encouraged Student Informant Culture" by Amy Gamm in the *Epoch Times* (February 25, 2023, https://www.theepochtimes.com/stanford-professors-push-back-on-university-encouraged-student-informant-culture_5082431.html).

[3] Victor Garcia, "Black Lives Matter leader states 'If US doesn't give us what we want, then we will burn down this system'," Fox News, June 24, 2020, https://www.foxnews.com/media/black-lives-matter-leader-burn-down-system.

[4] Olivia Land, "California activist Deon Jenkins threatens 'serious backlash,' demands more in reparation payout," *New York Post*, December 16, 2022, https://nypost.com/2022/12/16/calif-activist-deon-jenkins-threatens-serious-backlash-over-reparations/.

[5] Jackie Salo, "'We got to take these motherf–kers out': Rutgers professor calls white people 'villains'," *New York Post*, 10/29/21, https://nypost.com/2021/10/29/rutgers-professor-calls-white-people-villains/.

[6] Samuel Chamberlain, "NYC shrink tells Yale audience she fantasizes about shooting white people in head," *New York Post*, June 4, 2021, https://nypost.com/2021/06/04/nyc-pyscho-fantasizes-about-shooting-white-people-in-yale-talk/.

[7] Yaron Steinbuch, "Yale law students disrupt bipartisan free speech panel, trigger police escort," *New York Post*, March 17, 2022, https://nypost.com/2022/03/17/yale-law-students-disrupt-bipartisan-free-speech-panel/.

[8] Adam Sabes, "Binghamton University slaps down professor's 'progressive stacking' section of syllabus for 'non-white folks'," Fox News, 2/21/22, https://www.foxnews.com/us/binghamton-university-slaps-down-professors-progressive-stacking-section-of-syllabus-for-non-white-folks.

[9] Kristine Parks, "California college trustee apologizes after 'threatening' remarks about faculty who oppose equity initiatives: A board of trustees member said the teachers needed to be 'roped' and taken 'to the slaughterhouse,'" Fox News, January 4, 2023, https://www.foxnews.com/media/california-college-trustee-apologizes-after-threatening-remarks-faculty-oppose-equity-initiatives.

[10] Barnini Chakraborty, "University of Chicago takes home top honors, DePauw University the worst in free speech poll, Nearly 20,000 college students participated in the survey," Fox News, 9/29/20, https://www.foxnews.com/us/university-chicago-top-honors-depauw-university-worst-free-speech-poll.

[11] Cortney O'Brien and Danielle Wallace, "Syracuse assistant professor 'disturbed' by how many 'white pundits' still talk about 9/11: Academic calls 9/11 'an attack on the heteropatriarchal capitalistic systems that America relies upon to wrangle other countries into passivity,'" *Daily Mail*, September 12, 2021, https://www.dailymail.co.uk/news/article-9984125/Syracuse-professor-says-9–11-attack-heteropatriarchal-capitalistic-systems.html.

12 Emma Colton, "Washington U lecturer warns medical students not to 'debate' her on 'systemic oppression': 'shut that' down: 'I have a really hard time being neutral around issues of systemic oppression,' the lecturer told medical students," Fox News, December 18, 2022, https://www.foxnews.com/us/washington-u-lecturer-warns-medical-students-not-debate -systemic-oppression-shut-down#:~:text=EXCLUSIVE:%20A%20lecturer%20for%20 Washington,s—%20down%20real%20fast.%22.

13 Kate Chesley, "In its last meeting of the autumn quarter, the Stanford Faculty Senate condemned the COVID-19-related actions of Hoover senior fellow and presidential adviser Scott Atlas," *Stanford News*, 11/20/20, https://news.stanford.edu/2020/11/20/faculty-senate -condemns-actions-hoover-fellow-scott-atlas/. Faculty Senate condemns COVID-19 actions of Hoover's Scott Atlas .

14 Conor Friedersdorf, "The Perils of 'With Us or Against Us': A healthy deliberative process needs to make room for dissent," *The Atlantic*, 7/9/20, https://www.theatlantic.com/ideas /archive/2020/07/perils-us-or-against-us/613981/.

15 Kenneth Garger, "Syracuse University professor disciplined for calling coronavirus 'Wuhan flu,' 'Chinese Communist Party Virus': 'Syracuse University unequivocally condemns racism and xenophobia,' the school responded," *New York Post*, 8/26/20, https://www.foxnews .com/us/syracuse-university-professor-disciplined-for-calling-coronavirus-wuhan-flu-chinese -communist-party-virus.

16 Paul Caron, "Harvard Law Students Petition Administration To Denounce Professor Adrian Vermeule's 'Highly Offensive Online Rhetoric,'" TaxProf Blog, 1/20/21, https://taxprof .typepad.com/taxprof_blog/2021/01/harvard-law-students-again-ask-administration-to -denounce-professor-adrian-vermeules-offen.html.

17 Victor Garcia, "Suspended UCLA prof says school used him as 'sacrificial lamb' to placate 'those who threaten to riot,'" Fox News, June 10, 2020, https://www.foxnews.com/media /gordon-klein-ucla-professor-suspended-sacrificial-lamb.

18 Daniella Genovese, "UCLA students urge replacement of top computer science professor. The petition has notched over 1,600 signatures," Fox News, September 9, 2020, https://www .foxnews.com/us/ucla-students-replace-computer-science-chair.

19 Jennifer Kabbany, "Embattled Stanford Professor of Medicine Jay Bhattacharya: 'Academic freedom is dead,'" The College Fix, November 9, 2022, https://www.thecollegefix.com /embattled-stanford-professor-of-medicine-jay-bhattacharya-academic-freedom-is-dead/.

20 Greg Lukianoff and Jonathan Haidt, "The Coddling of the American Mind," *The Atlantic*, September 2015, https://www.theatlantic.com/magazine/archive/2015/09/the-coddling-of-the -american-mind/399356/.

21 Jon McWhorter, "Academics Are Really, Really Worried About Their Freedom," TaxProf Blog, 9/8/20, https://taxprof.typepad.com/taxprof_blog/2020/09/academics-are-really-really -worried-about-their-freedom.html#more.

22 Brian Flood, "Cornell Law professor says 'coordinated effort' launched against him for criticizing Black Lives Matter, condemns insinuations he's racist," Fox News, 6/11/20, https: //www.foxnews.com/media/cornell-law-school-professor-black-lives-matter.

23 Melkorka Licea, "'Deplorable' NYU professor sues colleagues for defamation," *New York Post*, 1/13/2018, https://nypost.com/2018/01/13/deplorable-nyu-professor-sues-colleagues-for -defamation/.

[24] Melkorka Licea, "Professor who tweeted against PC culture is out at NYU," *New York Post*, October 30, 2016, https://nypost.com/2016/10/30/nyu-professor-who-opposed-pc-culture-gets-booted-from-classroom/.

[25] "Affirm Prof. Dorian Abbot's Right to Free Speech and Uphold the Chicago Principles," Change.org, 11/26/20, https://www.change.org/p/university-of-chicago-president-robert-j-zimmer-affirm-prof-dorian-abbot-s-right-to-free-speech-and-uphold-the-chicago-principles.

[26] Nina Agrawal, "Controversy over USC professor's use of Chinese word that sounds like racial slur in English," *LA Times*, 9/5/20, https://www.latimes.com/california/story/2020–09-05/usc-business-professor-controversy-chinese-word-english-slur.

[27] Robert Dailyda, Campus Speech, July/August 2020, https://campus-speech.law.duke.edu/campus-speech-incidents/robert-dailyda-stockton-university/.

[28] Vandana Rambaran, "Dean fired after saying 'BLACK LIVES MATTER, but also, EVERYONE'S LIFE MATTERS' in email: Leslie Neal-Boylan sent an email to the nursing school community addressing the ongoing social justice protests," Fox News, 7/20/20, https://www.foxnews.com/us/dean-fired-after-saying-black-lives-matter-but-also-everyones-life-matters-in-email.

[29] Niall Ferguson, "A Cardinal Sin," Quillette, 3/5/21, https://quillette.com/2021/03/05/a-cardinal-sin/.

[30] Michael Lee, "Hamline University professor fired for showing images of Muhammad had warned students in syllabus: Hamline University President Fayneese Miller said respect for Muslim students should supersede academic freedom," *New York Post*, January 8, 2023, https://nypost.com/2023/01/08/hamline-university-professor-fired-for-showing-images-of-muhammad/.

[31] Caleb Parke, "LSU professor vows to 'drop' students on 'hate speech' list," Fox News, 6/11/2020, https://www.foxnews.com/us/lsu-professor-hate-speech-black-lives-matter.

[32] Brian Onorio, "The Intolerance of Tolerance," TECHNICIAN ONLINE, Feb. 26, 2004, http://technicianonline.com/story.php?id=00894.

[33] Michael Powell, "M.I.T.'s Choice of Lecturer Ignited Criticism. So Did Its Decision to Cancel." *New York Times*, 10/20/21, https://www.nytimes.com/2021/10/20/us/dorian-abbot-mit.html.

[34] Keith John Sampson, "My 'Racial Harassment' Nightmare, *New York Post*, May 9, 2008, https://nypost.com/2008/05/09/my-racial-harassment-nightmare/.

[35] Patrick Reilly, "Michigan school board member facing calls to resign after tweeting 'whiteness is evil,'" *New York Post*, 1/20/2023, https://nypost.com/2023/01/20/michigan-school-board-member-slammed-for-tweeting-whiteness-is-evil/

[36] John Murawski, "How California Is Embracing Mandatory Racial-Injustice Study for All of Its 1.7 Million High Schoolers," *Epoch Times*, March 12, 2021, https://www.theepochtimes.com/how-california-is-embracing-mandatory-racial-injustice-study-for-all-of-its-1–7-million-high-schoolers_3727957.html.

Chapter Seven

[1] Kimberle Crenshaw, "*On Intersectionality,*" *Essential Writings*, The New Press, NY 2019).

[2] Post Editorial Board, "De Blasio's DOE takes its war on learning to a new extreme with 'no honor roll' push," *New York Post*, 9/1/21, https://nypost.com/2021/09/01/de-blasios-doe-takes-its-war-on-learning-to-a-new-extreme-with-no-honor-roll-push/.

3   Monique Beals, "Student test scores fall for first time in national test's history," The Hill, October 14, 2021, https://thehill.com/homenews/state-watch/576870-student-test-scores-fall-for-first-time-in-national-tests-history/.

4   Victor Davis Hanson, "The woke university implosion—and what comes next," *New York Post*, December 25, 2022, https://nypost.com/2022/12/25/the-woke-university-implosion-and-what-comes-next/.

5   Isabel Vincent, "NYC New School students demand 'A' grades, refunds after faculty strike." *New York Post*, https://nypost.com/2022/12/17/nyc-new-school-students-demand-tuition-refunds-after-faculty-strike/.

6   Tom Lindsay, "The 'Other' College Scandal: Grade Inflation Has Turned Transcripts into Monopoly Money," *Forbes*, March 30, 2019, https://www.forbes.com/sites/tomlindsay/2019/03/30/the-other-college-scandal-grade-inflation-has-turned-transcripts-into-monopoly-money/?sh=46e9b2664182.

7   Emma Colton, "Professor says grading system is racist, proposes labor-based system: 'White language supremacy': Labor-based grading would weigh papers based on how much 'labor' students put into their assignments," Fox News, November 9, 2021, https://www.foxnews.com/us/arizona-state-professor-white-language-supremacy-labor-based-grading.

8   Karol Markowicz, "Every parent should fight back vs. the left's war on merit," *New York Post*, January 22, 2023, https://nypost.com/2023/01/22/every-parent-should-fight-back-vs-the-lefts-war-on-merit/.

9   *New York Post* Editorial Board, "De Blasio's DOE takes its war on learning to a new extreme with 'no honor roll' push," *New York Post*, September 1, 2021, https://nypost.com/2021/09/01/de-blasios-doe-takes-its-war-on-learning-to-a-new-extreme-with-no-honor-roll-push/.

10 Georgia Worrell, Susan Edelman, Mary Kay Linge, Rich Calder and Jacob Geanous, "Nearly half of NYC DOE grads at CUNY need remedial classes," *New York Post*, February 25, 2023, https://nypost.com/2023/02/25/nearly-half-of-nyc-doe-grads-need-cuny-remedial-classes/.

11 Danielle Wallace, "University of California agrees to nix SAT, ACT in admissions decisions in settlement with minority students," Fox News, May 16, 2021, https://www.foxnews.com/us/university-of-california-sat-act-admissions-settlement-minority-students.

12 Bill Pan, "California State University Permanently Ends Standardized Test Requirements for Admissions," *Epoch Times*, March 25, 2022, https://www.theepochtimes.com/california-state-university-permanently-ends-standardized-test-requirements-for-admissions_4357369.html.

13 Emma Colton, "California backtracks on woke math curriculum overhaul after stern opposition: Hundreds of professionals in math and science fields signed an open letter denouncing the plan as one that will 'de-mathematize' math," Fox News, July 13, 2021, https://www.foxnews.com/us/california-math-curriculum-equity-pushed-back.

14 Sam Dorman, "Oregon promotes teacher program that seeks to undo 'racism in mathematics': A toolkit includes a list of ways 'white supremacy culture' allegedly 'infiltrates math classrooms'," Fox News, February 12, 2021, https://www.foxnews.com/us/oregon-education-math-white-supremacy.

15 George Lowery, "Tougher grading is one reason for high STEM dropout rate," *Cornell Chronicle*, April 2, 2010, https://news.cornell.edu/stories/2010/04/tougher-grading-one-reason-high-stem-dropout-rate.

16 Adam Sabes, "NYU professor fired after students said class was too hard urges 'tough love' from college, end to 'coddling': The NYU professor said that he saw signs 'trouble' even before

the coronavirus pandemic," Fox News, October 20, 2022, https://www.foxnews.com/us/nyu -professor-fired-students-complained-class-too-hard-says-colleges-must-apply-tough-love.

17   Ibid.

18   Drew Desilver, "U.S. students' academic achievement still lags that of their peers in many other countries," Pew Research Center, February 15, 2017, http://www.pewresearch.org /fact-tank/2015/02/02/u-s-students-improving-slowly-in-math-and-science-but-still-lagging -internationally/.

19   John Mac Ghlionn, "The Chinese Regime Versus the US, and the Battle for Scientific Dominance," *The Epoch Times*, July 10, 2021, https://www.theepochtimes.com/opinion/the -chinese-regime-versus-the-us-and-the-battle-for-scientific-dominance-3895282.

20   Heather Mac Donald, "As China's military tech dominates, Congress demands science bow to racial 'justice,'" *New York Post*, March 14, 2022, https://nypost.com/2022/03/14/as-chinas -military-tech-dominates-us-science-bows-to-racial-justice/.

21   Bill Pan, "American Medical Association Embraces Critical Race Theory, Rejects Meritocracy," *Epoch Times*, May 12, 2021, https://www.theepochtimes.com/us/american-medical-association -embraces-critical-race-theory-rejects-meritocracy-3812858.

22   Tyler Olson, "American Medical Association pushes pro-critical race theory materials in 'Health Equity' guide: Document cites AMA guide for how to advocate for critical race theory," Fox News, November 10, 2021, https://www.foxnews.com/politics/american-medical-association -health-equity-guide-critical-race-theory.

23   Bill Pan, "Critical Race Theory Makes Its Way Into Mandatory Trainings at Top US Medical Schools, New Database Shows," *The Epoch Times*, February 21, 2022, https://www .theepochtimes.com/us/amid-opposition-from-the-left-more-states-push-for-curriculum -transparency-4326617.

24   Matt McGregor, "'Diversity to the Exclusion of Merit': Physician Criticizes Woke Initiatives in Medical Schools," *Epoch Times*, November 18, 2022, https://www.theepochtimes .com/diversity-to-the-exclusion-of-merit-physician-criticizes-woke-initiatives-in-medical -schools_4870249.html.

25   David Christopher Kaufman, "In the name of 'equity,' companies are now ignoring educational achievement," *New York Post*, December 31, 2022, https://nypost.com/2022/12/31/in-the -name-of-equity-companies-are-now-ignoring-education/.

26   Brian Flood, "Success of Asian Americans debunks critical race theory, 'Inconvenient Minority' author says:," Fox News, July 13, 2021, https://www.foxnews.com/media/asian-americans -critical-race-theory-inconvenient-minority-kenny-xu.

27   Timothy H.J. Nerozzi, "White people banned from off-campus UC Berkeley student housing common areas: The Berkeley co-op also states that residents must alert others when they intend to bring White guests to the house," Fox News, August 20, 2022, https://ifunny.co/picture /full-circle-back-to-segregation-mlk-not-gonna-like-this-ri4oj3wp9.

28   Hannah Grossman, "'Angry and bitter' Michigan school board member claims 'Whiteness is evil,' faces backlash for divisive tweets: Michigan school board member Kesha Hamilton claimed White people more dangerous than animals," Fox News, January 20, 2023, https: //www.foxnews.com/media/angry-bitter-michigan-school-board-member-claims-whiteness -evil-faces-backlash-divisive-tweets.

29 Fox News Staff, "Horace Cooper calls out anti-racism speakers for making 'racist' assumptions," Fox News, February 22, 2022, https://www.foxnews.com/media/horace-cooper-anti-racism -speakers-assumptions.

Chapter Eight

1   Albert Schweitzer, *The Decay and The Restoration of Civilization* (London/Bloomsbury, A&C Black 1923), 75.
2   *See* Paul Goodman, *Compulsory Mis-Education and the Community of Scholars* (New York, Random House 1966), 196.
3   Mark Bauerlein, "The Strange Obedience of the Professorate," *The Epoch Times*, October 20, 2021, https://www.theepochtimes.com/opinion/the-strange-obedience-of-the-professorate -4055973.
4   William Brooks, "To Defend Academic Freedom, a Canadian Professor Calls for 'Dangerous Universities'," *Epoch Times*, October 23, 2022, https://www.theepochtimes. com/william-brooks-to-defend-academic-freedom-a-canadian-professor-calls-for-dangerous -universities_4812511.html.
5   *Mao Zedong on the Dangers of "Liberalism"* (1937). Alphahistory.com, https://alphahistory .com/chineserevolution/mao-zedong-dangers-of-liberalism-1937/.
6   Dr. Martin Luther King Jr., "The Purpose of Education," in *The Papers of Martin Luther King Jr., Volume 1: Called to Serve*, January 1929-June 1951 (1992).
7   Malcolm X, Speech at Founding Rally of the Organization of Afro-American Unity (28 June 1964).
8   Nelson Mandela, Speech at Madison Park High School, Boston, 23 June 1990.
9   Ibid.
10 John A. Moses, "The Fallacy of Presentism in History," *The Quadrant*, January 8, 2022, https: //quadrant.org.au/magazine/2022/01/the-fallacy-of-presentism-in-history/.
11 Jack Phillips, "Portland State University Professor Resigns, Says School Is a 'Social Justice Factory'," *The Epoch Times*, September 8, 2021, https://www.theepochtimes.com/us/portland -state-university-professor-resigns-says-school-is-a-social-justice-factory-3987686.
12 Walter E. Williams, "The Fight for Free Speech," *Epoch Times*, October 7, 2020, https://www .theepochtimes.com/the-fight-for-free-speech_3528032.html.

Chapter Nine

1   Mattias Desmet, "The Psychology of Totalitarianism," *Epoch Times*, August 31, 2022, https: //www.theepochtimes.com/the-psychology-of-totalitarianism_4702827.html.
2   Paul Tournier, *The Meaning of Persons*, trans. Edward Hudson (Hymns Ancient & Modern Ltd; Reissue edition 2012, East Sussex, UK, 1957), 40.
3   Eric Hoffer, *The True Believer: Thoughts on the Nature of Mass Movements*, Harper & Row, New York, 1951), 127.
4   World Economic Forum, "Now is the time for a 'great reset,'" Jun 3, 2020. https://www .weforum.org/agenda/2020/06/now-is-the-time-for-a-great-reset/.
5   Walter E. Williams, "*The Fight for Free Speech*," 10/7/20, https://www.creators.com/read /walter-williams/10/20/the-fight-for-free-speech.

6   Harry Lee and Jan Jelielek, "Heather Higgins: Silencing People and Forcing Them to 'Accept Guilt' Not the Way to Unity," *The Epoch Times*, January 22, 2021, https://www.theepochtimes. com/mkt_app/us/heather-higgins-silencing-people-and-forcing-them-to-accept-guilt-not-the -way-to-unity-3666734.

7   Chris Pandolfo, "Federal judge heckled at Stanford says 'don't feel sorry for me,' says mob behaved like 'dogs**t': Federal Judge Kyle Duncan warns that the intolerance of students at Stanford Law School for speech they dislike will be a problem when they become lawyers," Fox News, March 11, 2023, https://www.foxnews.com/politics/federal-judge-heckled-stanford -says-dont-feel-sorry-me-says-mob-behaved-like-dogs-t.

8   David Rutz, "Ugly Stanford Law protest of judge shows 'something has gone very wrong culturally,' student says: 'People are yelling really horrible things about him, about his family members being raped,' Stanford student says of left-wing protest against Judge Kyle Duncan," Fox News, March 20, 2023, https://www.foxnews.com/media/ugly-stanford-law-protest -judge-shows-something-gone-very-wrong-culturally-student-says.

9   Nikolas Lanum, "Hundreds of silent masked students surround Stanford Law dean for apology to heckled federal judge: 'Eerie': Jenny Martinez's whiteboard covered in fliers from student activists denouncing her and Judge Kyle Duncan," Fox News, March 14, 2023, https://www .foxnews.com/media/hundreds-silent-masked-students-surround-stanford-law-dean-apology -heckled-federal-judge-eerie.

Chapter Ten

1   "George Soros on China: Remarks Delivered at the Hoover Institution," January 31, 2022, https://www.georgesoros.com/2022/01/31/george-soros-on-china-remarks-delivered-at-the -hoover-institution/.

2   Jeffrey A. Tucker, "Leviathan Must Be Stopped," *Epoch Times*, February 3, 2023, https://www .theepochtimes.com/leviathan-must-be-stopped_5032634.html.

3   Steve LeVine, "Artificial intelligence pioneer calls for the breakup of Big Tech: Yoshua Bengio, the artificial intelligence pioneer, says the centralization of wealth, power and capability in Big Tech is 'dangerous for democracy' and that the companies should be broken up," Axios, September 21, 2017, https://www.axios.com/artificial-intelligence-pioneer-calls-for-the -breakup-of-big-tech-2487483705.html.

4   Mary Pascaline, "Edward Snowden Warns Against Relying On Facebook For News," Yahoo News, November 17, 2016, https://ca.news.yahoo.com/edward-snowden-warns-against-relying -092615819.html.

5   Ibid.

6   Russell Jacoby, *The End of Utopia: Policy and Culture in an Age of Apathy* (New York, Basic Books 2000), 105.

7   Ibid.

8   Ibid, 110.

9   John McWhorter, "Academics Are Really, Really Worried About Their Freedom," *The Atlantic*, September 8, 2020, https://www.theatlantic.com/ideas/archive/2020/09/academics-are-really -really-worried-about-their-freedom/615724/.

10 Ibid.

11 Ibid.

12 Paul Rossi, "NYC teacher: We're damaging kids with 'Critical Race Theory,'" *New York Post*, April 13, 2021, https://nypost.com/2021/04/13/nyc-teacher-were-damaging-kids-with-critical-race-theory/.

13 Ibid.

14 "Language, Politics, and Composition. Noam Chomsky interviewed by Gary A. Olson and Lester Faigley," *Journal of Advanced Composition* 11, no. 1 (1991), https://chomsky.info/1991____/.

15 Ibid.

Chapter Eleven

1 Daphne Patai, "Speak Freely, Professor—Within the Speech Code," *Chronicle of Higher Education*, June 9, 2000, pg. B7.

2 Mary Joe Frug, "A Postmodern Feminist Legal Manifesto (An Unfinished Draft)," *Harvard Law Review* 1045 (1992).

3 Rich Lowry, "Woke claim that 'rational thinking' is a white male thing is both insulting and absurd," *New York Post*, October 26, 2021, https://nypost.com/2021/10/26/woke-claim-that-rational-thinking-is-a-white-male-thing-is-insulting-absurd/.

4 Christopher F. Rufo, " Going All In: The NEA pledges to bring critical race theory to a public school near you," *City-Journal*, July 15, 2021, https://www.city-journal.org/article/going-all-in.

5 Ayaan Hirsi Ali, "Ayaan Hirsi Ali: On September 11, here's what Islamists and 'Wokeists' have in common: Adherents of both pursue ideological purity, refuse to engage in debate and demand submission," *Wall Street Journal*, https://www.wsj.com/articles/what-islamists-and-wokeists-have-in-common-11599779507, *Wall Street Journal*, 9/11/20; Joseph A. Wulfsohn, "Ayaan Hirsi Ali says wokeism has 'remarkable similarities' to White supremacy: 'The rotten idea of our time': Hoover Institute scholar: 'If you think that White supremacy is the biggest domestic threat that we face . . . get a grip,'" Fox News, November 2, 2021, https://www.foxnews.com/media/ayaan-hirsi-ali-wokeism-white-supremacy.

6 Ruth Nanda Anshen, *Language: An Enquiry into Its Meaning and Functions* (New York, Harper, 1957).

7 Nikolas Lanum, "Colleges only getting worse by 'manifesting authoritarianism' with 'word policing', professor warns: William Jacobson said word banning is a form of 'repressive tolerance' to neutralize opposition," Fox News, January 17, 2023, https://www.foxnews.com/media/colleges-getting-worse-manifesting-authoritarianism-word-policing-cornell-law-professor.

8 Roger Kimball, "The Purity Spiral Turns, as Courage Goes Missing," *Epoch Times*, June 28, 2020, https://www.theepochtimes.com/the-purity-spiral-turns-as-courage-goes-missing_3404905.html.

9 Ibid.

10 Harry Lee and Jan Jekielek, "Heather Higgins: Silencing People and Forcing Them to 'Accept Guilt' Not the Way to Unity," *The Epoch Times*, January 22, 2021, https://www.theepochtimes.com/heather-higgins-silencing-people-and-forcing-them-to-accept-guilt-not-the-way-to-unity_3666734.html.

11 Christopher F. Rufo, "Critical race theory has taken over academic life at this Florida university: Education bureaucrats have inserted radical 'diversity, equity, and inclusion' programs into

almost everything at Florida International," Fox News, March 2, 2023, https://www.foxnews
.com/opinion/critical-race-theory-academic-life-florida-university.

12   Adam Sabes, "University language guide says 'grandfather,' 'housekeeping,' 'spirit animal' are
'problematic' words: The language guide, created by the university's information technology
department, states that 'grandfather,' 'housekeeping,' 'minority,' 'ninja,' and 'lame' are considered
'problematic words,'" New York Post, January 22, 2022, https://nypost.com/2022/01/23
/university-of-washington-language-guide-says-grandfather-housekeeping-spirit-animal-are-
problematic-words/.

13   Bryan Jung, "Stanford Updates Guide to Canceling 'Harmful Language' Including Words
Like 'Man' and 'American,'" NTD News, December 21, 2022, https://www.ntd.com
/stanford-updates-guide-to-canceling-harmful-language-including-words-like-man-and
-american_889899.html.

14   It is available at: http://works.bepress.com/david_barnhizer/106/.

15   Amy Gamm, "Stanford Professors Push Back on University-Encouraged Student Informant
Culture," Epoch Times, February 25, 2023, https://www.theepochtimes.com/stanford
-professors-push-back-on-university-encouraged-student-informant-culture_5082431.html.

16   Kendall Tietz, "University of Wisconsin-Milwaukee alters 'bias reporting system' following
First Amendment challenge: The university clarified that students would not be punished for
protected First Amendment speech," The Atlantic, March 6, 2023, https://www.theatlantic
.com/magazine/archive/2023/04/us-extremism-portland-george-floyd-protests-january
-6/673088/.

Chapter Twelve

1   Crimestop, Technovelgy.com. http://www.technovelgy.com/ct/content.asp?Bnum=565. From
G. Orwell, 1984.

2   Bill Pan, "Tackling Critical Race Theory: What It Is and Where It Is Being Banned," The Epoch
Times, December 2, 2021, https://www.theepochtimes.com/us/tackling-critical-race-theory
-what-it-is-and-where-it-is-being-banned-4108055?u.

3   Joe Silverstein, "Cambridge Dictionary changes definition of 'man' and 'woman': '1984 wasn't
supposed to be a how-to manual': One commentator argued the Cambridge Dictionary is
'ceding linguistic territory to the radical Left,'" Fox News, December 13, 2022, https://www
.foxnews.com/media/cambridge-dictionary-changes-definition-man-woman-1984-supposed
-manual.

Chapter Thirteen

1   Albert Camus, Defense of Intelligence, [Speech given at a meeting organized by L'Amitie
Francaise on March 15, 1945] https://www.scribd.com/document/131898952/Defense-of
-Intelligence-Albert-Camus.

2   Deborah Tannen, The Argument Culture: Moving From Debate to Dialogue (New York, Random
House 1998).

3   Allan Bloom, The Closing of the American Mind, How Higher Education Has Failed Democracy
and Impoverished the Souls of Today's Students (Ann Arbor, University of Michigan Press 1987),
18.

4   Adolf A. Berle, Power (San Diego, Harcourt Brace 1969), 92.

5   Xaviaer DuRousseau, "We are not your victims, liberals: Slavery reparations are an insult," *New York Post*, March 17, 2023, https://nypost.com/2023/03/17/we-are-not-victims-liberals -slavery-reparations-insulting/.

6   Adam B. Coleman, "The Culture War: Recognizing the Battle for Society's Direction," *The Epoch Times*, 7/29/23, https://www.theepochtimes.com/opinion/the-culture-war-recognizing -the-battle-for-societys-direction-5420276.

7   Ella Kietlinska and Jan Jekielek, "Wokeism Is Costume Elites Wear to 'Signal Virtue' and 'Hide Greed, Corruption': Former Levi's Executive," *The Epoch Times*, December 2, 2022, https: //www.theepochtimes.com/us/wokeism-is-costume-elites-wear-to-signal-virtue-and-hide -greed-corruption-former-levis-executive-4899644.

8   Ibid.

9   Masooma Haq and Jan Jekielek, "Affirmative Action Perpetuates Racism: Author Vivek Ramaswamy" *The Epoch Times,* 11/20/22, https://www.theepochtimes.com/us/affirmative -action-perpetuates-racism-author-vivek-ramaswamy-4873216.

10 Joseph Bernstein, "Alienated, Alone And Angry: What The Digital Revolution Really Did To Us: We were promised community, civics, and convenience. Instead, we found ourselves dislocated, distrustful, and disengaged.," BuzzFeed News, December 17, 2019, https://www.buzzfeednews.com/article/josephbernstein/in-the-2010s-decade-we-became -alienated-by-technology.

11 Ibid.

Chapter Fourteen

1   Anthony J. Diekema, *Academic Freedom and Christian Scholarship*.Wm. B. Eerdmans-Lightning Source; New Stiff Wraps edition (August 8, 2000) Grand Rapids, MI and Cambridge, UK, 34.

2   Wiley Miller, "Non Sequitur," *St. Louis Post-Dispatch*, August 23, 2002, E5.

3   Charles Creitz, "Bill Maher roasts woke 'presentism': 'A magic moral time machine' where you always win: 'It's not all up in the air to change or delete or make up based on what makes you feel better today,'" Fox News, September 17, 2022, https://www.foxnews.com/media/bill -maher-roasts-woke-presentism-magic-moral-time-machine-you-always-win.

4   David Barnhizer, *The Warrior Lawyer: Powerful Strategies for Winning Legal Battles* (Bridge Street Books,Irvington-on-Hudson, NY 1997).

5   David R. Barnhizer, "A Chilling of Discourse," *St. Louis University Law Journal* 361 (2006).

6   Martha C. Nussbaum, *Cultivating Humanity: A Classical Defense of Reform in Liberal Education* (Cambridge MA, Harvard University Press, 1998).

7   Albert Camus, "Defense of Intelligence," in *Resistance, Rebellion, and Death*, trans. Justin O' Brien (New York, : Alfred A. Knopf, 1961), 38.

Chapter Fifteen

1   Ella Kietlinska and Joshua Philipp, "Identity Politics Is a Tool to Break Down America," *Epoch Times*, February 19, 2021, https://www.theepochtimes.com/identity-politics-is-a-tool-to -break-down-america-expert_3700658.html.

2   Heather Mac Donald, "Law School Humbug," *City Journal* (Autumn 1995), 46, 48–49, https://www.city-journal.org/article/law-school-humbug.

3   Bruce Abramson and Robert B. Chernin, "China, the True Enemy Within," *Epoch Times*, February 20, 2021, https://www.theepochtimes.com/china-the-true-enemy-within_3691541.html.

4   Jan Jekielek and Masooma Haq, "Universities Are 'Propaganda Mills,' Teach a 'New McCarthyism': Former Harvard Law Professor Alan Dershowitz: This will impact generations of leaders," *The Epoch Times*, September 24, 2022, https://www.theepochtimes.com/us/universities-are-propaganda-mills-teach-a-new-mccarthyism-former-harvard-law-professor-alan-dershowitz-4751039.

5   Ella Kietlinska and Joshua Philipp, "Identity Politics Is a Tool to Break Down America," *Epoch Times*.

6   Bob Zeidman, "How Diversity Is Dividing Us," *Epoch Times*, December 2, 2022, https://www.theepochtimes.com/how-diversity-is-dividing-us_4896634.html.

7   *Furman v. Georgia*, 408 U.S. 238, 467 (1972) (Rehnquist, J., dissenting) (quoting J.S. Mill, *On Liberty* (1885), 28).

8   Hannah Grossman, "North Korean defector: I am terrified of the 'massive indoctrination coming from the left' in public schools: North Korean defector Yeonmi Park draws a parallel between Nazi ideology and the left-wing indoctrination," June 5, 2022, https://groups.google.com/g/soc.retirement/c/LyNeA6BbLKs?pli=1.

9   Marx wrote this passage in 1843 as part of the introduction to Critique of Hegel's Philosophy of Right, a book that criticized philosopher Georg Wilhelm Friedrich Hegel's 1820 book, Elements of the Philosophy of Right. This introduction was published in 1844 in a small journal called Deutsch–Französische Jahrbücher; however, the book itself was published posthumously. First published: in *Deutsch-Französische Jahrbücher*, 7 & 10 February 1844 in Paris; Transcription: the source and date of transcription is unknown. It was proofed and corrected by Andy Blunden, February 2005, and corrected by Matthew Carmody in 2009. https://www.marxists.org/archive/marx/works/1843/critique-hpr/intro.htm.

10   ReviseSociology, "The Marxist Perspective on Religion," Updated on February 24, 2023 by Karl Thompson. https://revisesociology.com/2018/07/10/marxist-perspective-religion/.

11   Ella Kietlinska and Joshua Philipp, "Identity Politics Is a Tool to Break Down America," *Epoch Times*.

12   Abraham Maslow, *Toward a Psychology of Being*, 2nd ed, 9 (New York, D. Van Nostrand Company; 2nd edition January 1, 1968).

13   Ibid.

14   Noam Chomsky interviewed by Gary A. Olson and Lester Faigley, "Language, Politics, and Composition," *Journal of Advanced Composition* 11, no. 1, https://chomsky.info/1991____/.

15   Ibid.

16   James Schlesinger, "Intellectuals' Role: Truth to Power?," *Wall Street Journal*, October 12, 1983, 28.

Chapter Sixteen

1   Bill of Rights Institute, Federalist Papers # 10 (1787), https://billofrightsinstitute.org/primary-sources/federalist-no-10.

2   Walter E. Williams, "The Fight for Free Speech," Creators.com, October 7, 2020, https://www.creators.com/read/walter-williams/10/20/the-fight-for-free-speech.

3   John Patrick Diggins, *The Rise and Fall of the American Left* (W.W. Norton, New York 1992), 276.

4   Adam B. Coleman, "*The Culture War: Recognizing the Battle for Society's Direction*," *Epoch Times*, July 29, 2023, https://www.theepochtimes.com/opinion/the-culture-war-recognizing-the -battle-for-societys-direction-5420276.

5   Richard Delgado and Jean Stefancic, *Critical Race Theory: An Annotated Bibliography*, Va. L. Rev 79 (1993), 461–463.

6   Lance Izumi, "The Critical Race Theory debate is turning parents into unlikely activists," *New York Post*, January 14, 2023, https://nypost.com/2023/01/14/the-crt-debate-is-turning -parents-into-unlikely-activists/.

7   Jan Jekielek and Masooma Haq, "Universities Are 'Propaganda Mills,' Teach a 'New McCarthyism': Former Harvard Law Professor Alan Dershowitz: This will impact generations of leaders," *Epoch Times*, September 24, 2022, https://www.theepochtimes.com/us /universities-are-propaganda-mills-teach-a-new-mccarthyism-former-harvard-law-professor -alan-dershowitz-4751039.

8   Ibid.

9   John Nolte, "Nolte: Left's Demand for Racism Far Exceeds the Supply," *Breitbart*, June 5, 2023, https://www.breitbart.com/the-media/2020/06/25/nolte-lefts-demand-racism-exceeds- supply/.

10 Hannah Grossman, "NYC forces all city employees to undergo radical critical race theory training: 'Really unfair': A source told Fox News that NYC wanted the contracts with the city and the hiring to be determined with a 'racial equity' lens," Fox News, January 30, 2023, https://www.foxnews.com/media/new-york-forces-all-city-employees-into-radical-racial -equity-training.

Chapter Seventeen

1   "Language, Politics, and Composition. Noam Chomsky interviewed by Gary A. Olson and Lester Faigley," *Journal of Advanced Composition* 11, no. 1, https://chomsky.info/1991____/.

2   Marshall McLuhan, *Understanding Media: The Extensions of Man* (New York, NY: McGraw-Hill, 1964).

3   Jacques Ellul, *Propaganda: The Formation of Men's Attitudes* (New York, NY: Knopf, 1968), 163–64.

4   Thomas F. Green, *The Activities of Teaching* (New Haven, CT: Yale University Press, 1982), 47.

5   Robert A. Dahl, *Dilemmas of Pluralist Democracy: Autonomy vs. Control* (New Haven, CT: Yale University Press, 1982), 45.

Chapter Eighteen

1   "Mao Zedong on the Dangers of "Liberalism,'" 1937, https://alphahistory.com /chineserevolution/mao-zedong-dangers-of-liberalism-1937/.

2   John McWhorter, *Woke Racism: How a New Religion Has Betrayed Black America* (New York, Penguin 2021).

3   Sam Dorman, "Black professor blasts 'dehumanizing condescension' of bestselling book 'White Fragility': Columbia associate professor warns tome teaches readers 'how to be racist in a whole

new way'" Fox News, July 17, 2020, https://www.foxnews.com/media/john-mcwhorter-white -fragility-robin-diangelo-atlantic.

4   Brian Flood, "Bill Maher compares woke liberals to KKK on Joe Rogan show: They see race 'first and foremost': 'You can be woke . . . but don't say that somehow it's an extension of liberalism,' Maher said," Fox News, 9/4/23, https://www.foxnews.com/media/bill-maher -compares-woke-liberals-kkk-joe-rogan-show-see-race-first-foremost.

5   Kristine Parks, "James Carville rips far-left Democrats on Bill Maher podcast: 'Most stupid, naive people you can imagine,'" Fox News, 9/26/23, https://nypost.com/2023/09/26/james -carville-rips-stupid-far-left-democrats-on-bill-maher-podcast/.

6   Olivia B. Waxman, "The White Supremacist Origins of Exercise, and 6 Other Surprising Facts About the History of U.S. Physical Fitness," *Time*, 12/28/2022, https://time.com/6242949 /exercise-industry-white-supremacy/.

7   Sophie Mann, "'Pantry porn is classist, racist and sexist': Chicago professor slams social media trend of showing off perfectly organized pantries and blames likes of Kardashian-Jenner family for pushing 'modern-day status symbol,'" *Daily Mail*, 3/16/2023, https://www.dailymail .co.uk/news/article-11869325/Chicago-professor-slams-social-media-trend-showing-perfectly -organized-pantries.html.

8   Adam B. Coleman, "We're not guilty for crimes of history," *New York Post*, February 24, 2023, https://nypost.com/2023/02/24/were-not-guilty-for-crimes-of-history/.

9   Ibid.

10 Masooma Haq and Jan Jekielek, "CRT Ideology Used in Schools Degrades the Individual: NYC High School Teacher," *Epoch Times*, April 6, 2022, https://www.theepochtimes. com/crt-ideology-used-in-schools-degrades-the-individual-new-york-city-high-school -teacher_4357926.html.

11 Carl Gustav Jung, *The Undiscovered Self* (Princeton, NJ: Princeton University Press, 1958), 2.

12 Michael Rectenwald, "Here's what happened when I challenged the PC campus culture at NYU: I'm on leave after a misunderstood Twitter experiment," *Washington Post*, 11/3/2016, https://www.washingtonpost.com/posteverything/wp/2016/11/03/campus-pc-culture-is-so -rampant-that-nyu-is-paying-to-silence-me/.

13 Evita Duffy, "Science Professor Harassed and Threatened For Supporting Merit-Based Selection and Hiring Practices at University of Chicago," The Chicago Thinker, https: //thechicagothinker.com/science-professor-harassed-and-threatened-for-supporting-merit -based-selection-and-hiring-practices-at-university-of-chicago/ Chicago Thinker.

14 Daniella Genovese, "UCLA students urge replacement of top computer science professor. The petition has notched over 1,600 signatures," Fox News, September 4, 2020, https://www. foxnews.com/us/ucla-students-replace-computer-science-chair.

15 Caleb Parke "UCLA professor suspended, under police protection after threats, Fox News, 6/9/20, https://www.foxnews.com/us/ucla-professor-suspended-under-police-protection-after -threats.

16 https://www.wilsoncenter.org/sites/default/files/media/uploads/documents/2020–07- HoldingAPenInOneHand-Brady_Update.pdf. Anne-Marie Brady, with Jichang Lulu and Sam Pheloung, "China's Exploitation of Civilian Channels for Military Purposes in New Zealand," July 2020, https://www.timeshighereducation.com/news/review-clears-new-zealand-scholar- over-china-criticism Review clears New Zealand scholar over China criticism. Joyce Law, "Anne-Marie Brady complied with policies and legislation, says Canterbury, but statement calls for 'clarity' amendments," December 11, 2020.

Chapter Nineteen

1   Walter E. Williams, "The Fight for Free Speech," October 7, 2020, https://www.creators.com
    /read/walter-williams/10/20/the-fight-for-free-speech.

2   Masooma Haq and Jan Jekielek, "CRT Ideology Used in Schools Degrades the Individual:
    NYC High School Teacher," *Epoch Times*, April 6, 2022, https://www.theepochtimes.
    com/us/crt-ideology-used-in-schools-degrades-the-individual-new-york-city-high-school
    -teacher-4357926.

3   Charles Axelrod, *Studies in Intellectual Breakthrough: Freud, Simmel, and Buber* (Amherst, MA:
    University of Massachusetts Press, 1979), 2–3.

4   Robert Paul Wolff, *The Poverty of Liberalism* (New York, NY: Beacon Press, 1968), 16.

5   John Patrick Diggins, *The Rise and Fall of the American Left* (New York, NY: W.W. Norton
    1992), 290.

6   Ayaan Hirsi Ali, "Ayaan Hirsi Ali: On September 11, here's what Islamists and 'Wokeists'
    have in common: Adherents of both pursue ideological purity, refuse to engage in debate and
    demand submission," *Wall Street Journal*, September 11, 2020, https://www.wsj.com/articles
    /what-islamists-and-wokeists-have-in-common-11599779507.

Chapter Twenty

1   Terri Wu, "Critical Race Theory Aims to Turn Students Into 'Red Guards,' Chinese American
    Warns," *Epoch Times*, September 10, 2021, https://www.theepochtimes.com/us/critical-race
    -theory-aims-to-turn-students-into-red-guards-chinese-american-warns-3988678.

2   "Falun Gong, a spiritual discipline which China banned in 1999 and calls an "evil cult." Along
    with Tibetans, Uighur Muslims, democracy activists and pro-independence Taiwanese, Falun
    Gong practitioners round off the "five poisons"—risks which the Chinese government has
    acknowledged as posing the biggest threat to its rule. What is Falun Gong?
        Falun Gong, which means "law wheel practice" in Chinese, is a set of meditation exercises
    and texts that preach the virtues of truth, benevolence and forbearance. It was founded in north-
    east China in 1992 by Li Hongzhi, a former trumpet player. Falun Gong draws on China's
    long tradition of qigong, a regimen of controlled breathing and gentle physical movements.
    But unlike other qigong-inspired disciplines that sprouted up in the 1990s, typically claiming
    nothing more than health benefits for practitioners, Falun Gong avows a path to salvation for
    the faithful." ("What is Falun Gong? China's government calls it an 'evil cult,'" *The Economist*,
    September 5, 2018, https://www.economist.com/the-economist-explains/2018/09/05/what
    -is-falun-gong.)

3   David Barnhizer and Daniel Barnhizer, *The Artificial Intelligence Contagion: Can Democracy
    Withstand the Imminent Transformation of Work, Wealth, and the Social Order?* (Atlanta: Clarity
    Press, 2019).

4   David R Barnhizer. "'Something Wicked This Way Comes': Political Correctness and the
    Reincarnation of Chairman Mao," Cleveland-Marshall College of Law Legal Studies Research
    Paper Series (2016). Available at: http://works.bepress.com/david_barnhizer/108/.

5   Michael Martina, Reuters Staff, "China's Xi calls for universities' allegiance to the Communist
    Party," Reuters, December 9, 2016, https://www.reuters.com/article/cnews-us-china
    -education-idCAKBN13Y0B5.

6   David Kopel, "Rage Mobs 1966 v. 2020: Part 2: Red Guards begin rampaging," December 9,
    2020, https://www.theepochtimes.com/rage-mobs-1966-v-2020_3604830.html. This essay is

adapted from David B. Kopel, "The Party Commands the Gun: Mao Zedong's Arms Policies and Mass Killing," pages 423–521, in online chapter 14 of "Firearms Law and the Second Amendment: Regulation, Rights, and Policy," by Nicholas J. Johnson, David B. Kopel, George A. Mocsary, and E. Gregory Wallace.

7   Charles Creitz, "Leftist mob riots after Charlie Kirk shows up at campus, tries to shut down free speech event," Fox News, December 2, 2022, https://www.foxnews.com/media/leftist -mob-riots-charlie-kirk-shows-campus-tries-shut-free-speech-event.

8   Philippe Naughton, "'F*ck You, Fascist!': Charlie Kirk Drowned Out by Protesters on Arizona College Visit," *Daily Beast*, 9/20/23, https://www.thedailybeast.com/fck-you-fascist-charlie -kirk-drowned-out-by-protesters-at-northern-arizona-university.

9   Epoch Newsroom, "People Marching With Antifa Attack Conservatives at Rally Against Big Tech: Conservative event organizer had front tooth knocked out," *Epoch Times*, October 17, 2020, https://www.theepochtimes.com/people-marching-with-antifa-group-attack -conservatives-at-rally-against-big-tech_3542911.html.

10   Jessica Chasmar, "Pro-Antifa teacher brags about turning students into 'revolutionaries,' undercover video shows," Fox News, August 31, 2021, https://www.foxnews.com/politics /video-antifa-teacher-bragging-students-revolutionaries.

11   Jessica Chasmar, "California teacher hangs 'F—the Police,' 'F—Amerikkka' posters in classroom," Fox News, September 16, 2021, https://www.foxnews.com/us/california-teacher -f-police-amerikkka-posters-classroom.

12   Darlene McCormick Sanchez, "Students Speak Out on Anti-white, Anti-Christian, Anti-American Culture at Florida University: Desantis's Stop WOKE Act called 'toothless,'" *Epoch Times*, December 24, 2022, https://www.theepochtimes.com/students-speak-out-on-anti -white-anti-christian-anti-american-culture-at-florida-university_4937887.html.

13   "CCP buys media influence by paying millions to US dailies, magazines: Report," ANI / Jul 4, 2021, https://timesofindia.indiatimes.com/world/china/ccp-buys-media-influence-by-paying -millions-to-us-dailies-magazines-report/articleshow/84109897.cms.

14   Judith Miller, "Rise and fall of *New York Times* writer Bari Weiss—a victim of far-left intolerance," *City Journal*, July 15, 2020, https://manhattan.institute/article/rise-and-fall-of -new-york-times-writer-bari-weiss-a-victim-of-far-left-intolerance.

15   Zachary Evans, "NYT Publishes Op-Ed by Chinese Professor Without Disclosing Ties to Beijing," *National Review*, July 23, 2020, https://www.nationalreview.com/news/nyt-publishes-op-ed-by-chinese-professor-who-mocked-trump-by-calling-aids-american-sexually-transmitted-disease-in-post-on-propaganda-outlet/.

16   Bret Stephens, "Bret Stephens: What The Times Got Wrong," *New York Times*, 6/12/2020, https://www.nytimes.com/2020/06/12/opinion/tom-cotton-op-ed.html.

17   Oliver Darcy, "Anger inside the New York Times as divided newsroom erupts in debate over recent controversies," CNN Business, February 11, 2021, https://www.cnn.com/2021/02/10 /media/new-york-times-donald-mcneil-andy-mills/index.html.

18   Charles Creitz, "Alex Berenson on 'censorship', free speech: 'Times have changed and the NY Times has changed,'" Fox News, February 26, 2021, https://www.foxnews.com/politics/cpac -alex-berenson-censorship-free-speech-ny-times.

19   David Bauder, "NY Times says it needs culture change, better inclusion," AP News, February 25, 2021, https://apnews.com/article/ny-times-culture-change-inclusion-1dbd01abdffb9c050 01ede64dcb68f5a.

20 Tamar Lapin, "New York Times union wants 'sensitivity reads' as part of editorial process," *New York Post*, July 31, 2020, https://nypost.com/2020/07/31/new-york-times-union-wants-sensitivity-reads-as-part-of-editorial-process/.

21 Joseph Wulfsohn, "Staff believed my columns were 'physically harming' them," Fox News, July 17, 2020, https://www.foxnews.com/media/ andrew-sullivan-new-york-magazine.

22 Conor Friedersdorf, "Why Matthew Yglesias Left Vox: He is the latest high-profile writer to abandon traditional media," *The Atlantic*, November 13, 2020, https://www.theatlantic.com /ideas/archive/2020/11/substack-and-medias-groupthink-problem/617102/.

23 Brian Flood, "The Intercept co-founder Glenn Greenwald quits, claims editors censored story critical of Biden," Fox News, 10/29/20, https://www.foxnews.com/media/glenn-greenwald -quits-the-intercepteditors-censored-story.

24 Joseph A. Wulfsohn, "British columnist Suzanne Moore on why she 'had to leave' The Guardian: I was 'bullied by 338 colleagues,'" Fox News, November 25, 2020, https://www .foxnews.com/media/suzanne-moore-the-guardian.

25 *Guardian* staff and agencies, "'Buildings matter': Philadelphia newspaper editor resigns after headline sparks uproar," *The Guardian*, June 6, 2020, https://www.theguardian.com /media/2020/jun/06/philadelphia-inquirer-editor-resigns-buildings-matter-too.

26 Noam Chomsky interviewed by Gary A. Olson and Lester Faigley.

27 Ibid.

Chapter Twenty-One

1 Tom Phillips, "Xi Jinping heralds 'new era' of Chinese power at Communist party congress," *The Guardian*, October 18, 2017, https://www.theguardian.com/world/2017/oct/18/xi -jinping-speech-new-era-chinese-power-party-congress.

2 Tom Phillips, "China universities must become Communist party 'strongholds', says Xi Jinping: All teachers must be 'staunch supporters' of party governance, says president in what experts called an effort to reassert control," *The Guardian*, December 9, 2016, https://www .theguardian.com/world/2016/dec/09/china-universities-must-become-communist-party -strongholds-says-xi-jinping.

3 "China's Impact On The U.S. Education System," Staff Report, United States Senate, Permanent Subcommittee On Investigations, Committee On Homeland Security And Governmental Affairs," Rob Portman, Chairman, Tom Carper, Ranking Member, https://www.hsgac.senate. gov/imo/media/doc/PSI%20Report%20China's%20Impact%20on%20the%20US%20 Education%20System.pdf.

4 Ethan Epstein, "How China Infiltrated U.S. Classrooms: Even as they face criticism, Chinese government-run educational institutes have continued their forward march on college campuses across the United States," *Politico*, January 16, 2018, https://www.politico.com /magazine/story/2018/01/16/how-china-infiltrated-us-classrooms-216327/.

5 Joseph Kahn, "Chinese General Threatens Use of A-Bombs if U.S. Intrudes," *New York Times*, July 15, 2005, http://www.nytimes.com/2005/07/15/washington/world/chinese-general-threatens -use-of-abombs-if-us-intrudes.html.

6 Miles Yu, "Inside China: PLA says war with U.S. imminent," *Washington Times*, June 27, 2012, https://www.washingtontimes.com/news/2012/jun/27/inside-china-pla-says-war-us -imminent/.

7 Evelyn Cheng, "US-China war increasingly a 'reality,' Chinese army official says," CNBC, January 29, 2017, https://www.cnbc.com/2017/01/29/us-china-war-increasingly-a-reality -chinese-army-official-says.html.

8 Jane Perlez, "A U.S. Admiral's Bluntness Rattles China, and Washington," *New York Times*, May 6, 2016, https://www.nytimes.com/2016/05/07/world/asia/us-admiral-harry-harris.html.

9 Thomas Gibbons-Neff, "Mattis Accuses Beijing of 'Intimidation and Coercion' in South China Sea," *New York Times*, 6/1/2018, https://www.nytimes.com/2018/06/01/world/asia/mattis -south-china-sea.html.

Chapter Twenty-Two

1 Bob Zeidman, "How Diversity Is Dividing Us," *Epoch Times*, December 2, 2022, https://www .theepochtimes.com/how-diversity-is-dividing-us_4896634.html.

2 Ibid.

3 *Where Next? Western Civilization at the Crossroads,* Encounter Books, New York and London 2022.

4 Roger Kimball, "Why the Diversity Industry Is so Homogenous," *Epoch Times*, February 21, 2023, https://www.theepochtimes.com/why-the-diversity-industry-is-so-homogenous_5071781 .html.

5 Ibid.

6 Russell Jacoby, *The End of Utopia: Politics and Culture in an Age of Apathy* (New York: Basic Books, 1999), 33.

7 Abby Budimn and Neil G. Ruiz, "Key facts about Asian origin groups in the U.S.," Pew Foundation, April 29, 2021, https://www.pewresearch.org/fact-tank/2021/04/29/key-facts -about-asian-origin-groups-in-the-u-s/.

8 Ibid, 53–54.

9 Martha Nussbaum, *Cultivating Humanity: A Classical Defense of Reform in Liberal Education* (Cambridge, MA: Harvard University Press, 1998).

10 Danielle Wallace, "Virginia's Winsome Sears says voters are 'tired of the Black against White'," Fox News, November 14, 2021, https://www.foxnews.com/politics/virginia-winsome-sears -voters-tired-black-against-white.

11 Bob Zeidman, "How Diversity Is Dividing Us," *Epoch Times*, December 2, 2022, https://www .theepochtimes.com/how-diversity-is-dividing-us_4896634.html.

12 Carrie Sheffield, "Critical race theory is teaching kids to hate each other," *New York Post*, March 8, 2023, https://nypost.com/2023/03/08/critical-race-theory-is-teaching-kids-to-hate-each -other/.

Chapter Twenty-Four

1 John Leo, "Free Inquiry? Not on Campus: And the college speech police threaten the liberty of us all," *City Journal*, Winter 2007, https://www.city-journal.org/article/free-inquiry-not-on -campus.

2 Meimei Xu, "More than 80 percent of Harvard Faculty Identified as Liberal," *Harvard Crimson*, July 13, 2022, https://www.thecrimson.com/article/2022/7/13/faculty-survey-political-leaning/.

3 Frank Luntz, "Inside the Mind of an Ivy League Professor," FrontPageMagazine.com, Aug. 30, 2002, http://www.frontpagemag.com/articles/Printable .asp?ID=2642.

4   John Leo, "Free Inquiry? Not on Campus: And the college speech police threaten the liberty of us all," *City Journal*, Winter 2007, https://www.city-journal.org/article/free-inquiry-not-on-campus.

5   "Political Party Affiliation Among Academic Faculty," C-Brief, National Communication Association, March 2017, Volume 7, Issue 1. https://www.natcom.org/sites/default/files/publications/NCA_C-Brief_2017_March.pdf.

6   "Political Party Affiliation Among Academic Faculty," National Communication Association Vol. 1, no. 1 (March 2017), https://www.natcom.org/sites/default/files/publications/NCA_C-Brief_2017_March.pdf.

7   Ibid.

8   Samuel J. Abrams and Amna Khalid, "Are Colleges and Universities Too Liberal? What the Research Says About the Political Composition of Campuses and Campus Climate," Heterodox Academy, October 21, 2020, https://www.aei.org/articles/are-colleges-and-universities-too-liberal-what-the-research-says-about-the-political-composition-of-campuses-and-campus-climate/#:~:text=The%20data%20for%20three%20campus,openness%20to%20non%2Dliberal%20viewpoints.

9   Joan Acker, Kate Barry, and Johanna Esseveld, "Objectivity and truth: problems in doing feminist research" in *Back to the Future: A Look at the Second Wave of Feminist Epistemology and Methodology*, ed. Mary Margaret Fonow and Judith A. Cook (Bloomington, IN: Indiana University Press, 1991), 133, 135.

10 https://en.wikipedia.org/wiki/Women%27s_studies. Women's studies, Text last edited November 1, 2023. No named editor.

11 Margaret H. McFadden, Women's Studies, Last updated June 8, 2018, https://www.encyclopedia.com/history/united-states-and-canada/us-history/womens-studies. Updated Jun 08 2018.

12 Stanley Rothman, Robert Lichter, and Neil Nevitte, "Politics and Professional Advancement Among College Faculty," *The Forum 3* (January 29, 2005), https://www.aei.org/articles/are-colleges-and-universities-too-climate/-liberal-what-the-research-says-about-the-political-composition-of-campuses-and-campus.

13 Mitchell Langbert, "Homogenous: The Political Affiliations of Elite Liberal Arts College Faculty," National Association of Scholars, 2018, https://www.nas.org/academic-questions/31/2/homogenous_the_political_affiliations_of_elite_liberal_arts_college_faculty.

Chapter Twenty-Five

1   Joe Schoffstall, "Top DEI staff at public universities pocket massive salaries as experts question motives of initiatives: Highest-paid diversity and inclusion employees rake in substantially more than the average full-time professor," Fox News, March 30, 2022, https://www.foxnews.com/politics/top-dei-staff-at-public-universities-pocket-massive-salaries-as-experts-question-motives-of-initiatives#:~:text=Top%20diversity,%20equity%20and%20inclusion,enforce%20a%20%22political%20orthodoxy.%22

2   Ibid.

3   Darlene McCormick Sanchez, "Florida University Conceals Rampant DEI, CRT on Campus, Insider Report Says: University of Florida has hidden programs from DeSantis probe, has ties to gender clinic performing mastectomies on teens," *Epoch Times*, February 4, 2023, https:

//www.theepochtimes.com/exclusive-florida-governors-office-only-scratched-surface-of-crt-at
-university-of-florida_5033252.html.

4 Christopher F. Rufo, "Critical race theory has taken over academic life at this Florida university:
Education bureaucrats have inserted radical 'diversity, equity, and inclusion' programs into
almost everything at Florida International," Fox News, March 2, 2023, https://www.foxnews
.com/opinion/critical-race-theory-academic-life-florida-university.

5 Rikki Schlott, "DEI failing because it 'promotes division instead of unity': DEI pro," *New York
Post*, July 31, 2023, https://nypost.com/2023/07/31/dei-industry-failing-promotes-division
-instead-of-unity/.

6 Ibid.

7 Zippia, The Career Expert, https://www.zippia.com/administrator-jobs/demographics/.

8 Samuel J. Abrams and Amna Khalid, "Are Colleges and Universities Too Liberal? What the
Research Says About the Political Composition of Campuses and Campus Climate," Heterodox
Academy, October 21, 2020, https://www.aei.org/articles/are-colleges-and-universities-too
-liberal-what-the-research-says-about-the-political-composition-of-campuses-and-campus
-climate/.

9 Roger Kimball, "Elite NYC Prep School's Faculty Issues Racist Demands," *Epoch Times*,
December 21, 2020, https://www.theepochtimes.com/elite-nyc-prep-schools-faculty-issue
-racist-demands_3628074.html.

10 Hannah Grossman,"Professor lambasts White people as 'damaging' who need to dismantle
their 'Whiteness,'" Fox News, February 4, 2023, https://www.foxnews.com/media/professor
-white-people-become-less-damaging-dismantle-whiteness.

11 AAC&U 2022 Conference on Diversity, Equity, and Students Success, https://secure.aacu.org
/iMIS/AACUR/Events/Event_Display.aspx?EventKey=DESS22.

12 Ninveh Mansour, "Introduction to the Work and Ideas of George Lakoff," NonviolenceNY
Network (Spring 2018), https://www.nonviolenceny.org/post/introduction-to-the-work-and
-ideas-of-george-lakoff.

13 Kyle Smith, "Black and Latino students did worse in schools with 'diversity officers,'" *New
York Post*, October 27, 2021, https://nypost.com/2021/10/27/black-latino-students-did-worse
-with-diversity-officers/.

14 Jay Greene, PhD, and James Paul, "Equity Elementary: "Diversity, Equity, and Inclusion"
Staff in Public Schools," Heritage Foundation, October 19, 2021, https://www.heritage.org
/education/report/equity-elementary-diversity-equity-and-inclusion-staff-public-schools.

15 Mark J. Perry, "Quotation of the Day: Booker T. Washington," AEI, July 22, 2013, https:
//www.aei.org/carpe-diem/quotation-of-the-day-booker-t-washington/.

16 Eli Steele, "Rooftop Revelations: Booker T. Washington predicted Black Lives Matter: Black
Lives Matter exploited the death of George Floyd for profit, Pastor Corey Brooks says," Fox
News, February 2, 2022, https://www.foxnews.com/opinion/rooftop-revelations-booker-t
-washington-predicted-black-lives-matter.

17 Isabel Van Brugen, "BLM Suspends Fundraising as States Question Financial Transparency,"
Epoch Times, February 3, 2022, https://www.theepochtimes.com/us/blm-suspends-fundraising
-as-states-question-financial-transparency-4254077.

18 Xaviaer DuRousseau, "We are not your victims, liberals: Slavery reparations are an insult,"
New York Post, March 17, 2023, https://nypost.com/2023/03/17/we-are-not-victims-liberals
-slavery-reparations-insulting/.

[19] Adam B. Coleman, "The Culture War: Recognizing the Battle for Society's Direction," *Epoch Times*, July 29, 2023, https://www.theepochtimes.com/opinion/the-culture-war-recognizing-the-battle-for-societys-direction-5420276.

[20] Kristine Parks, "Fed-up staff seethe over Boston U's antiracist center: 'Colossal waste of millions of dollars': Ibram Kendi's Center for Antiracist Research accused of mismanagement amid layoffs," Fox News, 9/22/23, https://www.foxnews.com/media/fed-up-staff-seethe-boston-us-antiracist-center-colossal-waste-millions-dollars.

Chapter Twenty-Six

[1] Kendall Tietz, "Arizona universities demand rigid allegiance to 'diversity,' suppress hiring of conservatives: study: Up to 80 percent of job applications at a U.S. university required students and faculty to submit a 'diversity statement'," Fox News, January 19, 2023, https://www.foxnews.com/media/arizona-universities-demand-rigid-allegiance-diversity-suppress-hiring-conservatives-study.

[2] "FIRE Statement on the Use of Diversity, Equity, and Inclusion Criteria in Faculty Hiring and Evaluation," June 2, 2022, https://www.thefire.org/issues/fire-statement-on-the-use-of-diversity-equity-and-inclusion-criteria-in-faculty-hiring-and-evaluation/.

[3] Duncan Kennedy, "Legal Education and the Reproduction of Hierarchy," *J. Legal Education* 32 (1982), 591, https://duncankennedy.net/documents/Photo%20articles/Legal%20Education%20and%20the%20Reproduction%20of%20Hierarchy_J.%20Leg.%20Ed.pdf.

[4] Insight Staff, "AAUP Releases First Tenure Study Since 2004, Revealing Major Changes in Faculty Career Tracks," *Insight Into Diversity*, June 27, 2022, https://www.insightintodiversity.com/aaup-releases-first-study-on-tenure-since-2004-revealing-major-changes-in-faculty-career-tracks/.

[5] "Brown University: Guide to Diversifying Faculty Searches: Diversity Statements and Evaluation Rubrics," https://cfaesdei.osu.edu/sites/diversity/files/imce/Brown%20Guide%20to%20Diversifying%20Faculty%20Searches%20Diversity%20Statement%20and%20Evaluation%20Rubrics.pdf.

[6] "Evaluating Faculty Candidates Diversity, Equity, and Inclusion Statements," https://eoaa.columbia.edu/sites/default/files/content/docs/Rubric_to_Assess_Faculty_Candidate_Contributions_to_D_E_I.pdf.

Chapter Twenty-Seven

[1] Peter Wood, "Regime Change: Repelling the DEI Assault on Higher Education," NAS.org, 6/13/22, https://www.nas.org/blogs/statement/regime-change-repelling-the-dei-assault-on-higher-education.

Topical Index by Chapter

Chapter One

They've Ruined the University

Chapter Two

As Marshall McLuhan Explained, the Medium Is the "Message" and the University Is a Very Powerful "Medium"

Chapter Six
The University Is Being Consumed from Within

Chapter Seven
The Degradation of Merit and Ability

Chapter Eight
We Need to Get Back to Having "Dangerous Universities"

Chapter Twelve
Orwell and "Protective Stupidity"

Chapter Thirteen
The "Argument Culture"

Chapter Seventeen
Heroes, False Prophets, and Demagogues

Chapter Eighteen
All Revolutions Need an "Enemy"

Chapter Nineteen
What Happens When the Revolutionaries Win?

Chapter Twenty-One
China's Strategy of Propaganda and Division Harms America's Universities

Chapter Twenty-Two
Real Diversity and Multiculturalism Contribute to Our Society

Chapter Twenty-Six
What Kind of Faculty Are DEI Systems Allowing Universities to Hire?

Index of Sources Cited